Svengali's Web

Svengali's Web

The Alien Enchanter in Modern Culture

Daniel Pick

Yale University Press
New Haven and London

Set in Adobe Minion
Printed in Great Britain by St Edmundsbury Press, Suffolk

Library of Congress Card Number: 00–100625

ISBN 0–300–08204–5

A catalogue record for this book is available from the British Library.

10 9 8 7 6 5 4 3 2 1

In memory of Tony Tanner
1935–1998

I am *Svengali*; and you shall hear nothing, see nothing, think of nothing, but *Svengali, Svengali, Svengali*!

George Du Maurier, *Trilby*

Contents

Illustrations

Acknowledgements

My thanks to my colleagues and students at Queen Mary and Westfield College, University of London, for offering a congenial environment in which to work and for providing many challenging ideas that bear on the themes of this book. In recent years, I have had the opportunity to present some of these ideas at conferences and in informal academic discussions, here and abroad, and I am particularly grateful to Bryan Cheyette, Laura Marcus, Gita Deneckere, Alessandro Pagnini and Antonello La Vergata for inviting me to present papers drawn directly or indirectly from this work.

A number of colleagues and friends have let me know their views on work in progress, and this has often led to substantial rewriting. I am much indebted once again to Gareth Stedman Jones for encouragement to pursue this inquiry in the first place, and for acute historical advice and clarification as the text took shape. At crucial stages, Lisa Jardine offered her support and incisive comments, and I am grateful to her on both these counts. I would also especially like to acknowledge the contribution of Ignês Sodré of the British Psychoanalytical Society for her subtle and helpful observations on the literature presented here, and on much besides. Alison Winter, Roy Porter, Lyndal Roper, Richard Bourke and Keith Jacobs have also been more than generous with their time; all of them have offered astute suggestions on the cultural and historical implications of 'Svengali' that have affected the form and content of this account.

For guidance on various nineteenth-century sources, I am grateful to Jacqueline Carroy, Robert Mighall, Matt Cook, Sarah Waters and Robin Straus. Katharina Rowold kindly advised me on some German material. A number of librarians and archivists in England and abroad have responded promptly to written questions and enabled me to track down some of the more obscure primary materials; thanks, particularly, to the staff who patiently assisted me at the British Film Institute Library, the archives of *Punch*, the

British Library, the Wellcome Library and the Académie Nationale de Médicine, Paris. Liz Mailer, until recently History Librarian at Queen Mary and Westfield, has been unfailingly helpful. I have appreciated written advice offered on biographical matters by several members of the Du Maurier family, also by Julie Coleman of Glasgow University Library and Jean Adams at the Hampstead Museum (Burgh House). Quotations from correspondence between Du Maurier and Edward Burne-Jones are by kind permission of the Syndics of the Fitzwilliam Museum, Cambridge.

Without the backing of research organisations, I would have had the greatest difficulty in seeing this project through to completion. I have been fortunate in gaining substantial support for my work from the Inman Trust, administered by the British Psychoanalytical Society. William Inman (1875–1968) was a distinguished ophthalmologist and member of the British Psychoanalytical Society who wrote extensively on the psychosomatic aspects of eye disorders. I hope that he might have considered the evidence presented here on mesmerism, fascination and the evil eye as being, at least, of tangential relevance to his own long-standing interest in cultural attitudes to vision. I would like to offer this preliminary acknowledgement to the Leverhulme Trust and the Wellcome Trust, whose generous funding for further work on which I am currently engaged, has also enabled me to see this study into print.

It has been a pleasure to work with Robert Baldock and Candida Brazil at Yale University Press. Special thanks to Margaret Hanbury, who dispensed, as required, good humour, trenchant opinions and cool-headed advice. I have received much able assistance from Yale's picture researcher, Sally Nicholls, and have also benefited from the input of an exceptionally committed copyeditor, Susan Watkins, whose thoughtful suggestions led to some substantial reorganisation of the material. Despite having more pressing matters to deal with at the time, Irma Brenman Pick read and commented on the book with a keen editorial eye. It would not have been possible to undertake this study at all without a very great deal of encouragement and sustained, practical support from my family, during a particularly demanding period of life. In this regard I would also like to express my appreciation to Rosie Munday and Cecilia Della Vedova for all their help. Above all, my thanks to Isobel, for helping me to clarify the issues at stake in this book, for retaining a sense of irony and of proportion during its drawn-out history, and, no less indispensably, for encouraging me to let go of it.

1
Svengali

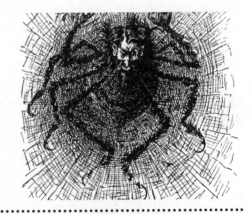

'Svengali, marvellous Svengali – a weird spectral, Satanic figure – he literally took away our breath.' Yes, it was a creation that took away one's breath with the sheer force of its genius, with its wealth, its unfathomable depths of fantastic, unpremeditated art. The creation was so rich, so rare, so subtle, that it was beyond estimation, and thus beyond praise.

Max Beerbohm, *Sir Herbert Beerbohm Tree*[1]

The image of a sinister hypnotist, lurking behind the scenes, ambiguously responsible for breaking and remaking another weaker character, has been given many literary, theatrical and cinematic forms. Medicine, psychiatry and psychoanalysis also offer up their cautionary tales about charismatic charlatans who have become the dire masters of their patients. But there is one such shadowy entrancer whose name has become synonymous with psychological manipulation: Svengali.

Mesmerist, musician and Jew, the original Svengali was invented by the Anglo-French illustrator and writer, George Du Maurier, in his novel, *Trilby*, a none-too-demanding tearjerker that was serialised in *Harper's New Monthly Magazine* and then published as a book in 1894. Du Maurier's story is set in Paris and London. Svengali, an itinerant conductor, is its villain. Described as being 'of Jewish aspect, well-featured but sinister' and with 'bold, brilliant black eyes' and 'long heavy lids',[2] Svengali attempts to win over the heroine of the book, a young artists' model named Trilby. He hypnotises her without her consent. She becomes 'haunted' by his eyes and by his name which rings in her head and ears until 'it became an obsession'. Trilby is eventually compelled to marry Svengali and is then transformed into an international concert star, who sings zombie-like, to ecstatic audiences while under Svengali's spell. When Trilby finally escapes the mesmerist's clutches in very public and dramatic circumstances it is only to collapse, broken and exhausted.

The tale quickly became a public sensation, the source of what one can only call a transatlantic craze. Booksellers and librarians could not keep up with the vast demand; indeed *Trilby* is generally thought to have been the best-selling novel of the last century. The story's run-away success and astonishing 'marketability' requires some explanation, but so does the fact that the protagonists loomed so large in the social imagination. Svengali brought together certain inchoate cultural fears and political ruminations. Even at the time, the level of collective interest in this fierce and impenetrable conductor was felt to be excessive and puzzling. And while the novel itself is now long forgotten, the name 'Svengali' has entered the dictionary,[3] and is routinely evoked on the political pages of the newspapers.

In Du Maurier's novel, the off-putting *and* charismatic Svengali appears in France, in flight from persecution in eastern Europe. He is dirty and poor but harbours vast dreams of success, involving both artistic and sexual conquest. Incapable of performing or excelling in his own right, he makes the helpless, poor and warm-hearted Trilby sing slavishly to his tune. Svengali is often 'off-stage', out of sight; much of the plot proceeds without him in evidence. Readers are often surprised at his relatively fleeting appearances; yet whether in the foreground or not, Svengali is the indispensable ingredient of Du Maurier's bestseller, and of the many adaptations for stage and screen that followed. *Trilby* has much to say on other topics, too, but it was the theme of the mesmerist and his psychic prisoner that became the major contemporary talking point. Not altogether surprising perhaps, for the adventures of Svengali and his stupefied bride were written in an epoch when experiment and conjecture about the nature of hypnosis and the unconscious were rife. Many writers of fiction, philosophers and scientists were exploring and challenging traditional accounts of the meaning of hypnotism in those years. Freud himself, after all, was consolidating his pioneering early discoveries in Vienna at the same time as Du Maurier was at work on his story about secret and morbid inter-personal communications.

Du Maurier himself made no particular claims for the book; indeed he was modest in the extreme. Few would have dissented from the description given in his obituary in *The Times*, which made much of his sweet and simple character, his 'unaffected modesty'.[4] As a stylist, admittedly, he had much to be modest about. Yet for all that, his Svengali seemed to draw the reader into ambitious and provocative conceptual territory. He was more than simply another cartoon scoundrel. Svengali personified a key philosophical theme of his day – the nature of unconscious influence – even as he reproduced the old cultural cliché of the odious alien fixer. For all of these reasons and more, Du Maurier's subliminal 'manager', Svengali, has come to intrigue me, despite his provenance in a novel whose maudlin tone is enough to make one cringe. Du Maurier's tales are in many respects poor; his incorrigible sentimentalism an embarrassment.[5] His books are full of twee evocations of the Paris of the Second Empire, clogged with platitudes about life, love and good fellowship in the happy times of his youth. But the cloying images of sugary childhoods, cheery camaraderie, wholesome sports and virtuous marriages clash with a mood of lingering melancholy: jolly escapades and songs are juxtaposed with strange sounds and dark scenes; whispers of the night, shadows of the occult, mysteries of dreams and of the cosmos itself.

For all his populism, inverted snobbery and anti-intellectualism, Du Maurier sought to raise surprising new questions about esoteric influences, forgotten ideas and nameless sensations, lamenting the blinkered nature of everyday material assumptions and the crass conventions of the day. Nostalgia was not only the mood of much of his writing, but also the frequent object of his investigations. Though Du Maurier was no Proust, he sought repeatedly to capture the curious persistence of the old in the new as well as the distressing knowledge that each moment is both stored and lost, haunting and yet irrecoverable. The compelling pleasures and pains of 'the remembrance of things past' were insistently evoked in his writing. His novels provide a strange confection of the mundane and the miraculous, the memorable and the mindless. *Trilby* may have been a sentimental tale, but it contained, as Max Beerbohm put it, that truly 'weird spectral, Satanic figure'.

The portrayal of Svengali was meant to be viewed with amusement. Even as it deals with intense states of envy, rage and melancholia, *Trilby* has an easy touch. The angry Jewish hypnotist was a witty prose sketch by a man renowned for his delectable pictorial illustrations of Victorian life in *Punch*, countless 'snap-shot' drawings of the passing foibles and fashions of the metropolitan scene. But Svengali was, nonetheless, a joke with a certain twist. Whatever his intentions, Du Maurier succeeded in creating a character with a peculiar intensity, and an enduring appeal. He linked the theme of mesmeric entrapment with persistent anxieties about the penetrating psychological powers of the Jews. Svengali was a dazzlingly memorable meeting point of such currents of fear and fascination: he brought into focus many of the *fin de siècle*'s forebodings about the nature of hypnosis, alien control and the unconscious.

Fears of the covert presence and evil eye of the adviser 'behind the throne' have persisted since ancient times, yet there are particular ways in which such preoccupations have been developed in modern political thought. Sometimes isolated outsider figures have been seen to acquire a magnetic hold, or even a near supernatural possession of their leaders, as in the celebrated case of Rasputin. Elements of fact and fantasy, observation and myth-making are extremely difficult to disentangle here, as the biographers of the Russian monk invariably show. The nature of such psychological power in the exceptional individual has generated a vast literature in its own right; but the 'sick influence' of certain groups has also been the object of intense scrutiny and, on occasion, not so much of psychological analysis as of the most catastrophic collective paranoia. Modern racism has luridly portrayed an entire people's surreptitious invasion of their 'hosts', and has proposed expulsion or elimination as the only means of restoring the peace of mind and integrity of body of 'the people'. It is not only in Hitler's *Mein Kampf* that it is claimed that 'every court has its "court Jew"'.[6] The original Svengali appeared at a time when preoccupations with both insidious hypnotists *and* with successfully insinuating Jews were strikingly evident in many works of literature, journalism and political thought on both sides of the Channel. It was commonly asserted that, deep-down and despite assorted apparent 'conversions', the Jews would not (indeed could not) convert from Judaism; on the contrary, they threatened, to quote that dread concept of the period, to 'Jewify' the gentile. In the 1890s, the Jews were often depicted as contaminating the mind and body of gentiles, as well as controlling everything from the stock market to public taste in art.[7] As the quintessential dark hypnotist of turn-of-the-century culture, Svengali gave a very particular edge to familiar prejudices in which the Jews were routinely cast as financial wizards, omniscient seers or mysteriously omnipotent bankers.

After a general introduction, the book's focus of inquiry shifts to the previous century. Chapters two to four move backwards in time, from the 1890s *succès de scandal* of the Svengali story to the aspirations and predicaments of mesmerism, or animal magnetism, as it was once known, in its original heyday on the eve of the French Revolution (chapter three). Chapter four provides a broader picture of the Victorian preoccupation with group psychology and the covert captivation of hearts and minds. The aim of these chapters is not only to trace major themes from the history of mesmerism and hypnotism, but also to show how certain structures of feeling and obsession, already faintly evident in those older traditions, would converge so sharply and compellingly in 'Svengali' at the close of the last century. Stories and reports about the erotic dangers of mesmerism and hypnotism, and the strange surrogate passions swirling around the 'inspired' artist, are the subjects of 'The Sexual Charge', and 'Queen of Song', respectively, chapters five and six.

Victorian racial discussions and images move to the foreground in the final section of the book where it is argued that broader hypnotic and psychological concerns could be fused with ongoing debates about the Jewish 'race', in late nineteenth-century Europe. Chapter seven ('Racial Hypnosis') brings together a number of Victorian accounts linking Judaism and states of gentile perturbation and entrancement. Chapter eight ('Evil Eye') considers the novelty, or otherwise, of the idea of an omnipotent and envious gaze and proposes some of the ways in which that particular motif was linked with racial fears. Chapter nine, 'The Training of Sorrow', reconstructs various theories, evident particularly in late nineteenth-century anti-Semitic writing, that were used to explain, often in quasi-scientific terms, how the Jews were psychologically menacing to gentiles, *à la Svengali*. The title of this chapter refers to an argument advanced by commentators at the time that the Jews were actually 'trained' by their historical sorrows, the racial beneficiaries of past cruelties – made fit, shrewd and vengeful by their long evolutionary struggle in a hostile world. The concluding discussion returns to the original 'Trilby' craze. It ponders some peculiarities of the narrative and describes the unhappy fate of Svengali. The staging of his fall was a dramatic event experienced, with manifest excitement, not only by readers, but also by a large theatre-going public on both sides of the Atlantic.

It would be a travesty of the truth to suggest that the sinister 'Svengalian' enchanters of modern culture and politics have always been cast as Jewish. Nor was the original Svengali just a cipher for anti-Semitism. Du Maurier's portrait was informed not only by the racial hatreds of the day but also by psychological debates about the nature of inter-personal forces, not least the role of others in the shaping of the self. What did contemporaries make of the mesmerising musical conductor and his diva? Why was the Jew's look understood at the time to be so particularly devastating? Can one even be sure that Svengali was a creation of the 1890s? How far our author had simply conjured up his doleful mesmerist out of nowhere remains to be explored. Was Svengali really, as Du Maurier's admiring son-in-law claimed, 'an entirely original conception, in character unlike anything previously described in fiction'?[8] Authorship and provenance are complex enough issues in literature, still more so in the field of mesmerism with which the story in question is engaged.

Svengali's ultimate creative origins may be obscure, but his cultural reach in subsequent years is apparent enough. Beyond *Trilby*'s passion-ridden triumph in the 1890s, the story of the mesmerist and his dubious possession of the pliant singer continued to be taken as a familiar cultural reference point well into the twentieth century, wryly and precisely evoked, for instance, in a novel by D.H. Lawrence.[9] This is no longer the case. Or at least while 'Svengali' remains a common word, it seems to have shaken off any direct connection with the original plot, setting, or wider cast of characters. Precisely what does 'Svengali' imply? How far does the expression in common parlance have anything to do with the original story, or with the undercurrents of nineteenth-century thought and fantasy that lie behind it? Du Maurier's villain was a creature of melodrama, with its stylised forms of horror and facetiousness, its 'larger than life' antics; but the portmanteau term that has passed into language signifies a more troubling psychological tie.

Svengali has slipped free of his original fictional setting. Thus when a journalist refers to the manager of the late Ella Fitzgerald as her 'Svengali', it is not necessary to have read *Trilby* in order to follow his account.[10] When a provocative teenage model apparently has the Dutch 'agonising over sex laws' (according to what is billed as a 'world news' report in the *Sunday Times*), she is said to be controlled by a secretive Svengali, but no first-hand knowledge of Du Maurier's narrative is assumed:

> Although her face and figure can be seen on posters everywhere, other details about [the model] remain a closely guarded secret. Her father, a Svengali-like figure who is believed to be the driving force behind her career, refuses to talk to reporters.[11]

'World news' or not, such stories are frequently recycled, and often express unease at the perceived manipulation both of the 'model' and of the public by Svengalis of one kind or another. The fashion industry, as the site of dangerous and even morbid public manipulation, has become a much discussed theme. During the 1990s, even the President of the United States famously added his voice to those concerned by the 'heroin look' that had come to epitomise what was *chic*. But was there not something *déjà vu* in all this? For the glazed and emaciated figures as the acme of style could one read, perhaps, an old aesthetic of deadly pallor, the morbid consumptive beauty that once aroused and troubled the Victorian muse? Tempting as such comparisons may appear, they are generally trite when pushed too far, although some punditry from around 1900 could be placed on today's opinion page's without looking amiss. Familiar commentaries, now and then, often refer to how slick, covert psychological manipulation and underhand commercial inducements have weakened moral fibre and the individual will.

Public figures are unlikely to identify themselves personally with Svengali, of course; the term always seems to describe an object rather than a subject. Indeed, the English journalist Julie Burchill, referring in a newspaper column to her widely publicised affair with another woman, facetiously disclaimed any resemblance to the mesmerist, insisting rather that she be seen as Trilby.[12] If these examples are frivolous in isolation, the fact of their accumulation, their continuing modern repetition, makes it worth asking what is at stake in the evocation of a Svengali and how this may relate to the fears and fascinations that clustered round the original version. On occasion the terms are directly topical and politically significant, as when Peter Mandelson, the well-known Labour Party figure, government minister, and long-standing confidant of the Prime Minister, was deemed to be seeking to conceal his reputedly vast secret influence. The image of 'Svengali' stuck, despite Mandelson's evident discomfort and attempts to shrug off the term. As one typical newspaper report put it in the run-up to the 1997 general election that returned Labour to power, Mandelson was 'trying to shed his image as a backstage Svengali'. The positive or negative qualities, scandals and machinations of this particular individual are beside the point here; what is so striking is how much work the term 'Svengali' accomplishes, and yet how little political analysis is ever offered of the historical scenario from which it emerged. The question of whether Mandelson's part-Jewish background has been 'in play' in the frequently repeated caricature of him is scarcely ever addressed.[13] Mandelson, it is implied in the press, simply *is* Svengali and no further questions need be asked. In cartoons, he has commonly been cast as a half-comic, half-sinister figure, even as a spider, again perhaps without deliberate reference to the 'spiderman' version of Svengali drawn by Du Maurier himself.[14]

'Svengali' is no less 'at home' in show business. Opera divas and other musicians are seen as especially prone to Svengalis, although perhaps reports of sport stars and their shady backers are now starting to achieve

Steve Bell, *Mandy Spider*, 1997.

equal prominence. What better demonstration of the power of the Svengalian impresario than the capacity to catapult stars into the limelight, and to dictate the terms on which they appear? Legend has it that Rasputin once sent an imperious note to the Court Secretariat demanding, on his authority alone, that an attractive young woman whom he had just met should be given the position of first lady at the opera.[15] The perceived mesmerism of the public by the stars, and of the stars by their managers, was already evident in the folklore that surrounded Victorian opera, and which provided the background to Du Maurier's tale. Adelina Patti, the great *prima donna* of La Scala and Covent Garden in the last decades of the nineteenth century, was said to have been held in a state of near-entrancement by her mentor: 'Strakosch exerted a Svengali-like influence over her earliest professional years.'[16] No surprise that Patti's triumphant London début was in the Bellini opera that features sleepwalking in its plot, *La sonnambula*. Erotic relationships and hypnoid states were continually entangled, both on the stage, in learned articles, in the pages of fiction and at practical demonstrations of trance induction. It is to the music of *La sonnambula* that George Eliot's heroine Maggie Tulliver nearly succumbs to the advances, and the relentless gaze, of the unworthy Stephen Guest in *The Mill on the Floss*, which appeared in 1860. Maggie tries to resist the dreamy pull of the man and the music, '[b]ut it was of no use: she soon threw her work down, and all her intentions were lost in the vague state of emotion produced by the inspiring duet – emotion that seemed to make her at once strong and weak, strong for all enjoyment, weak for all resistance.'[17] (In Eliot's *Daniel Deronda*, however, this theme takes another form, when the charismatic Jewish musician, Klesmer, refuses to enter into this kind of musical 'duet' with Gwendolen Harleth or to confirm her fantasy of a glorious singing career.)

The theme of Svengalian hypnotic domination is perhaps no less familiar in the world of cinema. There are many references to omniscient men 'behind the scenes', shaping the actress or the diva as the potter moulds his clay. The belief in the success of the megalomaniac man often casts the woman as little more than his passive sleepwalker. This representation goes beyond the suggestion of gender inequality to convey absolute psychic domination. This has become culturally familiar, even stereotypical. It would be hard to imagine a feature piece on, say, Maria Callas without such insinuations about the men who drove her ('blindly') to lunatic musical feats. In various celebrated tales about Hollywood stars, the man's 'Svengalian' manipulation of the woman is shown to absolutely determine her success. Garbo, for instance, had Maurice Stiller as her Svengali: 'a hypnotic director who made over even her very soul'.[18] Conversely, of course, Citizen Kane's ultimate powerlessness and demise is exemplified by his *failure* to turn his tuneless wife into the musical triumph he craves her to be.

It is not only women who are portrayed as the passive theatrical, cinematic or musical victims of their Svengalis. Male pop stars have also been cast as hopelessly hoodwinked by their Svengali managers. From the Beatles' Brian Epstein to Elvis' Colonel Parker, or Bob Dylan's Albert Grossman, for that matter, the image evoked is always that of 'Svengali', namely of covert manipulation, insidious exploitation, a world divided between the passive and the active, the puppet and puppet-master. One cannot doubt the probability – often the incontrovertible fact – of grotesque advice and malign influence, as well as youthful naivety, financial or otherwise; the reality of double-dealing and the existence of self-interested ruses by promoters and agents is not in question. It may be the role of the historian, however, to point out that both such practices and their florid shaping narratives are less novel than we think, and that components of social reality and of fantasy are deeply, sometimes inextricably, intertwined.

What is so intriguing is the endurance of the particular image of the cynical, colourful and strangely omnipotent musical manager, operating as a kind of bad surrogate parent, a malignant hypnotist rather than a real carer.

A recent history of British pop management entitled *Starmakers and Svengalis* concludes: 'The irresistible power and influence of the Svengali, like that of the charismatic leader in politics, has a universal appeal that will ensure its cyclical revival at appropriate moments in future rock history.'[19] In music journalism, Svengali is chronically shown to exploit and reshape the 'stage property'. Thus the dismissal of a manager (the so-called brain behind that pop bubble of the 1990s) was announced in dramatic terms on the front pages of popular papers; a typical Sunday tabloid headline: '£10 million pay-off for Svengali Spice'. In accompanying features, he was described as guru, minder, strategist and elusive operator, rolled into one. His zealous interference was said to extend to the smallest and most intimate aspects of the singers' private lives, to say nothing of a sexual affair with one of them; the word that recurred on each page of the overblown article, and a hundred others: 'Svengali'.[20]

An earlier generation read of Colonel Parker, 'the man behind Elvis Presley', who was represented, to quote the words of one of the many biographers of the singer, as a 'Svengali, both cunning and benign'. An indignant commentator takes up something of the general myth as well as the specific Presley story when he recounts how 'this extraordinary showman–salesman of the decaying American South . . . is selling Elvis off, like his popcorns and balloons, on the safest lines imaginable'. And 'the King' himself 'let it happen with no sign of resistance – he is passive, a living ghost'.[21] Presley, as another chronicler declares, 'was the Colonel's dream, the perfect vehicle for all the Colonel's elaborately worked out and ingenious promotional schemes. Elvis was the purest of post-war products, the commodity that had been missing from the shelves in an expanding marketplace of leisure time and disposable cash.'[22] Bob Dylan's Jewish manager, Albert Grossman, could be described in terms still closer to Du Maurier's original: 'He enjoyed recreating the artists he represented to suit his messianic ambitions.' He was said to be cryptic, arrogant, condescending, shrewd, underhand, cut-throat, even diabolical. 'He was by his own description, a "Jewish businessman", a cagey operator who lived by the Teutonic theory that those who strike first and fastest usually eat best.'[23] Corrupting, manipulative and bewitching in studied ways; diabolic and seductive – something of a Svengali.[24]

Such references and associations in modern culture have an undoubted rhetorical resilience, which depends perhaps as much on their vague allusiveness as on anything else. The very ambiguity of the concept means it can be construed in different ways. The 'Svengalian model' implies not only an inspiring and troubling presence, but also a complicated group dynamic which has in fact informed the literature of mesmerism and hypnotism from the beginning. To conjure a Svengali (or a Mesmer) is implicitly to invoke the matching figure, or figures, upon whom he operates, as well as the troubled but excited spectators. In the hypnotic phenomenon in general, and the Svengalian encounter in particular, the process may be thought of in terms of a dyad, but it can perhaps also be conceived as a triad involving not only the hypnotist and the hypnotised, but also a third party: the excluded lover, the bemused public audience, the scandalised critic. Like some marginalised but fascinated child, the watching crowd witness once, twice, a dozen times, the primal mesmeric scene. The strange intimacy of the pair, even in the most public of settings, is part of the *frisson* of so many hypnotic performances in the last two hundred years. Moreover the 'third party' is often pulled in, bewitched in turn. The anxiety generated by such close encounters, above all in the late nineteenth century, turned both on their dangerous privacy – depraved sexual deeds behind closed doors – and their alarming public aspect – theatrical participants, audiences, even entire national populations, at the mercy of the devious persuader. *Trilby* is, after all, a story about watching as well as about participating – although the identities of the sexual couple and the voyeurs keep shifting, as the other characters are themselves shown covertly observing Svengali who is slyly watching the woman and her lover. After a while, with underhand tricks, the Jew steps into the lover's place.

In Du Maurier's novel and in the spate of films which have followed it, Svengali is a master of stealth, creeping in from the wings, hiding behind screens (explicitly so, in an early cinema version), pulling the strings, watching, manipulating. The underhand character of Svengali is, proverbially, part of his nature. But does he fall captive to the very process he has engendered? Is Svengali in love with, and in thrall to, his creation, or is it merely his victim who is entranced by him? How far is 'being in love with the object' the same as being psychologically enslaved by it? According to Freud the question is best considered within the wider enigma of the hypnotic process; as he wrote in *Group Psychology*: 'There is the same humble subjection, the same compliance, the same absence of criticism, towards the hypnotist as towards the loved object. There is the same sapping of the

subject's own initiative.' Is it because Svengali takes us back to this complicated set of emotional ties, involving love and dread, devotion and abjection, slavery and mastery, that he is such a very suggestive and problematic
figure ?

Svengali makes the rest of the cast feel impotent and anxious; he is an
insidious, even macabre adviser, or *alter ego*. Sometimes he is deployed in
even more extreme terms, as a latter-day Mephistopheles, or a demonic
seducer. The theatre critic William Archer, commenting on the actor-
manager Beerbohm Tree's famous performances as Svengali in the 1890s,
related the character to imagery from the Middle Ages:

> [It is a] fantastic fairy-tale . . . Not for nothing does Svengali wear the
> features of a gargoyle from some medieval minster. He is lineally
> descended from the Devil of the Miracle Plays . . . It stands on a low
> plain of art, because it is not an effort of observation and composition,
> but of sheer untrammelled fantasy . . .[25]

Or, as one historian of hypnotism declared a few years later, Svengali has
become 'a twentieth-century Mephistopheles – [who] possesses all the
mystic powers of the mystery worker of romance, with a suggestion of decadent demonism'.[26]

Critics have occasionally drawn on Du Maurier's Svengali to characterise gender and racial relations; he has been linked, for instance, to the
Victorian stigmatisation of the talented woman. The flourishing female
artist was cast as abnormal – hysterical, somnambulistic, or worse – as
though only via the man, the Svengali, could 'the second sex' be allowed a
certain automaton-like 'success'. But clearly the issues are more complex
than such a bald interpretation would allow, for Du Maurier's male and
female characters are quite often presented as sexually unstable in attitude
or appearance, belonging less than completely to one gender or the other.
Thus Trilby makes her first appearance 'clad in the grey overcoat of a
French infantry soldier, continued netherwards by a short striped petticoat,
beneath which were visible her bare white ankles,' while 'her toes lost themselves in a huge pair of male slippers'.[27] The racial complications surrounding the mesmerist and the mesmerised add further dimensions of
ambiguity and difficulty to this picture. Some commentators have sought
to draw attention to the anti-Semitic meaning of Svengali. Edmund Wilson
observes that Svengali gave a new name to the perceived double aspect of
the Jews as a people, accredited with supernatural powers and talents but

also ascribed abhorrent and damnable qualities. In addition, he highlights
the idea of the Jews' ventriloquism: 'What is really behind Svengali is the
notion, again, that the Jew, even in his squalidest form, is a mouthpiece of
our Judaico-Christian God, whose voice he has, in this case, transferred
ventriloquially, to the throat of Trilby.'[28] Wilson refers to the Jews' various
designated roles in cultural history: from malignant devil to spirit from an
alien world. The Jew has been reviled and yet attributed a sometimes
uncanny prestige, a capacity to speak in a divine tongue. Another commentator recently wrote: 'Black magician, wandering Jew, malignant
Orpheus, devil-god, and spider cat – Svengali's paradoxical character is a
rich composite of archetypes that will continue to touch our deepest emotions.'[29]

This kind of insistent symbolic reference had already featured in Du
Maurier's own account. He called Svengali an 'incubus', a kind of evil spirit
which afflicts the sleeper, and which has found expression in literature
since classical times.[30] Perhaps most memorably he is described as sticky,
haunting, long, lean, uncanny, black and spider-like, 'if there is such an animal outside a bad dream'. It is an image that observers frequently picked
up; an important physician, Ernest Hart, for instance, congratulated Tree
for recreating Svengali on stage as 'the weird, unclean, spider-like mesmerist of the school of the popular imagination'.[31] A particularly powerful
illustration of Svengali as a spider was provided in the original serialisation
by Du Maurier and might be cross-referenced to the gruesome figures produced around this time by the symbolist painter, Odilon Redon; perhaps it
was also intended to refer obliquely to *Punch* cartoons of the virtuoso musician Paganini in the 1840s, 'with his great spidery arms and legs, his wild
huge eyes and wilder hair'.[32] To compare Svengali to a spider was to emphasise not only his speed and guile, but also his horror; the arachnid is, after
all, the very emblem of entrapment. The *Oxford English Dictionary* entry for
this 'eight-legged animal of the order *Araneida*' gives: '*spider and fly*, fig.,
ensnare & ensnared'. In an essay entitled 'The Fear of Spiders', the Italian
writer Primo Levi saw such creatures as suggestive of silence and secrecy, as
well as decay and oblivion. Spiders appear through 'invisible fissures', veil
their works, enveloping them 'as though in a shroud'.[33] In the Bible itself,
images of the spider and the web are a powerful expression of the iniquity
and evil of those who have turned away from God.[34] The spider's connotations, at least according to Freud and his follower Karl Abraham, go beyond
the signification of evil or entrapment to take in unmistakably sexual
elements. Abraham discussed at some length clinical material relating to

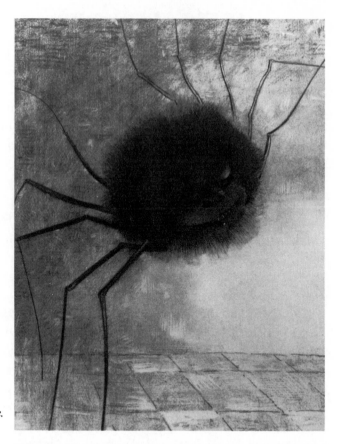

Odilon Redon,
L'Araignée souriante.
Louvre.

spiders which were in turn associated with male and female genitals, or with an amalgamation of the two. A patient's picture of a spider suggested a graphic infantile representation of 'horrible' sexual intercourse. The overdetermined figure of the spider is also said by Abraham and Freud to symbolise castration.[35]

Pertinent though such accounts of the spider and its sexual connotations may be to understanding his cultural resonance and survival, myths of Svengali cannot be explained exclusively in those terms; notions of universal psychological terrors and desires, shared symbolic investments in, say, spider images, only take us part of the way. Svengali is not merely a function of some ancient 'arachnophobia', primitive dreams of being engulfed, poisoned or entrapped; neither is he to be located solely in terms of some overwhelming unconscious infantile phantasy of parental intercourse between a 'dirty' intruding father and a 'hypnotised', castrated mother; still less is he the mere recapitulation of pre-modern tales of devils and satyrs, incubi or, for that matter, the perennially wandering Jew; he must surely also be sited within a definite cultural and scientific epoch, in which the psychology of races, mesmerised couples and crowds provoked extensive debate and important lines of thought in the human sciences. The emancipation of the Jews in nineteenth-century Europe had fuelled new anti-Semitic fantasies, although with highly variable implications and political consequences in different states.[36] Svengali's very freedom of movement and expression, combined with his relentless rancour in the face of persecutions old and new, real and imagined, appeared a truly formidable threat to his easy-going British 'friends'. Svengali shaped and was shaped by a particular British bemusement and ambivalence, a reflection of intensely conflicting Victorian attitudes to Jewish-gentile relations in an age of growing 'toleration'; his portrayal was further inflected by the traditions of melodrama and music hall, as well as by more specific concerns with the nature of suggestion, hypnotism and the emerging 'psychotherapies' of the day.[37] In short, a sense of time and place needs to be introduced alongside such broad-brush accounts of Svengalian myth if we are to make real sense of his cultural, political or psychological significance.

2
The Violence of Publicity

....

What I see certainly is that no such violence of publicity can leave untroubled and unadulterated the source of the production in which it may have found its pretext. The whole phenomenon grew and grew till it became, at any rate for this particular victim, a fountain of gloom and a portent of woe; it darkened all his sky with a hugeness of vulgarity.

Henry James, on the success of *Trilby*[1]

Nobody was more surprised than Du Maurier by the intense passions his story evoked amongst countless readers on both sides of the Atlantic. In England, *Trilby* was in its seventh edition by the end of 1894. However gratified by the novel's success, he clearly abhorred the sheer excess of enthusiasm, the salacious gossip and the inane curiosity of strangers, to say nothing of the worrying legal problems that cropped up in the wake of the story. He felt beset by reporters, subjected to an unpleasant and exploitative inquisition. In an interview in the year after the publication of *Trilby* he did not point the finger at anyone in particular, but spoke of money in general as 'filthy lucre'.[2] Even some of his friends cashed in, with or without his blessing. Biographical reports about the author's own experiences of mesmerism, for instance, appeared in a book, *In Bohemia with Du Maurier*, written by his old companion and fellow amateur magnetist, Felix Moscheles. Such experimentation in the induction of trance states was far in Du Maurier's past and was something of which he had long sickened, although he seemed to have borne Moscheles himself no grudge for writing it up.

Du Maurier was in many ways a self-effacing man; he gained only meagre pleasure from his immodest riches, and found the cascade of attention deeply intrusive. As the money poured in, so did rumours and gossip about his life and work. For a while the public was truly gripped by the most minute detail of the tale and the history of its composition. Du Maurier died in 1896 and the 'Trilby' craze itself subsided before the turn of the century (although Svengali's cinema career was only just beginning). If the story remained well known for years to come, it ceased to generate headlines in the newspapers as it had in the mid-nineties. The Du Maurier family name has remained in the limelight in the twentieth century less because of intrigue about this late-Victorian novelist and his fictional *personae* than because of the huge popularity of the stories of George's granddaughter, Daphne (1907–1989). Her father, George's son Gerald (1873–1934), was also very well known in the inter-war period as an actor and an all-round man of the theatre. His name became a byword for a certain debonair style. 'Du Maurier' was further publicised by a brand of cigarette to which, for a fee, the matinee idol agreed to lend his image.[3] The colourful earlier history of the Du Mauriers was a subject dear to George (so dear that he apparently sometimes embellished the truth), as well as to Daphne, who explored the saga of her French forbears in *The Glass Blowers*.[4] She also sought to reignite interest in her grandfather, the increasingly forgotten author of *Trilby*, publishing various books connected with his work and life.

George Louis Palmella Busson Du Maurier was born in Paris in 1834, the eldest son of an impecunious Frenchman, Louis Mathurin (whose own parents had fled the Terror), and Ellen Clarke, the daughter of Mary Anne Clarke. The latter, an actress and one-time mistress of the Duke of York, had caused a scandal in 1810, after her abandonment by the Duke, by threatening to publish certain love letters unless she was paid a large sum.[5] As a child and young man, George lived in altogether less exalted and flamboyant circles, but he always kept an interest in the romantic and aristocratic worlds – on both sides of the Channel – with which his family had such dubious associations. Perhaps the tittle-tattle about his amorous predecessors played a part in fostering his concern with sexual mores and particularly his criticism of intolerant 'Victorian' attitudes to female promiscuity – themes which feature prominently in *Trilby*. In any event cultural variations in morals and manners were plainly evident to the young Du Maurier, an artistic 'free spirit' on extended tour in Europe. He frequently contrasted England and France in his visual and written work. He was as much at home in Paris as London, and moved effortlessly between the French and English languages. He had been a student at University College, London as well as at the Sorbonne, although he left both before completing any course of study. By the time of his father's death, George had abandoned London and an incipient career in chemistry, for which he had no love, and headed back to Paris to train as an artist.[6] In 1860 he returned to England, where he was to support himself, his wife Emma (whom he married in 1863) and, in due course, their five children, by contributing drawings to illustrated novels and magazines, including *Punch*; by 1864 he had become a permanent member of the *Punch* staff. It was only later in life that he tried his hand at fiction and found the most stunning popularity. Versions of his youthful and later experiences as artist and writer, from novice in the studios of the Latin Quarter to creative writer and *pater familias* in London, are extensively explored in his novels.[7]

Whilst it is not the biography of Du Maurier or even the rebounding personal impact of his novel that primarily concerns us here, the life of Svengali cannot be entirely split off from the author's tribulations and attitudes. In some ways the cosmopolitan Du Maurier with his bohemian circle, his 'arty' European and American friends, was, like Svengali, a border-crossing 'outsider' himself. Moreover, George manifestly reviled Victorian chauvinism, provincialism and narrowness as much as did his eastern European villain. Yet a sense of domestic rootedness and even stolid bourgeois respectability was also clearly something he craved and worked very hard to create. An obituarist referred directly to the suburban setting of his art.[8] In his novels, foreigners or even Martian aliens break through the mental and physical boundaries of hitherto dull and unambitous characters, with both disturbing and creative effects. The author's insistent message is that the world around us is in fact never quite as boringly controllable, respectable or materially self-evident as it seems; homely complacency and provincial certainty are shaken up by travel or by the impact of a visiting foreigner. The alien and charismatic Svengali can be located within Du Maurier's extensive gallery of such outlandish and challenging 'other-worldly' types.

The enigma of Svengali's 'mind-reading' power was part of the wider human mystery to which this story-teller insistently drew his readers' attention in all three of his novels. Whatever his 'cosiness' of style or, indeed, his tendency to revel in the label of 'English philistine',[9] Du Maurier shared with many of his contemporaries a certain scepticism about the grander pretensions of Victorian society, to say nothing of the arrogance he associated with modern secular beliefs. While one of his fictional characters, Svengali's rival, Little Billee, was shown militantly brandishing Darwin's

Origin of Species before an appalled country vicar, the author himself was evidently critical of the imperialistic claims of science, or at least deeply intrigued by other realms of knowledge and experience, uncolonised by modern systems of thought. Such literary gesturing towards the unknown, the enigmatic, the occult, was an increasingly fashionable stance taken by sophisticated commentators of the time. Hypnotism itself was on the cusp between tawdry theatre, mysticism and the medical curriculum; between erotic enchantment, spiritual mystery and salubrious scientific pursuit. Nowhere was its fascination more successfully exploited in this period than in Du Maurier's own work: he took advantage of hypnotic expectations as surely as did his Svengali. For Du Maurier, as more significantly for Freud, the whole historical tradition of animal magnetism and hypnotism raised profound questions, but no satisfactory answers: the subject of entrancement was crying out for re-examination.

Du Maurier was neither a doctor, a neurologist nor a psychoanalyst; the word 'psychoanalyst' was only coined, after all, in 1896, the year of his death. Like many creative writers of this period, he used his fiction to point out the inadequacy of orthodox science, materialist medicine or Darwinian explanations of psychology, in which human emotions were understood to be a function, merely, of long-term 'natural selection'. Such models would not do; he reached towards another language, in search of the invisible and the ineffable, the motivating but unknown psychological and social forces of human endeavour which had, as yet, no adequate name. Freud was soon to conceptualise much of the psychic terrain and the unspeakable desires to which other writers of the period seemed to be vaguely alluding, in terms of sexual fantasy, repression, the dynamic conflict between consciousness and once-known, but then intolerable, thoughts. Such a vocabulary remained out of reach for Du Maurier (whatever he would have thought of it) but, alongside many of his contemporaries, he knew himself to be haunted by intuitions of unconscious mental states and intense social frustrations, as well as by a painful sense of 'the unknowable' in the human spirit and in the heavens; a perception of forces and powers which lay beyond the edge of any conventional materialist *or* religious system. He wrote about this experience on many occasions, seeking to acknowledge, as best he could, 'the unseen, unspeakable, unthinkable Immensity we're all part and parcel of, source of eternal, infinite, indestructible life and light and might'.[10]

Du Maurier endeavoured both to capture such obscure feelings and spectral intuitions in his writing and to defamiliarise everyday appearances, insisting upon the sheer strangeness of our emotional possibilities and communications. Conventional scientific approaches would not do. This was a frequent theme in fiction of the day. Thus the hapless doctor Harker in Bram Stoker's *Dracula* (1897) (another best-seller of the period) has to be instructed in open-mindedness by that indefatigable vampire hunter and free-ranging investigator of both science and folklore, Van Helsing. The physicians in *Trilby* are also shown to be inadequate to the task, out of their depth, disconcerted by the psychosomatic obscurity of the maladies they encounter as they attempt to save Trilby from her rapid decline after Svengali's disappearance. The unmistakable message was that orthodox medicine and science had overreached themselves and that their practitioners were deluded if they believed they held, or could ever hold, all the keys to enlightenment. Du Maurier himself had had his fair share of medical vexation and knew something about the patient's feelings of disaffection when cheated and fobbed off by arrogant, inept or cynical physicians. As a young artist he had sought treatment on the Continent after the sudden descent of blindness in one eye in 1857. Whilst Du Maurier was never to find himself fully 'in the dark', he dreaded complete blindness and felt he had been given due warning of its possibility; he had seen the world cloud over and temporarily disappear before him. It was an experience, he later confided, which 'poisoned my whole existence', but which evidently also stimulated his interest in more inward forms of 'vision' and which also encouraged him, eventually, to turn from the visual arts to writing. He completed *Peter Ibbetson, Trilby* and *The Martian* in the space of a few years towards the close of his life.

Du Maurier's novels display a continuing preoccupation with ventriloquism, alienated voices, transferred thoughts. His last tale, for instance, features a visitor from Mars. This demure female time traveller, Martia, flees to earth as a refugee, since she is not judged biologically worthy of bearing children by her compatriots. She enters the head of Barty, a young man whose eyesight is extremely precarious. Under her influence he has extraordinary visions and through her galvanising effect he becomes a celebrated writer. The narrative teases the reader with its unanswered questions and hint of irony behind its own matter-of-fact version of 'magic realism'. Is Barty a genius, a madman or just a cipher? Does he imagine this sweet eugenic outcast, this forlorn inter-planetary voyager, or does she lend him her own creative faculties? In any case, is such 'thought-transference' really a possibility? Certainly many investigators remained poised between adherence to and repudiation of Victorian natural science as they pursued such psychical riddles and occult enigmas in the last decades of the nineteenth century. The Society for Psychical Research, founded in 1882 and dominated by various Cambridge dons, is the best-known example of the gathering fascination with such topics, but there had also been earlier, equally high-minded Victorian inquiries into ghosts and other similarly tendentious phenomena. The Society's discussions, researches and committees ranged broadly across the terrain of 'the mysterious', from water divining to haunted houses, from dreams 'coincidentally' experienced by two individuals to animal magnetism, from telepathy to automatism.[11] Such themes (particularly shared dreams, trance states and telepathy) were all major preoccupations in the writings of Du Maurier, as well as of many others, in the century's dying years. Even Freud (later a corresponding member of the Society) was to argue that telepathy was 'the original, archaic communication between individuals'. He later came to hold the view that in the modern world such direct psychical transference and intuition remained in the background, to be reactivated under certain conditions, 'for instance in passionately excited mobs'.[12]

If the communication between *Trilby* and its readership involved no telepathy, it certainly seemed that something strange, below board and even archaic was going on. Or at least so Henry James concluded, as he chronicled the astonishing reception of his friend's novel. As the subliminal storm of enthusiasm gathered, James thought that the author of the hypnotic saga was being stifled by the passions of his fans. 'The phenomenon grew and grew', as the sad and incredulous James would afterwards declare; it seemed to know no bounds, no limits, no decorum.[13] Strikingly, Du Maurier's plot had described an analogous and ultimately deadly cultural *éclat*; it dwelled insistently on the commerce of art, the group psychology of audiences, the spleen of critics and the manipulation of the heroine by her sleazy impresario. It was almost as if the novelist intuitively predicted the fate of his story, not least the 'deafening roar' of the audience. The word 'phenomenon' is often on the lips of the protagonists. The fatuous musical commentators of London society, acidly portrayed in *Trilby*, speak dismissively of the music emanating from Trilby's 'phenomenal larynx' (mere sour grapes on their part, of course) whilst friendlier onlookers recognise the uncanny greatness and disturbed public reaction to the musical triumph which the singer has achieved (even if it is decidedly a surrogate kind of genius). As the maestro's lugubrious sidekick, the violinist Gecko confides: 'She was a *phénomène* monsieur! She could keep on one note and make it go through all the colours in the rainbow – according to the way Svengali looked at her.'[14]

As that record of contemporary events and affairs, the *Annual Register*, reported with reference to the stage production, 'Mr Tree's fantastic representation of the hypnotising Jew Svengali was so full of cleverness and power, and Miss Dorothea Baird's representation of the hypnotised "model" Trilby was so full of simplicity and charm that London lost its head over the production, and "Trilby" soon counted among the phenomenal successes in which managers delight.'[15] London 'lost its head': it was as though the very reception of the book and the play manifested the hypnotic problem described in its plot – readers and viewers falling prey to the same captivation, disorientation and irrationality conveyed on the page. As one reviewer remarked, 'One simply abandons oneself to the book.'[16]

Du Maurier's novel opens with a group of British friends, three aspiring artists, temporarily resident in Paris. The adventure subsequently moves from the French to the English capital via various rural escapades; it is predominantly 'a tale of two cities', but most memorably it is set in the artistic circles of the Latin Quarter of Paris during the Second Empire. Indeed Du Maurier's novel played a significant part in fostering the modern legend of Parisian 'bohemia'. Into this fondly recalled scene of relaxed manners and artistic camaraderie, a sinister but dazzling musician appears. He is something of a leech, exploiting men and women, 'milking' his associates for their money, abusing their good will and then getting right under their skin. He comes not from a Transylvanian castle, like that closely contemporaneous bloodsucker Dracula; rather from the beleaguered German-Polish Jewish community.[17] He sponges off his own family as well as his Parisian contacts. He needs a mouthpiece, a vehicle for his genius: the hypnotised woman. He dreams of achieving a wider conquest: the conversion of 'the public' into an adoring, quivering mass. In his egoistic fury, Svengali is determined to triumph over gentile men and, above all, gentile women. He longs for vast riches and a future in which hundreds of ladies will flock to him, falling at his feet. He has already made certain conquests amongst his own 'race' – a forlorn Jewess is one such victim of his charms and tyranny – but he dreams of other triumphs.

His central hypnotic drama is to be with a certain Trilby. She is cast as cheerful, free and easy, a good sport. Trilby is partly Irish, older than her years, of mixed ethnic descent. Her father was a drunken ex-priest, her mother a *grisette*. She is poor and seems plebeian, although her social origins are somewhat confused. Adopted by others when orphaned, she is soon fending for herself, down but not out in Paris. She is a wild and highly vulnerable figure, semi-autonomous, unprotected as she seeks to care for

Sir Herbert
Beerbohm Tree and
Dorothea Baird in
Trilby.

her younger brother. Whilst no Frenchwoman, she has been brought up
(after a fashion) in the French capital. She is the sentimentalised child of the
Left Bank and of low-life, but has inherited both aristocratic and lowly,
sound and degenerate elements. Her family history involves a sad tale of
drink and desertion, gambling and fighting. In sum, she is, within the
medico-psychiatric terms of debate in that period, extremely vulnerable to
hypnosis. Svengali influences (or forces) her to fall for him without much
difficulty, turning her not only into 'Madame Svengali' but also into an
irresistible 'nightingale'. He snatches her from the sanctuary of those happy
British artists, Taffy, the Laird and Little Billee who occupy their Paris studio and who had happily patronised her, trying to bring out 'the lady' they
detected beneath her rough and ready manner (shades of Pygmalion).
Until the fatal intrusion of Svengali's powers, all had gone well. Under their

care, she 'grew more English every day; and that was a good thing'. They cannot but be shocked, however, by her promiscuous ways; Little Billee (who has fallen deeply in love with her) is particularly excruciated and leaves Paris when he discovers Trilby's career as nude model. Shocked by his shock, she endeavours to become 'decent', taking up as a laundress. Thus re-moralised, Little Billee can accept her, although the class difference remains wide.

The story emphasises social, racial and national differences, conflicting moral values, the abyss between classes and the incomprehension between the sexes. But the narrator parodies the codes underpinning such distinctions, noting that they are absurd and exact a heavy human price. It is as though Du Maurier carefully marks out the lines of the social order only to show that in fact they are blurred. None of the discriminations turns out to be as straightforward as it appears. Intriguingly, the two central lovers, Trilby and Little Billee, are both described not only as of mixed ancestry, but also as neither clearly male nor female in appearance. It turns out that Little Billee (Svengali's chief rival for Trilby's love) is English but also has a touch of Jewish ancestry. Fortunately for the world, 'and especially for ourselves, most of us have in our veins at least a minim of that precious fluid, whether we know it or show it or not. *Tant pis pour les autres!*' Or again:

> And in his winning and handsome face there was just a faint suggestion of some possible very remote Jewish ancestor – just a tinge of that strong, sturdy, irrepressible, indomitable, indelible blood which is of such priceless value in diluted homeopathic doses, like the dry white Spanish wine called montijo, which is not meant to be taken pure; but without a judicious admixture of which no sherry can go round the world and keep its flavour intact; or like the famous bull-dog strain, which is not beautiful in itself; and yet just for lacking a little of the same no greyhound can ever hope to be a champion.

A faint suggestion, a remote ancestor, a homeopathic dose or judicious admixture of the Jews is tolerable; indeed thus diluted, the Jew's blood can be of 'priceless value'.[18] And after all the 'Anglo-Saxon' would be deluded to imagine such a thing as a pure non-Jew. But happily a little of that alien blood goes a long way. Strike too rich a vein and out flows something decidedly malignant. Little Billee has a touch of that 'indelible blood'. Svengali has it, as it were, in pure culture.

Little Billee gets along well with Taffy and the Laird. Unfortunately, his family learn of his passion for Trilby and persuade the poor young woman to give him up, which she does. She forsakes him for the good of his name and his future in what was very much a tragic trope of the period. Little Billee suffers intensely from her withdrawal and is furious with his friends and family, but goes on to make his fortune as a sad and empty but glitteringly successful society painter. Underneath the social facade, however, we learn of his illness, brain disorders, mental maladies as well as physical ailments, never quite fathomed by the doctors. In due course, Trilby reappears in London converted into La Svengali, the companion of the malevolent and possessive musician. He has realised the potential in her rich but tuneless voice and, under hypnosis, has transformed her into the greatest singer in Europe. The novel revels in the folklore of opera and, as much as any Puccini, relishes the world of café society, swashbuckling artists and the pathos of 'La Bohème'. It all ends in tears for the participants, but let's leave the precise nature of their sorry end to be considered later.[19]

Before things come to grief, Svengali is depicted as having taken over the mental functioning of the woman; their bodily relations are always more in question. While the young Irishwoman became 'Madame Svengali', nonetheless the hypnotist was rumoured to have a wife elsewhere. Marital scruples evidently provided no bulwark against his fiendish psychological, sexual and musical designs. He refused to be constrained by social niceties and conventions. Du Maurier was more constrained of course than his character, although when he gave voice to his fantasies, he made it clear that he longed to be free of such respectable morality. No 'Mr Hyde' in his daily dealings, the author was yet troubled by certain less than 'civilized' dreams, the beckoning of a quite different world of nocturnal possibility. He wrote of sexual and moral liberation, yearning to 'break free', 'to indulge in every riotous excess', to carry on 'the most shameless intrigues'. He did not know if he could restrain himself from performing a war dance, he once daringly confided to his betrothed.[20] But when people he knew actually lived too close to the moral edge, he recoiled, appalled as much by transgression as by the Victorian 'straight and narrow'. Thus he dubbed his 'Svengalian' companion Moscheles (who was the godson of the composer Mendelssohn) 'Mephistopheles'. Anyway, in Du Maurier's eyes, the Jewish Moscheles was always too much the charlatan, too violent in his self-publicity. In his painting, music and money-making, Moscheles was deemed crude, altogether too 'unenglish' (sic).[21]

Respectability and Englishness were constant sources of tension in Du Maurier's work and life. His fictions, so highly conventional in some respects, also repudiated stultifying social restrictions. He likened the villain and heroine to father and daughter, but when Trilby was not free from the mesmeric influence, the nature of her intimate relationship with Svengali was anybody's guess; the author offered no sure guarantees to an anxious reader who wrote to him on the subject.[22] And anyway, just how innocently fathers and daughters, particularly somnambulistic or hysterical daughters, were perceived to live with one another in the age of Svengali, or, rather, the age of Sigmund Freud, was an increasingly moot point. Together with his older colleague Joseph Breuer Freud had become deeply involved in the clinical complexities, the transference and countertransference intensities, of hysteria; a series of patients, most famously 'Anna O' (Bertha Pappenheim), were using words as a kind of 'chimneysweeping', a 'talking cure', involving the attention and participation of their physicians. For various reasons, Breuer took fright at the amorous turn things were taking with Bertha and broke off the treatment. For a while, Freud had taken literally the hysterical women patients' painfully recovered declarations of sexual interference by relatives. As case piled upon case in the 1880s and 1890s, and as he began to draw upon material from his own 'self-analysis', Freud came to doubt and then to disbelieve the view that parental sexual intrusion was really so widespread as the evidence of these patients implied; he argued that it could not be the shock alone of such inter-personal events that was the cause of the psychic disturbance. Instead, he emphasised the role of phantasy, desire and repression.

Out of his growing hesitation about the literal historical accuracy of his patients' 'recovered memories' came a more subtle account of the aetiology of trauma. This did not imply for Freud that gross acts of parental abuse were necessarily made up or always falsely recalled by his patients (as he was at some pains to make clear on later occasions), or that such actions were harmless in themselves; but it did allow, at the least, for the role of phantasy, displacement and projection and, moreover, indicated the ambiguous relationships between thought and action, passivity and activity, past and present, subject and object, child and parent that might be functioning in the patient's memories, feelings and discourse. (The so-called 'seduction theory' came and went in the very early history of psychoanalysis; more recently it has again been the subject of intense controversy and re-examination. Sometimes the way Freud's struggles *and* errors, enthusiasms *and* revisions have been 'recollected' in recent polemics might itself seem tantamount to 'false memory': radical distortion and gross simplification of the attitudes and actions of the 'father of psychoanalysis'.)

In *Trilby*, Du Maurier describes a woman who has no idea what has been done to her under hypnosis. There were many readers in the 1890s who cared passionately about the fate of Svengali's more or less 'paternal' liaison with the singer and demanded clarification, even reassurance, about the status of the Jewish impresario's 'daughter-wife', reassurance which the author was reluctant to provide. When mesmerised, she had no defences, but even fully conscious, she was decidedly 'bohemian' and sexually available. Du Maurier tried to keep in the background, but when he was obliged to respond to the letters of distant admirers, his comments were as brief as possible:

NEW GROVE HOUSE, HAMPSTEAD HEATH,
October 31, 1894.

Dear Sir: In answer to your letter of September 24th, I beg to say that you are right about Trilby. When free from mesmeric influence, she lived with him as a daughter, and was quite innocent of any other relation. In haste, yours very truly,

G. DU MAURIER.[23]

Trilby was certainly a most equivocal 'daughter' to Svengali, and he the most problematic of 'fathers', but Du Maurier's haste was understandable enough, for the mountain of inquiries and the proliferation of publicity showed no signs of abating. By 1895, theatrical versions of the tale brought the story's renown to a still greater pitch of intensity on both sides of the Atlantic, but the release of the novel itself had already started the publicity ball rolling. People Du Maurier had never met were declaring their devotion, clamouring for attention, begging for answers to any number of questions about the author, his story and the characters. Little wonder that the shy writer felt increasingly under siege. Such had become his fame and such the extent of 'Trilbyana' that a newspaper as far away as San Francisco had published the paltry letter above, which had arisen in response to an inquiry from a correspondent in New Jersey concerned about possible sexual impropriety between the heroine and Svengali.

If Du Maurier had provoked widespread enthusiasm, he had also unwittingly fostered his own notoriety; either way, his name and story were doing the rounds. This was not without irony. Du Maurier had been known for his mockery of *fin-de-siècle* hype and self-promotion from his leafy Hampstead retreat. He was renowned for his wry, critical drawings of Oscar Wilde and the cult of decadence. Derision of pretentious modern 'sexo-maniacs', decadents, aesthetes and literary posers of all descriptions was the hall-mark of his prolific artwork for *Punch*. It was also the enduring refrain of his novels. Henry James had even called it Du Maurier's 'crusade'.[24] As it happened, Wilde's career was on the brink of disaster just as Du Maurier's own stock rose to new heights. At the beginning of 1895 Wilde's *An Ideal Husband* was playing at the Haymarket Theatre; by the end of the year, the playwright was 'in disgrace', and an adaptation of Du Maurier's fiction was a triumph at the same venue. As his legal status shifted from prosecutor to prosecuted, Wilde's predicament became more compelling to his contemporaries than any of his stories or plays. His trials were undoubtedly an important cultural and sexual dividing line at the mid-point of the final Victorian decade.[25]

The imprisonment of Wilde for acts of gross indecency (under legislation passed in 1885, which in effect criminalised homosexuality, in private or in public) aroused enormous public interest and crystallised complex currents of social, sexual and cultural hostility that had been in evidence for some time. As Jonathan Grossman has recently remarked, the writer's demise was 'the completion of a contemporary cultural rage'. Was Wilde not indeed cast by his accusers as the 'Svengali of homosexuality', who had beguiled and commandeered the very souls of his youthful and less brilliant associates?[26] Was it the case, as Grossman suggests, that Svengali was meant to personify (in disguised form) the arrogance and egotism of Wilde at the peak of his celebrity?[27] He was after all the most famous aesthete and cultural entrancer of the age, the man whom Max Beerbohm called effeminate and magnetic in equal measure: 'Deeper than repute or wit – Hypnotic'.[28] In his own work Wilde had himself raised many of the probing questions about suggestibility that would finally come to haunt him in the law courts. Five years after its publication in 1890, Wilde's novel, *The Picture of Dorian Gray*, was to be cited by the prosecuting lawyers as evidence of the author's depravity and of its immoral effects on his associates. It was apparently no defence to differentiate writer from story, or to show how the tale itself had engaged precisely with the question of the *danger* of the forces of psychological interference.[29] Although in many ways Wilde and Du Maurier (to say nothing of *Dorian Gray* and *Trilby*) were poles apart, images of bohemianism, art for art's own sake, hypnotic influence, seduction and the destruction of the innocent love object were evident in both tales. Various critics have even detected a repressed homoerotic strain beneath the saga of muscular, sporty camaraderie that Du Maurier so evidently relished.[30] And yet Du Maurier's own pictorial ridicule of aestheticism in general and Wildean artistic (or sexual) posturing in particular had long featured in *Punch*, most notably in the character of Jellaby Postlethwaite. Indeed the close antagonistic relationship between Wilde and Du Maurier had given some piquancy to a facetious inquiry addressed to the two men by the American painter, James Abbott McNeil Whistler: 'I say, which one of you two invented the other, eh?'[31]

An element of mutual invention and playfulness, perhaps – but denunciation of decadence, distaste for homosexuality *and* aestheticism were more directly apparent in Du Maurier's work, above all in *The Martian*, published soon after the author's death. There are passages of the narrative that appear to be taken straight out of *Degeneration*, Max Nordau's notorious pot-boiler on cultural, sexual and mental pathology in which Wilde and his artistic contemporaries had figured so large. *Degeneration* was a sensational bestselling diatribe on the diseases of modern art and thought, written in German in 1892 and rapidly translated across Europe and beyond: the English-language edition was published in 1895. Nordau offered his blast against contemporary culture, fulminating at every opportunity about the diseased thinkers and artists he encountered all around him. Du Maurier's protagonist, the writer Barty Josselin, directly meets such degenerates and hysterics on his spiritual journeys across Paris and London. He is temporarily and dangerously led astray in a decadent milieu where 'artists' grotesquely boast about their own disorders:

> [T]here were others he got to know, rickety, unwholesome geniuses, whose genius (such as it was) had allied itself to madness; and who were just as conceited about the madness as about the genius, and took more pains to cultivate it. It brought them a quicker kudos, and was so much more visible to the naked eye.

In case the reader missed the point the narrator adds:

> Like Barty, I am fond of men's society; but at least I like them to be unmistakably men of my own sex, manly men, and clean; not little misshapen troglodytes with foul minds and perverted passions, or self-advertising little mountebanks with enlarged and diseased vanities;

creatures who stand in a pillory sooner than not be stared at or talked about at all.[32]

Du Maurier's novels, for all their whimsy, entered forcefully into the discussion of social and sexual pathology, contributing to a widely rehearsed medico-psychiatric debate about the potential malignancy of the artist that would reach its unexpected culmination in Wilde's own sad citation of Nordau in a confession to his own degeneracy penned in Reading Prison.[33] Of course, Du Maurier could not know Wilde's fate at the time he was completing his famous tale of hypnotism in 1894, but it was clear enough to him that the destiny of Svengalian enchanters should turn out to be unhappy in life as in fiction.

The irony remains. Du Maurier derided Wilde's self-publicity and apparently sought the quiet life for himself. But then, of all unlikely things, he found he had promoted intense dissension and a vulgar cultural craze of his own; his work and person became transformed into the most debased and sought-after of commodities. Strange passions were in play and the author did not like them. He recoiled from the pandemonium, the intrusions, the manic reviews and odious insinuations. He confided the strength of his feelings to a friend: 'I hate it'; 'I have always wished to gain a reputation through my drawing and it is rather bitter for me to get a success by what I consider my worst work.'[34]

Du Maurier's 'worst work' had brought a landslide of breathless reviews, fan mail and lugubrious inquiries about the sexual ethics of his characters. Still more unpleasant than letters from unknown overseas admirers and critics was the acerbic correspondence which had come his way from another artist, and one whom he had known since his student days in Paris: Whistler. This one-time friend had responded viciously to his literary portrayal, and his hatred had spilled over into the public domain. It seemed to the hapless Du Maurier just as massively disproportionate a response as the adoration he received elsewhere. Nonetheless the mild and reclusive figure, so resistant to the gossipy pretensions of London 'society', became embroiled, via his characters, in one of the most acrimonious literary disputes anyone could remember (except perhaps the 'friend' in question, who was rather more used to them than most).[35]

The source of the grievance was a little satirical sketch of Whistler included in the initial version of *Trilby*.[36] Du Maurier cast the American painter as 'Joe Sibley' in the *Harper's New Monthly Magazine* serialisation of his novel. It has been suggested by biographers that the real target was

George Du Maurier, *The Two
Apprentices*, 1894.

not the young man of the late 1850s (whom Du Maurier had known as a
fellow student at the Atelier Gleyre in Paris), but the older, more illustrious
and, for many, insufferably pompous Whistler of the 1890s. Nonetheless,
the description of this 'idle apprentice, the king of Bohemia', an untrustworthy associate akin to Svengali in his powers of manipulation, was hardly
going to revive their friendship, but neither did Du Maurier realise the
intense enmity his joke would cause.

If Whistler had any doubts that he was the object of attack, the accompanying illustration by Du Maurier resolved them. The American threatened legal action although this never came to court since the publisher
offered an apology and stopped the sale of the March number of *Harper's
Magazine* in which the offending account occurred. It was agreed that the
passage would be removed and an alternative provided.[37] When the novel

eventually appeared in book form, the character had been rewritten and renamed as 'the yellow-haired Anthony, a Swiss who became a household name in two hemispheres'. The whole episode was both startling and painful to the author but, given the intemperate attacks upon him, Du Maurier did not want to grovel. Whilst Whistler's legal menaces subsided, his rage left a deep and enduring impression. The affair may have appeared petty to bystanders, but to Whistler the literary portrait was evidently intensely offensive. When he first read the relevant number of the story, the artist's reaction was extreme, or at least so it seemed from his public pronouncements. He suggested that it was Du Maurier who was eaten up with malice. Emotions were not only stirred up but also seemed to be projected back and forth between the two men. The aggrieved painter fired off a letter which appeared under the byline 'Mr Whistler on friendship' in the *Pall Mall Gazette*, a paper which more than matched the flamboyant litigator himself in its love of the sensational:

May 15, 1894

Sir, – It would seem, notwithstanding my boastful declaration, that after all, I had not, before leaving England, completely rid myself of that abomination – the "friend"!

One solitary unheeded one – Mr George Du Maurier – still remained hidden in Hampstead . . . Now that my back is turned, the old *marmite* of our pot-a-feu he fills with the picric acid of thirty years' spite, and, in an American Magazine, fires off his bomb of mendacious recollection and poisoned rancune.

The lie with which it is loaded, *à mon intention*, he proposes "for my possible future biographer" – but I fancy it explodes, as is usual, in his own waistcoat, and he furnishes, in his present unseemly state, an excellent example of all those others who, like himself, have thought a foul friend a finer fellow than an open enemy. The compagnon of the pétard we guillotine. Guineas are given to the popular companion who prepares his infernal machine for the distinguished associates in whose friendship he had successfully speculated.[38]

These were heavy charges: as though the mild-mannered George was some demented anarchist (of whom there were admittedly quite a few in the 1890s). Du Maurier was cast not only as dangerous but as self-deluding, self-defeating, self-destroying; a fermentor of chaos whose bomb had exploded in his own pocket; closer to a fiend than a friend, poisonous, mendacious, duplicitous. Du Maurier was bemused by such torrents, and wrote to a friend that 'J.W. seems to me to have gone crazy – however there's nothing I can do now – and I don't see what he's aiming at unless it's notoriety . . . Nor can I, after all this virulence on his part, attempt anything in the shape of an apology.'[39] He confessed himself at a loss when interviewed on the affair by the *Pall Mall Gazette* a few days later, pointing out that Whistler had spent much of his life 'making enemies', and that he had even published a book on that 'gentle art'.

The author ostensibly found it hard to understand what all the fuss was about, even insinuating that Whistler might be suffering from a mental illness. In this case, Du Maurier seemed to hint, one would have to turn to the doctors for an explanation of jokes and their relationship to the unconscious. Whistler's wit (or wits) seemed to have been overcome by an extreme negative passion. The episode was certainly painful to Du Maurier: he was genuinely dismayed that the fun had turned so quickly to fury (however useful for his sales); and yet, interestingly, his story was centred on the very phenomena – altered states of mind, the transfer of emotions and talents from one person to another, wounding underhand attacks, cultural and emotional parasitism – that it now provoked. Whistler's reaction made the point, disclosing his slavery to deep passions, perhaps to unknown or unconscious forces triggered by the other man. Was it a case of 'monomania', as Du Maurier believed? Whether truly the victim of uncontainable emotion, or the master of simulated rage, the cantankerous plaintiff continued to pen an uncensored stream of letters against his former Parisian friend. This tirade was sent to the President of the Beefsteak Club in the West End, an establishment frequented by both men: 'As good faith and good fellowship are your essentials it becomes plain that Mr Du Maurier & I cannot both continue as members. Either I am a coward, or he is a liar – *That* is the issue.'[40] His request that the letter be hung in the Club dining room was refused, and it was pointed out that Du Maurier had already given up his membership. In response to this miserable fiasco with its bathetic ending, a humorist forged a letter by Whistler in the first number of Harry Furniss's publication, *Lika Joko*, feigning indignation that the painter had been cut out of the revised version of Du Maurier's book. Here in this latest twist to the satire, Whistler was cast as a Svengali-like egoist to cap them all:

It was I, Ich, Io, Yo, Ego, – I in all the languages of whose alphabet Mr. Du Maurier holds the secret – who was the sympathetic, charming, irresistible, unreliable, idle, sarcastic, clean, graceful, famous-notorious worshipper of Himself and art: but I also, the terrible, the contentious, the launcher of elaborate epigrams, the two-penny cane wielder, the turbulent libel auctioneer, the scalp-hunter – I, as some trumpery outsider, I think Oscar has called me, the rowdy and unpleasant.[41]

Apparently some readers fell into the trap and took the letter to be genuine, although it is hard to see how they could have, given the crude nature of the parody.[42]

This scandal proved an omen of the way in which the book's influence, notoriety and popularity would run out of control amidst the literary rumour-machines, the 'new journalism' and the gossip circuits of the 1890s. It was, after all, a period renowned for its preoccupation with, and perpetuation of, cultural hype. 'New' was a constant epithet: new hedonism, new paganism, new drama, new unionism, new humour, new realism, new woman, new spirit, new journalism, new Grub Street.[43] And, of course, the years around the turn of the century were also a time of self-consciously modern inquiry into unconscious psychological states, into the strange processes of forgetting and recall, the irrational forces of anger and hatred, cravings and desire, apparently exacerbated by the impossible hypocrisies, as well as by the sheer pace, stress and expectations of modern life. It was also the era of 'sexology' in which various specialists became renowned for their 'scientific' preoccupation with sexual relations, and even of new definitions of sexuality itself. The sensational mesmeric story of Svengali and Trilby was celebrated by all and sundry as a newsworthy development. It was an 'original' phenomenon, a sign of the times. Here was a tale professedly trading on the hypnotic, sexual and artistic mysteries which so exercised doctors and scientists at that moment. It was, in Freud's later sense of the word, 'uncanny': familiar and unfamiliar, homely and unhomely, all at once. Du Maurier not only combined the elements of mesmerism and the enchantments of strangers in an unprecedented way; he also connected with other stories and histories of bodily and mental possession which spanned the nineteenth century.

While there had been many earlier fictions of trance, possession and hypnotic depravity, there was nothing which evoked quite the reaction of *Trilby*. Something very exceptional had taken place between this novel and its readership. Reviewers wryly celebrated the fact that in 'juggling' with hypnotism, Du Maurier had surpassed the scientists. A piece in the *Atlantic Monthly* argued that:

While psychologists are experimenting with this occult force, and coming out of their laboratories from time to time with partial results, thinking perhaps to give a therapeutic turn, or to account by means of it for
mob action and other half understood vagaries of human nature, our
trifling novelist and artist gayly possesses himself of the secret of the
whole matter, and applies it to the life of that loveliest object in nature,
a maiden stepping over the threshold of womanhood.[44]

Even within the medical press, close attention to Du Maurier's plot was the
order of the day and here, too, caution was thrown to the winds. Svengali's
author was said to have written something not only out of the ordinary, but
unique. An article in the *British Medical Journal* declared *Trilby* an exceptionally accurate rendition of the hypnotic relationship, insisting that 'Mr.
Du Maurier may be congratulated on having produced, for the first time, a
literary masterpiece, in which the conditions of hypnotism are used with
the power of genius'. While it was acknowledged that he had not fully
analysed the phenomenon, Du Maurier had apparently presented the
process with laudable scientific appropriateness. The *BMJ* continued:

Under the conditions, which Mr. Du Maurier carefully and accurately
indicates, of perfect hypnotic subjection, of complete abstraction from
interfering external or internal influences, Trilby, when she sings, is in a
perfect hypnotic sleep; she is unconscious of her audience and unaware
of her surroundings. She is, like all thorough hypnotics, reduced to the
state of a marvellous machine, capable of receiving the most perfect
training and in complete subjection to the will and the suggestion of the
operator.[45]

Neither is it every potboiler of the day that ends up with its villain and its
eponymous heroine in the dictionary. At one time the word 'trilby' was
slang for 'foot' as well as, more enduringly, the name for a particular type
of hat. For a while you could sell virtually anything by naming it after
Trilby. If the laboured pathos of the story now causes us to flinch, it should
be remembered that many of Du Maurier's contemporaries were as deeply
absorbed and affected by the novel's themes as they were keen to buy
'Trilby' accessories. Adopted (via the stage play) as an alternative name for
the soft felt hat, there were to be 'Trilby parties' (involving readings from
the text), Trilby high-heel shoes, 'an ornament to any foot' (price $3), as
well as Trilby sweets and lozenges. There were Trilby sausages from

Philadelphia ('something new' which 'fills a long-felt want'; they 'melt in your mouth'), Trilby hearth-brushes and hams; and of, course, concert performances of the music cited in the novel (from Schubert and Chopin to 'Ben Bolt'). There were Trilby musical scores (published in pamphlet form by Oliver Ditson and Company), not to mention soaps and tooth-pastes. *Life's Monthly Calendar* offered a series of cash prizes for the best set of replies to ten questions which included: What was Svengali's real name? In what places does the author compare Gecko to a dog? How old was Trilby when she died? What was Little Billee's physical explanation of his inability to love? What incidents of the story are inconsistent with the author's own argument on behalf of the nude in art?[46] Then there were Trilby and Svengali waltzes, for which, of course, the sheet music was in heavy demand. There was even a town of Trilby in Florida with its Svengali Square and Little Billee Lake.[47] Even as earnest discussions of the heroine's morals proceeded, there were lucrative appropriations of her name for domestic products of dazzling variety.

These points are not merely anecdotal; neither are they simply 'extra-textual', for ventriloquism, gossip, exploitation and stardom are central themes in the novel. The euphoria of the audiences at Trilby's performances in the tale is made weirdly extreme, and almost hysterical. Remarkably, the story reflects, disturbs, interacts with, its own overblown reception. In other words, the history of the novel's reception and the story contained in the novel overlap to a significant degree. Idealisation and idolisation are explored in the narrative ('La Svengali's' image plastered in shop windows; her name the talk of the town); the tale becomes a legend. The distasteful and even deranged crowd fanfare before 'the diva' and the process of hero-worship is recounted in the text (whole audiences overwhelmed, men and women of every rank entranced); yet the fiction is outdone by the extra-fictional 'drive' to turn the novel's author into public property. Sexual chicanery as well as artistic ventriloquism are themes of Du Maurier's nar-rative and in turn inform the debate about its 'ethics'. Squabbles and fights occur on *Trilby's* pages; and journal articles reported cases of real couples in America fighting over the question of the heroine's honour.

To a bizarre degree, the novel was also appropriated in moral and reli-gious discussions of the time. Through making some association with the story, serious-minded commentators and preachers sought to gain greater public attention for otherwise unfashionable or controversial topics.[48] This was a seminal story of the *fin de siècle*, but it also introduced to an unprece-dentedly large audience an ongoing discussion about induced states of

"TRILBY."
By Napoleon Sarony.
ALFRED HICKMAN, AS LITTLE BILLEE

From the New York
production, 1895.

incapacity (or special capacity), with all manner of associated confusions. So many people loved the story that *Trilby* virtually became an industry. As one commentator, with little exaggeration, declared, 'Its presentation has given employment, onerous or enjoyable, honorary or remunerative, to thousands; hundreds of thousands have read it, and hundreds of thousands seen it on the stage.'[49] It was noted that American libraries had been inundated by excited readers in search of a copy. At one major library in New York it was found necessary to circulate a hundred copies of the book. The Chicago Public Library found its initial purchase of twenty-six copies insufficient. In the librarian's words, 'I believe we could use 260 and never find a copy on the shelves. Every one of our 54,000 card-holders seems determined to read the book.'[50]

Henry James was alert to the damage such extreme commercial success and publicity inflicted on Du Maurier; perhaps he felt some responsibility, having had a hand in the original concoction.[51] The creator of Svengali and Trilby did not long survive the production of his mesmerising novel and

James came close to suggesting that its very success was responsible for Du Maurier's physical decline. It was as though Du Maurier became so despondent about finding any peace that he gradually gave up the ghost, taking to his grave as another might have taken to his bed. He was the languishing phantom of his own opera. In his delicate obituary essay, James exempted Du Maurier from explicit criticism on the score of promoting the tasteless pandemonium. He spoke as though the base commercialism and the popular curiosity lay simply and inexplicably in the wake of the novel. For whatever reason, the beast had been unleashed unwittingly by the author. 'It became a mere immensity of sound, the senseless hum of a million newspapers and the irresponsible chatter of ten millions of gossips.' Indeed in James' view, the problem started with the crowd, that 'many-headed monster', as he put it, only then rebounding damagingly on 'the victim'.[52]

Du Maurier's fortuitous idea for the characters in *Trilby* had first been described to James in the late 1880s, when the two men were out walking together.[53] Du Maurier had long been seeking an alternative to drawing and painting. It was the habit of the two friends to stroll the streets of London or to ramble along the coast. They sometimes shared their ideas about stories. The novelist complained of lacking a good plot, whereupon Du Maurier offered him an intriguing scenario, as a kind of gift, which James duly noted down. Svengali and Trilby were not mentioned by name, but the characterisations were roughly sketched by the great American writer. Here was the adventure of a servant girl with a wonderful voice but no musical genius, who was 'mesmerised and made to sing by a little foreign Jew who has mesmeric power [and] infinite feeling'. In James' version, the Jew and the servant girl seemed mutually dependent, each sparked off by the other. The girl 'is really all the while only galvanized by her mate'; 'she had the glorious voice, but no talent – he had the sacred fire, the rare musical organization, and had played into her and through her. The *end*, as regards her, miserably pathetic.'[54] James was clearly rather taken with the story but urged his friend to write it, since he felt that his own want of musical knowledge would have hampered him from proceeding with the task. A few years later the novel emerged, but only after Du Maurier had completed another, his first 'romance', *Peter Ibbetson*, published in 1891, also about strange inter-personal communications and intra-psychic events. That the prospect of *Trilby* was passed back and forth between these two companions, that it was the loose change of George and Henry's banter, could even be seen to have a relation to the tale itself, where the heroine was divided between the creative men as, much earlier in Du Maurier's life, a young

Belgian woman had been uneasily shared between himself and Felix Moscheles.[55]

In the story, Trilby passes from the protection of the loving artist into the clutches of the malevolent musician – yet in the end she is not fully possessed by either. Instead she is shown to take a strange hold over the controlling men, somewhat like the intriguing potential characters passed back and forth between James and Du Maurier. One could speculate endlessly about the relations of Du Maurier's work, social experience and friendships. 'Fountains of gloom', 'violence of publicity', 'miserably pathetic endings' might characterise aspects of his life and thought as well as of his prose. Many questions can be asked about the interweaving of mesmeric tales and real-life case histories, extraordinary interactions of 'text' and 'context'; real cases of individuals affected by entrancing strangers which were said to lie behind novels of somnambulism; couples whose behaviour was rumoured to have been influenced and modified by the assumptions of the story-line; a dozen Svengalis and Trilbys who worked mysteriously together to produce music – and sometimes worse. So many questions and half-truths, hints and puzzles remained unresolved, complained some of Du Maurier's devotees at the time. What on earth was the author up to? Private correspondents as well as journalists beseeched and besieged the poor man for interviews, begging him for some definitive clarification as to the meanings and motivations of his story. He was deeply reluctant or, perhaps, truly unable to respond to their demands. It was clear enough that he experienced such inquiries as the most violent of intrusions.

The 'clink of gold' was insufficient compensation for the intrusive public furore and the unpredictable nastiness of surrounding events (not least the Whistler episode), but the scale of the demand, especially in the United States, can hardly be overstated. The tale became an instant best-seller even at the relatively high price of $1.75. By February 1895, more than 200,000 copies had been sold, 75,000 as a triple-decker, the rest in a new one-volume illustrated version. The US sales in turn led to greater British sales. Du Maurier tried to lie low, remaining holed up in Hampstead as the clamour worsened. Then in June 1895 he and his family moved from New Grove House to a central London residence (in Oxford Square, near Hyde Park). This was puzzling to his friends, given his protestations of dislike for metropolitan life. It was said he was never as happy there as he had been close to the greenery and quiet of Hampstead Heath. His friends looked on with concern and not a little amazement at the entire '*Trilby* madness'. While the creator of the horrible 'spider', Svengali, had initially spun the web in which he was now entrapped, it was equally clear that he had not known what he was letting himself in for when he released the book.

Critics have continued to speculate about the real origins of the charac-ters, including Svengali. Many of the minor figures could be clearly located as portraits of Du Maurier's friends and colleagues, but the origins of the Jew remain a mystery. Was he perhaps, as some thought, loosely derived from a particularly egotistical Greek acquaintance Du Maurier had made in Paris?[56] Whatever the biographical provenance of Svengali and the rest of the novel's cast, they were evidently acquiring the most extraordinary life of their own. By 1896, a friend of Du Maurier's referred to the phenomenon of the story's public reception as 'Trilbyism' and 'Svengalism'.[57] The stage version of 1895 produced in the United States by Paul M. Potter soon crossed back to the London stage (thanks to Herbert Beerbohm Tree) and to theatres elsewhere in Britain. It was a smash hit, and even as it ran at the Haymarket, parody versions were doing the rounds, cashing in at the box-office.

The *Illustrated London News* referred to the 'Trilby boom', and a whole series of overblown articles drew attention to the remarkable crowds queuing for tickets to see the play. Not everyone liked the dramatised ver-sion. Max Beerbohm admitted that he had thought the play dismal when he had attended a performance in New York, but his half brother, Herbert, took a very different view. On seeing Potter's *Trilby*, he bought up the rights during the interval, returning to London with the contract in his pocket.[58] Kate Terry Gielgud (John Gielgud's mother), who attended the first night in London, considered it bad art and had serious reservations about Tree's 'Leviathan Svengali of the most grotesque type among a cast of pigmies', whilst the Princess of Wales was not amused by the exposure of Trilby's naked feet on stage.[59] Amidst the 'general fund of excitement on this red letter day' (the opening night), Trilby-style dress, as worn by the actress Dorothea Baird, was *de rigeur* for the ladies.[60] Whether loyal repli-cas, free adaptations or sardonic take-offs, the theatre craze for *Trilby* reached astonishing proportions. It has been calculated that by 1896, there were twenty-four productions running simultaneously in the United States. In one take-off entitled *Drilby* ('a parody in verse'), Svengali, Little Billee and company take a train across America where they have numer-ous absurd adventures. Yet the novel itself was already there before the spin-off satires had been penned; it became virtually a license to print money. Such was the aura surrounding it that the London Fine Arts Society placed the original manuscript on exhibition in a locked glass case.

Meanwhile the New York Knoedler Gallery featured a series of Trilby paintings.[61] In the same city one might also attend a Trilby Coterie and Chowder Club.[62] As early as 1899, a brief film based on Svengali showed a man bringing two ballet dancers to life from the billboard in front of him, thereby inaugurating a sustained tradition of large screen versions of the tale.[63] Mesmeric stage acts under the name of 'Svengali' were also to remain features of popular culture long after the original.

Du Maurier and the writers and artists who formed his social circle had often charted with dismay the processes of mass modern enthusiasm which they deemed to have so corrosive an impact on the individual's capacity for aesthetic judgement, let alone mental stability. But what more powerful illustration than Trilby and Svengali of the volatile and even hysterical mood of 'the public'? If it was not the acclaim itself that was responsible for Du Maurier's own depression, it was said to be the vile accompanying cacophony. The author was immured in what Henry James called a 'landslide of obsessions, of inane incongruous letters, of interviewers, intruders, invaders'.[64] Henry shuddered in sympathy for poor old embarrassed George. That the exquisite American stylist half craved such a windfall for himself is not in doubt; but neither is his genuine horror at the 'vulgar' uproar.

If James was the most exalted, he was by no means the only champion of Du Maurier's tale to lament the plebeian response. One wonders, of course, whether James' fondness for Du Maurier was greater than his respect for the novel. But certainly there were others who were genuinely moved, even overwhelmed, by the tale, and wanted to distinguish and preserve the original story from cheap travesty. Nonetheless, the mawkishness, as well as the insistent 'anti high-culture' tone of the original, made it a strange candidate for the high-minded protectionism that, *inter alia*, James and George Bernard Shaw advocated on behalf of Du Maurier. It was as though the admirers of a brash literary form took offence at the idiotic subculture which grew out of it. Svengali had been travestied, Trilby belittled – or at least, so it seemed to Du Maurier's friends. It was the blatant sexual and racial innuendoes of the sequels that were most resented. In one tawdry pamphlet, there was lewd emphasis on Trilby 'posing for the figure'.[65] The very names of the characters were pulled about and mocked in coarse ethnic send-ups.

Such ribald comic renditions contrasted with more staid entertainments in the novel's aftermath, such as 'An Evening with Trilby', held in Omaha in the United States (on 17 October 1894), in which various gentlemen were reported to have given papers with titles such as 'The Story of Trilby', 'Trilby's Voice and Method', 'The Identity of the Artist in Trilby' and 'Trilby as a hypnotic subject'.[66] On stage, too, Trilby and Svengali had their serious interpreters; but they also suffered unspeakable indignities. While the official version was running at the Haymarket, other, less respectful, performances quickly appeared elsewhere. '"Thrillby," A Shocker in One Scene and Several Spasm' (sic), by William Muskerry, boasted a mixture of songs and dialogue. The comedy commented upon (even as it amplified) the whole *Trilby* fad, lampooning, in its feeble verse, the heroes of this 'modern romance', 'the craze and the rage' of the day.[67] In this version, Svengali was marked out not only by his strong stage make-up but also by his heavy 'Jewish' accent. He compulsively answers questions with questions ('Everyding dat I blay ends vid a "note of interrogation"'). Malleable, slippery, untrustworthy, Muskerry's Svengali is, in the worst sense of the word, 'cosmopolitan'. He speaks German, Italian, Spanish and English (with an Irish accent too, if required).[68] He is 'polyglot', a concept allied here with his decentred, composite mind and his socially contrived position. Here Svengali is an ethnic confection with no real soul or centre. He is a creature of cosmetic arts and crafts. Sometimes, it seemed to be the thespian Herbert Beerbohm Tree just as much as the Jewish mesmerist Svengali who was the target of satire. It was said that an actor who could play Svengali on one night, Hamlet on another, must be a strange man indeed. The question of fraud and masquerade, of mystery and despotism, of hypnotic and erotic powers are all lightly touched on in this 'Svengali song':

SONG (SVENGALI) – 'The Polyglot Manager'

If you doubt my identity, I'm a nonentity
Shown in my entity, nightly by Tree –
A being mysterious, haughty, imperious,
My name is – I'm serious! –
Keep it dark – Svengali!
I'm slightly despotic, I'm highly hypnotic,
My temper's erotic – when out on the spree!
Tho' my conduct's outrageous, I'm far from courageous,
Still my laughter's contagious –
Ho, ho, ha, ha (laughing), hee! hee!

Banal, without question; but in fact even this ghastly verse was recapitulating themes anxiously discussed in European medico-psychiatric journals, as they considered the dangerous antics of stage 'magnetists'. In the spoof, Svengali is shown to be a victim of self-delusions. He grossly exaggerates his own abilities as hypnotist. The process works, in so far as it does in this account, through the power of Svengali's eyes. In an aside, Svengali offers the woman 'Thrillby' a salary if she will fake the state of mesmerism, a proposal with which she willingly complies:

> THRIL. Oh, if it's a paying game. Oh! 'Mai! Aie!' (becomes cataleptic and
>   presses her hand to her brow)
> SVEN. (Making passes) It's all in her eye![69]

The exchange ridicules the fear aroused by hypnosis in this period, by suggesting that the whole thing is an elaborate farce. Thus when Svengali asks the supposedly mesmerised subject what she sees, the reply is:

> Well, candidly speaking, not much, beyond an inordinate quantity of
> 'No. 5' grease-paint, and a shocking bad wig.[70]

Here the mesmerising Jew is cut down to size, exposed as an impotent fraud – unlike in the original novel. And yet, the enigma remained: how was one to explain Svengali and company's massive cultural appeal? Was it the tale's complicity with anti-Semitism, the charm of its picture of bohemia, its fascination with mesmerism, or the mournful and melancholic rendition of a lost Paris which inspired the violent passions and ensured that the names of the villain and the heroine would enter permanently into the language? Tales of *Trilby*'s original impetus, whether true or apocryphal, all blended together, became part of the mythic structure of the novel and its world, reverentially documented in various publications of the time. Du Maurier's was more than just an instance of the best-seller phenomenon. It was a novel which interestingly disturbed the dichotomy between its content and its context, inside and out, playing around with its own considerable limitations and prejudices. The Jew's fury, Little Billee's prostration and Trilby's martyrdom, their mutual experiences of compulsion, coercion and nervousness, were 'all the rage' in the 1890s. James was surely right to conclude that the tale had something extraordinary about it; a passion had been unleashed in excess of any evident logic, and for reasons which had little to do with literary merit. Du Maurier had let loose the elements and 'they did violence to his nerves'.[71]

3
Mesmerism

SVENGALI Yes, I can work magic (*laugh*). At least, what
fools call magic. You saw me cure her pain just now?
GECKO A trick of magnetism!
SVENGALI It was the beginning. Trained by me, she shall
sing for the world's delight. Hers will be the voice, mine the
knowledge – mine the genius . . . I have not studied
Mesmer's art in vain.

Paul Potter, *Trilby*[1]

Pondering the startling work of Franz Anton Mesmer (1734–1815), that
had first came to the attention of the European public in the years leading up to the French Revolution, the twentieth-century cultural critic and
follower of Freud Stefan Zweig, remarked: 'In a word the power evoked
by Mesmer burst the boundaries of its proper sphere, the sphere of medical science, and filled the whole of France with a dangerous and infectious fluid. There was a sort of collective frenzy, of universal hysteria.
Everyone suffered from mesmeromania.'[2] Whether late eighteenth-century onlookers were for or against this intriguing healer, they were
obliged at least to address the question of his strange, dangerous and
infectious achievement. What was the 'rapport' Mesmer claimed and the
crisis he induced? How far was it a deception of individuals and groups,
and anyway, even if it was a deception, an effect of the charlatan, what had
actually occurred? How had his clients' 'gullibility' been secured? In
short, what was the medical, political and moral significance and the
long-lasting effect of this Viennese adventurer who had, at least for a
time, taken Parisian society by storm?

Mesmer was not the first person ever to have drawn attention to the healing properties of magnets; neither was he by any means the last. A number of historians have shown that there was interest in the health-giving powers of magnets before the late eighteenth-century craze associated with Mesmer's name; but it was above all this particular practitioner who brought certain inter-personal or, in his terms, inter-bodily forces to the forefront of public discussion and controversy.[3] Like many later 'Svengalis', Mesmer was to be accused of malevolently and rapaciously interfering with his 'patients'. Whilst he was something of a maverick, he was not working in isolation, even if he often failed to gain the prestigious 'Academy' recognition for which he longed. His ideas were novel enough to startle and impress; they were also familiar enough to be given some credence. He was intellectually indebted to a man of the Church, Father Hell, Professor of Astronomy at the University of Vienna and court astrologer to the Empress Maria Theresa. The churchman had manufactured magnets and applied them to diseased parts of the body, although he made rather less far-reaching claims for the efficacy of the procedure than the ambitious novice who took up his idea. Anyhow, before long the two magnetists fell out and became enemies. Mesmer also owed a debt to the thought and practice of the Jesuit priest Gassner, who employed something akin to what was later to be termed hypnotism, albeit in an explicitly religious guise, for the purpose of casting out devils. Gassner's dramatic performances attracted large and enthusiastic crowds, and the anxious attention of the Vatican.[4]

Mesmer concluded that the success of Gassner's exorcisms was due to magnetism rather than some spiritual struggle with the devil. In other words, he provided a distinct explanatory framework for the effects Gassner achieved. The importance of this development, at least in Mesmer's own view, could not be exaggerated: he announced that he had found a universal method for curing and preserving mankind. Illness was nothing else, he grandly insisted, than a perturbation in the progression of the movement of life.[5] Once liberated from Jesuit rhetoric, and with the technique packaged with increasing suavity, 'the wizard from Vienna' quickly made his mark; indeed he was to prove fascinating, electrifying, to people from all walks of life.[6]

Mesmer had entered university in Vienna in 1759 to study medicine. His interests were wide-ranging and encompassed philosophy, law and music. He was deemed both an able alchemist and a talented musician, claiming friendship with Glück, Haydn and Mozart (who made his famous reference to Mesmer's magnets in the opera *Così fan tutte*). In Mesmer's doctoral dissertation of 1766, on the influence of the moon and planets on the course of disease, the themes which were to occupy him for much of his later life were already evident. In the 1770s, he developed ideas about bodily tides, seeking, through the use of magnets, to apply his insights to the needs of the patients who began to consult him at the rather grand house in the Landstrasse in which he was by then installed, thanks to a wealthy widow whom he had married in 1768. An early success was with a 29-year-old woman, a Miss Oesterline, whom he treated for aches and pains (especially of the teeth and ears), delirium, mania, blackouts and nausea. This patient, amongst others, appeared to make impressive progress.

Mesmer's 'discovery' of a superfine fluid that enters into and surrounds all bodies had cosmic as well as human implications, but it was above all the therapeutic promises which attracted supporters. He claimed that the magnetic movement in the body determined health and illness; uneven distribution or irregular rhythms were deemed harmful and sickness occurred where there was an obstacle to the flow of fluid though the system. This could be alleviated by massaging the body's 'poles', thereby easing the obstruction. This process would often induce a 'crisis', perhaps in the form of convulsions. Whereas Mesmer initially used metals in his endeavours to bring the patients' magnetic fluids back into harmony, he found that such aids were not strictly necessary hands alone sufficed. He increasingly relied on manual 'passes' over the body. In other words he came to the conclusion that animal magnetism could be conducted directly through his own person and that his own, physical intervention might therefore restore equilibrium in the sufferer.[7]

Amongst the more notorious episodes early on in his career was the case of a certain Maria-Theresa Paradis whom he began seeing in Vienna in January 1777. Mesmer claimed to have achieved a miraculous improvement in the condition of this young pianist, sightless from early childhood, as a result, it was thought at the time, of paralysis of the optic nerves, brought about, perhaps, through a sudden fright caused by a loud noise.[8] Initially, Miss Paradis' parents had been enthusiastic, even overjoyed by the charismatic intervention that Mesmer made in the life of their daughter. She had earlier endured, apparently in vain, treatment with leeches, purgatives and electricity – hundreds of shocks had been administered. But her mother and father gradually came to the conclusion that the young woman had escaped from one gruesome regime only to be transferred into the hands of a monstrous charlatan;[9] the nefarious physician had taken her over in the most sinister fashion. When Stefan Zweig came to examine the case many years later, he remarked, as it were with hindsight, that the girl's blindness was probably caused by a psychical disturbance rather than optic nerve atrophy, and that Mesmer had somehow intuited this although, even now, critics debate the organic or psychogenic origins of her problems.[10] This is not the place to speculate on what was really wrong with the patient, or to guess at Mesmer's private intuitions and intentions; rather, the point is that this tale of music and mesmerism provides, albeit in different form, an 'advance copy' of the narratives of suggestibility, sexuality, musical recovery and physical sequestration disseminated in later years. In short, the dread of the swooping emotional kidnapper and the vulnerable musical proxy, so prominently encountered a century later in the case of Svengali and Trilby, was already powerfully written into the original history of Dr Mesmer and Miss Paradis.

Maria-Theresa Paradis' talents had been clear from an early age. As a seven-year-old she had begun to listen with rapt concentration to church music; soon, others were to attend to her performances with equal devotion. She had an exceptional ear and a good voice. Before long, she was playing the organ and singing soprano in the Church of St Augustin in Vienna. It is said that Mozart attended one of her concerts and that the Empress Queen had been so moved by her recitals as to settle a life pension upon her. When she was placed under the care of the 'celebrated empiric', as one English report in *The Gentleman's Magazine* dubbed Mesmer, Miss Paradis was still in her teens.[11] He promised to cure her blindness, as well as the melancholy which reduced her at times to a state of delirium. Whether on the basis of this undertaking, or some other less transparent motive (or compulsion), she became a boarder in his house for several months. Relations with the family deteriorated, however, and Mesmer refused to grant her parents access. Eventually she was taken away by force, on the express order of the Empress. Mesmer claimed she had been cured, whilst others grumbled that she remained blind. The disgruntled magnetist 'had the diabolical malignity to assert that she could see very well, and only pretended her blindness to preserve the pension granted to her by the Empress Queen'.[12] The pension was stopped on the Empress' death. Paradis' musical career was resumed and she toured to great acclaim, arousing, in equal measure, admiration for her fortitude and pity for her misfortunes. In Paris she received huge approbation; and when she moved to England she captured the enthusiasm of the Court and of various eminent musicians. A cantata in German was written for her by an esteemed professor of mathematics, himself blind. She was said to have executed this

Faustine Parmentier,
Marie-Theresa Paradis,
1784.

piece in an able and truly affecting manner. The young and accomplished visitor presented letters at court and played to their majesties, who became her patrons, as did the Prince of Wales. Maria-Theresa never recovered her sight and died in 1824, at the age of sixty-five.

The rights and wrongs of Mesmer's conduct in the case continued to divide later commentators. According to Richard Harte, in an extensive history of hypnotism produced at the end of the nineteenth century, it was Mesmer's misfortune to be victimised by the Paradis family and Vienna's establishment doctors. Their failure to support him, Harte complained, was typical of the arrogance, stupidity and self-interest of official medicine throughout modern history. The case of Paradis struck this sympathetic writer as a good example of the intransigence of orthodox scientific opinion and the persecution of men with new and eccentric ideas.[13] In his view, the much-maligned magnetist may have been a little insouciant, but he had certainly cured the girl. It was the duplicity and impatience of her family,

along with their dull physicians, who conspired to rob him of the achievement. Some evidence for this more generous view of Mesmer was contained in a remarkable statement made by Herr Paradis himself, writing in
the first flush of his daughter's ostensible recovery. His descriptions of the
gradual improvement of her vision were certainly poignant. Whether one
chooses to side with Mesmer or believes Herr Paradis, the latter's initial
declaration was a moving account of the blind patient's painful progress.
The first person she recognised on apparently recovering some vision was
Mesmer himself, but she admitted to preferring the sight of a large dog, also
brought before her. She never quite got used to the human face, and found
noses particularly offensive: 'They seem to threaten me, as if they would
bore my eyes out.' Gradually, her father continued, she became reconciled
to the human countenance but her appreciation of objects and colours was
always marred by the harsh effect light had upon her. To avoid dizzy spells,
she sometimes requested that her eyes be bound up again, although when
blindfold she walked without the confidence she had possessed whilst previously sightless. The judgement of distances was a great problem too.
Dipping a rusk in chocolate and lifting it to her mouth, she was convinced
it was too large ever to be consumed. Conversely, a remote reservoir
appeared to her to be a mere soup-plate, and the Danube a white stripe.[14]

Such gentle descriptions are a far cry from the fracas that ensued after
relations had deteriorated between the young lady's parents and her magnetist. By all accounts, undignified scenes occurred in which father and
mother (especially mother) actually came to blows with the doctor, as they
sought to retrieve the helpless victim from his clutches. The story of her
blindness and musicianship, her equivocal residence with the magnetist,
and her even more doubtful physical improvement, combined to make the
case a *cause célèbre* and to face Mesmer himself with the stark choice, communicated by one of Viennese society's medical grandees, of abandoning
either his activities or the city itself; he chose the latter.[15] It seems that difficulties in Mesmer's marital life also contributed to his decision to leave
Vienna; his relationship with his wife had already deteriorated before he left
the city (without her), on his odyssey towards Paris, where he was to arrive
in February 1778.[16]

The perceived dangers of the practice and the person of Mesmer are
clear enough in this episode; so, too, the therapeutic confusion, allure and
excitement. The patient was, on the one hand, to enter a kind of trance, on
the other, to be offered a greater acuity of vision. In addition to the material amelioration which might be achieved in so many physical ailments, it

was claimed that mesmerism offered, in a more general sense, to bring an invisible world to light. Indeed, the capacity for 'internal visualisation' was advertised as a function of the mesmeric state, and was described by several subsequent English and French supporters.[17] While some scoffed at Mesmer's ability to pull the wool over the eyes of his devotees, others catalogued the startling physical and mental improvements that they had enjoyed as a result of his efforts. Improvement of vision was but one of many reported effects, although the full significance of eye contact in producing the mesmeric state itself would only be addressed later.[18]

The charismatic healer had been rudely dispatched from Vienna in the wake of the Paradis debacle, yet he was never to be an altogether lonely wanderer abroad. From the early days, there had been considerable attention to his work in various European countries. He had quickly generated some interest in Bavaria (where, in a rare official accolade, he was made a member of the Academy of Science), and he also did well in Switzerland and Hungary.[19] It was not long before fresh episodes of 'enthusiasm' broke out across numerous European cities, and even further afield. The circle of those he treated was increasingly only a fraction of the much wider public who were aware of his dramatic work. The *Society of Universal Harmony*, which he and his followers founded in Paris in the 1780s, came to have a membership of hundreds or even thousands, with branches established in many towns.[20] Mesmer had soon gathered a number of well-connected pupils and aristocratic sympathisers, as well as a court physician.[21] There was, admittedly, also a growing number of disillusioned erstwhile devotees. In Paris, Mesmer became the talk of the town during the decade of social and intellectual turbulence leading up to the French Revolution, as has been most memorably shown in Robert Darnton's fine study, *Mesmerism and the End of the Enlightenment in France*. Both the enthusiasm and the ambition of participants in this new movement were considerable. By 1784, one of Mesmer's followers had travelled to the New World to announce the discovery of animal magnetism and to establish groups of followers.[22] It was not long before both straight-faced and satirical books on Mesmer's Parisian 'splash' were appearing all over the place. It was the bouts of ridicule rather than the bursts of applause, however, that seemed to make the deeper impression on the *maestro*. Popular acclaim was not enough; he wished to be taken seriously by his peers.

Mesmerism has long raised an interpretative dilemma for historians: is it best seen as a late-flourishing example from a vanishing world of 'folk' credulity? Is it convincing to argue that, in so far as mesmerism endured into the nineteenth and twentieth centuries, it has been as a 'survival' of some primitive or at least pre-modern 'mentality'? Certainly the assumption is often made that 'modern mesmerism' is a contradiction in terms; rather, the mesmerist emerges from – and is always redolent of – the *ancien regime* of the soul. Even in such sinister modern tales of mesmerism as Thomas Mann's *Mario and the Magician* (1929), set in Italy, and written in the shadow of fascism, the stupefying 'magician', Cavaliere Cipolla, is very much cast as a man from the old world. This is how Mann describes his mesmerist:

> A man of an age hard to determine, but by no means young; with a sharp, ravaged face, piercing eyes, compressed lips, small black waxed moustache, and a so-called imperial in the curve between mouth and chin . . . Perhaps more than anywhere else the eighteenth century is still alive in Italy, and with it the charlatan and mountebank type so characteristic of the period.[23]

The figure has piercing eyes, of course (so often this is a stock image in literary depictions of the mesmerist), but he also has a faintly anachronistic air: the mesmerist is an eighteenth-century charlatan. But is it true to say that mesmerism became increasingly 'outlandish' as the nineteenth century wore on? Darnton suggests it did, compellingly explaining the phenomenon in terms of a social order still committed to a belief in the 'fantastic'. He argues that eighteenth-century folk continued to have great difficulty in differentiating 'the real' from 'the imaginary' and that in certain crucial ways their credulity was quite unlike that of their descendants.[24] In the age of mesmerism's first triumphs, elastic shoes for walking on water were also greeted with artless enthusiasm. Such beliefs, contends Darnton, declined in the nineteenth century, although he evidently allows (as does Mann) for its indomitable upsurge here and there in the modern age. 'So strong was the popular enthusiasm for science', Darnton remarks of Mesmer and his epoch ('the end of the enlightenment'), 'that it almost erased the line (never very clear until the nineteenth century) dividing science from pseudo-science.'[25] But was the line really so sharp *in* the nineteenth century? Did developments in scientific theory and knowledge really establish so solid a boundary as Darnton's account might imply? Whether one agrees that a world of endless and charmingly preposterous eighteenth-century 'gadgeteering' gave way to a less fantastic order of knowledge depends, of course, on many other assumptions about truth, progress, science and pseudo-science, and also on the weight given to the very many nineteenth-century phenomena of transported 'hearts and minds', as well as persistent interest, both popular and learned, in 'the occult'. At any rate, it is striking that the practices that Mesmer had inaugurated in the 1770s endured throughout the nineteenth century. It was not even the case that 'hypnotism' (a term coined by a Scottish-born surgeon, James Braid, in the 1840s) eclipsed erudite scientific or popular belief in Mesmer's original ideas: various magnetic and metallurgical explanations of trance states and so forth were still being canvassed in the 1870s and 1880s.[26]

It was not so much that mesmerism was eclipsed, as that its style and explanation shifted; in the age of Mesmer himself, its *coups de théâtre* seemed akin to the enchantments of Mozart operas; a century later, under the mantle of scientific authorities such as Charcot, Liébeault and Bernheim, it appeared closer to the naturalist idiom of Zola's novels or Ibsen's dramas. In other words it moved from the salon to the hospital, from the concert hall to the laboratory (as well as back again in the opposite direction). In Mesmer's seances in the French capital in the 1780s, the magnetic rites and props were certainly enchantingly and elaborately staged. Patients sat around an oval vessel, or *baquet* as it was known, filled with water and iron filings. (On occasion, so many people sought to attend that Mesmer was forced to transfer to larger rooms and install four special tubs, including one for those who were unable to meet his high fees at the standard basin.) In what followed, Mesmer orchestrated the most extraordinary participatory theatre. At the *baquets* in the Hôtel Bullion, where he installed his main operation, everybody held hands and pressed their knees together to facilitate the passage of 'fluid' from one to another. From the vessel emerged long rods which patients applied to the afflicted part of their bodies. Mesmer appointed young assistants, whose task it was to channel the force across the patients and to apply various other techniques, such as embracing their legs or rubbing their spines and breasts. All of this was performed to the music of a piano or harmonica, or with the accompaniment of an opera singer. As the tension mounted, Mesmer would appear in a robe of lilac-covered silk embroidered with gold flowers, bearing a white magnetic baton.[27]

Extreme emotional reactions were catered for in the very layout of his rooms, which included mattress-lined crisis areas for violent convulsives. The main action was around the tub where a new initiate might expect to find an eager throng. The *baquet*, in turn, became the stuff of folklore. To sit to the north of the container cured avarice, lying and idleness, while the west end

H. Thiriat, *Mesmer's Tub; Or, a Faithfull Representation of the Operations of Animal Magnetism.*

was particularly recommended for the arrogant.[28] As the crowds grew uncomfortably large and plebeian, Mesmer fortuitously discovered the magnetic properties of trees. Henceforth interested groups, however uncouth, could be accommodated *en plein air*. Throngs gathered around a particular elm on which the master had worked his magic in a Paris street. Ropes were swung over branches and then wrapped around the diseased limbs of the man or woman below. The participation of socially heterogeneous groups (from aristocrats to peasants) was a striking feature of the social history of mesmerism as also of hypnotism. Mesmer's own methodological eclecticism was matched by the diversity of his clientele. He ministered to the nobility, the bourgeoisie and the common people.[29] This motley patronage as well as the varied political nuances drawn from the practice, added to the excitement and the political unease. This was no simple aristocratic country game; it was also ammunition in the hands of firebrands. Around the time of the French Revolution, the analogy drawn between unhealthy blockages of fluid in the body and noxious effects of patronage and privilege in society became strident. If the Revolution splintered mesmerism, it notably strengthened its radical wing. Unjust legislation was likened to a disruption of the atmosphere and hence of human health; obstacles to social harmony were compared with the dangers of obstructions to the circulation and equilibrium of magnetic forces.[30] Mesmer's practice, then, could be seen as erotically, politically and socially transgressive.

The faithful, no doubt, had a variety of expectations, as the expert ran his fingers over their bodies in his search for their poles. To establish 'rapport', it was deemed best to rely on the body's 'stable' magnets, such as the fingers and the nose. Mesmer forbade the use of snuff since it might disturb the nose's magnetic equilibrium. It is, of course, difficult for the modern reader not to delight in the more arcane rules and regulations then prevailing. (All that needs to be said on the ludicrous pomp and touching solemnity of mesmerism across the first hundred years of its history is contained in chapter eight of Flaubert's incomparable *Bouvard and Pécuchet*, 1881.) What transpired in the mesmerised subjects was sometimes bizarre and always ambiguous: how far was it the patient and how far the subsequent story-teller who had been carried away? Who knows what really went on, for instance, when (as reports had it) a mesmerised woman went into convulsions while looking at a mirror because her own fluid was being reflected back to her, passing over her head?[31] Theories proliferated about the magnetic map of the body: from the head as north pole to the feet (deemed the best receptors of terrestrial magnetism) as south pole. Amid the general buzz created by Mesmer, and the fashionable tittle-tattle that drew the curious to his doors, one should not forget the real suffering which drove so many to seek him out. Mesmer would touch the site of pain with his fingers or palm, following the direction of the nerves for as far as he could. If some attended with vague feelings of *ennui*, others were desperate to find a cure for the most pressing physical complaints, from blindness to life-threatening illnesses. The urgency of such sufferings and anxieties, as well as the barely suppressed erotic *frisson* of more casual participants, all need to be taken into consideration, as we picture the patients earnestly clenching their knees between the mesmerist's own. In other words, this was not simply some frivolous circus or trivial sexual titillation – at least, not for everyone; nor was it merely some 'medico-operatic' leisure pursuit. For many people, animal magnetism was sought as a remedy for desperate conditions. High hopes rested on Dr Mesmer who had, after all, stimulated intense public aspirations in the first place by promising that his technique would not only add to human knowledge but would also increase the sum total of human happiness.[32]

Mesmer rejected the idea that his technique should be understood in mystical terms or via the occult; neither would he have accepted any designation of it as the primarily theatrical experience perhaps implied here. Nonetheless, the props he used were heavily suggestive and dramatic. There were mirrors, luxurious rugs, the *baquet*, astrological symbols, to say nothing of the flamboyantly dressed master, wagging, as the historian of hypnotism, Alan Gauld, put it, 'his singularly potent index finger'. But however 'potent' his gestures, this pioneer remained continually exasperated by the obstruction of the authorities. Two Royal Commissions were established in Paris to investigate his claims: membership of one was drawn from the Academy of Medicine, the other, from the Royal Academy of Sciences, included Antoine-Laurent Lavoisier and Benjamin Franklin amongst its members.[33] The magnetic pretender's work was loftily dismissed by this august company in 1784, albeit with some caveats and minority dissent (so many crumbs of comfort) from within the investigating groups. The majority concluded, however, that Mesmer's 'successes' were attributable to the power of the imagination, rather than that of animal magnetism. The long drawn-out institutional cold-shoulderings, frustrations and prevarications even led Mesmer to send an exasperated and bitter letter to Marie-Antoinette, his most regal of sympathisers, despite her efforts to secure a pension on his behalf.

It seems, however, that there was something about mesmerism which enabled it, in the short and long term, to survive as a popular practice, despite the scepticism of the French scientific elite in the 1780s, and a further negative assessment in an inquiry of the 1830s.[34] It was not Mesmer himself, however, but his followers who would investigate 'mesmeric somnambulism' and it was probably one of them, the Marquis de Puységur, who first showed how the magnetised subject could be brought into a docile dialogue with the mesmerist, of which nothing would be recalled afterwards.[35] Indeed the scope of mesmerism was enlarged in many startling ways by these early freewheeling practitioners. In 1784 de Puységur and his brother placed a shepherd boy under mesmeric influence on their estate at Buzancy near Soissons; he fell asleep, but then stood up and blindly obeyed instructions, walking and talking according to the will of the other. The mesmerising Marquis de Puységur's experiments grew increasingly large-scale and extravagant. Thus his hapless peasants were literally roped in, tied together around a magnetised tree. It was also reputed that one somnambulist could see his own insides whilst mesmerised, thereby making a diagnosis of his ailments, anticipating the precise moment of his recovery, to say nothing of communicating with absent friends and even with the dead.[36]

A new, non-magnetic approach to the field emerged with the work of a Portuguese priest, Faria, who pursued his therapeutic work in Paris during the second decade of the nineteenth century, and proposed a theory of lucid sleep, brought about through concentration. Faria rejected the explanation of 'animal magnetism' and stressed the role of the patient's mind. He was also celebrated for his technique of looking the patient in the eye and using an imperative form, such as 'Sleep!'[37] Reports on hypnotic acts in the late nineteenth century suggest that much the same technique as Faria's was often still employed: the performer would stare hard and speak commandingly, at which point the subject would be rooted to the spot, transfixed by the master's overwhelming presence.[38]

Mesmerism continued to be the subject of some sporadic curiosity and inquiry in Britain, too, although it also attracted considerable criticism due to its close association with the French Revolution. By the late 1820s, there is evidence of widening interest (for example, one of Mesmer's followers, Richard Chenevix, demonstrated the medical applications of the technique at St Thomas' Hospital in 1829). It was also increasingly tied in to prevailing ideas about phrenology; the argument went that each bump in the skull might be worked over, to mesmerise specific faculties of the brain. Meanwhile, a burgeoning number of 'variety acts' featured magnetic couples. A certain Gerald Massey, for instance, toured with his wife 'Somnambule Jane' in 1850, while the following year, another clairvoyant, Mlle Prudence and her magnetiser, M. Roux, starred in a show in Piccadilly which promised the most audacious '*soirées Parisiennes et artistiques*' in the heart of London, much to the amusement of *Punch*.[39] Mesmerism also featured in the repertoire of various travelling lecturers who appeared in taverns, halls and fairs, alongside jugglers, clowns and fortune-tellers.

By the middle of the century there was talk of 'mesmeric mania'; the vogue was also becoming intertwined with spiritualism (a movement which emerged in America in the late 1840s and arrived in Britain soon after). After 1850, such erstwhile carnival mesmerists and popular pedagogues tended either to be dismissed as charlatans, or were absorbed into the new educational institutions as serious-minded lecturers.[40] Yet, at least to some extent, this robust and ribald world of magnetic attractions remained a part of the music hall and theatrical tradition throughout the late Victorian years, culminating, among other things, in the carnivalesque Svengalis who popped up in cartoons, poetic spoofs and plays, in the aftermath of Du Maurier's triumph. Mesmerism became both a vogue and a matter of real concern and alarm, cutting across intellectual boundaries and social groups. It was increasingly perceived to be running out of control, as the enthusiasm spread back and forth from West End drawing rooms to working mens' lecture halls and rural inns. The apparent irrationality of these enthusiasms continued to generate caustic social comment. The magnetic craze had featured prominently in Charles Mackay's critical study, *Extraordinary Popular Delusions and the Madness of Crowds* (1841), that early precursor of crowd psychology. There had also been a long tradition of political concern about magnetic 'invasion'. In the 1790s, as well as in the 'mesmeric mania' of the mid-nineteenth century (when Louis Napoleon's intentions towards Britain were the subject of considerable anxiety), talk of magnetising spies hopping across the Channel to bewitch the somnolent population was commonplace. In the middle of the century, mesmerism was generating a bewildering range of writing, discussion and activity in Britain and elsewhere. It was the subject of extensive gossip, satire, newspaper reports, learned articles and books, although, on the whole, official reaction had always been muted, at least compared with establishment attitudes in France. On this side of the Channel there had not been prominent official inquiries, or elaborate and authoritative condemnations of mesmerism during its early days. Where the magnetic pursuit was opposed, this was more often through gossipy insinuation and ridicule rather than direct state hostility, although certainly there were medical careers which foundered on these dangerous rocks.[41]

Hostile British commentators often combined a tone of religious distaste with more xenophobic mutterings: mesmerism as blasphemous import. Despite that, specialist journals as well as infirmaries were opening up, promising great things of magnetic treatment. Whilst critics complained that the public was being 'mesmerised' by the cultural phenomenon at large, men of action set about the business of making money from it. Certainly, such therapies were caught up in a burgeoning world of merchandising, one among many cures being sold with a vengeance to the Victorian public. By comparison with other prevailing treatments, it was presented as a pain-free and even pleasant regime. On the other hand, some sceptical critics – as well as sombre story-tellers on both sides of the Atlantic – presented a less innocuous account. Nowhere was the horrific face of mesmeric medicine more dramatically portrayed than in the macabre tale by Edgar Allan Poe which appeared in 1845, and which many took to be an authentic report.

'The facts in the case of M. Valdemar' describes a man mesmerised at the actual point of transition from life to death. The story explores, in detail, and in seemingly deadly earnest, how M. Valdemar is brought into a trance state, whilst *in articulo mortis*: 'The glassy role of the eye was changed for that expression of uneasy *inward* examination'; the subject is now looking inwards, in a manner 'which is never seen except in cases of sleep-walking, and which it is quite impossible to mistake'. Thus M. Valdemar is placed in suspension, left glassily staring, fixed in the interim of dying. Perhaps this image captured something of the mesmeric effect in general, the hiatus it involved in conscious volition. Caught between life and death, Poe's subject is even able to articulate the moment of his own passing away, making the impossible declaration, 'I am dead.' Seven months after the initiation of this cruel death-in-life interval, in a state unbearable to behold, a series of manual manoeuvres finally brings the man forth from the trance, leading instantly to the resumption of the loathsome bodily decomposition which had been held at bay. Poe spares his readers little in describing the physical scene, dwelling, for instance, on the horrific state of the victim's face, as nature resumes its course and pungent yellow liquids seep from the corners of the eyes.

Such a liaison of mesmerism with death had Poe's very particular signature; but whether one looks earlier or later in the century, serious and enduring, if generally less macabre, doubts about the safety of such procedures for individuals or for groups, continued to be expressed. Nevertheless, the blithe commercial exploitation of the practice now had its own unstoppable momentum. In response to the appearance of a patented magnetic brush in 1860, *Punch* satirically proposed going into business itself to produce a magnetic nightcap.[42] A few years later, *The Magnetic Review* was busy extolling the virtues of a variety of restorative contraptions and clinics. It was said that the 'Magneticon' could cure conditions ranging from lumbago and nervous debility to rheumatism, from bronchitis, sleeplessness and spinal complaints to weak knees, lameness, heart disease and severe colds. There were advertisements for 'magnetic rooms' in a Cheltenham establishment which welcomed the bearers of all conditions: dropsy, indigestion, sprains, tumours, consumption, paralysis, sciatica and asthma were all within its remit. In adjacent pages, the Victorian reader was offered throat protectors, ladies' belts, friction gloves and lung invigorators. If these were not enough, they were advised to sample the medical miracles of a specially built compressed-air chamber.[43] (This is perhaps less strange than it initially looks, when one considers the demand today for 'oxygen bars' in New York and elsewhere.) 'Self-help' manuals in amateur mesmerism were also available for the Victorian enthusiast. The marketing potential of such voguish medicine was evident; so too were the possibilities of religious appropriation.[44] For every cleric who was interested in mesmerism, there was another muttering that it should be condemned, alongside 'table-turning', as the work of the devil.

One notable mesmeric enthusiast to risk public disapproval was Dr John Elliotson, a radical medical reformer and professor of practical medicine at University College Hospital. He was the editor of *The Zoist: A Journal of Cerebral Physiology, and Mesmerism,* which promoted magnetic cures for cancer and ulcers, rheumatism, coughs and even blindness in the 1840s, although it should also be added that Elliotson himself made a great point of rejecting payment for his 'scientific' work with his subjects.[45] He was well-known for his ability to place his subjects in deep trance. Especially good at achieving rapport, Elliotson established intense contact with his epileptic or hysterical patients by prolonged eye-to-eye contact. Certainly he detected a decisive alteration in the patient's state of mind 'under the influence', whether in the direction of death-like sleep or intense, wakeful devotion. But as he immersed himself in such treatments and experiments, mesmerism was also dragging his career into deep and dangerous waters. He found himself beleaguered at University College and in due course had to resign, after his star patients, the O'Key sisters (who sang, danced, and supposedly possessed 'second sight' at his bidding) were exposed (at least in some eyes) as frauds, with the doctor cast as their dupe or, alternatively, as a fellow knave. Whatever these medical set-backs to his fortunes, the charismatic Elliotson had stimulated the interest of a wide number of observers, who had attended his demonstrations at the hospital. Thackeray and Tennyson as well as Dickens were all deeply intrigued.[46] Elliotson also went on to found the London Mesmeric Infirmary.

By the 1840s, new terms and experiments were shifting the European landscape of mesmerism. Braid elaborated his theory of hypnotism, thereby fanning the flames of public interest, although this again was in the face of considerable hostility and sometimes indifference from the majority of the medical establishment.[47] 'Hypnotism' drew attention to the special form of sleep into which the subject could be placed, and conveniently pushed aside (for the time being) the magnetic model which had been so dear and so costly to Mesmer. Hypnosis was no ordinary state of sleep, for while that was achieved through a kind of mental dispersal, Braid's entranced patients were said to lose consciousness through singular concentration. Braid was at some pains to dissociate himself from any notion that his hypnotic theory could be allied with 'modern materialism'. Still less was he happy to see hypnosis linked with pre-modern magic, obscure cults, or ancient Jewish traditions (he did not elaborate on precisely what he had in mind). Such speculations, he suggested, might lead to the unwarranted prejudice that his techniques were inimical to Christianity. He was no

Svengali, after all, and he insisted very specifically that far from aiming to blaspheme, his intention was to show the wonderful, God-given power of the patient's own mind.[48]

Braid developed various techniques to bring his patients under his influence. As a later sympathetic commentator noted, his characteristic approach was as follows:

> He took a bright object, generally in his lancet-case, and held it in his left hand about a foot from the patient's eyes, and at such a distance above the forehead that it could not be seen without straining. The patient was told to look steadily at the object and to think of nothing else. The operator then extended and separated the fore and middle fingers of the right hand, and carried them from the object towards the patient's eyes.[49]

This often led his subjects to close their eyes, but if this did not happen spontaneously he repeated the process. The patients were instructed to let their eyes close when his fingers moved towards them. They were urged to keep their eyeballs fixed in the same position and to concentrate on the object. While frequently successful, Braid found such fixed gazing was on many occasions followed by pain, so he altered the technique somewhat, urging the patients to close their eyes at an earlier stage of proceedings. Most strikingly, he found that he could induce hypnosis in the blind as well. It has been argued that these various discoveries led him to abandon his physical theory and to conclude that the influence was exerted through the mind, and not through the optic nerves, let alone magnetic fluids.[50]

Braid also realised that hypnosis seemed to become easier to induce after several earlier episodes. 'In such cases if the patients believed something was being done which ought to produce hypnosis, the state appeared.'[51] Conversely, the most skilled practitioner would fail in situations where the subject did not know what was expected. Eventually Braid concluded that direct verbal suggestion was the best conductor and judged the earlier physical methods to be nothing more than indirect suggestions whose efficacy depended upon the underlying mental state they fostered. Nevertheless, fixation of the gaze continued to be the most frequently chosen method, albeit not the exclusive one, deployed by Braid, as well as by many subsequent practitioners. Braid believed that in hypnosis, the mind was thrown out of gear, so that the higher faculties 'become dethroned from their supremacy', giving place to imagination, credulity, docility and passive obedience:

so that, even whilst apparently wide awake . . . they become susceptible of being influenced and controlled entirely by the suggestions of others upon whom their attention is fixed . . . they *see* and *feel* as REAL,
and they consider themselves *irresistibly* or *involuntarily fixed*, or *spellbound*, or *impelled to perform whatever may be said or signified by the
other party upon whom their attention has become involuntarily and
vividly riveted* . . .[52]

Those tempted to become involved in seances and to succumb to
trances were in very good company indeed. Numerous writers, artists and
scientists had plunged in at the deep end, not only as patients but as would-
be practitioners, seeking to acquire the techniques for themselves. In
France, Balzac claimed during the 1820s to have mastered the procedure
and several of his friends and acquaintances noted that he had 'the mesmeric eye', 'lightning-like glances, so brilliant, so charged with magnetism'.
The great chronicler of the human comedy was only one of many Parisian
men of letters to practice, preach and portray mesmerism.[53] Mesmerism
and hypnosis were also fashionable leisure pursuits in Britain during the
early years of Queen Victoria's reign. The fact that the famously genteel
opera singer Jenny Lind attended the demonstrations of Dr Braid in the
1840s should not cause surprise.[54] More or less salubrious expositions of
the art were common in those years. But creative writers and artists were
also sometimes drawn in further than they (or their loved ones) wished. It
is easy to multiply examples of this uneasy curiosity and this heavily com-
promised voyeurism; more difficult indeed to find an example of a major
novelist not interested in (and ambivalent about) such events. By the 1840s
and '50s, practically 'anyone who was anyone' in polite literary and scientific London society, took the time at least to attend demonstrations. Even
by Victorian standards, however, the radical writer Harriet Martineau was
seen as taking her enthusiasm for animal magnetism a bit far: on one occasion when her own mesmerist was unable to attend her, she trained her
maid to imitate his 'passes'.

Jane Welsh Carlyle provides a different but equally striking reaction. She
was interested in the phenomenon but struck a decidedly cautionary note
about her experiences in a letter to her uncle, in which she described a mesmerist she had encountered at an afternoon tea party in 1844. It was idle,
she declared, to deny that animal magnetism existed, but it was too close to
witchcraft and demonic possession for her liking. She acknowledged the
man's powerful attraction; she had felt enticed and repelled at the same

time. At the party, she witnessed a young woman being worked upon by the
dark-eyed figure. After a quarter of an hour in which he had simply stared,
Jane Carlyle observed that he had reduced the unfortunate girl to the very
image of death. The mesmerist then challenged Jane herself: he would mag-
netise her, too. She sought to defy him, initially confident in the force of her
own volition and in her self-protective contempt for the unrefined man
before her; she was convinced that someone so incapable of saying his
aitches was unlikely to work any magic on her! Nonetheless, even as she
pondered why she would not surrender, she found herself falling, experi-
encing a flash, and then something crossing her body from head to foot.
She saved herself, but only just. She vowed never to experiment again, for
it is 'a damnable sort of tempting of providence'.[55]

While commentators have correctly stressed the fact that Braid's radical
redefinition of the mesmeric procedure was an important staging post on
the road towards medical respectability, the field certainly remained riven
with controversy, doubt and anxiety. Already in the 1840s, *Punch* had
warned of the dangers of the legal abuse of mesmerism – fallacious
appeals against criminal sentence based on claims of mesmeric incapacity
(thereby anticipating the shape of things in the last decades of the century).[56] Unscrupulous law-breakers might doubly exploit the practice –
first, to procure the acquiescence of an accomplice; second, to plead lack of
responsibility in court.[57] Selfish ends might be masked by the paradoxical
claim that 'the self' was altogether absent from the deed. But perhaps the
accomplice was herself merely faking the state of hypnosis. Female felons,
it was suggested in the late nineteenth century, might be consummate performers – no less so, perhaps, than some of Professor Charcot's patients,
those equivocal 'actresses' at his famous neurological clinic at the
Salpêtrière hospital in Paris.[58] The theme of the dependent and depraved
'second string' brought forensic debate a high degree of prominence, especially in late-nineteenth-century France.

It was above all Jean-Martin Charcot (1825–93), a renowned doctor,
teacher and neurological specialist of his day, whose investigations of hypnosis and hysteria opened up major new interest in the subject, and in no
small part paved the way towards Freud's own radical hypotheses. (Freud
studied under him in 1885.) Charcot certainly drew the subject of hypnotism closer towards medical respectability, by dint of his very interest in it:
nobody would dare doubt his *bona fides*. He sought to show the precise
relationship between induced hypnotic conditions and the sequence of
hysterical manifestations in the patient. He argued that it was possible to

Laurent-Gsell, *A Lecture at the Salpêtrière.*

provoke hysterical symptoms artificially through hypnotism and, conversely, that hypnotism was a particular propensity of the hysteric, whose condition he understood as, at least in part, a function of hereditary degeneration.[59] In his relentless pursuit of organic explanations for the causes of hysteria, Charcot was blind to other possibilities, unable to attend to what his patients were saying or to the thoughts and feelings that might inform their words. In that respect the doctor, like the hysterics themselves, pushed everything into the body, insisting on the material basis of the condition and, in the process, taking too little heed of what his patients were actually saying (or whispering). Freud was first entranced, then increasingly sceptical of Charcot's explanations; but the student's very dissatisfaction with the master was a major stimulus to new thinking. Charcot was, as Freud once remarked, a *visuel,* a man who sees. Had Charcot listened more carefully to what his hysterics were saying, he might have entered into less familiar nineteenth-century territory.

Charcot's lectures at the Salpêtrière become an international attraction; the man was, as has often been said, doctor and impresario, scientific authority and showman rolled into one. But by the 1880s Dr Hippolyte Bernheim was becoming a major counterweight, publishing influential work refuting Charcot's contention that susceptibility was restricted to hereditarily tainted subjects. Bernheim, who was appointed to a chair in the medical faculty of the university in the French provincial town of Nancy, believed suggestion to be a psychological fact. 'Suggestion' had been deployed throughout the ages, he argued, wrapped up in other guises by superstition, ignorance and charlatanism. He took the view that the mesmeric phenomenon always depended on 'faith' and 'imagination' rather than on some mysterious ethereal or organic effect. Everybody was vulnerable to hypnosis, since everybody was prey to suggestion.[60]

Bernheim and his colleagues (collectively known as 'the Nancy School') believed that crimes committed 'under the influence' of another were a distinct risk for non-hysterical personalities as well as for the psychiatrically disturbed;[61] the debates on hypnosis and general criminal responsibility were frequently merged.[62] Charcot continued to claim that hypnotic vulnerability was tied to hysteria, but this was further challenged at the Second International Congress of Psychology in London in 1892. What was increasingly difficult to avoid, however, from any of these vantage points, was a recognition of the fundamental complexity and intra-psychic 'hiddenness' of much mental life. Whether late-Victorian specialists sided with 'Nancy' or 'Paris', the enigma of hypnotism remained a major concern. Even Charcot never definitively claimed to have located the anatomical lesions which he postulated might exist in the brains of his hysterical patients. Whilst Charcot fought a rearguard action to keep these topics in the realm of the pathological, claims for a relationship between hypnotism and the 'normal' psychic state were gaining ground.

As an admirer of the renowned late-nineteenth-century stage hypnotist Donato wrote, the state of fascination produced in the subject amounted to a dissolution or perhaps doubling of the '*moi*'.[63] In the cabinet of Dr Bernheim, the theatre of Donato, or the concert hall of Svengali, hypnosis profoundly reinforced doubts about mental 'singularity'; it complicated Victorian ideas about the nature of the self, the subliminal aspects of *all* relationships, the indeterminate border between covert command and creative collaboration, inspiration and interference, partnership and possession. Narratives in which even sceptics wavered and then succumbed to 'the spell' became almost routine. In other stories of the 1890s, such as Arthur Conan Doyle's 'The Parasite', lives were permanently disrupted and destroyed by the slightest dalliance with the mesmerist – in this case, a sinister foreign woman. It seemed that the divide between audience and cast, onlooker and volunteer was often unwittingly crossed.

Many commentators took for granted women's special vulnerability to such procedures. While they were never viewed as exclusively prone to hypnotic and hysterical conditions,[64] even before shellshock decisively changed the sexual landscape of mental breakdown during the First World War, women were generally seen as more susceptible than men. The reasons for such views are complex; suffice it to say that perceptions of differences in the propensity to hysteria and hypnotism were part of a wider set of social, political and medico-psychiatric ideas about woman's nature, about which much has been written in recent years. To take a notoriously extreme but not entirely outlandish example of the exploration of gendered sensibility at the turn of the century, consider the much-quoted book, *Sex and Character*, written in 1903 in Vienna by a highly troubled young man, Otto Weininger. Weininger was known to, and discussed by, Freud and his circle (not least because of his suicide so soon after completion of his book). It was his bizarre self-destruction that caused many to pay heed to his provocatively stated thesis. The argument brought together a number of well-rehearsed theories and metaphors of the day. Crucially, Weininger contended that women lived an unconscious existence to a greater degree than men. Women, he insisted, were in their essence only sexual, while men could transcend the carnal appetites altogether; erotic excitement was the supreme force in a woman's life, and it was necessary to bind this otherwise uncontrollable force in marriage. Whereas a woman's relations with her husband and children completed her life, the male naturally aspired to more than this private familial world. Weininger also claimed it to be impossible for women, as purely sexual beings, to recognise their sexuality, since knowledge of anything requires duality. Dominated by and yet never fully conscious of their sexual passions, women were *in need* of psychological domination. It followed (apparently) that they wanted to remain always and throughout purely passive, to live under another's will. This was their essential womanhood. They demanded only to be desired physically, to be taken possession of, 'like a new property'.

Weininger had converted from Judaism to Protestantism, and excoriated Jews with much the same passionate hatred he directed towards women. In such writing, racial and sexual fears coalesced in the vision of a debilitating, passive and suggestible modern culture. He concluded that modernity had reached rock-bottom, amidst all these Jewish and feminine influences. But if 'woman' could be so easily possessed, was she responsible for her actions? The outcome of criminal cases could turn on expert deliberations and debates around precisely these questions, although a sceptical legal profession in the

second half of the nineteenth century not infrequently derided the pretensions and interventions (whether on behalf of the prosecution or the
defence) of the increasingly vocal psychiatric fraternity. Even if dismissed as
fakery, however, it seemed that the social dangers of this hypnotic terrain
could not be ignored. Sex and character were indeed key issues in the wider
politics of *fin-de-siècle* mesmerism and hypnotism. Where it was believed to
constitute a real subliminal phenomenon, the problem was all the greater.
What happened to the concept of responsibility when some alien force penetrated into the deepest mental layers of the enthralled 'volunteer'? Could
people at large, and most especially women, be hypnotised against their own
judgements, and then induced to seduce men, or even kill them? And if individuals could be thus afflicted, what about groups, cultures, entire nations?
Even the theosophical pioneer, the larger-than-life Madame Blavatsky,
wagged her finger at the hypnotists. Late in her life, she sought to spell out the
dangers of such abuses, speaking of maidens carried away by charming mesmeric rogues. It was a nice valedictory warning from a woman who was
herself no stranger to charges of hoaxing, gross manipulation, and worse:

> Do you not see the tremendous evils that lie concealed in hypnotism?
> Look at Charcot's experiments at the Salpêtrière! He has shown that a
> quite innocent person can be made to perform actions quite against his
> or her will; can be made to commit crimes, even, by what he calls
> Suggestion. And the *somnambule* will forget all about it, while the victim
> can never identify the real criminal. Charcot is a benevolent man, and
> will never use his power to do harm. But all men are not benevolent. The
> world is full of cruel, greedy, and lustful people, who will be eager to
> seize a new weapon for their ends, and who will defy detection and pass
> through the midst of us all unpunished.
>
> Yes, Sir! Witch-tales in this enlightened age! And mark my words!
> You will have such witch-tales as the Middle Ages never dreamt of.
> Whole nations will drift insensibly into black magic, with good inten-
> tions, no doubt, but paving the road to hell none the less for that![65]

The subject which had engaged and enraged so many writers and practitioners, doctors and lay healers across the century that had passed since
Mesmer, gradually found its way back to scientific credibility. Many
Victorian doctors contributed to this process, demanding that the phenomenon be viewed as a scientific question, a matter for serious and rational debate.[66] But most of all it was Charcot who tipped the balance. It was

not only Madame Blavatsky who insisted that he was an honourable and exceptionally benign man – the polar opposite of the untrained charlatan. Doctors journeyed to France to see Charcot and Bernheim at work, studying carefully their demonstrations of hypnotic states in a salubrious clinical setting. Sometimes scientific visitors even brought their cases abroad with them; Freud, for instance, transported a patient all the way to Nancy to consult Bernheim.

And yet these doctors demonstrated the power of fascination in their very person. As several observers recorded, not only could Charcot's manner be seen as powerful suggestion in its own right, but the experience of witnessing him at work was reminiscent of being an awed spectator at the theatre. A German doctor, Max Nonne (who would himself become famous when he spectacularly revived the use of hypnotism with traumatised soldiers during the First World War), recalled rather critically: 'I had the impression that Charcot's lectures, at that time, in the twilight of his life, more closely resembled a theatre performance than a lesson attended by interested doctors.'[67] As we have seen, Freud also had growing doubts about what he witnessed at the Salpêtrière and came to favour the approach of Charcot's rival, Bernheim; but Freud's first reaction to Charcot was intensely positive. Like Nonne and many others, he wrote about the state of deep enchantment into which he had fallen. Freud acknowledged that there was a certain 'magic that emanated from his looks and from his voice'; he was powerfully gripped by the lectures he heard, and remarked that as a teacher, 'Charcot was positively fascinating'. In a letter to his betrothed, Martha, in 1885, he spoke of the considerable power the Frenchman now exerted over him:

I think I am changing a great deal. I will tell you in detail what is affecting me. Charcot, who is one of the greatest of physicians and a man whose common sense is touched by genius, is simply uprooting my aims and opinions. I sometimes come out of his lectures as though I were coming out of Notre Dame, with a new idea of perfection.

Or again:

My brain is sated, as if I had spent an evening at the theatre. Whether the seed will ever bear any fruit, I do not know; but what I do know is that no one else has ever affected me in the same way . . .[68]

4
Hearts and Minds

And in a minute or two it is all over, like the lovely bouquet of fireworks at the end of the show, and she lets what remains of it die out and away like the afterglow of fading Bengal fires – her voice receding in to the distance – coming back to you like an echo from all round, from anywhere you please – quite soft – hardly more than a breath. Then one last chromatically ascending rocket, *pianissimo*, up to E in alt, and then darkness and silence!

And after a little pause the many-headed rises as one, and waves its hats and sticks and handkerchiefs, and stamps and shouts . . . 'Vive La Svengali! Vive La Svengali!'

Du Maurier, *Trilby*[1]

While images of the dangerous hypnotist gave expression to specific *fin-de-siècle* preoccupations, they also reflected longer-standing Victorian anxieties about irrational influences and the transport of hearts and minds to unseemly and dangerous places. There were many altered psychological states that had aroused public debate and fear. Unlike, say, opium and alcohol, however, which might be abused by individuals acting alone, mesmerism and hypnotism characteristically involved at least two human subjects: these treatments were most typically carried out, voluntarily or otherwise, by one person upon another, although discussion of self-induced hypnotic states was by no means unknown. Such psychic or bodily transformations called the very notion of the subject's self-control and self-possession into question. Moreover, the encounter between the hypnotiser and the hypnotised was fundamentally unequal. If its causes and meanings were opaque, its observable effects were often unmistakable, and were frequently cast as an insidious infiltration of a subject's mind by the untrustworthy practitioner.

Hypnosis provoked deep philosophical uncertainties about identity, and the role of identification with others in the very constitution of the self; the increasingly elaborate technical vocabulary that surrounded it provided important new terms for considering various emotionally charged dynamics: from love affairs to political disturbances. Hypnosis offered a language to conceptualise what was really going on in individuals and groups who had, as it were, lost their hearts and minds to politicians, lovers, musicians or enchanting theatrical performers. In Victorian times, the experience of drama was increasingly conceived in terms drawn from the medico-psychiatric literature: the spectators manifesting, say, unconscious imitation, the effects of suggestion, or even something like hypnosis. Some such explanation was clearly needed to explain why it was that when the great actress Sarah Bernhardt coughed during a performance as the dying heroine of *La Dame aux camélias* in Moscow, the entire audience reached for their handkerchiefs as well.[2]

The puzzle of hypnotism stimulated long-standing debate amongst Victorian scientists and doctors; it inspired and troubled novelists; it aroused popular wonderment, even childlike devotion, as well as much alarm from social commentators. It disturbed the boundaries between high and low culture, education and entertainment, fact and fiction, medicine and quackery, waking states, sleep and dreams; it seemed to return its subjects to some long-lost state of being, an irresponsible world, free of the conventions of grown-up 'self-mastery'. But it was not only the hypnotic pair who were thus mutually engaged: the encounter was scrutinised by others, enjoyed as a spectacle and a social phenomenon, or challenged by sceptics. Hypnotism became the scene (to borrow an image from Thomas Carlyle) of 'swarmery' and – whether, despite or because of, this notoriously messy cohabitation of the polite and the vulgar – continued to command both awed and squeamish public attention.

From one end of the nineteenth century to the other, creative writers and philosophers pondered the nature of such emotional – or even, they thought, magnetic – processes, and sought to theorise in new ways the nature of the interaction between the charismatic personality and the group. The nature of 'sympathy', much discussed in the eighteenth century, remained a hotly debated question, that led off in many different directions, eliciting endless metaphorical variants and competing schools of thought to account for the nature of the emotional impact of one person upon another. Napoleon Bonaparte had once likened his own impact to that of an intense electric charge: 'I had the gift of electrifying men.'[3] Hypotheses about the impact of electrical charges had indeed been invoked as one possibility to account for the success of Napoleon, as well as Mesmer and other influential personalities, leaders or healers of the day: 'animal electricity' was the characteristic title of a treatise in 1805.[4] By the mid-nineteenth century, explanations of fascination and hypnosis via the effects of electricity on the nervous system were part and parcel of psychological debate, as were claims and counter-claims for the therapeutic effects of mild shocks. An elaborate theory of 'electrical psychology' was advanced in the 1850s by a certain John Bovee Dods in America, while in France a book was published in 1855 under the title *Electro-dynamisme vital*.[5] The poet Heinrich Heine mused about the mysterious nature of emotional captivation in the following terms:

> Is there some mysterious aura radiating from exceptionally strong personalities? Do we glimpse some such effulgence with our mind's eye, invisible though it be to our bodily eye? Perhaps the moral thunderstorm in an extraordinary personality has an electric effect on young people who approach him with unblunted minds, as a physical thunderstorm has on cats.[6]

It seemed that the pull of one body or mind on another might be not only invisible to the eye but also, at least for the present, inaccessible to the powers of reason. It was often feared, moreover, that emotional influence was a growing rather than diminishing problem in the modern age. While some novelists charted a loss in the very capacity to wonder and experience enchantment under the impact of modern life, other writers perceived a new efflorescence of irrational and uncontrollable states of mind in modern society. For all the discussion of material progress, evolution, utilitarianism and the dull inexorability of market forces, many Victorian critics were convinced that industrialisation, urbanisation and 'the cash nexus' had not done away with unbounded, intoxicated or downright erotic states of entrancement. Strange nervous conditions were now perceived to be fostered by the stimuli of modern capitalism and city life. Moreover, even the very discoveries in medicine, science and technology could be viewed as the catalysts of public excitability, fascination and irrational enthusiasm. Thus

Frederick Harrison (a leader of the English positivist group who had followed and developed the scientific 'religion' first promoted by Auguste Comte) became alarmed that the late-nineteenth-century trend was not towards the growing rationalisation and *dis*enchantment of the world at all, but rather towards the flourishing of vulgar and occult forces, inimical not only to mental health but even to the maintenance of civilisation. He described this rather helpless collective state of public naivety in the face of scientific advance as:

> an enchanted world, where everything does what we tell it in perfectly inexplicable ways, as if some good Prospero were waving his wand, and electricity were the willing Ariel – that is what we have – and yet, is this civilisation?[7]

Du Maurier sought to render the intensity of such feelings of exhilaration and confusion in his fictions. When Little Billee, Taffy and the Laird hear the hypnotised Trilby sing, they marvel at the public emotion – the sheer hysteria – before being swept up in it themselves. Du Maurier offered extended descriptions of the unrestrained enthusiasm of musical audiences, grown men and women across Europe brought to their knees, laughing and sobbing, delighted and overwhelmed by the soprano's voice, and, behind it, by the presence of the story's own macabre 'Prospero', Svengali. Such accounts of emotional intoxication and the return to infantile states connected with a wider, scientific and fictional literature on mesmerising conductors and captivated players (or listeners), as well as with dark warnings about the ravages caused by politicised crowds and their dazzling demagogues. The fascinated mob was frequently likened to the volatility of infancy as well as to the figure of the hysterical or sleep-walking woman. Continental crowd specialists tended to cast the leaders of the masses either as demonic and wilful manipulators, or as mere suggestible stooges who were no less entranced than the groups to whom they spoke. Group enthusiasms, or as Charles Mackay put it in a prescient book title of 1841, *Extraordinary Popular Delusions and the Madness of Crowds*, cried out for explanation as well as description.

Political 'prophets' from both home and abroad (*especially* from abroad), were observed to exploit a quasi-sacred aura and to foster irrational emotional ties to striking (and self-serving) effect. Du Maurier's story was set in the Second Empire of Louis Napoleon, who was in power throughout the 1850s and 1860s; but it was not only that particular

The audience during one of Jenny Lind's performances at the opera house in Stockholm.

French leader who exemplified the ruses of pretenders and crowd manipulators in modern society, or who made disturbing political bargains with the Church. Far from diminishing the role of emotion and passion in political life, the rising 'secular age', if such it could really be called, only seemed to be re-inventing it in more dangerous and insidious forms. Or at least, so it was argued in a plethora of anxious analyses of crowd delusions.

A dramatic new language of the crowd was beginning to emerge amongst historians and human scientists in the second half of the nineteenth century, a language replete with a psychiatric and criminological vocabulary more powerful and harder-edged than anything that had existed at the time of the French Revolution, even in Edmund Burke's famously horrified and horrifying 'reflections'. Thomas Carlyle's history of the Revolution, written in the 1830s, had combined the volcanic metaphors of Romanticism with strident zoological-sounding flourishes, as he sought to render the primitive frenzy of the throng. But stronger still – and far more scientifically impressive – was the crowd analysis of

Hippolyte Taine, who began writing his history of the French Revolution, *Les Origines de la France Contemporaine*, in the 1870s, after Charles Darwin, Herbert Spencer and a host of other crusading evolutionary commentators had brought the issue of human 'descent' to the forefront of European debate. Here the latest expressions of evolutionary biology, medico-psychiatry and anthropology were brought to bear on history and politics with devastating force. In the very nature of the French Revolution itself, as well as the anarchic events of 1870 and 1871 – the French defeat in the war with Prussia and the short-lived revolutionary turmoil of the Paris Commune – Taine glimpsed (in his apocalyptic 'Darwinian' terms), the rise of the 'wanton baboon'. In Taine and his successors, earlier literary conceptions of the mysterious charismatic pull of certain orators were subsumed within, or displaced by, newly proclaimed scientific laws of group behaviour.

Whilst some commentators sought to differentiate the fundamental behaviour of crowds in different nations, situations or epochs, others now argued that the deep structure of the group was much the same everywhere. Admittedly, few English writers rendered their crowd psychology in quite the remorselessly gruesome fashion of Taine. A more light-hearted view was often called for, even a sigh of relief that Victorian England was so different from the land across the water that had produced revolutionary guillotines, barricades and ferocious reaction. Nonetheless, there were also sporadic warnings, crescendoing during the political and social upheavals in the English capital during the 1880s, about the thin psychological and political line that separated the peaceful British worker from the bloodthirsty foreign ruffian. The Channel-hopping Du Maurier was clearly interested in such crowd psychology, but always retained his light and whimsical touch. He did not write of urban riots, but of wild bourgeois passions at the theatre. Yet the fact that, behind the scenes, a foreign, low-life Svengali could orchestrate the emotions of the audience hinted at this darker and more sinister world of group manipulations. While it may be fanciful to detect, in the 'i' that ends Svengali, direct echoes of the names of political and national leaders – for instance the Italian nationalist figures Mazzini and Garibaldi, or even, closer to hand, the English conservative politician Disraeli – the nomenclature of mesmerism itself *was* seen to be highly relevant to the interpretation of such spell-binding figures abroad on the European political stage. Certainly the sequels to Svengali played up the Italian angle, albeit in the form of the lampoon: in one spoof, Svengali's name became 'Spaghetti';[8] in another, he spoke thus:

Who am I? – Who? Tausend teifels! Sapr-r-isti! – Carambo! –
Macaroni! – Poloney! – Polenta! "This is the most unkindest cut of
all!" No! – that's what I say when I'm doing Hamlet at the Haymarket!
Why, I'm the Polyglot Manager, and the Press always compliment me
on my make-up.[9]

Whilst such verbal excitability and malleability suggested that he was
from nowhere and everywhere, it also spoke to a stereotyped 'italianicity';
it belonged to a tradition of Victorian cartoon and theatrical representation
of entertaining Mediterranean characters. At a directly political level, however, Italian enchanters provoked much comment and no shortage of concern in the early and mid-Victorian years. Mazzini had been a long-time
resident in London (an exile from the reactionary powers that still divided
and ruled Italy). Both he and Garibaldi were to arouse much comment on
the nature of political charisma; indeed, amongst notable outsiders visiting
or living in the English capital, none had aroused more speculation on
political irrationalism than the Italian nationalists who had set out to liber-
ate their country from foreign rule and despotism. Mazzini's political
dream was indeed for a 'secular religion' to regenerate the nation. For all
their anti-clerical polemics, their diatribes against the papacy, neither
Garibaldi nor Mazzini ever doubted the political advantage of inculcating a
quasi-religious faith in their followers; but the attraction was widely perceived to go beyond any conscious strategy or chosen aim. Du Maurier's
friend Moscheles, an admirer of Mazzini at the mid-point of the century,
attributed the Italian's impact to mesmeric force and charismatic eyes:

> His eyes sparkled as he spoke, and reflected the ever-glowing and illu-
> minating fire within; *he held you magnetically.* He would penetrate into
> some innermost recess of your conscience and kindle a spark where all
> had been darkness. Whilst under the influence of that eye, that voice,
> you felt as if you could leave father and mother and follow him, the elec-
> tive Providence, who had come to overthrow the whole wretched fabric
> of falsehoods holding mankind in bondage.[10]

The terms of this description are drawn from the mesmeric tradition, suggesting an unknown physical or psychological effect on the bystander. Not
everyone agreed with such ecstatic portraits of this particular national pioneer, but they were certainly commonplace at the time.[11] Still more recurrent and intense, however, was the attribution of a profound and even

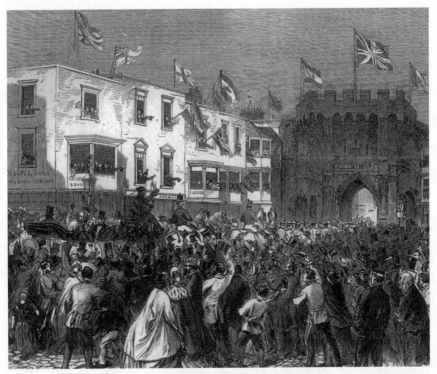

Garibaldi arriving in Southampton, April 1864.

magical power of fascination to the Italian military hero Giuseppe Garibaldi. During his visit to Britain in the 1860s, Garibaldi provoked the boundless social enthusiasm which would eventually be diagnosed more formally by the crowd psychologists in their textbooks. Many of those who knew 'the General' or even read of his escapades felt they had fallen in love. Nobody in the nineteenth century attracted more astonishing adulation. Countless men and women, from all nations and walks of life, declared themselves enchanted. 'I have seen today the face of Garibaldi; and now all the devotion of his friends is made clear as day to me. You have only to look into his face, and you feel that there is, perhaps, the one man in the world in whose service you would, taking your heart in your hand, follow blindfold to death,' said one admirer.[12]

Admittedly some – Queen Victoria and Disraeli amongst them – resisted the communal rejoicing during the unusually attired Italian's tumultuous tour. Disraeli himself, however, (no less sartorially challenging in his own way) was also to provoke charges of mesmeric manipulation, although in his case more often by his enemies than his friends. Again, the essential 'alien' status of the enchanter was crucial to the representation. Some of Disraeli's critics conflated the language of political magnetism with the image of Jewish infiltration. Nowhere did the anxieties and dreads surrounding the puppet master and the gullible political subject appear more strongly than in the debate about this Tory politician, cast as the Jewish manipulator *par excellence* in numerous analyses, quips, rhymes and cartoons, not least in the magazine most closely associated with Du Maurier, *Punch*.[13] To explain Disraeli's achievements and electoral successes with the growing Victorian electorate, notions of conjuring and even hypnotism became common currency.[14] It is true, of course, that Gladstone also received his share of such diagnoses as mass manipulator. But whether given a specifically racial edge – *à la Disraeli* – or not, there remained, across the Victorian period, abiding conceptual uncertainties about the nature of modern political orchestration and its relationship to states of entrancement; especially so in the aftermath of the Second Reform Act of 1867.

Doubts endured about the possibility of a scientifically materialist explanation of hypnotic processes and of crowd psychology. Was there really some organic change, some 'lesion' in the body of the hysteric and the *somnambule*, some hitherto undiscovered physical process of transmission across the excitable crowd? If there was some invisible but actual bodily change in the individual case, how was one to explain the aggregated phenomenon? Could it be some magnetic force or some as yet unknown physical phenomenon? The fundamental 'bone of contention' was organicism itself. For was hypnosis, as Charcot's adversary, Dr Bernheim, suggested in France in the 1880s, in fact merely part of a larger and indeed unavoidable *psychological* reality of 'suggestion'?[15] These questions remained both a stimulus and an annoyance, touching on deep uncertainties about the nature of the individual mind-body relationship and the social influence of minds and bodies upon one another. Scholarly debates, and sometimes more openly vitriolic personal disputes, broke out about the singularity or plurality of 'centres' in a person's mental world.

There were, of course, scientific writers who dismissed all trance confessions, somnambulistic demonstrations and theories of crowd hypnosis as mere hocus-pocus, at least until the interventions of Charcot in Paris in the 1870s. But there were others who recognised that they had to take very seriously the issues opened up by various Victorian physicians (if not by the shady Mesmer himself). At times, they ventured into misty realms of philosophical speculation in trying to understand what was going on in the mind of the mesmerised patient. Take an example from the 1840s – an editorial by Dr Thomas Wakley (editor of the medical journal, the *Lancet*), who was an acerbic but thoughtful critic of mesmerism. The phenomenon of induced sleep-walking, followed by amnesia, was used by Wakley to challenge the notion that the mind could be considered a single entity, transparent to itself. He noted how traditional conceptions of consciousness were at odds with the new findings of physiology and pathology:

> For example, that 'consciousness is *single*' is an axiom among the mental philosophers, and the proof of *personal identity* is made by those gentlemen to rest chiefly on the supposed universality or certainty of that allegation. But what would they say to the case of a somnambulist who evinced what is regarded as a double consciousness – the operations of the mind being perfectly distinct in the state of somnambulism from its developments in the wakeful condition? With reference to such an individual, the proof of *his* personal identity must rest with others, not with himself, for his memory in one state takes not the smallest cognisance of what he thought, felt, perceived, said, or did, in the other.[16]

That the assurance of identity might rest with others, not with the self, was a potentially important insight, to be taken up much later by psychoanalysts. Wakley's comments might no doubt be extended in several ways. The perceived inseparability of identity from the recognition and 'regard' of another person opens up questions that go beyond that of the hypnotised subject: there is surely a broader significance in the idea that our sense of ourselves is powerfully informed by the experience, or even the shaping gaze, of the other. Equally importantly, Wakley rejected the idea that somnambulism was caused by any actual magnetic process, as had been argued by the early mesmerists. He considered the explanatory term 'animal magnetism' absurd in understanding the nature of somnambulism, concluding that the real explanation remained a mystery, an example of the imperfection of our state of knowledge of nervous functions.

Perhaps it is misleading to detect an incipient Freudian understanding of the mind in such Victorian explorations and critiques of mesmerism, but there is no doubt that unconscious worlds and mental hinterlands were a common point of discussion in the human sciences. Commentators drew attention, with or without explicit mention of 'the unconscious', to mental processes operating beyond the limits of will-power and of self-knowledge. Discussion of mesmerism and hypnotism often interacted with these broader psychological issues and obscurities. The word 'unconscious' was itself foregrounded in various European philosophical inquiries (such as Hartmann's *Philosophy of the Unconscious*, published in 1869). Eleven years later, Samuel Butler's *Unconscious Memory* moved towards the threshold where an older romantic idiom would give way to a new scientific desire for experimental or conceptual rigour, and to the dreams of a modern psychology. The cultural preoccupation with 'altered states of mind', as the historian of science, Alison Winter, has so effectively shown, was extremely pervasive throughout the Victorian period, and cut against equally pronounced views of the mental stability and self-mastery that could be attained and sustained in the healthy individual.[17] In the work of W.B. Carpenter (*The Unconscious Action of the Brain*, 1871), a large component of mental life was viewed as 'automatic', an effect of reflex action. Carpenter attributed trance behaviour to the severance of the connections between mental reflexes and the will. The eccentric but influential Victorian medico-psychiatrist Henry Maudsley deployed the term 'subconscious' as well as, more casually, 'unconscious' (in the sense, for example, of inherited memory). In France, the clinician and theorist Pierre Janet went on to speak of the subconscious and additionally coined the term 'dissociation'.[18]

The hidden transmission of symptoms between individuals, as well as within parts of the individual body, was increasingly exercising the specialists on hypnotism and nervous disorders. A number of doctors had noticed, in experiments conducted on hysterics, how pains and disabilities would move around the body on command, or even shift from one patient to another. The process came to be called 'the law of transfer', an expression which itself had been transferred from the world of finance to medicine, after a routine morning visit to the bank inspired the Parisian neuropathologist Amédée Dumontpallier to adopt the phrase in the 1870s. As Charcot wrote, 'It appears with these hysterics, that the nervous fluid, if one will pardon the expression, does not transport itself to one side until after it has in part abandoned the other.'[19] Attitudes as much as physical symptoms might move and transform themselves within or between patients.[20] But there were other ways, too, in which the obscure process of transmission from individual to individual – with or without the command of a charismatic doctor – was provoking new debate. There were multiple attempts to explain the passage of brains, intellect or thoughts, not only across space – from one person to another – but also across time, from generation to generation. Family trees of delinquency, madness and other pathologies were compiled with enthusiasm by psychiatrists and criminal anthropologists of the period. So, too, were possible links between art, genius and insanity. Questions of transmission and of transfer necessarily raised others, not least about the nature of inter-personal psychological power. How and why might one person invest or invade another's mind, and with what consequences? Many later nineteenth-century fictions, political commentaries and scientific projects entered into these speculations, exploring them singly or in combination, often through the presentation of mesmerism, spiritualism, telepathy and other such possibilities.

From mesmeric turns at the Victorian music hall to sedate drawing room entertainments, from public house tricks to clinical demonstrations and solemn scientific inquiries, the widespread vogue for, and experience of, induced trances had powerfully challenged the idea that *any* human consciousness or will could be understood as a single entity. In these varied contexts, mental life could not be confined to the thoughts or memories of which the subject was aware, or capable of becoming aware. In the later part of the century investigators went further, opening up in a new way the issue of how what is forgotten may in fact be the most formative factor in our characters, even before Freud's decisive intervention. The brain itself was declared, by no less an authority on memory and consciousness than Théodule Ribot (whose celebrated scientific career culminated in his appointment to the prestigious Collège de France in Paris), to be 'like a laboratory full of movement, where thousands of tasks are performed at once . . . Consciousness is the narrow gate through which a very small part of this work appears to us.' Or, as he summed up these startling revelations, 'the conscious person is a compound, a result of very complex states'.[21] A large scientific literature on 'multiple personalities' was produced between 1870 and 1900, much of it emanating from France. Again, the recognition of such psychic ramifications and divides between the mind's different *personae* could not just be confined to the realm of the pathological 'cases'.

Ribot and his colleagues also pointed out that conscious memory was not a precondition for effective action by the subject. Somebody might even go on performing a task of extreme complexity while quite oblivious to what they were doing. Musicians provided several of Ribot's most effective examples. Thus he referred to a violinist struck by loss of consciousness during his concerts, who was able to continue playing while remaining in absolute ignorance of his surroundings. Further illustrations of the power of unconscious memory followed, involving skilled string players or accomplished ballet dancers functioning, as it were, on autopilot: 'In such cases it seems as if consciousness had taken upon itself the task of exposing its own peculiar sphere, of reducing its *rôle* to proper proportions, and of showing, by sudden absence, the supplementary part which it plays in the mechanism of memory.'[22] Unconscious memory, somnambulism (whether spontaneous or induced by hypnosis) and multiple personality, then, were all examples of a wider set of challenges to the notion of the commanding, single, fully-conscious self.[23]

A dizzying array of social phenomena were pulled together in late nineteenth-century explorations of human irrationality. Commentators sought to shed some scientific light on the polyphonic psychic drama taking place inside individuals as well as crowds. Taine had perhaps glimpsed the scientific future when he referred to the mind itself as a kind of theatre, comprising many conflicting voices.[24] Numerous such statements can be found in those last decades of the nineteenth century, never elaborated into a full blown theory of intrapsychic – and interpersonal – conflicts, but nonetheless appearing to foreshadow the Freudian discoveries to come. In addition to insidious, sexual magnetism between couples, and outright mob behaviour, there were discussions of *public* entrancement, whether amongst crowds of rough labourers or genteel participants at vicarage tea parties. Social 'enthusiasms' of various kinds became potential symptoms in the new medico-moral discourse of suggestibility; dark warnings multiplied about theatrical vogues, medical crazes, newspaper gossip, stock-market panics, boardroom battles and literary fashions. New mass literacy had fuelled fears of a world of debased popular taste, in which books were just as often cast as agents of mental anarchy as they were celebrated as the sources of edification and education. While such anxieties and diatribes were not new, the sprinkling of neurological and degenerationist terms that characterised the later-Victorian discussion gave the whole subject of dissolute cultural tastes a particularly alarming and portentous scientific tone. Vulnerable readers were thought by some authorities to be entering into virtual trance states as they absorbed the latest vulgar best-seller:

> Some books are so exciting to the attention, to the imagination, to the passions that they produce a mental debauch . . . in reading the mind is often in a passive state, like that of dreaming or reverie, in which images flit before the mind without any act of volition to retain them. In rapid reading [the mind] is nearly in the same states as yours is when you are whirled through a country in a railway-carriage or post-chaise.[25]

Women were seen as especially prone to such literary excitability and dreaminess. Indeed, elaborate physiological and neurological theories of women's constitutional propensity to cultural hypnotism of one sort or another were frequently rehearsed in the gloomy anti-feminist polemics of Victorian doctors, including, notably, the psychiatrist Henry Maudsley. The sheer range of modern stimuli was seen by many commentators as harmful to the mental equilibrium of vulnerable members of both sexes. Numerous social processes came to be examined in this way, listed at length on the pages of disparate Victorian tomes like some motley crowd in their own right, jostling for attention. Clamorous specialists insisted that the problem of bewitchment would only get worse as 'progress' advanced.[26]

With the growth of the new discipline of sociology in the 1880s and 1890s, and of the study of crowd psychology within it, these pervasive views and visions were extensively theorised in the human sciences; acrimonious discussion as to the universality or particularity of hypnotic susceptibility littered the specialist European periodicals. Gustave Le Bon, the best-known, most widely translated and arguably the most hysterically alarmist of the period's crowd psychologists, made clear to a wide readership in and beyond France that hypnosis and hysteria were indispensable explanatory terms when dealing with collective behaviour, even if such terms only threw up further enigmas.[27] By this time, the nature of charisma had become a central concern in social and political thought (most famously developed in the work of the major sociological pioneer, Max Weber), part of a growing preoccupation with irrational factors in individual and collective human behaviour.[28] While some specialists identified these phenomena with primitive, or at least pre-modern tendencies, others argued that the rising tide of mass democracy signalled new waves of collective infatuation with orators and 'crowd pleasers'.

Despite intellectual rivalries and academic divisions, much was shared by *fin-de-siècle* commentators on crowd hypnotism, such as the Italian Sighele, or his French rivals, Tarde and Le Bon. It was evident to all of them that beyond the conscious relationship of politicians and crowd, speaker and audience, buyer and seller, lay a more shadowy world of social communication and mutual psychic entanglement. Some took this argument further, envisaging an interaction in which both parties communicated with each other unconsciously as well as consciously.[29] In their writings, the potential or actual violence of the group was almost always a prominent theme. Thus the emergence of the discipline of crowd psychology formalised a much wider political and cultural language warning of the dangers of the irrational.[30] Tarde summed up a plethora of contemporary ideas in particularly dramatic terms when he declared, in 1890: 'The social state, like the hypnotic state, is only a form of dream, a dream of command and a dream of action. To have ideas only suggested and to believe them spontaneously: such is the illusion of the somnambulist, and of social man as well.'[31] Again, the masses of modern society were cast as especially vulnerable to political magnetism, although Tarde drew attention to the fascinating effect of strangers on both 'primitive' and 'civilised' minds.[32] The *somnambule* revealed the essentially emotional and fantastic dimension of all social and political relationships; fascination and imitation were ubiquitous. As Tarde glumly concluded: 'Society is imitation, and imitation is a form of somnambulism.'[33] He rejected the idea that there was a clear divide between rational and irrational forces in society, exploring rather the powerful hypnotic investment in all political and commercial relations, the bewitching features of the most material of objects and the most ephemeral of social exchanges.

Such ominous analyses of the crowd in the street, and the crowd in the head, often presented themselves as entirely aloof from the emotions they explored – as cool, 'scientific' appraisals of a vulgar age, which was doomed by the uncivilising effects of the widening franchise for men (let alone the prospect of votes for women). Many gloomy forecasts were written to the effect that 'ballots' heralded barbarism or, more specifically, evolutionary regression. Votes or higher education for women were transmuted into the language of national – and racial – crisis, diagnosed as features of a neurasthenic and hysterical modernity. Whether they included themselves in the picture or not (and Bernheim and Tarde were less hubristic on this score than some of their rivals) crowd psychologists concluded that humanity remained the chronic victim of suggestibility; indeed, in some ways, more so now than ever before. The very idea of the human being, Bernheim argued, was inconceivable outside the concept of suggestion. From our early infancy, he noted, we are all inescapably caught up in the dynamics of influence. But modernity created special new difficulties: the public was subject to an impossible succession of commercial, political and social pressures, strained by the speed, confusion, industrial complexity, motley information, sexual hypocrisies and general urban confusion of the day. The result: so many epidemics of hysteria and hypnoid confusion. 'Mass culture' as well as 'mass politics' were the source of medico-psychological dread. After 1900, cinema was increasingly to become a source of such apprehension, attributed with responsibility for

fostering a disturbed dream world in which dangerous patterns of suggestion were unavoidable. It was commonly argued that the susceptible
'masses' would be sent into nervous convulsions or trance conditions as they
sat together in the new, darkened pleasure palaces.[34] Louis Haugmard's pre-
diction in 1913 that the 'charmed masses will learn not to think anymore,
to resist all desire to reason, to construct, to open their large and empty eyes
only to look, look, look', was not atypical.[35]

* * *

While it has long been common for historians and social theorists to stress
the processes of secularisation which have transformed Europe in the modern age, other recent commentators, following a less well-worn route, have
tracked, on the contrary, the quasi-religious and magical beliefs re-emerg-
ing within this changing world: wondrous beliefs and beliefs in the power
of wonder, arguably as apparent at the end of the nineteenth century as ever
before. Capitalism, so it is now recognised, did not demystify social relations nearly as much as Marx and others had sometimes hoped. Industrial
modernisation and psychological enchantment turned out to be deeply
compatible.[36] Far from pitilessly tearing asunder the veils and bonds of a
feudal yesteryear, modern industrial society was found to be caught up in
an infinitely complex set of desires, displacements and projections.

Old eighteenth-century debates about taste and the marketplace were
conceived a century later in terms of mass suggestion, popular atavism and
group psychological regression. The recognition that products were sold on
the basis of their verbal or pictorial association with something else were
described by various social commentators, as were the subliminal desires
projected into literary, political and consumer artefacts themselves. Many
of the real and fictional personages who feature in the pages of this book
wittingly or unwittingly lent themselves to goods, provoking wonderment
at the public's inordinate craving for novelties and a bite-sized 'piece of
their heroes': from Garibaldi biscuits and Jenny Lind sweets to Trilby
lozenges. In the 1870s, Du Maurier mocked the latest craze for collecting
products, even referring to the taste for old blue and white china as 'Acute
Chinamania'. (The *Trilby* saga which would come to embarrass the sardonic illustrator was still twenty years away.) Recognition of such emotionally laden fashions, tastes and cross-references between one thing and
another, in contexts remote from traditional religious sites, provides a necessary corrective to older histories which have equated, say, capitalism with
secularism and disenchantment. There is now an extensive secondary

literature on this issue: much has been written since Roland Barthes' wry demonstration that even steak and chips, or wine and milk, let alone the face of Garbo or the brain of Einstein, are saturated with 'spiritual' meanings in modern societies.[37]

The Great Exhibition of 1851 has often been seen as a defining moment in the Janus-faced history of commercial and industrial experience, inaugurating the era in which the very scrutiny of commodities was to provide a mass leisure pursuit.[38] In later years, other products would be greeted at industrial fairs with public awe and fascination, a fact noted with appreciation or dismay by early chroniclers. The advent of bicycles, chemical dyes, electric lighting and automobiles, radioactivity itself, were received by some admirers in the most breathlessly reverential and even mystical terms.[39] Perhaps no less than the amazed sightseers who witnessed hot-air balloons in the late eighteenth century, commentators a hundred years later gave themselves over to the fantastic – indeed the phantasmagoric – experience of industrial products. In short, the experience of consumer society was frequently cast as wondrous. Take this 1904 description of ranked automobiles on display at the Grand Palais in Paris:

> You come at nightfall. Coming into the world from the entrance to the Métro, you stand stupefied by so much noise, movement and light. A rotating spotlight, with its quadruple blue ray, sweeps the sky and dazzles you; two hundred automobiles in battle formation look at you with their large fiery eyes . . . Inside, the spectacle is of a rare and undeniable beauty. The large nave has become a prodigious temple of fire; each of its iron arches is outlined with orange flames; its cupola is carpeted with white flames, with those fixed and as it were solid flames of incandescent lamps: fire is made matter, and they have built from it. The air is charged with golden haze, which the moving rays of the projectors cross with their iridescent pencils.[40]

Paeans to industrial progress were matched by numerous critical reflections; if priests, metaphysicians and sometimes novelists worried about the spiritual toll of modern production and consumption, physicians concerned themselves principally with the physiological and neurological bill to be paid by society. Medico-moral diagnosis of the impossible bodily and mental strain was reiterated in 'degenerationist' commentaries (culminating in Max Nordau's *Degeneration* in the 1890s). Artefacts and new social experiences were said to come at the citizen in a disorderly and impossible deluge: the brain was simply overwhelmed by the miscellany of items in the shops and the newspapers – an inane and insanely motley output of tit-bits, from cookery to shares, solemn state occasions to the most tawdry gossip, vague metaphysical discussions and reports of the latest in science and industry. This mad flow of news was said to make rationality difficult for any but the best attuned minds. As Frederick Harrison lamented in the 1880s: 'Our human faculties and our mental forces are not enlarged simply by multiplying our materials of knowledge, and our faculties of communication.' Telephones and steam-presses were all very well but they led to no enlargement 'of the brains of the men who heard Moses speak, and saw Aristotle and Archimedes pondering over a few worn rolls of crabbed manuscript'.[41]

Harrison chronicled with some pain the way books corrupted as well as inspired the spirit, mesmerising rather than enlightening the masses. Authorial celebrity was becoming a function of the sales figures to a quite new degree. The fame of a novel was thus not only a cause of the revenue it generated; the sales themselves fuelled the fire of demand, and were discussed in magazines dealing with the book trade itself. Success was publicised – placed on the sales lists – which in turn fostered further purchases. The notion of the publishing 'phenomenon' gathered pace: the successful text was recorded in newspaper columns and authors were spotlighted through interviews and feature stories as never before. In the later nineteenth century, newspapers, those quintessential 'one-day best-sellers', were not only undergoing a noteworthy quantitative change – new titles and expanding circulation figures – they were also very often changing form. Personal slants, interviews and anecdotes were dramatically foregrounded. Correspondence columns, human interest angles, individual exposés and scandals would be pioneered in the investigative journalism of such high-profile figures as W.T. Stead, who had taken over the *Pall Mall Gazette* from the far more staid editorship of John Morley. (Here, not surprisingly, the Whistler–Du Maurier mini-scandal would be extensively aired.)

The very notion of journalism as a distinct profession, with its own ethos and protocols, its circuits of gossip, whispering campaigns and bureaucracy, fully came of age in the 1880s, institutionalised in new formations such as the Institute of Journalists; the Institute of Women Journalists followed in 1895. While there were great social gains and exciting cultural and political possibilities in the fact of widening literacy, expanding readerships and innovative techniques of news representation

and inquiry, these seemed to connect all too seamlessly with an imperative
of selling at any cost, and the constriction of writing to predictable formu-
lae. Laments on the decline of public taste, the cynical fostering and
exploitation of vulgarity, the gathering vogue for frivolous entertainment
rather than edification, led some to despair.[42] The 1880s and 1890s saw a
tide of titillating and moralising 'easy reading'; it was a world in which
Pearson's Weekly, Tit-Bits and *The Star* all flourished. By 1894 there were
four halfpenny evening papers in London. In May 1895 the *Daily Mail* was
launched, with its self-consciously middlebrow image, its sentimentality,
sensational sagas and general patriotic noise.

While it is true that Victorian commentators often characterised the age
in terms of natural-scientific triumph or the advance of Reason, there were
also some very powerful counter-currents to any correlation of, say, widening education or literacy, let alone technology, industry and science, with
the inevitable extension of social enlightenment. The art critic John Ruskin
was not alone in wishing that the railways had never been invented. And
anyway the extent and nature of modernisation was open to debate. Not
only was there a striking 'persistence of the old regime' in politics, but also
a notable tenacity of religious enthusiasms, new and old. The fact that railways were spreading did not necessarily and automatically mean that the
age of religion was declining, although it had been axiomatic for many
commentators that industrialisation would be reflected in the worldly triumph of 'mechanical beliefs' (whatever they might be). But, to take one
notable example, how were such commentators to accommodate the fact
that new cults of Mary were emerging in Europe in this period (more followed during the First World War), arguably the signs of a contradictorily
modern faith rather than the mere survival of older 'tradition'?

The divide between 'the secular' and 'the religious' was itself anything
but clear. Music and dance, for instance, while largely beyond the aegis of
'the Church', acquired ever more religious overtones, as was often
observed. Witnessing the ballerina Fanny Essler's performance in Boston in
the 1840s, Margaret Fuller is reported to have whispered to Ralph Waldo
Emerson, 'This is poetry', to which he replied: 'No, Margaret. It is religion.'
Such an 'invitation to ecstasy' (as the historian Peter Gay deftly puts it),
emerging from ideas of sensibility in the eighteenth century and the cultural fashions of Romanticism, spread widely. It became, for many commentators, a kind of spiritual duty to 'succumb' to music. It was not just
that music taps powerful emotional experiences and primitive, sometimes
unspeakable, affects, but that it was seen as culturally and even therapeutically

important to submit oneself to this process. While one view stressed this openness to the musical spiritual flood as a kind of moral imperative (the best means to emotional rejuvenation for the jaded), others viewed precisely such acquiescence as a dangerous entrancement, opening up perturbing psychological possibilities. A variety of commentators and connoisseurs divided over whether audiences *should* allow themselves to be thus engulfed. But certainly there was a notable shift in manners, whereby hushed and even awed attention became *de rigeur* during concert performances, to enable each subject's private experience of release from events 'outside', and full emotional connection inside the concert hall.

A veritable ethics of listening, with elaborate protocols for entering into the required quasi-mystical state, crystallised during the nineteenth century, while technical virtuosity, in the manner of Paganini, was celebrated with ever greater wonderment. The great composers of the past were more or less deified. It became increasingly unlikely that distinguished musicians would be required to enter noblemen's houses through the tradesmen's entrance, as had happened to the Jewish pianist Ignaz Moscheles, or that a rope would be required to separate the musicians from the guests in *salon* performances (the celebrated Victorian singer Charles Lablache marked and enhanced his status, by dramatically kicking one aside).[43] In Wagner, such notions of musical dignity – and sublime intensity – reached their culmination. At his Bayreuth Festival (which opened in 1876 with the *Ring* cycle), audiences entered (or at least were expected to enter) into a very special state of mind, a kind of rhapsodic listening. In Gay's words, they 'surrendered their individuality for a shared spiritual bath and a collective adoration of the genius who had brought them there'.[44]

In the 1860s, Matthew Arnold had famously proposed the elevation of the role of culture as a necessary antidote to the mechanical age he witnessed all around him. Culture was to be a kind of substitute or surrogate for religion, since he accepted that society *had* profoundly lost its spiritual orientation. The only way to avoid anarchy, he suggested, was to disseminate across classes a quite different language of worship from the old one. Poetry was to have a crucial place; this was, as a scholar of modern literature has observed, the crucial point of departure for a new 'social mission of English criticism'.[45] But on a broader European stage, it was not at all clear that subsequent decades bore out such an analysis of spiritual bankruptcy and religious decline. Thus when, late in the last century, the novelist Emile Zola visited Lourdes in south west France, he soon concluded that here was the hot topic of the age. The town had become the scene of an

Théophile-Alexandre
Steinlen, *Emile Zola at
Lourdes*. Musée Pyrénéen,
Lourdes.

extraordinary cult around a grotto spring, prompted by the visions of a
shepherdess, Bernadette Soubirous, in 1858. Interpretation was not simple
for Zola. Were the crowds a sign of new times or a vestige of the past? Zola
marvelled at the pilgrims and the miracle cures. He found himself
enthralled by the spellbound thousands who flocked to this new holy place,
displaying in their very actions a profound resistance to the kinds of scientific triumphalism which he had made his own.[46] In the pilgrimage phenomenon, as Ruth Harris argues in her history of Lourdes, lay 'the lure of
the miraculous and the individual encounter with the supernatural, a
vision of community and of selfhood entirely at odds with secular creeds'.[47]
One way of trying to account for – or explain away – the phenomenon
was, of course, in terms of collective hypnosis.[48]

Meanwhile, at Marpingen in Germany, a group of young girls had seen
a vision of a woman carrying a child, and soon after thousands were
streaming into the village. These were modern consumers on a grand scale,
as was evidenced by the roaring trade in prayer books, rosaries, photos,

brooches and flasks. The writer and Catholic convert J.-K. Huysmans referred to such commercialisation as he witnessed at Lourdes as 'the Devil's revenge', while at Marpingen German Catholics complained that the profits of such modern pilgrimage were being siphoned off by Jews and Protestants.[49] As David Blackbourn insists, in a recent history of the subject, Marpingen 'did not represent a clash between tradition and modernity, but fed off many conflicts of an uneven, uneasy world'.[50]

In France, Zola richly chronicled human irrationality in all its manifold guises, while in England George Gissing wrote somewhat dour novels in which political mobs appeared no less deranged. Distinct inflections of style notwithstanding, both novelists recorded how crowds were easily reduced to the baboon-like condition that Taine had so influentially described in his *Origins of Contemporary France*. Gissing also chronicled more mundane forms of suggestion in the modern age. Like Zola and Taine, he was deeply interested in the whole panoply of group psychological disturbances. His *New Grub Street* (1891) drew attention to the modern degradation of writing as a profession. There were indeed new kinds of commercial techniques at work. Novels had never as yet been so caught up in 'promotion', thereby raising in a different form the question of collective manipulation. Books constantly fed off one another and cross-referenced each other in the wider market. This can be seen at an early stage in Dickens' career, where parody texts such as *Oliver Twiss* and *Martin Guzzlewit* (sic) appeared hardly a moment after the ink on the author's own texts was dry.[51] Prescient readers could see the commercial shape of things to come in the ever-more strident promotion of Dickens' novels, or the spin-off products (from perfumes to dances) which followed a literary success such as Wilkie Collins' *Woman in White*. When *Our Mutual Friend* appeared in the mid-1860s, there were posters advertising the work on omnibuses and steamboats, as well as publicity at the major outlets of W.H. Smith, notices at railway stations and bills around gas lamps; and the first instalment of the novel itself in *All The Year Round* was accompanied by advertisements for Mudie's Select Library, crinolines, Slack's electro-plates, Cash's cambric frilling, metallic pen-makers and the Passport Agency.[52]

Dreams and desires, as advertisers demonstrated with growing ease, could be fostered in the most leaden material goods as well as in the most apparently ephemeral of tales. This is not to suggest, however, that such Victorian commercial manipulations were entirely new, of course, or that they could be guaranteed to work in advance; not even the most scheming entrepreneur could ensure a product took hold, any more than today a

Hollywood producer can bank with certainty on any one film, however close to the previously successful formula. But the superficial and the ephemeral were frequently viewed as overwhelming works of real cultural and moral worth. They 'crowd out the immortal poetry and pathos of the human race, vitiating our taste for those exquisite pieces which are a household word, and weakening our mental relish for the eternal works of genius!' as Harrison complained in a typical fulmination on the state of the culture. It was true, he concluded sadly, that the contemporary public would rather read M. Zola's seventeenth novel in preference to Homer. Indeed 'they' were mostly quite incapable of understanding Homer at all, whether in Greek or in translation.[53]

In the world of letters, sport and the arts, the mysterious phenomenon of the 'craze' was gathering pace in those late nineteenth-century years as, too, the concept of the 'fan'; the word itself was a product of the 1880s.[54] The sudden popularity of croquet in America in the 1860s, the dance crazes that spread from continent to continent in the 1880s and 1890s, the mass vogue for roller-skating and cycling, or 'ping pong fever' in 1901, ignited public discussion about the social-psychological implications of these endless 'modern fads'.[55] Henry James was characteristically eloquent about, and troubled by, the 'many-headed monster' of popular fashion. Even in his beloved Italy, he saw, by the last three decades of the century, a rampant tourism in the process of ruining the very sites the visitors had come to behold. The popularisation and values of tourism, as well as the vulgar press, were perceived as deeply troubling and morally distracting, indicating a kind of inexorable modern slide towards superficiality and ephemeral suggestion. It might also be recalled here that Coca-Cola was invented and first sold in Atlanta in 1886 and was first bottled in 1894. It was not long before its advertising budget was measured in hundred of thousands, if not millions.[56]

The messenger was often deemed as idiotic as the message in these new times. A newspaper, quipped Oscar Wilde, was an indispensable source for the discovery of all that was uninteresting and stupid about the age. 'By giving us the opinions of the uneducated, it keeps us in touch with the ignorance of the community. By carefully chronically the current events of contemporary life, it shows us of what very little importance such events really are. By invariably discussing the unnecessary, it makes us understand what things are requisite for culture, and what are not.[57] Books and newspapers were themselves becoming congested advertising sites for other products. It has been calculated that, by 1882, the *Daily Telegraph* was devoting more than sixty per cent of its space to advertising.[58] Although advertising agencies as such were not new, their numbers mushroomed in and beyond the 1870s. According to one estimate, by 1900 there were several hundred advertising agencies in London alone.[59] It was a world, then, of proliferating sales and selling activity, and swelling angst-ridden commentaries on that activity; a world in which the industry surrounding 'consumption' was increasingly disjoined from 'production'. Literature was inevitably part of this dynamic and shifting marketing world. While Gissing had chronicled *New Grub Street*, Henry James' short story 'The Next Time' came out in one of the new magazines still most closely identified with Decadence, *The Yellow Book* (first published in 1894) and told the tale of an author who found it impossible to lower himself to the 'the voice of the market', the 'age of trash triumphant' and the contemporary standards of the best seller.[60] The relationship between this so-called descent of taste, this downward slope towards the trash-heap of civilisation and the hypnotic nature of group psychology were very much part of the cultural conversation of the *fin de siècle* in general, and the work of Du Maurier in particular.

But if the florid vision of Svengali's power over hearts and minds connected clearly with a particular kind of Victorian unease with emotional manipulation and the heavy selling of crass and ersatz values, it also reflected worries and passions about seduction and 'medical' abuse that had been very prominently stirred up in Europe much earlier still. Du Maurier's 'odd couple', after all, came more than a century after the practice of animal magnetism had caused an international sensation. The fundamental uncertainties about the nature of the sexual interaction between the mesmerist and the mesmerised subject, dramatically inaugurated in the last decades of the eighteenth century, were re-activated by a long line of controversial practitioners, performers and theorists thereafter.

5
The Sexual Charge

And there is not a sign of effort, of difficulty overcome. All through, Trilby smiles her broad, angelic smile; her lips well parted, her big white teeth glistening as she gently jerks her head from side to side in time to Svengali's bâton, as if to shake the willing notes out quicker and higher and shriller . . . Svengali steps on to the platform by his wife's side and kisses her hand; and they both bow themselves backwards through the curtains, which fall, to rise again and again and again on this astounding pair!

(Du Maurier, *Trilby*)[1]

That mesmerism could be a method of sexual *and* political control had been noticed by various Victorian writers. The issue was discussed in many journals, not least in the pages of *Punch*. Thus an article in 1841 on 'the advantages of animal magnetism' proposed facetiously that the practice might be used by governments to pacify the Chartists, as well as by husbands to secure their wayward wives.[2] It was suggested there that emotional leverage could be used to achieve a kind of compliance and stability. The idea that such entrancement could provide beneficial sedation or cure for mental distress was canvassed often enough. Similarly, in late-nineteenth-century sexology, hypnotism was on occasion advocated as an important therapeutic means of helping patients *abandon* perceived sexual depravity of one sort or another. But the main thrust of much journalistic and scientific comment throughout the period concerned the risks of malign fascination and, while there were diverse political and legal responses in different European countries, the terms of the ethical debate were often very similar. Many commentators focused on the ways in which such techniques could be used to lure crowds, criminal accomplices or adulterous partners towards their moral doom. Political leaders, as well as lovers, were said to be quite literally mesmeric, or hypnotic, their very success bypassing any rational appeal to the mind. Often the words lost any direct association with a particular theory of hypnosis, standing in more vaguely for a kind of alien interference: the catastrophic and irresistible take-over of a spouse by a stranger, or of a group by a demagogue.

In London, there was much discussion of the exotic foreign aspects of mesmerism and considerable public interest in the flamboyant activities of several continental practitioners.[3] Reports of their activities became ever more outlandish. The dazzling Charles Lafontaine, for instance, caused a sensation during his visit to Britain in the early 1840s by apparently magnetising a lion at London Zoo.[4] Critics smelled a rat, of course; but at one demonstration, a sceptical observer failed to provoke any sensation (or at least any physical reaction) when he stabbed Lafontaine's side-kick – a 'mesmeric boy' from France – to see if he really was insensible. No sooner had such mesmerists set foot on British soil than warnings proliferated about the risks of allowing such foreign 'scoundrels' access, particularly to native British women.[5] Salacious stories, and cases reminiscent of the unfortunate affair of Dr Mesmer and Miss Paradis, continued to be reported. Mesmerism and hypnotism were frequently likened to emotional, or sometimes even bodily, kidnapping. Reports had occasionally circulated in Britain of mesmeric orgies in Parisian hospitals, of parasitic and lascivious magnetists deflowering their patients.

In the Victorian period, medical journals such as the *Lancet* expressed unease at the depth of the social curiosity about such adventurers. Sober critics scoffed at reports about the therapeutic prowess of the doubtful continental mesmerists who 'set up shop' in London, yet some explanation had to be offered for their exciting effects on individuals and groups. After all, the impressive Lafontaine (with his piercing eyes and long beard) apparently caused women in the West End of London to cry out and cover their faces when he walked past, while the missing thumb of one 'Baron' Dupotet was said to be the source of his nefarious powers. Nobody seemed quite sure how it worked. Did the 'influence' of these figures bypass the minds of their victims? Was it a straight 'body to body' communication? Furious debates raged as to the merits and demerits of the practice among radical medical reformers and literati, while the clergy were dramatically divided.[6]

LES MALADES ET LES MEDECINS.

LE MÉDECIN MAGNÉTISEUR.

– Indiquez nous la maladie de monsieur ?
– Monsieur a un rhume de cerveau chronique compliqué d'une douleur rhumatismale dans le mollet gauche c'e
ce qui est cause de la souffrance qu'il éprouve au creux de l'estomac...il doit prendre pendant trois mois une infusi
de violette édulcorée avec un petit verre de Cognac...et puis venir nous consulter régulièrement tous les jours !

An 'exotic' doctor magnetises a young woman.

Such debates were still in full swing towards the end of the century, often amplified by sensational medico-legal cases. Claims of sexual and moral irresponsibility under hypnosis were dramatised in celebrated Parisian trials. Meanwhile, hypnotic entertainments remained a feature of popular theatre in a number of European countries. Long-simmering forebodings boiled over in the case of 'Donato'. Donato was the stage-name of a Belgian ex-naval officer, D'Hont, who became the most notorious of all late nineteenth-century mesmeric charmers to entertain European audiences – and trouble respectable opinion in the process. He could tame the rowdy as easily as he could arouse the lethargic subject. In Liège, early in his career, he was reputed to have magnetised more than one hundred people successfully, to the outrage of many orthodox religious believers. Editorial comment in a Catholic journal made no bones about the fact that he was doing the work of the devil. Donato went on 'grand tours' across Europe, reaching Paris in 1875, almost a century after his illustrious predecessor Mesmer's initially triumphant sojourn in the same city. As so often the case, it was the magnetiser's effect on a woman – in this case a certain Lucile – which attracted the most notice, although Donato's influence over both sexes was certainly remarked. In Donato's work, eye contact was everything. Through his gaze, as one admirer put it, he did not simply mesmerise, he 'Donatised' the subject.[7]

'Donatism' was meant to rival the term 'mesmerism', describing the particular phenomenon of fascination at which the Belgian excelled, although admittedly this flattering terminology never really caught on.[8] Instead, it was the scurrilous charges against him that stuck. Donato protested his innocence and his seriousness, but did not help his own case when he mischievously insisted that Jesus Christ was no miracle worker with the sick, merely a mesmerist who got there about eighteen hundred years ahead of the pack![9] There were frequent calls for his demonstrations to be curbed and for his inflammatory presence to be removed altogether from one town or another.[10] When the first international congress of hypnotism opened its proceedings in Paris in 1889, the issue which came highest on its agenda was a proposal to ban hypnotic performances by untrained (that is to say, non-medical) entertainers.[11]

Implicitly or explicitly, the fear of sexual confusion and moral violation lay at the heart of most Victorian mesmeric narratives. The Paris-based British artists in Du Maurier's tale had to comfort themselves with the knowledge that, deep down, their beloved Trilby loathed her beguiling Jewish companion; the idea of her conscious acquiescence – let alone active sexual interest in Svengali – would have been too upsetting. Yet however distasteful to them her 'conjugal' liaison may have been, she became 'La Svengali'. Not everybody took the issue so much to heart, of course, as did Du Maurier's forlorn, jilted and love-sick expatriots. But those who lampooned the magnetists and derided the abilities of the motley entrancers to be found on stage, in the boudoir or the consulting room, were still prone to warn the public of the sexual and emotional risks run by the vulnerable patient, or the gullible spouse. Even where popular performances in the manner of Donato were acknowledged to depend upon mere trickery (paid stooges in the audience), and thus to be offering (at best) mere 'entertainment', there was often a serious 'health warning' attached. It was argued that the theatrical accomplice might lose control, cause injury and attack the audience. In short, it was thought possible for the faking of hypnotism subtly to transmute into the genuine article, and with dire consequences.[12]

Amongst the most fatuous of all the 'Trilbyana' products of the *fin de siècle* was a poem, 'Drilby', penned by Leopold Jordan, comically rehearsing the sexual charge against the rapacious and captivating Jew. Published in New York in 1895, it presented 'Du Haurier's' (sic) characters, as Zvengali, Toffy, the Baird, Bill and Jecco. They travel across America in search of Drilby. Zvengali is a very different creature from his companions: lascivious, predatory, racially ridiculous and intellectually pretentious. He has shaggy hair, eagle eyes, bony fingers and heavily accented speech:

> 'Och, Got!' Zvengali cried, 'I'll show
> Zese beoples who am I,
> As on ve go I'll hypnotize,
> Or know ze reason vhy.'

The Jew's sinister sexual prowess in the original story is displayed as incompetent bumbling in this doggerel counterpart. Zvengali is deluded about his occult powers. His musical credentials are portrayed as equally ridiculous; he has an aptitude at most for comic songs at the piano. The jokes turn on Zvengali's puffed-up claims for his own abilities and his pathetic pursuit of the woman. Drilby is also presented as physically hideous, rather than as the strange statuesque beauty of Du Maurier's imagination. She is, however, shown to be sceptical about and immune to Zvengali's hypnotic and musical capabilities.

The poem follows Du Maurier's narrative in its gloomy denouement. But here the deaths of the two lovers, Bill and Drilby, are presented as a suicide designed to thwart the sexual designs of Zvengali:

> Let this story be a warning,
> It's written on that plan,
> Don't introduce your sweetheart to
> Von hypnotizing man.[13]

The period was marked by many such exhortations, frivolous or otherwise, to beware the enchantment of strangers and, in particular, the dangers of sexual conquest through hypnosis by unknown men. 'One catches flies with honey, and not with vinegar', declared Dr Auguste Forel, former director of the Zurich lunatic asylum, as he pondered the not inconsiderable historical catalogue of such abuses. So many unscrupulous and lascivious

'Svengalis' seemed to be operating in the twilight of the 1880s and 1890s, arousing undue sympathy, effecting some form of sedation or pacification, and thereby achieving their illicit ends. There were parallel discussions about how drugs might be used to dominate a sexual prey, but hypnosis was viewed as the more pervasive technique, the more insidious weapon in the armoury of rogues. It was feared that as well as burglaries, blackmails and murders, sexual conquest amounting to rape might be facilitated by the trance: sexual violence concealed by the appearance of mutual agreement within the hypnotic couple. Newspapers and journals were often agog with speculations about the passion that became possession and the seduction that was but somnambulism under another name.[14] Experts continued to disagree about the appropriate treatment or punishment for the stupefied offender. If a prostitute could be made to renounce her trade through hypnotic interference, why might not a virtuous woman be perverted by the same method?[15] Racial and gender differences in susceptibility to the manipulation of the will were often implicated in such debates, pornographic or otherwise. Different groups, it was thought, possessed unequal inborn capacities for self-control.

It is true that some commentators, such as the philosopher Joseph Delboeuf, championed a 'free market' in hypnosis and rejected calls for banning public displays and the experiments of lay practitioners. But at the 1889 Paris Congress he was roundly condemned for this misplaced liberality.[16] Protests against 'lucrative exploitation' carried the day. The names of mesmeric players on the European stage (including Hansen, Donato and Léon) were often on the lips of the doctors. Medical authorities, not least Charcot himself, had often spoken with distaste and condescension about lay abuses, as though something precious had been stolen from 'Science' by these mountebanks; in fact, the physicians had certainly learned a thing or two from the performers they denounced. The intellectual and theatrical debts were two-way, but sober medics were largely resolved to widen the division between the professional and amateur, the respectable and the disreputable.[17] Earnest doctors admonished their patients to treat any claims by 'Svengalis' and 'Donatos' they met with a large dose of salt; meanwhile alarming exhortations peppered the learned periodicals and popular novels of the day. Here hypnosis was but one chapter, albeit a particularly tendentious one, in the wider debate about standards – and standardisation – in the medical field. There were extensive discussions about how effectively to police plebeian displays and treatments and, on the other hand, concern to consolidate the position of the technique within the orthodox training of the physician: hence proposals emerged at the Paris Congress that instruction in hypnotism should become a compulsory feature of the medical curriculum.

For all the anxious warnings and horrified moral reactions which had plagued this borderline therapeutic and theatrical technique in the late nineteenth century, mesmerism, neo-mesmerism and hypnotism had endured and even flourished.[18] So, too, had gossip about the vulnerability of wives or husbands (but especially the former) amidst the surreptitious magnetic manoeuvrings, flashing eyes and operatic posturings of charismatic dinner guests. It was a piquant conversation, which seemed to go on in many nations and from one end of the century to the other. Long after Mesmer and Paradis, tongues wagged about the notorious musical and sexual liaison in early Victorian London of the conductor and harpist Charles Boscha and Anna Rivere Bishop (wife of the composer Sir Henry Rowley Bishop). This scandal was later recalled and recounted to a popular weekly by Frederick Lyster, a musician personally acquainted with the couple.[19] Boscha, reputed by some to be a forger and a bigamist, was clearly an effective charmer. Once under his fascination, Anna never looked back, abandoning Bishop and their children and travelling far afield, from Moscow to Cape Town, Hong Kong to Salt Lake City. Apparently Lyster claimed that Svengali and Trilby were based on Boscha and Anna Bishop, or at the least, that Du Maurier was acquainted with the family and knew of the scandal. When Mrs Bishop had met the ageing, but still charismatic, Boscha, it was said that something extraordinary emerged, a quality to her voice which she had never before possessed. Unlike Trilby, however (whose voice reverts to its tunelessness as soon as Svengali languishes), Anna sang on for many years beyond her Svengali's death. What could be more apt than that her career should hit a high note when she starred in Bellini's *La sonnambula* at the Old Broadway Theatre in New York in 1847?[20]

Musical or theatrical manipulation often went hand in glove with tales of hypnotic sexual conquest. Was it new-found virtuosity or enforced ventriloquism? This indeterminate scenario of melodic magnetism, repeated in many guises, itself came to have a special hold on story-telling and social commentary – tuneless women acquiring perfect pitch; uneducated provincials manifesting, with lightning speed, a command of foreign languages, through the dramatic influence of another.[21] It is tempting to see this as a kind of underlying, shared cultural narrative, repeated in many specific yarns and case histories across the century. In this insistent 'story within the story', the reader was shown the limits of psychological autonomy; against the image of the discrete self-knowing individual was set a compelling picture of inter-personal influences and moral transformations. Nobody could say for sure who owned the intellectual, musical or artistic property which resulted from such subliminal interactions.

Some decades before turning to fiction, George Du Maurier had also ventured into this experimental field. The claim that *Trilby* referred to his own youthful contact with mesmerism owed much to the subsequent reminiscences of his friend Felix Moscheles, who had known the young George and described their explorations in a book which appeared soon after Du Maurier's death, at a time when there was still a storm of public interest in his life. *In Bohemia with Du Maurier* (1896) even carried a posthumously published endorsement from Moscheles' old companion. It described the two young men's companionship and experiences together in Antwerp and Malines, as well as their shared infatuation with the cryptically named Octavie L., or simply 'Carry'. Moscheles put the facts candidly, or almost: 'The truth of the matter is that we shared fraternally in the enjoyment of her good graces'. He speculated that this woman was the model for the figure of Trilby. Carry was delightful in her easy manners; but these were matched by a 'ladylike reserve' where appropriate. She was the daughter of an organist who had held a good position at one of the principal churches of Malines, and her mother was the proprietor of a shop selling tobacco. There the two artists regularly encountered her. Apparently they had both been fascinated by her. Through mesmerism, they succeeded in becoming fascinating to her. Moscheles confided in the book that for him, personally, such days of dangerous mesmeric dabbling were decidedly in the past: 'Now I have not touched the fluid (sic) for some thirty years; I swore off because it was taking too much out of me.' Before their time together in Belgium, the youthful Felix had already attended various seances in Paris where he discovered that he possessed a certain gift: 'I could mesmerise'. He also found 'a truly remarkable mesmeric subject', a cleaner named Virginie Marsaudon:

It needed but little to lead her from a state of docile and genial dependence to one of unconscious mesmeric subjection, and so, a few passes shaping her course, I willed her across the boundary line that separates us from the unknown, a line which, thanks to science, is daily being extended. Madame veuve Marsaudon was herself an incorrigible disbeliever in the phenomena of mesmerism, but as a subject her faculties were such as to surprise and convert many a scoffer.

This was a rather intriguing comment, stating that the boundary line *separating* us from 'the unknown' was being extended 'thanks to science'; as though 'the unknown' was not being diminished, or conquered, but simply cordoned off by modern 'advances'. In any event, Du Maurier and Moscheles experimented in those dreamy frontier areas of art and science where fantasy easily lost itself in the depths of the intra-psychic and interpersonal mystery:

> We loved that never attainable Will-o'-the-Wisp, 'Truth,' for its own dear Bohemian sake; so, guided by Fancy and Fantasy, we made frequent inroads into the boundless land where unknown forces pick up our poor dear little conception of the Impossible, and use it as the starting-point of never-to-be-exhausted possibilities.

Both men explored the power of mesmerism; but it was Moscheles who initiated Du Maurier and had, perhaps, led him further than he wished. It seems that the novice mesmeriser had himself fallen too far 'under the influence' of his teacher. It may be supposed that their friendship had come under some strain; perhaps their relations with 'Carry' had become increasingly problematic. In any event, Du Maurier scrawled 'Mephistopheles' on a drawing of his magnetic collaborator. The 'midnight presence of the uncanny' was evidently too much for George and he became, at the least, playfully suspicious. As he complained: 'Why should you make nervous fellows' flesh creep by talk about mesmerism, and dead fellows coming to see live fellows before dying, and the Lord knows what else? Why, Gag! It's horrible!'[22]

Horrible perhaps, but the practices of mesmerism and hypnotism remained invested, as earlier in the century, with considerable hopes and dreams. The ambivalent late Victorian reactions prompted by such dabblings in the scientific or even occult mysteries of 'lucid sleep' can be linked to the original history of mesmerism itself which, from the very start, had provoked such cultural ambivalence: horror, scepticism *and* wild enthusiasm. Victorian hypnotism continued to exist on the border between the medically sober and the erotically intoxicated, science and theatre, work and abandon, treatment and amusement. Although not a late nineteenth-century invention, of course, hypnosis still seems particularly redolent of those last decades. Indeed it is almost a defining image of the 'Victorian twilight' or the *Belle Époque*. As the *Revue de l'Hypnotisme* stated in its first number in 1887, such induced states of trance had become 'the order of the day'.

Moscheles, or Mephistopheles? which

Drawing of Felix Moescheles by George Du Maurier.

Successful Victorian practitioners were frequently recognised as social or national outsiders of one kind or another, a feature on which critics leapt with alacrity.[23] Fictions of mesmerism often played up the connection between alien origins and depravity. Worse still, according to some specialists, the 'wandering science' of mesmerism could dissolve a sense of nationhood altogether, enabling, for instance, the *émigré* to speak another language as a native, and a native to lose command of the mother tongue. The foreign features and dubious marital status of charismatic entrancers were apparent enough in Victorian stories such as 'The Poisoned Mind' or 'The Notting Hill Mystery', illustrated by Du Maurier.[24] On occasion, mesmerism in less respectable fiction was likened to a taint, or even seen as akin to a sexually-transmitted disease contracted overseas.[25] Consider a particularly salacious example, an anonymously penned tale, *The Power of Mesmerism: a Highly Erotic Narrative of Voluptuous Facts and Fancies*, published in 1891. Here the terrain of De Sade collided with late-Victorian magnetic speculation to produce a tale of outrageous incestuous couplings in the Etheridge family. Strikingly, all the main characters have a foreign connection: the Etheridges' sexually adventurous son, Frank, learns his mesmerism in Germany. Their equally lascivious daughter, Ethel, has been to school in Paris. The handsome but depraved Mr and Mrs Etheridge are the products, respectively, of Italian and Spanish stock. Such equivocal family romances, stimulated by the flow of magnetic currents, were certainly part of the fictional and theatrical tradition. Although it is true that English husband and wife teams provided 'magnetic' entertainments on stage in Victorian London, it was often said that the riskiest and most stage-worthy liaisons were with foreigners. The 'provoked' rather than 'spontaneous' state of somnambulism was said, by some experts, to be more easily prompted by the impact of a stranger than a partner – or at least, that was one theory. Others argued that it was not the spectacular and exotic skill of the hypnotist, foreign or otherwise, that was crucial to the efficacy of the procedure; rather, it was a question of the patient's willingness to succumb, whether to friends, enemies or enchanting strangers.

Outrages against Modesty, a French treatise on hypnotic sexual abuse published in 1894 – the very year that *Trilby* appeared in book form – attempted, *après* Charcot, to explain such susceptibility to trance states through the model of hereditary degeneration.[26] Its author, Dr Ernest Mesnet, assumed that the suggestible subject was already tainted by a degenerate ancestry and that intergenerational disturbances lay behind her current malady. He also insisted that night-time sleep-walking among children was so common that the term '*noctambulisme*' was required to describe it.[27] Women and children shared a particular propensity to trance states. Simple pressure on the eyes, or a firm look, might be enough to send certain of these especially weak creatures into the special state of sleep. The hypnotic relationship which produced the symptom of somnambulism (once attributed to devilry and sorcery) was, he confidently concluded, today firmly in the realm of science. His alarming study of sexual outrages was in fact stronger on description than on any convincing explanation, as it explored the overthrow of a normal sense of shame and decorum, sometimes through the mere gaze of the hypnotic exploiter. It seemed that even some extremely inhibited and polite women were instantly transformed into shamelessly lascivious beings.[28] Mesnet recorded the powerful agitation and desire that patients exhibited in his own presence. Some subjects were overwhelmed by the intensity of their feelings; he recalled how in one case a suggestible lady fell into hypnotic slumber at the mere mention of the word 'Mesnet'. As the doctor details the procedures and experiences in the hospital, readers cannot but be struck by the sheer manipulation and emotional exploitation of the patients. In short the violence, the collusion and the deception were not merely, as Mesnet implied, 'out there' beyond his hospital doors.

Of one thing, at least, we can be sure: those who concern themselves with such clinical and historical matters, now as then, would do well not to protest too much their own dispassionate motivation and impartiality. Mesnet, on the contrary, did assume his own neutrality, even as he showed how to secure the patient's acquiescence in his own desires. This particular authority on hypnotic scandals wrote tellingly of the ease with which women could be seduced without even knowing it; the skilful hypnotist had no need of narcotics, chloroform or alcohol. But his 'clinical' account quickly reveals not only its own excitement but its cruelty, despite the fact that such passions are claimed to be located elsewhere, amongst the amateurs and quacks. He spoke about hospitalised women who resisted examination with the speculum being tamed by hypnosis, and reported the way in which struggling subjects were brought under his medical domination, referring, for instance, to the acquiescence of an impoverished young woman to whom he offered the present of a brooch. Initially, she was delighted and moved. He then ordered her to hand it over to an attendant. The patient first resisted, then reluctantly obeyed. This was achieved, he was convinced, through hypnosis. When her memory was tested, she was unable to recall the interaction, or at least to recount it to him. It might, of course, be asked whether she was unwilling rather than unable to participate. Nonetheless, Mesnet took the case as proof that in the somnambulistic state, all memory was eradicated. To confirm his theory, he then played out the sadistic game with her all over again.

* * *

There had been other fictions of sexual mesmerism and musical ventriloquism before Svengali, some much finer – and stranger – than Du Maurier's; mesmerism and literature have enjoyed a long liaison. Amongst others, Balzac, Poe, Charlotte Brontë, Flaubert, Hawthorne and James were all deeply intrigued by states of enchantment and automatism.[29] Historians and literary critics have often chronicled how mesmerism touched the lives of writers, poets, and social prophets, from Dickens and Darwin to the Brownings and the Carlyles. Quite how much of the earlier mesmeric literature was known to the creator of Svengali we cannot be sure, but some literary connections proposed in later versions of the tale surely had no place in Du Maurier's original conception. Thus in the 1955 film version,

Svengali was linked to 'Coppola', a frightening figure from E.T.A. Hoffmann's extraordinary tale, 'The Sandman', published in 1816. Fastidious literary critics might object to the conflating of Hoffmann with Du Maurier in this way; in fact, Hoffmann's story does contain, albeit in a more complex form, elements of the sexualised and demonic mesmeric saga of the manipulative 'conductor' and the automaton singer, which the later writer went on to explore.

Hoffmann's rich tale involves the presentation of an automaton, the figure of Olimpia, with whom the disturbed protagonist, Nathanael, falls in love. Unable to respond to his betrothed, Clara, Nathanael becomes captivated by the singing machine, behind which lies a certain wily operative. He attends a concert at which Olimpia plays the piano with great skill and performs a bravura aria in a clear, almost shrill, voice, like a glass bell. Nathanael is enraptured by the 'performer'. Olimpia's gaze gives off no ray of light; her gait is equally bizarre. She has the soulless timing of a machine when she plays, sings and dances. Despite a friend's warning, Nathanael is sure that he can arouse the loving regard of this wax doll. He declares, moreover, that 'only in Olimpia's love do I recognise myself'; he needs no words from her, only her look: 'Words? What are words! The look in her heavenly eyes says more than any terrestrial language.' Nathanael is finally forced to be aware that his object can neither see him nor speak: she is but an automaton. There are 'just black caverns where eyes should be; she was a lifeless doll'.

As the complicated story-line develops, involving an outlandish cast of characters, eyes become ever more prominent, disturbing and dangerous for Nathanael. Hoffmann's intricate narrative charts the central character's final descent and suicide, beautifully conveying, in the process, the delicate link between sanity and vision; it demonstrates how our psychic state affects what we see, and how the way we are seen, in reality or in phantasy, profoundly affects our psychic economy. We experience, but also project meaning into the other's eyes; moreover, we introject some sense of the thoughts and feelings, the love or hate, that lie behind those eyes. The primary significance of visual contact both in sanity and in the state known as 'fascination' is enormously heightened here – the very apparatus of vision taking on phantasmagoric qualities: what Hoffmann portrays is not only the quality of visual hallucination, but the way in which the eye is itself the powerful and dangerous object that is hallucinated.

The story took up not only the theme of psychic disturbance and ocular fascination, but also the moving statues which had intrigued a diverse

European public. The design of automata had proceeded apace in the later eighteenth and nineteenth centuries and various models had been displayed at prominent events across the continent, from Vienna to Paris to London. As a young boy, the English inventor Charles Babbage, later to become famous for his 'calculating machines', had been enchanted by the dancing exhibits at a mechanical museum, first established in Hanover Square in the 1780s by an impresario of such modern wonders of machinery, appropriately named Merlin. Recalling a mechanical dancer he had witnessed, Babbage declared: 'The lady attitudinized in a most fascinating manner. Her eyes were full of imagination, and irresistible.' The figure was one attraction amongst a host of others to be witnessed around this time in London and a number of other capital cities. There was a 'Musical Lady', originally brought to England by a Swiss clock maker in 1776. The public were particularly drawn by her moving eyes and heaving breasts. In a richly suggestive article on the vogue for such machines, the historian of science Simon Schaffer has remarked on the motifs of passion, exoticism, mechanism and money in play here. 'Seduction was an indispensable accompaniment of the trade in automata.'[30]

Since the 1760s, a number of London-based designers and merchants had sold their gesticulating exhibits in Canton, or had exchanged them (via the East India Company) for tea. If the automaton was a product sold by the West to the East, famous Orientalist images of the automaton caused a stir in European capitals, and interacted with current stereotypes of the machine-like Asiatic character. The idea of the calculating but less-than-fully human near-Eastern adversary was also exploited in the famous case of 'the Turkish chess player'. Built at the end of the 1760s as an entertainment for the Empress Maria Theresa, it featured a seated Turk, playing chess. The automaton (originally built by an inventor called Wolfgang von Kempelen) travelled triumphantly across Europe, like that closely contemporaneous sensation, Mesmer himself. Von Kempelen's inventiveness extended beyond the building of automata. He had, for instance, made a printing machine that helped Mesmer's one-time patient, the blind Miss Paradis, to write letters.[31] As Schaffer writes:

> The Turk's arrival in Western Europe coincided precisely with that of another Viennese guru, Franz Mesmer – while von Kempelen had the ability to build an automaton which displayed human intelligence, mesmeric séances seemed able to reduce the most rational humans to the condition of automata.[32]

It seems that von Kempelen may have been explicitly attempting to steer public attention away from animal magnetism. Whatever his intent, his critics accused him of dallying with the devil; much the same charge levelled against Mesmer, the creator of human rather than mechanical automata. Nonetheless, significant numbers of people remained highly enthusiastic about both men's achievements. Story-tellers recounted how 'the Turk' had mystified not only the ordinary public but also great leaders: 'Even Bonaparte who made automata of Kings and Princes at his will, was foiled in an encounter with the automaton chess player.' E.T.A. Hoffmann took a particular interest in the movable Turk after the machine fell into the hands of a fellow musician and engineer, Johann Maelzel, in Vienna. Hoffmann took up the theme in his stories, while Maelzel sought to exploit the marvel more directly. He had bought the figure upon von Kempelen's death in 1814 and proceeded to display it across Europe, for instance in England in 1818, where it appeared in an exhibition held in tasteful but conveniently dimly lit rooms.[33] Maelzel's own designs became increasingly elaborate, and he even went on to build a complete orchestra of automata. But the mechanical Turk remained the greatest attraction. (Although there had been speculation about a possible hoax, a hidden child or dwarf inside the Turk's body, it was not until 1820 that his hidden operators were revealed as William Lewis and Jacques Mouret.)[34]

Certain themes and images unite the disparate episodes and fictions of Olimpia and her manipulators, Maelzel and his Turk, Svengali and his Trilby: the depiction of those mesmerising but vacant eyes, the beguiling music of the automaton, the sinister figure who creates the inhuman player or diva and then mocks the besotted lover or public. Mesmerism and hypnotism were sometimes said to produce a state of human 'automatism', but this only begged further questions about the meaning of the mechanical condition to which the subject had been reduced. Was the 'sleeper' imprisoned or liberated, dehumanised or brutalised by the entrancer's commanding eye?[35] There were no shortage of moralists prepared to denounce the whole enterprise as a war on human relations and spiritual values. From the 1840s, the Catholic Church established a series of decrees condemning such activities. Many subsequent religious denunciations linked hypnotism with spiritualism, and castigated both as unnatural.[36] On the other hand, the erotic aspect of the magnetic encounter, that had scandalised so many pious commentators right from the beginning, was on occasion denied altogether by magnetic practitioners, or else defended as harmless, indeed even therapeutically beneficial.[37]

The subject could scarcely be evaded. As Victorian readers turned the pages of fictions, newspapers, medical and legal reports in the major periodicals, it would have been hard indeed to avoid discussion of such phenomena for very long. The prospect of a woman morbidly and disastrously enthralled or in some other way imprisoned by a repulsive man featured in many of the most memorable novels of the period, of course, from *The Woman in White* (1859-60) to *The Portrait of a Lady* (1881). Evidently new, however, in the later nineteenth century was the interaction of the language of mesmerism with the 'blood and guts' sensibility of literary naturalism, with its characteristic emphasis on the physiological workings of the body and the power of biological inheritance. Thus stories and reports explored the medical, or even neurological, aspects of fascination, or described, in unsparingly explicit detail, the erotic component of subliminal rapport. Zola's compelling novella *Thérèse Raquin*, published in 1867, provides a case in point, describing with quasi-clinical interest, the way an intense and semi-conscious sexual fascination bound an adulterous couple, producing quite ferocious instinctual energy. Right from the start, Thérèse, married to the feeble Camille, is disturbed and captivated by her husband's friend, the artist Laurent. In particular, his direct stare gets to her: he 'seemed to look right through her'.

Zola justified this controversial tale in terms of scientific inquiry into 'the mysterious attraction that may spring up between two different temperaments'. He famously claimed a quasi-medical neutrality in relation to such nervous violence. He also introduced a racial factor into the tale, drawing on a theme from contemporary anthropology. Thérèse was seen as particularly impressionable and volatile because of her mixed racial descent: 'All the instincts of this highly-strung woman burst forth with unparalleled violence; her mother's blood, the African blood that burned in her veins . . .' Thérèse and Laurent's liaison smoulders and then explodes, leading inexorably to the murder of Camille, and its aftermath, the persecuting remorse and madness consequent upon their crime of passion. Although inspired by a newspaper story, the novel was soon criticised by reviewers for its obscenity; neither were such accusations forestalled by the authorial defence of 'forensic accuracy'. Zola's thriller connected seamlessly with certain real cases that followed it. It anticipated, in certain respects, the terms of the trial in 1890 of Gabrielle Bompard and her lover Michel Eyraud, whose sexual and murderous debacle drew wide public attention. Here the woman had claimed not to be responsible for her participation in a capital crime, on the grounds that she had been reduced to a kind of automaton through the hypnotic powers of the man.[38] Such a defence, drawing on the notion of the woman's seduction and helpless descent, encountered some scepticism, although Bompard's plight does seem to have been considerably helped by supporting medico-psychiatric argument. Admittedly, the experts squabbled, casting doubt on who had manipulated whom. Some argued that it was the man who held the woman captive, others that the woman had enslaved the man, or again it was contended that the 'criminal couple' jointly beguiled the authorities.

The process of malign mesmeric seduction is recounted more obliquely by Du Maurier's friend Henry James in 'Professor Fargo', published in 1874. Predating James' more famous example of the vulgar exploitation of animal magnetism on stage in *The Bostonians* by some twelve years, 'Professor Fargo' depicted the tawdry appeal and predatory sexuality of the stage hypnotist of the title. Professor Fargo's theatrical career takes him to New York where he appears under the auspices of an impresario, described (in the same expression that James would later apply to Svengali) as 'a little Jew'. This dubious theatre manager 'had a dirty shirt-front, a scrubby beard, a small, black eye, and a nose unmistakably Judaic'. The Jewish impresario; the down-at-heel Professor; one might speculate, perhaps, on how far Svengali conflates elements of both these characters. In his black evening suit, with an immense turquoise ring, Fargo is presented as a man 'of the conjuring class', who was not without a certain mysterious charisma, emanating particularly from his 'impudent eyes': 'It was his eyes, when you fairly met them, that proved him an artist on a higher line. They were eyes which had peered into stranger places than even lions' mouths.' The narrator (who first comes across this equivocal figure in the town of 'P—') is a sceptical guide through the sad case that follows.

The antics of the Professor become ever more alienating to his sidekick, Colonel Gifford, whose own music-hall talent consists of the ability to make lightning calculations. The Colonel becomes suspicious of his sinister theatrical partner and eventually reveals it in both his smouldering eyes and his words. Fargo ('the perpetrator of vile frauds') is sexually successful with several young girls but his mesmeric reach is shown to be strictly limited. Yet this is not just a tale of swindlers or charlatans: the Professor is a showman, a clever manipulator of occult practices who promises spiritualist contact with the dead, but his true interest lies in the mesmerist's capacity 'to exercise a mysterious influence over living organisms'. Such domination, he tells a crowd of drinkers, can be achieved with the eye, the voice and motions of the hand, or just through setting your mind on it: 'It's called *magnetism*', he informs his bemused audience. Fargo claims to believe the Lord has bestowed the power upon him personally and proposes to make 'noble' uses of the gift. Magnetism, he declares, warming to his theme, can make people sick or well, love or hate, just as the operator pleases. The Colonel at this stage makes a fatal decision by denouncing his colleague as a fraud; Fargo takes revenge by capturing the Colonel's daughter. Here lies the curious double edge: this is a world of illusion and masquerade, yet the narrative presupposes that *something* quite real and effective is actually at work on the body and psyche of the mesmerised subject, producing an unmistakable effect on the behaviour of Miss Gifford. By the time the Colonel has separated from his stage partner in disgust, it is too late; his daughter's 'charming eyes' are now fixed forever on Professor Fargo's 'gross, flushed face', awaiting his commands: 'She had no will of her own.' 'Spiritual magnetism' may be evil, then, but it is not bogus. The Colonel ends up in an asylum while Fargo and Miss Gifford go off together, acting out their 'sensation'.[39]

A few years earlier, Charles Dickens had also provided his most explicit engagement with the erotic dynamics of mesmerism in his unfinished final novel, *The Mystery of Edwin Drood* (1870). Dickens had been interested in mesmerism throughout his career as a writer and had attended John Elliotson's mesmeric demonstrations in the later 1830s.[40] Before long, he swapped his role as admiring spectator for that of amateur practitioner, plunging into mesmerism himself. Travelling through Italy in 1844, he achieved a notable success with his strong 'visual ray' on the wife of a Swiss banker in Genoa (somewhat to the chagrin of Mrs Dickens). The depictions of mesmerism in his novels, however, are more complex. In his fiction, Dickens was less interested in the miraculous curative promises of the art than in the twists and turns of psychic power and slavery, human infatuation and captivation. *Edwin Drood* begins in a fantastic and depraved oriental realm, filtered through the drugged imagination of the languishing addict John Jasper. The 'East' of the dream reverie with which the novel opens turns out to be an East End opium den; the white elephants, Turkish robbers, ten thousand scimitars and thrice ten thousand dancing girls are illusions. But the 'Far East' intrudes in other, less chimerical, ways: we are introduced to Neville and Helena, orphan twins, who have recently arrived in England from Ceylon and who enjoy a near telepathic rapport with each other.

This is a Dickensian world dangerously devoid of parents, where women are exposed to strange forces of fascination and men to the desire for

Illustration for *Edwin Drood* (1870) by Luke Fildes.

unspeakable debauchery. As later on in the case of *Trilby*, the novel picks up the wider belief that an orphan condition was a predisposing factor in the mesmeric or hypnotic state.[41] Although we first meet him in a seedy East End den, Jasper is in fact a most respectable provincial citizen, an official and organist at Cloisterham cathedral.[42] The outcome of the plot remains part of 'the mystery', since Dickens only completed six of the twelve instalments before his death, but it seems that Jasper may have murdered his nephew, Edwin Drood. Whilst the denouement remains in doubt, the presence of evil, threatening but unseen, is perceptible enough, at least to certain especially sensitive characters. The novel is remarkable for its whispered sense of menace, its off-stage sounds, its atmosphere of foreboding. If there are no actual ghosts in this story, there are faint ghostly sounds in the night which cannot easily be explained.

The musical Jasper is cast as a restless and dissatisfied figure. He is shown to feel stultified by the 'cramped monotony' of his existence, suffering an 'unhealthy state of mind', as Edwin quickly discovers. It seems that the uncle is victim to an obscure illness, 'subject to a kind of paroxysm, or fit – I saw him in it once – and I don't know but that so great a surprise, coming upon him direct from me whom he is so wrapped up in, might bring it on perhaps.' There is something even feminine about the man, 'with me [Jasper] is always impulsive and hurried, and, I may say, almost womanish'. Jasper has some awareness of his own obscure sickness. As he declares, 'I have been out of sorts, gloomy, bilious, brain-oppressed, whatever it may be.' Meanwhile, the reader has been shown how the arranged betrothal between Edwin and the beautiful Rosa Bud lacks any real passion. Neville and Edwin have a fierce argument over Rosa, before Edwin's disappearance (presumed drowned) on Christmas Eve. The really dangerous scenes and mesmeric moments occur between Jasper and Rosa, despite the woman's distaste for the man. Jasper is engaged in a kind of sexual blackmail, exploiting her feelings for the vulnerable Neville. But blackmail cannot explain away the strange inner compulsions which drive her towards the 'Svengalian' figure she loathes. This is picked up by Neville's sister, Helena, who remarks to Rosa: 'There is a fascination in you.'

Unprotected by the love of a parent or a betrothed, Rosa is exceptionally exposed to these invisible but powerful forces emanating from Jasper. Sexual desire, as such, is presented as Jasper's alone. That desire, located in (or perhaps projected into) the figure of the vile and isolated mesmerist, is seen as coming back at the bewildered object with a vengeance; the threat moves from outside to inside. Rosa's dread is of an irresistible psychic intoxication and bodily invasion; she cannot help registering the inner nature of her 'music-master', and is forced to experience his invasive quality, his insidious *rapport* with her. Dickens describes the powerful and puzzling nature of the contact between them; Jasper's gaze, whether penetratingly clear or dreamily glazed over, impinges disturbingly on the mind of his pupil, bringing her an unwanted knowledge, which she can only vaguely articulate but which somehow concerns her teacher's desires. 'Even when a glaze comes over [his eyes] (which is sometimes the case), and he seems to wander away into a frightful sort of dream in which he threatens most, he obliges me to know it, and to know that he is sitting close at my side, more terrible to me than ever.' Jasper's crazed and murderous secret self comes to preoccupy or even, literally, to occupy Rosa. Whether because of, or despite, his symptoms, he exerts this formidable hold over his prey, whose final resolution remains just one of the many mysteries of *Edwin Drood*: 'The fascination of repulsion had been upon her so long, and now culminated so darkly, that she felt as if he had power to bind her by a spell.'[43]

6
Queen of Song

He has made a slave of me with his looks. He has forced me to understand him, without his saying a word; and he has forced me to keep silence, without his uttering a threat. When I play, he never moves his eyes from my hands. When I sing, he never moves his eyes from my lips. When he corrects me, and strikes a note, or a chord, or plays a passage, he himself is in the sounds, whispering that he pursues me as a lover, and commanding me to keep his secret. I avoid his eyes, but he forces me to see them without looking at them.

Dickens, *The Mystery of Edwin Drood*[1]

She was a *phénomène*, monsieur! She could keep on one note and make it go through all the colours in the rainbow – according to the way Svengali looked at her.

Du Maurier, *Trilby*[2]

Nowhere were mysteries of entrancement and the enigmas of psychological take-over more evident than in the musical field, as has already been briefly recounted in previous chapters, from the cases of Dr Mesmer and Miss Paradis and the scandalous departure of the conductor Charles Boscha with the singer Anna Bishop, to the fictional triumphs of Svengali and Trilby themselves. Musical experience was itself sometimes likened to a form of mesmerism in late-Victorian commentaries: in each experience lay the possibility of a radical loss of boundaries, even a felt dissolution of the self. Music and mesmerism, it seemed, could both access worlds of sensation unknown in ordinary waking life. Conan Doyle's mournful violinist and drug-taker Sherlock Holmes struck a contemporary chord late in the century when he said with regard to music: 'There are vague memories in our souls of those misty centuries when the world was in its childhood.'[3]

Musicians were thought to be especially prone to hypnotic processes, and sometimes, it was claimed, this vulnerability could actually be used to cure them of hysteria and other disorders. A British contributor to the 1893 proceedings of the Société d'Hypnologie in Paris, for instance, drew attention to the nervous troubles of musicians. He noted the close connection between 'the artistic temperament' and psychological impressionability. The audience was informed of the successful use of hypnosis in clearing various physical symptoms, as well as in restoring the confidence, talent and prospects of a number of unfortunate performers. There was even, *à la Trilby*, a report about an exceptionally vigorous, if neuropathic and hysterical, Irish musician, whom the doctor was able to restore to health, or at least in whom he managed to effect some symptomatic change. Through hypnotism, her nervous cough disappeared; she was then pronounced cured. This particular medical account collated evidence on several young unmarried women opera singers and piano soloists.[4] Hypnotism was said to have led them back to theatre stage and concert hall, as it had led various sufferers from aphasia to recover their language.

The representation of such musical and hypnotic states was typically gender-specific and assumed the transfer of thoughts – as well as talents – from man to woman. It was often remarked that a discordant singer could only 'tune in' through her male conductor and often specifically via the compelling effect of his gaze. The provenance of the voice in such cases was highly ambiguous. When the conductor or hypnotist transformed a woman's talents, whose sound was it that she 'found'? To whom did the achievement belong when, at another's edict or even unspoken wish, the subject could turn a hitherto dismal voice into that of a nightingale? Could she be said to possess, albeit temporarily, that talent? Was she, once 'transported', any more mindful and soulful than some clockwork figure?

Alongside the terrifying mesmerist, a new stereotype was emerging to cultural prominence: the all-controlling conductor. The dominant style of musical direction had gradually shifted from a previously favoured 'impersonal' attitude towards a more self-conscious stress on the power of personal expression and even the demonic force of individual genius. Not only the time-keeping function but also the theatrical authority of the conductor was enhanced by the arrival of the baton, a regular accoutrement of the profession only from the 1830s and 1840s. The successful conductor was cast as a kind of colossus, possessed of a remarkable reservoir of energy. His mind, body and very glance cast a spell. It was remarked, particularly of Mendelssohn, not only that he used his stick to good effect when conducting, but that he directed the players with his whole body. Indeed the baton was but an instrument, an extension of his powerful personality. Mendelssohn was said to control the orchestra with the merest look or turn:

> The eyes of the musicians were all, as it were, focused within his own; he communicated with them as if by electricity – made them sympathize with his spirit, catch the impulses, and partake of the emotions of all that was to be interpreted before the thronging multitude, who were listening with blended awe, excitement, and admiration, to every feeling symbolized, and every thrill evoked.[5]

The conductor moved increasingly into the Victorian cultural limelight. No longer a mere 'accompanist' or 'timekeeper', this figure was, in his very isolation from and influence over the orchestra, perceived as the music's presiding genius, its moving spirit. In *Musical Elaborations*, the cultural critic Edward Said remarks on the unprecedented preoccupation with virtuosity which emerged during the nineteenth century. He detects a growing historical investment in the idea of performing genius and a relative demotion in the priority accorded to the musical text. Images of the performer's power were increasingly detached from the correlative skills of composing. Paganini's arrival on European stages in the late 1820s provided 'the great archetype of the preternaturally skilled and demonic performer on endlessly fascinating display'.[6] In that context, the image of the supremely gifted musical leader or director of the orchestra came to be associated with psychological penetration, even clairvoyance and telepathy, as though the mental space of the humdrum players could be entered – and modified – by the omniscient and omnipotent overseer.

Showmen-composers such as Philippe Musard and Jullien, household names during the Victorian period, were said to have mesmerised both onlookers and players.[7] In pursuit of the origins of Du Maurier's Svengali, the Frenchman Louis Jullien is a good candidate for attention, with his astonishingly successful commercial career, intensity, energy, lavish riches, debts, descent into madness and pathetic, premature death in 1860. While Jullien does appear in *Trilby* (thinly disguised as 'Monsieur J'), he is in fact not cast as a powerful mesmeriser but as the hapless conductor who takes over the orchestra when Svengali's doctors forbid him to conduct, and who is quite incapable of persuading Trilby to sing after Svengali, catching sight of Little Billee, is consumed by rage. Yet Jullien's history is certainly no less outlandish than that of the mesmeric villain in Du Maurier's fiction. The real-life musician died in an asylum in France, a few days after his admission, following his demented attack on his niece, whom he was training to be a singer. Armed with a large knife, he had told the fifteen year old, 'Come here, I am going to let you hear the most marvellous of all my music, the Grand Concert of the Angels; I am going to kill you!' Struggling free, the girl fled.[8]

Jullien had come to London in the late 1830s and, within a few years, had acquired an unprecedented reputation both for his skills as a musical director and for his acumen in promoting his performances. He understood the needs of advertising and advance publicity, as well as informal gossip, in generating interest in his concerts. As a result, the charge of charlatanism was never far away. Felix Moscheles took his family to see this dark-eyed dandy gesticulating at his orchestra, and later described it as akin to visiting a circus.[9] Jullien's cartoon portrait became a frequent feature of *Punch* in the 1840s and 1850s. He was the very image of the modern, flamboyant and captivating conductor, perceived at the time to be treading and sometimes crossing the line between breathtaking musical powers and sheer theatrical vulgarity. Images of mesmerism featured strongly in his depiction at the time: As the *Musical World* put it in 1860: 'There was, too, between him and [the audience] a kind of magnetic sympathy.' 'The mere personality of the man exercised a spell, a fascination, which rendered it a forlorn chance for a rival, no matter what his gifts, no matter what his experience, no matter what his acquirements, to attempt to fill the post if Jullien was known to be alive, still more if Jullien was known to be at hand.'[10]

A more direct and significant precursor of our Svengali figure, also descending from East to West, was Anton Rubinstein. His extravagant musical ability aroused both public fascination and anti-Semitic suspicion. Rubinstein was a child prodigy in the 1840s, and a greatly revered pianist throughout his adult life. The question of whether this Jew could be a genuine independent talent was much discussed. Rubinstein happened to die in the very year that Du Maurier's Svengali first appeared in book form, and was mourned by many music lovers across Europe. Both Anton and his highly gifted brother, Nicholas, had suffered directly from the anti-Semitism prevalent in their native Russia, yet both had been widely admired – even there – Anton was eventually honoured by the Tsar. In

St Petersburg there was a saying: 'We don't like Jews, but that doesn't mean Anton Gregorovitch.'[11] He had many supporters and enthusiasts in England as well, although when he returned to the London stage to conduct an opera, *The Demon, Punch* did not let its readers forget he was an acquisitive Jew. An article used the original Italian title, *Il Demonio*, to quip that, given Anton's large takings from the performances, he could be renamed 'De-money-o'.[12] It also so happened, in a nice anticipation of the Svengali plot, that Rubinstein had an intense relationship with a young Irish girl (Lillian Macarthur) who was said to have been enchanted – she had run away from home to be with him, having first heard him play in Dublin.[13]

The example of Rubinstein not only demonstrates the continuing significance of racial prejudice in relation to nineteenth-century arts, but also indicates the intense cultural interest in the mental state and personal history of the musical virtuoso. At major concerts, the appearances of performing stars were increasingly carefully choreographed and, as we might say, 'hyped', set off against the nameless obscurity of the ordinary players. Some recent social commentators have scrutinised the cultural relationship that has existed since the nineteenth century between the superhuman 'genius' figure, the transfixed accompanying players and the mesmerised audience, using it to describe the charismatic nature of group processes at large. In his famous inquiry, *Crowds and Power*, the Nobel Prize-winning novelist Elias Canetti argued that there is no more obvious expression of power in the modern age than that of the great conductor. Such a person may believe himself to be merely the servant of music, but in fact he has other symbolic functions, as he stands facing the orchestra. In Canetti's account, it goes without saying that such a figure is male, and the very symbol of sexual and creative mastery. He silences the orchestra at will, and then brings in different players through a mere gesture or look: 'He has the power of life and death over the voices of the instruments; one long silent will speak again at his command.' Meanwhile, it is well understood that the audience must sit still and store up their emotions until the end. Only then can they break loose, as the conductor eventually surrenders to their applause, returning repeatedly as though at their will, bowing before their climactic tribute. But for all this acquiescence, it is the conductor who remains master; it is he who receives the 'ancient salute to the victor, and the magnitude of his victory is measured by its volume'. What the conductor enacts, suggests Canetti, is a kind of 'world rule', as well as a form of hypnotic process in which each member of the crowd is 'penetrated' by the leader's eye:

His eyes hold the whole orchestra. Every player feels that the conductor sees him personally, and, still more, hears him . . . He is omniscient . . . He is inside the mind of every player. He knows not only what each *should* be doing, but also what he *is* doing. He is the living embodiment of law, both positive and negative.[14]

An overblown description perhaps, but reference to the hypnotic quality of the charismatic musical director is common enough.

Twentieth-century conductors have continued to be ascribed the most extraordinary sexual, hypnotic and artistic powers; the 'deification' of men such as Arturo Toscanini or Arthur Nikisch is a case in point. Nikisch was said to have effortlessly magnetised not only his players but virtually anyone he met. He seemed to draw adoring fans into his net where they languished in helpless fascination, as Norman Labrecht recounts in a history of 'the maestro myth':

Nikisch was not naturally good-looking. His supreme asset was a deep-set pair of dark eyes that drew men and women to him like a silken web: soft, brooding, somewhat sombre, unfailingly hypnotic. There was nothing demagogic in his look, just a seductive hint of infinite consolation, like a siren's distant song. The top of his baton became an extension of those remarkable eyes, hypnotizing the players with its slightest tremor as he stood almost motionless on the rostrum.[15]

Contemplating such phenomena, Labrecht has described how each epoch's cultural fantasies of the genius conductor relate to wider political fascinations of the time. The age of Mussolini, Hitler and Stalin, for instance, had its disturbing musical corollaries, representations of the stick-wielding hero who would brook no opposition. There is, Labrecht argues, a pronounced modern cult of the conductor which cannot just be explained as a 'natural' response to an individual's overwhelming talent.

Hypnosis and hysteria became intricately linked with narratives of musical possession. Certain virtuoso talents had been said to operate blindly through the machinations of their teachers or managers, their mesmerists and sinister inspirers, well before Gaston Leroux penned his hugely popular Parisian tale, *The Phantom of the Opera* in 1910, or, for that matter, Du Maurier his saga of 1894. Perhaps no 'true-life' Victorian musical story of virtuosity and hype was more famous than that of 'the Swedish nightingale', Jenny Lind, to whom Du Maurier himself compared his hero-ine.[16] Born in Sweden in 1820, Lind was a musical child prodigy. By the time of her maturity, she had become an international opera sensation. She was known for the purity of her morals as well as of her voice, but this did not entirely eradicate salacious speculation: there were, for instance, rumours of a secret marriage to a young Swede with whom she was vio-lently in love; there were equally vehement denials. It was said that she had disappeared to Paris to recuperate from the affair.

Like some blueprint version of Trilby, it turned out that Lind had been the illegitimate child of parents with colourful sexual pasts. Jenny became, apparently in stern reaction to the sexual freedom enjoyed by her mother, a strikingly puritanical figure. Indeed her fame was inseparable from her image as pure of body and heart, as well as voice. It was her renowned virtue as well as her virtuosity that led to unprecedented offers of hospitality by bishops (although inevitably some tongues wagged) and even some per-sonal intimacy with her admirer Queen Victoria. By 1850, it was said that part of the responsibility for the great improvement in the moral reputation of the stage belonged to Jenny Lind.[17] Even after the marriage that led many to lose interest in her, a Berlin critic proclaimed that 'Jenny Lind-Goldschmidt is the musical demon of the century; to fight against such a power is a futile effort for any other artist'.[18] His choice of metaphor admit-tedly made this a somewhat barbed compliment. Perhaps it accurately reflected the view that, however virtuous the entrancer, the effect on the object was always in some sense sinister and disturbing, as well as seductive and delightful. In Lind's case, certainly, appreciation and admiration were the more typical and dominant responses, although when she had toured Italy in the 1840s, it was said that she left a 'dark-browed Italian *prima donna* louring, Medea-like, in the background, and looking daggers when-ever the name "Questa Linda!" was uttered'. In Vienna, she was followed to her house by large adoring crowds ('thirty times she was called to the win-dow'). By the time Lind took up residence in England in 1847 she was a reg-ular source of public interest. 'From the first moment of her entrance she kept us in a state of enchantment,' remarked one admirer. It was said that to call her 'the Swedish nightingale' was to flatter the bird.[19] Her talent and her name were traded with a vengeance. The most extensive merchandising of her image occurred in America, but enthusiasts on both sides of the Atlantic could sport a Jenny Lind dress, cravat, scarf or gloves, and could procure 'Lindiana' products ranging from chocolate boxes to tulips, matchboxes to furnishings. In other words, 'her name had invaded every-

A printed song-sheet: all part of 'Lindomania'.

thing. It had crept into families and entered their very bed-rooms'.[20] Or as a doggerel song had it:

> Yes, all is Jenny Lind now,
> In ev'ry shop she's found;
> Jenny Lind you get there retail
> By the yard, quart, pint, or pound.
> We've Jenny Lind shirt collars,
> And round my neck – oh fie!
> I've fastened lovely Jenny Lind,
> A charming op'ra tie.[21]

As the lyrics suggest, the name of Lind became a goldmine.[22] But if she was a trade phenomenon she was also an ambassadress for serious music, the very acme of respectability. Towards the end of her life, she became, at the express request of the Prince of Wales, professor of singing at the newly established Royal College of Music in South Kensington. On her death in 1887, a plaque was placed in Westminster Abbey.

Lind was not only an exceptional musical talent, but also an ambiguous medico-psychological case. The Victorian public became familiar with the story of her remarkable early recovery from loss of voice; rumours of an acute and enduring nervousness were sometimes seen as part of her charming naivety. Whatever her emotional state in adulthood, it was well-known that in her youth, she had suddenly – and shockingly – fallen silent. As a fan publication, *Lindiana*, put it in 1847: 'At the age of twelve years Jenny Lind was menaced by one of those misfortunes – yes, the poor girl's favourable prospects seemed irremediably ruined, by her entirely losing her voice.'[23] She recovered her confidence and her powers of sound four years later and starred in Meyerbeer's opera, *Robert Le Diable*; the audience was electrified. In subsequent years, *La sonnambula* was perhaps her greatest triumph. The mysterious crisis of her voiceless period, as well as her tenacity as a young woman in persevering with her career after rejection by a distinguished teacher in Paris, all became part of this elaborately mythologised life.

Lind's sources of inspiration, not least her teachers, were also discussed. In particular, the sound of the young Lind playing to and for Mendelssohn attracted public notice. Lind was reported to have succumbed to his musicianship and his personal charm at the home of a German sculptor:

> Now, in the hours they spent together talking and making music at the Wichmanns', she discovered a companionship deeper and more satisfying than anything she was ever to know for the rest of her life. Mendelssohn would sit at the piano and extemporise . . . his eyes large and brown, always the focal centre of his beautiful mobile essentially Jewish face, would dilate until they turned almost black, and Jenny would be carried completely out of herself.[24]

The composer was presumed to have enchanted the girl, with his talent and personality, as well as his penetrating 'Jewish' eyes. Mendelssohn apparently recognised her at once as a kindred spirit – 'one of ourselves', a fellow member of what he called 'the invisible church'.[25] Another Jewish composer, Giacomo Meyerbeer, had also been an early inspiration, a guiding star in her voyage back to health and confidence, but it was above all Mendelssohn who transformed Lind's prospects after the misfortunes of her youth.[26] A deep bond with these celebrated and wealthy men was one

Jenny Lind in
La sonnambula.

thing, however; infatuation and sexual union with an obscure German Jewish pianist, Otto Goldschmidt, quite another.[27] The notion that her marriage to Goldschmidt constituted a bathetic end for the pure-eyed diva still remains the conventional assumption of commentators on her life. Lind's equivocal relationship to the Jews became a kind of defining image. In a burlesque of Disraeli's grandiose style, Thackeray had even facetiously associated Lind with 'the Chosen People'. 'Lind is the name of the Hebrew race; so is Mendelssohn, the son of almonds'.[28]

Lind, who so excelled in *La sonnambula*, was perceived by many former admirers to have made a mistake by, as it were, sleepwalking into marriage with this 'unattractive' Jew (who had himself apparently become entranced by her when, earlier in the 'nightingale's' career, he heard her sing to the accompaniment of Mendelssohn). Take this recent description of Lind's fall from the dizzy heights of her mid-century popularity:

The situation was exacerbated by the man she married in Boston, Otto Goldschmidt, a short and serious German Jew, nine years younger than

Lind, who had been a pupil of Mendelssohn. He had no glamour or publicity value whatsoever, except as a 'model of virtue, industry and domesticity' (thus did his wife describe him to a friend) and the way in which his second-rate pianism was blatantly pushed forward at every Lind concert infuriated audiences.[29]

There are few simple 'facts' in the case. The negative judgements on Goldschmidt's talent and Lind's marital choice are difficult to separate from social attitudes of the day. That audiences cooled off somewhat or even recoiled is not questioned here, but how far this was a consequence of 'second-rate musicianship' and how far a distaste at the union between the Jew and the gentile is hard to resolve. The reader will no doubt recognise familiar elements in this 'historical' record of a 'little Jew' shamelessly pushing himself forward before the bemused and then disenchanted crowd. There is some evidence that Lind did not think Goldschmidt so ineffectual a musician, neither did she view him as a mere parasite feeding off her success. She apparently considered him a great pianist. Clearly stung by the insinuations, she made the classically complicit response of seeking, as it were, to 'clear his name' of the wrongful accusation: 'His family is Jewish, though he is as little Jew as I.'[30] Her opinion of his talent and his equivocal racial nature could be put down to the vagaries of love, or, no doubt, even to the hypnotic state the Jew had induced.

The point here is not to seek to equate this celebrated case with Du Maurier's later story, but to record the compelling and highly stereotypical aspects of the saga. Whilst Goldschmidt was not exactly cast as Lind's 'Svengalian' creator, references abound to the Swedish diva as a kind of sleep-walker:

> Not only the looks and movements are those of a somnambulist, but the ringing is that of the dreamy state – internal, addressed to the objects in the dreamy circle of the brain when in the cold ecstasy of the night. The sensation it excites in the spectators is one of deep sympathy, not unallied with the feeling with which are contemplated powerful phe-nomena unexplained and bordering on the preternatural . . . When she awakes, the transition from the dreamy world of spasmodic thought and chequered happiness to the positive reality of lost joys suddenly restored is rendered with a wonderful effect.[31]

Even allowing for operatic hyperbole, most commentators on the diva agreed she was very special and had a long way to fall. Almost everybody

CORONATION OF JENNY THE FIRST—QUEEN OF THE AMERICANS.

Jenny Lind's American reception.

who had encountered the singer (once restored from her nervous condition) felt affected; Lind was able to reduce an audience to tears. Admittedly, Thackeray and Carlyle dissented, but they were deemed eccentric in their refusal to share in the general rejoicing at her London performances.[32] It was above all in America, under the auspices of the exuberant and swashbuckling impresario Mr Barnum, that her most spectacular and lucrative tour was conducted, as well as her doubtful marriage. Under Barnum's direction, she gave one hundred and fifty concerts; her large fees (and share of the profits) were raised still higher as the storm of applause intensified.[33] According to Lind's biographer Joan Bulman the singer's American reception smacked of 'mass hysteria'. Barnum's daring in agreeing to reward her so handsomely was in its turn amply justified by the scale of the gate receipts.[34] In the New World, audiences were so overcome by her voice that it was said 'a spirit was among them, weird and mighty in its fascination'. But by the end of her extended transatlantic sojourn some felt that the spell was wearing off, even murmuring that they had been milked just a little too much. Her marriage to Goldschmidt had come as a shock. And while the public at large had willingly paid for Miss Lind, some clearly resented the prices charged by Mrs Goldschmidt.

Some years earlier, Jenny Lind had made the acquaintance of the specialist on hypnosis, Dr James Braid. At their meeting, which occurred while the singer was on tour in the north of England during the 1840s, something very strange indeed was reported to have happened. Precisely how Braid and Lind turned a tone-deaf woman into a virtuoso – a second 'nightingale' – was never revealed for sure, but a number of witnesses confirmed the following remarkable story, recounted afterwards in the *Phrenological Journal* of 1847. The singer, accompanied by some friends, attended a seance at Braid's house. First the doctor showed them the method for putting his patient to sleep, as well as other aspects of his technique. He did not touch the head of his subjects, but sought to excite into action those muscles in the face, or other parts of the frame, which in the waking state gave active physical manifestation of certain passions or emotions he sought to foster. After these preliminaries began the most extraordinary part. Eye witnesses confirmed that Braid brought two working-class girls before his audience. They were dressed in their work clothes and were introduced as employees in a local warehouse. Having thrown them into a strange slumber, Braid sat down to the piano, and the moment he began playing both somnambulists arose and approached the instrument, joining him in singing a trio. He focused on one of the two and declared to the assembled company that although his somnolent subject had little grammar when awake (even in her own tongue), under hypnosis she could sing songs in *any* language requested. He promised that she would produce both notes and words correctly. Everyone was incredulous, but Braid was said to have been proved right. A Mr Schwabe tested her in German song: she gave the notes simultaneously with him. Another gentleman tried her out in Swedish: again there was notable success. Next, the Swedish 'queen of song' herself sat down to the instrument, played and sang 'most beautifully a slow air', with words in her own mother tongue: the somnambulist apparently accompanied her in the most perfect manner, both in words and intonation.

Lind now resolved to test the powers of the girl to the limit. She put her hypnotised protégé through a formidable range of roulades, cadenzas and even some of those extraordinary *sostenuto* notes, 'with all their inflections from pianissimo to forte crescendo, and again diminished to thread-like pianissimo', for which the singer was so famous:

> but in all these fantastic tricks and displays of genius by the Swedish nightingale, even to the shake, she was so closely and accurately tracked by the somnambulist, that several in the room could not have told,

merely by hearing, that there were two individuals singing – so instantaneously did she catch the notes, and so perfectly did their voices blend and accord.[35]

Further tests followed, all of which were impressively passed, although there was some doubt as to whether the dazed apprentice was defeated by one of Lind's highest notes. (Braid acknowledged this was possible, although confessed that he had failed to notice it himself.) When the subject was awakened, she had no memory of her achievement. The hypnotist declared that such powers stemmed from the enhancement of the senses and muscular abilities at a certain stage of the sleep. The 'abstracted state of the mind' enabled total concentration and confidence. It was miraculous indeed and not easily talked away. Braid's rather paltry explanation begged many questions.

At the time, such feats were certainly seen as amazing, but fraught with dangers and puzzles. As earlier discussed, the possibilities and risks of such techniques were trawled in erudite scientific journals as well as in popular tales. They had already aroused concern in the age of Mesmer, but both worries and enthusiasm mounted to further heights in the final Victorian decades. More than a century after Mesmer and Miss Paradis, and fifty years after Braid and his hypnotised nightingales, the question of music and mesmerism was still very much on the agenda. 'Svengali' was a case in point. The *British Medical Journal*, responding to Du Maurier's singer and mind-influencing Jew, pointed out that it *was* scientifically credible; no miraculous factors were involved in the famous fictional interactions everyone was reading about. 'The elaborate lessons of Svengali in vocalisation and dramatic passion might quite conceivably transform Trilby, who possesses a magnificent vocal organ, into a dramatic singer of the highest order.' Indeed the phenomena the novel described were seen as quite natural, 'the transformation effected in a perfectly natural and physiological manner in the subject under the influence of external or auto-mental suggestion'. Such factors were not uncommon, they pointed out; many such cases had been observed in which feats of strength and agility, intense dramatic expression, matchless emotional effects, were achieved under hypnosis. No new ingredient or endowment has been 'injected into the subject'; rather the inhibitory influence of fear, shyness and other 'interfering mental emotion' had been removed. 'In the hypnotic state and under the influence of suggestion inhibition ceases, the individual is unconscious of danger, and *pro tanto* insusceptible of fear.' And yet, paradoxically, it was also held that the removal of inhibition, far from emancipating the inner-most nature of the subject, actually made the woman in question into a mere vehicle of another's will. Du Maurier was also said to have rendered this enslaving process most acutely in the character of Trilby: 'She is, like all thorough hypnotics, reduced to the state of a marvellous machine, capable of receiving the most perfect training and in complete subjection to the will and the suggestion of the operator.'[36]

7
Racial Hypnosis

Svengali was a bolder wooer. When he cringed, it was with a mock humility full of sardonic threats; when he was playful, it was with a terrible playfulness, like that of a cat with a mouse – a weird, ungainly cat, and most unclean; a sticky, haunting, long, lean, uncanny, black spider-cat, if there is such an animal outside a bad dream.

It was a great grievance to him that she had suffered from no more pains in her eyes. She had; but preferred to endure them rather than seek relief from *him*.

So he would playfully try to mesmerize her with his glance, and sidle up nearer and nearer to her, making passes and counter-passes with stern command in his eyes, till she would shake and shiver and almost sicken with fear, and all but feel the spell come over her, as in a nightmare, and rouse herself with a great effort and escape.

Du Maurier, *Trilby*[1]

Mesmerism and hypnotism provided rich sources for challenging the assumptions of rationalism and individualism in the nineteenth century. Even if such complex intra-psychic and inter-personal processes of entrancement could be explained magnetically, they appeared to leave the notion of the discrete and self-possessed individual in some disarray. In the late nineteenth century, specialists were divided over whether only the nervous, degenerate or otherwise abnormal person was prone to such states; but whatever the conclusion, there were serious implications for the understanding of mental processes and social relationships more generally. That a Jew such as Svengali could so successfully hypnotise and transform a vulnerable gentile woman added a further complex aspect to these contentious issues, since the psychological, physical and artistic distinctiveness of races was itself an important, and much debated, feature of thought within the human sciences at the time. How far Victorian writers argued or believed that the 'virtues and vices of a long-oppressed race',[2] namely the Jews, included special powers of psychic manipulation will be considered in this chapter.

The hypnotising Jew, Svengali, was clearly seen by many contemporaries as Du Maurier's personal creative departure. His friends at *Punch*, for instance, evidently felt that the invention of the captivating Jewish character was the most novel element in *Trilby* and they offered this somewhat backhanded tribute:

> Svengali, the weird unwashed Hebrew, the fantastical, musical magician, so dominates the story that the author of his being will be remembered as GEORGE JEW MAURIER. And Svengali the Satanical, marvellously impersonated by Mr. BEERBOHM TREE, stands out as the central figure of the strange, unconventional drama at the Haymarket. It isn't *Trilby*, the hypnotised subject, but *Svengali*, the fearful 'object,' the dirty demoniac hypnotiser, on whom all eyes are fixed, and in whom the interest is centred.

Svengali, *Punch* insisted, is 'Shylock and Fagin, Mephistophesized'; he is 'as loathsome as Hyde without Jekyll'. If he has something of the genius of a Paganini, he is nonetheless a 'brutal slave-driver'.[3]

Early in Du Maurier's plot, Svengali swoops on Trilby while she is suffering from a severe attack of neuralgia. As Svengali commands her to look into the whites of his eyes, she grows still and then becomes completely spellbound; meanwhile the pain has gone. As Trilby's friend, the Laird, explains afterwards: 'He mesmerised you . . . They get you into their power, and just make you do any blessed thing they please – lie, murder, steal – anything! and kill yourself into the bargain when they've done with you!'[4] 'They' are Jews and mesmerists – indeed, a fearsome configuration of the two. While in a sense this creative linkage belongs to Du Maurier, speculation about the relative powers of enchantment and susceptibility to hypnosis amongst races had started earlier, as, too, the imagined association between Jews and special musical powers. In some views, Jews were profoundly musical; in others, they could at best achieve a superficial, if enchanting, expressive power.[5]

Commentators were also split as to whether the supposed mesmeric, artistic or clairvoyant powers of the Jews were fundamentally benign or malign. Svengali's creator was no doubt conversant with the complicated exploration of enchantment and race in George Eliot's *Daniel Deronda* (1876). Du Maurier could hardly have failed to notice her intense, idealised presentation of the penetrating powers of the ascetic Jew, Mordecai, a literary portrait much discussed at the time; neither, presumably, had he forgotten her resonant accounts of the irresistibly beautiful voices of the two central Jewish women characters in the story. Not only does Mirah sing beautifully, but so does Daniel Deronda's mother. When he finally meets her and discovers his Jewish parentage, he is also told about her mesmerising musical and romantic career: 'I was a great singer, and I acted as well as I sang. All the rest were poor beside me. Men followed me from one country to another. I was living a myriad lives in one. I did not want a child.'[6]

The putative connections between Judaism, genius and fanatical states of mind featured sporadically in various minor stories of the time as well, although no doubt these were less likely to have been known to Du Maurier or his circle than Eliot's major treatment of Judaism. Thus, to take a rather different plot from a contemporaneous novella (that seems to have died without leaving much trace), an entranced Jewish violinist turns on his betrothed, a soprano. At the climax of this tale, entitled *A Jewish Musician's Story*, the woman sings, her disturbed lover lapses into a reverie, whereupon he murders her. Whilst the Jews are shown to excel in music, they are also cast here as especially prone to the sort of volatile emotional and hypnotic states in which deadly impulses are acted upon.[7]

In other words, although *Trilby* – and Svengali – was a creation of the 1890s, its particular cluster of themes, involving both secret Jewish psychological powers and a kind of musical ventriloquism through mesmerism, was not entirely new. Particular aspects of these mesmeric and racial motifs had occurred in various earlier combinations. The most prominent example in which a Jew was conceived in terms of magnetic power was not from a novel at all, but from the immediate political past: the case of Benjamin Disraeli. In a cogent article on anti-Disraelian sentiment, the historian Anthony Wohl has recently shown the widespread dissemination of such views. The Tory politician and Prime Minister endured a quite remarkable degree of vilification, and the language used was often explicitly racial. Crucially, he was seen to have a very special power of insinuation and penetration. A pamphleteer remarked not untypically: 'Events appear to show that Englishmen have cause to share in that fear', for they are led by 'a man who is a Jew in race, in heart, and in practice . . . a man who has risen to a position, where he controls all England, by skilfully playing upon the prejudices and weaknesses of those around him'.[8] 'Disraeli the wizard' was an increasingly familiar stereotype in the 1870s and beyond. The question then of *how* he had risen to power was sometimes answered by recourse to the ominous vision of the Jew who could 'cast a spell' over the gentile. To the medieval 'ring' of such utterances, however, there was also added a specifically modern reference to charismatic powers. These caricatures revived and also profoundly reshaped much older fears of Jewish cabalistic magic, supernatural and occult practices. Traditional wiles and mysterious new arts, wizardry and novel mesmeric powers, were all attributed to this politician. In 1878, the *Spectator* invited its readers to consider, 'This great Israelite magician [who] appears and with his wand transforms the whole political horizon.' Disraeli, the article went on, has 'a half-belief in the cabalistic sorcery, with all its wild spiritual machinery'. Or again: 'What is the strange talisman by which Lord Beaconsfield achieves the strange victory over . . . typical Englishmen till they become the most plastic of all materials?'[9]

It has been argued that Victorian depictions of the Jew shifted from an earlier more ramshackle racial rhetoric (evident in the mocking banter of the crowds to whom the young Disraeli spoke) to the harder-edged anthropological theories so evident by the 1870s. The association of Jews and the diabolic, or more specifically of Disraeli and nefarious power, also became more pronounced.[10] Disraeli was cast as the devil himself in disguise:

> And how do you think the devil look'd?
> Or black, or cruel, or sinister?
> Not at all, not at all, but his shoulder was crook'd,
> And his head it was bald, and his nose it was hook'd –
> He look'd like a Cabinet Minister![11]

There was a heightened perception, Wohl suggests, of Disraeli and Anglo-Jewry not only as 'un-English', but more specifically as anti-English. This shift can be seen as part of a wider transformation from representations of comic, exotic or usurious stage-Jews to what is sometimes called the 'scientific racism' of later Victorian Britain. Disraeli came to be presented as a psychologically dangerous voice, playing like a sorcerer on the minds of an emotional public; he was the puppet-master of the masses as well as of press and parliament. It was also said that he was following a treacherous, secret Jewish agenda.[12] Disraeli was not simply the passive receiver of such debate and vituperation. Arguments for the superiority and spiritual power of the Hebrew race were liberally distributed throughout his own novels. Moreover, his fictional character, the powerful Jew Sidonia, warned that, if not appeased, the 'Chosen People' could indeed prove an unconstrained and socially destructive force.[13] These arguments were alluded to by some of Disraeli's critics as proof of his suspect personal sense of patriotism, or even as evidence of the rancorous and conspiratorial nature of Jewry at large.

The language of magic and of blinding mesmerism often seemed interchangeable in political attacks on Disraeli. To the social critic Carlyle, Disraeli was 'a superlative Hebrew conjurer, spellbinding all the great Lords, great parties, great interests of England'.[14] Whatever his official religion as a convert, or his nationality by birth, Disraeli was depicted as being a Jew in his bones. He was English 'only by adoption'. In other formulations, the politician was the dazzling 'Arch-Deceiver' of the nation, his 'bewitching' character effectively robbing the victim of sight. 'Has this Jew juggler clean put out her eyes,/ That she may dance complaisant to his piping?', a poem of 1877 asked.[15] Imperialism was part of the bait the wily politician was said to have used to hook the nation. On the one hand, such commentators painted a picture of a spellbound public, on the other, an image of the supreme mind-reader and mass manipulator, replete with stereotypical 'Jewish' features: 'that little yellow god', with 'huge nose' and 'cunning eye', 'around whose heavy-lipped mouth a smile of satisfaction reigns?'[16] In the period before the general election of 1880, this is how *Liberal World, A Monthly Journal and Review for Young Men*, made the case against him:

> Oh! England, though for long thine eyes
> Were blinded by the rays
> The Israelite so deftly cast
> On dark and crooked ways.[17]

Such imagery of the evil eye (further explored in chapter eight) conflated Victorian ideas about states of fascination with a conscious anti-Semitic 'medievalism'. Anti-Disraelian rhetoric certainly provides the most conspicuous instance of such entwined racial and mesmeric imagery, at least before Svengali was placed before his massive readership. Nonetheless there are a number of other examples and episodes one might add – certain figurative and sociological associations between the Jews and magnetic dabbling of some relevance, even if of an altogether lower cultural profile. Obscure anecdotal evidence from the annals of mesmerism can be adduced, for instance, to show that some Jewish merchants in London had been involved in promoting publications on the subject in the 1820s. There were also occasional reports of Jewish stage hypnotists during the early Victorian period. But whatever else it was accused of, for much of the nineteenth century the practice of pioneering magnetists and hypnotists (Mesmer, Braid and the rest) had not been seen as the occult science of the Jews in particular.[18] Rather, there was a trickle of disparate Victorian stories and medical case studies which gradually formed a stream, combining anti-Jewish with anti-mesmeric innuendo.[19] By the last decades of the nineteenth century, psychiatric texts, political diatribes and fiction all contributed to the pool of writings about the disturbed minds *and* mesmeric powers of the Jews.

In turn-of-the-century histories of hypnotism, it was sometimes noted that the real origins of trance-induction lay not in Vienna or Paris, but much further to the East. Indeed, the assumed connection of mesmerism and the Jews was greatly overshadowed by another set of stories and speculations about Asiatic and Middle Eastern peoples more generally. A respected European expert on the subject in the late nineteenth century, Dr Albert Moll, himself Jewish, typically gestured towards remote eastern origins in his major study of hypnotism. From ancient Egyptian divination to Japanese devotions, from the Persian magi to the Indian yogis and fakirs 'who throw themselves into the hypnotic state by means of fixation of the gaze', Moll had gathered numerous examples of such phenomena. In addition, there were 'uncivilized peoples' in other non-European places whose primitive customs of trance merited consideration; he suggested that hypnotism was a feature of Aborigine life in Australia, and was widely practised amongst tribes in Africa. The doctor briefly mentioned hypnotic activities amongst the Jews, as well as drawing the reader's attention to the role of suggestion in Islam. It was not clear whether the differentiation of 'civilised' and 'uncivilised' races helped his argument much, since it was also pointed out that ultimately hypnosis functioned in the same way regardless of who was on the receiving end. Moll cited Nietzsche in support of the view that the dream state of the civilised person is the waking state of the savage. Or, put the other way around: 'We are all savages in our dreams'.

Moll sought to link modern hypnosis with a much wider array of mysterious mental states that had been intuited or 'tapped' by other cultures.

Powers of suggestion and entrancement were exercised in all societies, he mused. He pointed out that in the past rulers had been ascribed special powers of touch. In some cases, healing was believed to occur through the very breath of the king. Yet it was consistently in the East that Moll found the most extreme and dramatic examples of rudimentary hypnotic techniques, as well as wilder processes of suggestion: 'Whoever has seen the howling dervishes of the East will have observed that the Sheik, in attempting to heal the sick, especially the children, breathes on them, or touches them, and often treads with the foot.'[20] The moral and emotional worlds described in such vignettes seemed a long way from modern reason, Moll admitted, but he granted that the essential nature of the hypnotic relationship had been instinctively recognised in all those faraway places and times. His readers were also informed that the nineteenth century had brought these hitherto vaguely known and poorly scrutinised processes towards the light; in other words the ancient world of hypnotism was now securely within the field of modern science.

This expert on hypnotism allowed that trances could lead to countless abuses and scandals (especially when practised by unauthorised entertainers), but he suggested that they could also be a force for immense therapeutic good – even surgery could be accomplished successfully when the patient was properly prepared. Moreover, while hypnosis could be a smoke-screen used by guilty defendants in court to mask their responsibility for a crime, it could also be a means of extracting the truth from unwilling witnesses and crooks. Hypnotism could be an instrument of deception, but it could also overwhelm the defences of the most wily and uncooperative police suspect. The concluding example which Moll brought in support of this contention was in fact not derived from the legal record at all, but from a much frequented play – *Le Juif polonais* [*The Polish Jew*] – which had dramatically disclosed the forensic miracles of mesmerism to enthusiastic audiences in France and England.[21]

It is worth examining the drama to which Moll refers in this discussion. Featuring a dead Jew and a truth-inducing mesmerist, the play was a major success. In London, the best-known version was renamed *The Bells*.[22] It opened at the Royal Lyceum Theatre on 25 November 1871, the first of one hundred and fifty-one consecutive performances.[23] For some reason, as the Russian actor-director Konstantin Stanislavski later noted, the story had captured the public imagination despite the poverty of the script. Something in this drama of the ghostly Jew, the tormented criminal and the mesmeric tribune of justice evidently appealed to Stanislavski himself. He,

too, staged the work, referring to it appreciatively as an 'hallucinatory symphony'.[24] Set in Alsace in 1833, *The Bells* features an innkeeper, Mathias,
and his family. Mathias' daughter, Annette, is to marry Christian, master of
the Gendarmes. The religious sub-text of the story could hardly have been
made more explicit than in that choice of name. Lurking behind this placid
and reassuring domestic surface, lies the repressed story of a Polish Jew,
Kovesky, 'a well-made vigorous man' who had vanished fifteen years earlier, leaving behind bloodstained clothes and a dead horse. The disappearance had long remained a mystery. At the time, two local brothers had been
held on suspicion of having unleashed their dogs and murdered him; they
were released after Mathias intervened on their behalf.

The original murderous events remain shrouded in darkness. But
Mathias' implication in this nocturnal crime gradually becomes apparent.
Under the pressure of subliminal forces, hallucinated reproachful eyes and
mesmeric suggestion, the truth spills out. Mathias is unable to escape the
sound or the image of the accusing Jew. The eyes of his victim continue to
appear before him, despite all efforts to forget: 'Those eyes! How he glares
at me.' When Mathias goes on a business trip to the capital, he sees a display of animal magnetism by a performer who 'sends people to sleep, and
when they are asleep he makes them tell him everything that weighs upon
their consciences'. Not only is Mathias troubled by his own crime, but the
whole area in which the murder took place is subjected to the sound of
mysterious bells, ringing out the evil. Mathias fears the dead Jew will return,
as eventually he does, in a sledge, with his face turned away. He is dressed
in a brown blouse, with a hood over his head, and carries an axe. The Jew is
finally seen face on, the eyes in his ashen face fixed sternly upon Mathias,
who utters a prolonged cry of terror and falls senseless.

Before he is brought to justice, Mathias is assailed by his own thoughts
and memories, besieged by phantoms, bad dreams, fevered sleep, desperate
thirst. This is indeed a haunted man: 'It was as if I had seen the ghost of the
Jew.'[25] As the pressure of his preoccupations intensifies, Mathias, dreading
a relapse in his own mental condition, insists that his daughter's marriage
be rushed through. He is unsure whether it is the mere talk of the Jew which
precipitates his fits, or whether it is something to do with the mesmerist he
encountered at the fair. Mathias desperately wants his prospective son-in-
law to come to his rescue. He seeks to mobilise the dutiful Christian, the
good policeman, against these multiple dangers. Yet he fears Christian to be
clever enough to discover the truth: namely that Mathias robbed the Jew of
his valuable girdle and its gold and then killed him in cold blood. When the

marriage takes place, Mathias gives the newly weds a huge gift of money, the fruits of his crime – as though insidiously investing Christian with the ill-gotten gold from the dead man. The bells ring out. Eventually the suspicions of those around Mathias become sufficiently intense to lead to his trial. The president of the court uses the bells as evidence against him and threatens to bring in the mesmerist to explain matters; the official suggests that the sounds are linked with the memory of the bells on the Jew's horse. Since there is no hard evidence, the court admits the mesmerist despite Mathias' protests that this is against precedent and justice. The accused tries to discredit animal magnetism as a fraud and conjuring trick; he refuses to be put to sleep, knowing he will be exposed. And indeed when finally Mathias goes under, the truth quickly pours out. In terror of the executioner's rope, the murderer collapses and dies.

It would be wrong to claim that the various stories and commentaries sketched in this chapter, alongside Du Maurier's character, all contained precisely the same description or dread of mesmerism and the Jews. But there was a striking relationship between these diverse images and tales of conjoined racial and trance-inducing power. Sometimes the Jew was seen as murderous, at other times as the victim of the murderous gentile assailant. If Mathias is the Jew's killer, he is also cast as his psychological victim. Perhaps the best-known representation from the entire period of the dangerous acumen of the Jew is provided by Charles Dickens in *Oliver Twist*. Like Mathias in *The Bells*, the Jewish criminal Fagin comes to live his last hours in the torment of promised execution, but for much of the novel he is the persecuting or even mesmerising master of others. Dickens' had had some experience of mesmerism during the 1830s, before writing the saga of Oliver, Fagin and company. It was reported that he knew, for instance, of the treatments being offered daily by 'Baron' Dupotet de Sennevoy in London. But in 1838 his interest was much heightened by demonstrations of the power of animal magnetism offered by Dr John Elliotson and it has been argued that *Oliver Twist* (which appeared between 1837 and 1838) was directly influenced by such encounters.[26] In any event, Dickens was deeply intrigued by the nature of fascination, acquiring an extensive library of works on the subject and exploring the intricate subliminal power relations for which mesmerism offered at least some model of understanding, albeit in a way which only generated further uncertainties. In *Oliver Twist* and elsewhere, Dickens drew attention many times to borderline states between assurance of self and loss of self, to the limits of mental individuality and willpower, the mysteries of fraternity and obscure,

interim states of mind between sleeping and waking. He highlighted enigmatic moments where the implementation of a personal choice was difficult to distinguish from external coercion, and where it was hard to assess
how far captivated underlings shared with their masters the responsibility for their crimes. Fagin, of course, has terrifying powers of influence
over his acolytes. He is a creature of the night, at home in the dark and
misty streets of the capital. From the shadows, he keeps others under
observation:

> The mud lay thick upon the stones, and a black mist hung over the
> streets; the rain fell sluggishly down, and everything felt cold and
> clammy to the touch. It seemed just the night when it befitted such a
> being as the Jew to be abroad. As he glided stealthily along, creeping
> beneath the shelter of the walls and doorways, the hideous old man
> seemed like some loathsome reptile, engendered in the slime and dark-
> ness through which he moved: crawling forth by night, in search of
> some rich offal for a meal.

The grotesque figure of the Jew inhabits and in turn exemplifies something of the reptilian underworld of the city. Fagin is presented as a revolting figure, 'a very old shrivelled Jew, whose villainous-looking and
repulsive face was obscured by a quantity of matted red hair.' Neither is he
the only Jew set out in such pejorative terms in the novel. Barney, for
instance, is 'younger than Fagin, but nearly as vile and repulsive in appearance'. Nonetheless even the brutish villain Bill Sikes regards the old man as
unsurpassed in his physical loathsomeness and diabolic genealogy: 'There
never was another man with such a face as yours, unless it was your father,
and I suppose *he* is singeing his grizzled red beard by this time, unless you
came straight from the old 'un without any father at all betwixt you; which
I shouldn't wonder at, a bit.' The Jew's extensively offensive appearance is
matched by the scale of his powers, especially over the bevy of homeless
waifs who come within his clutches. Fagin is ascribed unusual force of character as well as a constant propensity to calculate his own self-interest.
'How, thought Fagin, as he mused on Nancy whilst creeping homeward,
can I increase my influence with her? What new power can I acquire?'

This 'mesmeric' aspect of Fagin's representation is easily overlooked. In
addition to the obvious visual economy (in which 'good' or 'bad' physical
features signal fixed moral values), the novel sets up an elaborate force field
of invisible emotional influences, which often operate through oblique and

George Cruikshank, *Oliver Introduced to the Respectable Old Gentleman*, 1846.

anxious eye contacts. Fagin is lynx-eyed, hawk-eyed and has an evil leer. He and his associates eye one another incessantly. Through many descriptions of such sidelong looks between the characters, Dickens produces a pervasively sinister atmosphere of surreptitious social observation. If he emphasises the eyes of the police and the law, he also suggests the operation of less obvious forms of inter-personal scrutiny, for instance, within the bedraggled company of the thieves. The atmosphere of vigil and control is complex and the relations of mastery and slavery between the characters keep reversing. This can be seen particularly in the hallucinatory quality of Sikes' final flight, after his murder of Nancy. Where earlier he had been a source of power, the controlling and brutal subject, he becomes the haunted, fleeing object. Eyes again take on a remarkably paranoiac quality, increasingly abstracted from the person; they become features in their own right, free-floating images of persecution and reproach. Thus Nancy's eyes live on, drawing attention to her absent, dead body, her destroyed life: '"The eyes again!" he cried in an unearthly screech.' At the height of Sikes' torment, her orbs follow him everywhere:

> Those widely staring eyes, so lustreless and so glassy, that he had better borne to see them than think upon them, appeared in the midst of the darkness: light in themselves, but giving light to nothing. There were but two, but they were everywhere. If he shut out the sight, there came the room with every well-known object – some, indeed, that he would have forgotten, if he had gone over its contents from memory – each in its accustomed place. The body was in *its* place, and its eyes were as he saw them when he stole away. He got up, and rushed into the field without. The figure was behind him. He re-entered the shed, and shrunk down once more.[27]

Earlier in the novel, Sikes had been shown to be less observant than the menacing Fagin. He was ignorant, for instance, of the glances flashed back and forth between Nancy and the Jew; neither was he able, as was Fagin, to read much meaning in her physiognomy or behaviour. He lacks 'the niceties of discrimination' and is untroubled by 'subtle misgivings'. Rather, he seeks to bludgeon Nancy into compliance with him. Certainly, however, the boorish Bill had succeeded in getting through to her in his own fashion ('a vision of Sikes haunted her perpetually') and the emotional tie is only broken, on Nancy's side, by death. But others have less obvious means of exerting control. In numerous passing references, eyes function both to dominate and to survey. If eyes are sometimes viewed as mirrors of love, they are also seen here as organs of seduction, control, censure and mastery. The spy Claypole had tracked Nancy, keeping 'his eye upon her.' Above all, however, it is Fagin who combines appraising glances with emotional manipulation. *Oliver Twist* builds up an elaborate structure of such visual, visceral and psychic interactions and intrusions, the characters frequently sizing each other up or dominating a vulnerable figure through controlling mental or ocular contact: 'The old man turned to close the door, as he made this reflection; the noise thus occasioned, roused the girl. She eyed his crafty face narrowly, as she inquired whether there was any news.' '"And about what I was saying my dear?" observed the Jew, keeping his glistening eye steadily upon her.' The pattern is to be reversed later in the novel, when the Jew in the courtroom is inquisitively scrutinised. Eventually, Fagin becomes the object of the public gaze and wherever he looks, eyes filled with hatred stare at him. 'As his eyes wandered to the gallery, he could see the people rising above each other to see his face: some hastily applying their glasses to their eyes.'[28] Instead of being subjected to a state of hateful fascination, Fagin's onlookers are now enthralled by their hatred of the prisoner.

Oliver Twist – and the murder of Nancy in particular – had special significance for Dickens and the audiences who flocked to his live readings. Initially, the scene had been deemed too upsetting to recite at public events at all. Dickens began to include the episode only in the 1860s, when his contemporaries often referred to its rendition as 'mesmeric' or 'hypnotic'. His stage instructions emphasise the grizzly fate of Nancy: 'Beckon down . . . Point . . . Shudder . . . Look Round with Terror . . . Murder coming . . . Mystery . . . *Terror To The End*.'[29] The disturbance provoked by the death was given space in various ways in the story and was also apparent in Dickens' attitude.[30] Evidently, both Nancy and Fagin's death scenes impinged upon their author to an exceptional degree, perhaps becoming a kind of obsession. His involvement – even identification – with the woman was clear. Dickens spoke of how he was 'nightly murdered by Mr W. Sikes'. Having earlier refused to include it at all, he eventually became so preoccupied with this particular reading that he gave it several times a week. A biographer of Dickens, Peter Ackroyd, goes so far as to suggest that he was suffering a 'monomania' in relation to the terrible deed. Sometimes Dickens seemed to place himself in the shoes of Sikes rather than the woman: 'I am murdering Nancy . . . I have a vague sensation of being 'wanted' as I walk about the streets.' He referred to 'preparations for a certain murder . . . The crime being completely off my mind and the blood spilled . . . my fellow criminals . . . I commit the murder again . . . imbue my hands in innocent blood . . . I have a great deal of murdering before me'.[31]

The ultimate cause of Nancy's subservience to both Sikes and Fagin is shown to be ambiguous, the result not only of bodily fear, or of some discernible pattern brought about by her nature and nurture, but of certain inexplicable currents of fascination. The environment cannot fully wipe out her original endowment, but neither can her intrinsic qualities completely survive her experience. The resulting character is in the end impossible to calculate or to trace back to source. Nancy's intense and mysterious investment in her man has its bathetic corollary in Charlotte's infatuation with Noah Claypole. This force of allure exceeds conventional reason or morality altogether. It has nothing to do with self-interest or even self-preservation. Hence the failure of the virtuous Rose, who seeks to convince Nancy that moral conversion is always possible and flight from Bill a potential choice. She appeals in vain to the fallen woman's original character, but Nancy proves incorrigible, unable to break with the thug and accept the forlorn invitation: '"It is never too late," said Rose, "for penitence and atonement."' The energy behind these attractions and desires surpasses her understanding or power of argument; it cannot be explained simply by heredity or by environment. When Rose asks Nancy, 'What fascination is it that can take you back, and make you cling to wickedness and misery?', there is no satisfactory answer.

Dickens' novel suggests obscure contacts, interactions, psychological communication beyond the realm of reason. Fagin is centrally implicated in these mysterious processes and his Judaism is unmistakably cast as a factor in his pathology. As conjuror or manipulator, master or slave, criminal or resentful victim, the Jew repeatedly spells trouble, giving expression to unease about the process of inter-personal corruption, as well as the boundaries of reason and the will. In some of the Victorian examples drawn upon in the present book, the issue is not simply the mesmerising and malign reach of an isolated Jew – a Fagin or Svengali – but a veritable 'Jewish system'. This in turn was placed under clinical and forensic investigation by racial scientists. By the late nineteenth century, various inquiries were initiated into both Jewish individuals and Jews at large, leaving no clue unexplored in pursuit of essential differences between races: from the quality of Israelite blood to the malignity of the Semitic gaze; from the global Jewish bond to the powers of the race's subliminal influence over the gentiles who come too close. The Jew's body and mind, expression and intent were prime suspects in such analyses of social purity and danger. It came to be argued that you could see not only present-day hatred but millennia of past malevolence in the very eyes of the Jews.[32] The Jews, it seemed, might be particularly effective hypnotists on account of their terrible historical experience.

While neither Semitic nor Orientalist themes appear to have played a decisive role in the original literature of mesmerism, the picture was gradually changing, as was evidenced in various Victorian plays, stories and scientific commentaries. In the 1840s, significant discussions and debates developed about the particular purchase of mesmerism in India. Stimulated by the work of a certain Dr James Esdaile who experimented on numerous Hindu and Muslim hospital patients in Bengal, the issue of relative racial susceptibility became more prominent both in the Raj and in Britain; so, too, did consideration of the relations between the European tradition of 'animal magnetism' and various indigenous Eastern practices of entrancement. Esdaile was confident that mesmerism made his Eastern subjects insensible to pain, and was notoriously 'gung-ho' when wielding his surgical knife. Claims for similarity between such 'native' insensibility to pain ('under the influence') and Western hypnotic susceptibility divided the specialists. Whatever nervousness Esdaile's patients may have felt as they faced their pioneering doctor, some of his colleagues, as well as government authorities, were jumpier still about imputed 'inter-racial unions' and other improprieties practised (so rumour had it) at his mesmeric hospital in Calcutta. Esdaile himself concluded that no religious or racial background, either European or Asian, offered complete protection or exemption from the universal mesmeric law, although he also took the view that the 'servility' of the indigenous people exacerbated their vulnerability. He speculated that the mesmeric state owed something to the nature of 'nervous influence', which could be transmitted through the fingertips into the body of another person.[33]

Where Esdaile had focused so equivocally and dramatically on mesmerising Bengalis, and Moll (half a century later) explored Eastern propensities to somnambulistic states, Du Maurier conjured up his Jewish mesmerist, albeit coining a name whose letters linked it with 'Bengali'.[34] Neither was the portrayal of Svengali the first occasion on which the author had conflated the image of Jews and devious entrancers. Du Maurier had illustrated various stories of hypnotism before turning to novel-writing himself. He had also contributed a cartoon to *Punch* entitled 'Hypnotism – a Modern Parisian Romance'; here he had already sketched the figure of the mesmerising, lewd and basely materialistic Jewish 'doctor'. As in the case of Svengali, the image strikingly combined anti-Jewish caricature with anxiety about unconscious manipulation. The pictures (which appeared in 1890) showed a villainous and repulsive man, stereotyped as Jewish, using his hypnotic powers to dupe an unwitting American billionairess and her daughter.

At one level, Du Maurier was working in a familiar tradition, even within the circles of *Punch*: from its earliest days it had published articles and drawings on mesmeric fads and hypnotic dangers.[35] In the 1840s, a contributor warned against the risks of dubious 'professors' who might use scientific jargon to get criminals off the hook with false claims about 'mesmeric coma'.[36] *Punch* also had a well-known line in anti-Semitism,

HYPNOTISM—A MODERN PARISIAN ROMANCE. (In Four Chapters.)

American Billionairess. "M. LE DOCTEUR, I SEE THE DUC DE SEPT-CADRANS IS A PATIENT OF YOURS. I WANT HIM TO PROPOSE TO MY DAUGHTER. A—ANY FEE THAT—A——" *Professor of Hypnotism.* "MADAM, I VILL YPNOTISE M. LE DUC. VE SHALL SEE!——"

"SORRY TO TROUBLE YOU AGAIN SO SOON, MONSIEUR! BUT MY DAUGHTER DECLARES SHE WON'T ACCEPT M. LE DUC, JUST BECAUSE HE'S A HUNCHBACK, AN IDIOT, AND A PAUPER!" "MADAM, LEAVE IT TO ME. I VILL YPNOTISE ALSO YOUR DAUGHTER!"

THE AMERICAN BILL'ONAIRESS BECOMES MADAME LA DUCHESSE DE SEPT-CADRANS. SHE AND HER HUSBAND ARE HAPPY, ALTHOUGH SHE HAS NO MONEY, AND THERE IS NO SUCH DUKEDOM AS SEPT-CADRANS, FOR THEY HAVE NOT YET LOST THEIR ILLUSIONS ABOUT EACH OTHER.

AND HER LOVELY DAUGHTER IS NOW THE PROUD AND ADORING WIFE OF THE GREAT HYPNOTIC SCIENTIST, WHO THEREBY BECOMES AN AMERICAN BILLIONAIRE. THEY MOVE IN THE SMARTEST SOCIETY IN PARIS, AND MANAGE TO DO A GREAT DEAL OF GOOD.

George Du Maurier for *Punch*.

although it had not previously fused this with anti-mesmerism. Amongst the assorted pet-hates of its mid-Victorian editor John Leech (according to Du Maurier) was 'the sweating Jew tradesman'.[37] *Punch* certainly displayed considerable relish in debunking the idea, floated in a lecture by Edward Hine, that the Anglo-Saxons might be one of the lost tribes of Israel. The weekly paper quipped that this perhaps explained the reluctance of English butchers to put real meat in their pork sausages and why the purveyors of liquor set their prices so steep.[38] Du Maurier's illustrations appeared

amongst such rum 'jokes' and sometimes directly presented the pretensions and social climbing of 'the Israelites'.

In these respects, *Punch* itself was part of a familiar, self-consciously
English tradition; the Jew was often set up in sharp contrast to (and in
uncomfortable proximity with) the venerable home-grown subject,
although this was generally done in a light-hearted teasing manner, without
the manifest violence of sentiment in certain notorious continental anti-
Semitic theorists of the age.[39] Whether done up in cheeky *Punch* style or not,
later Victorian Jews were often represented as 'Svengalian' – ingratiating,
seductive, dangerously alluring. This in turn was recognised as a problem for
gentiles: the Jews were shown to be all too good at undermining others,
through emotional 'kidnapping' of various types. From Fagin to Svengali,
Victorian fictional Jews were many times to be cast not only as repulsive, but
also as psychologically penetrating. They were captivating, even as they (or
at least the men) were physically revolting. In numerous instances, Jews
were shown to evoke a confused and disturbed mental reaction in their companions, just as, in the wider culture, they were often said to confound the
gentile, to produce an intolerable *bafflement.*

On the one side, discussion turned on the psychopathology of the hypnotist; on the other, the disordered internal state of his object. By the late nineteenth century, argument raged as to whether patients who reliably
succumbed to the entrancer were in fact biologically degenerate, hysterical, or
both. Doctors often postulated hereditary causes of hypnotic susceptibility,
although again this was the source of much learned discussion. Racial 'degeneration', as we have seen, was proposed as relevant to the understanding of
the hypnotic process and the uneven results it achieved on different character 'types'. As one Italian authority later suggested, in an age of accumulating
racial disorder, the name of Mesmer would certainly continue to be relevant.[40] Jean-Martin Charcot, the best known of all the period's investigators
of hypnotism and hysteria, offered a neurological and psychiatric assessment
of the Jews which gave some comfort to rabid French anti-Semites of the
time. Charcot had often pointed to the idea of an innate Jewish nervousness;
he developed various accounts of peculiar racial conditions and declared Jews
to be the finest subjects for the study of nervous disease. It seemed to Charcot
and some collaborators that the tale of the wandering Jew was but the prototype for the modern psychiatric condition of the race.[41] According to legend,
a spiteful Jew had refused Christ rest as he passed on his way to crucifixion.
Christ looked sternly at him and said, 'I will stand here and rest, but you must
walk!', the fate of 'the wandering Jew' thereafter.[42]

In 1893, Charcot's follower, Dr Henri Meige (later to become the editor of the prestigious journal, *Revue Neurologique*), produced a psychiatric study of homeless Jews, who, he argued, landed up in unnaturally large quantities, like so much disintegrating flotsam, at Paris hospitals. Reviewing his work, the *Revue de l'hypnotisme* claimed that this over-representation of the Jews in the wards was not surprising given their propensity to neurosis. Charcot also insisted that the Jews were disproportionately prevalent amongst hysterics, epileptics, neurasthenics and diabetics. This work was seized upon by the notorious racial writer, Edouard Drumont. In place of suffering leprosy on the skin, he concluded, Jews today were afflicted most typically with cerebral disorders; or, as he put it in more macabre fashion, surface leprosy had seeped into their very brains.[43] The legend of the wandering Jew was thus linked to concepts of psychological and physical pathology. Discussion ensued of the Jews' 'travelling insanity', 'neurasthenia' and the mental dissolution attendant upon the race's lack of a geographical or personal 'homeland'. Meige wrote at length about the exotic 'types' who ended up in psychiatric clinics. A dismal room full of Jewish patients, from Hungary, Turkey, Armenia, Russia, British India and Tunisia, seemed to him incontrovertible evidence of the race's hereditary weakness. He took his readers on a kind of 'ward round', moving swiftly from case to case. If he seemed touched by the terrible mental suffering of these fellow creatures, he was also convinced of the peripatetic racial illness they shared, the nomadism which made them so psychically similar to one another, so alien to the mental world of the well-rooted Frenchman. One is asked to picture Mr Klein, a Hungarian Jew who ended up as a wreck at the Salpêtrière after years of miserable and fruitless journeying from land to land, or to attend to the symptoms of 'Moser B', a Polish Jew, perpetually and pointlessly pursuing doctors in the mistaken hope that they could alleviate his ills. Each day this sad case would come to the hospital, where he was treated with electricity, a procedure, according to Meige, which he enjoyed so much that he asked Charcot to give him a certificate so he could seek more treatment elsewhere. He supposedly wished to present his document to M. Rothschild so that he could obtain money and return for treatment in Russia, where he hoped to end his days. Then came the musical Siegmund S, a polyglot and eternal wanderer, as well as the chronic sufferer and lost soul, Rosa A. Meige hesitated to estimate the precise percentage of Jews who suffered this morbid condition of travelling insanity, but was sure it was high. He noted the chronic insomnia, nightmares, somnambulism, hypochondria, hysteria, hallucinations and (perhaps most characteristically of all) eye complaints amongst the unsettled Jews he had treated.[44]

Such medico-psychiatric images of the Jews were far more than clinical accounts; they extrapolated from the particular to the general, implying a chronic propensity to movement, mental uncertainty, emotional home-lessness and tormented waywardness in the race at large.[45] Jews were often discussed in these terms, perceived to stray in both minds and bodies, drift-ing where they were not wanted, driven hither and thither by compulsive internal as well as external forces. The same volume of *Harper's New Monthly Magazine* which carried the original serialisation of *Trilby* offered several explicitly anti-Semitic and highly cautionary articles with titles such as 'The Mission of the Jews', about the 'labile' population of Eastern Jews and the danger of applying the same concepts to them as one would to other groups. A further piece meditated more specifically on 'wandering Jews'.[46] There are many variants of such discussions with quite antithetical racial representations: Jews differentiated by virtue of their weakness as much as by their exceptional durability; lauded for their tenacity while at the same time diagnosed as infirm and constitutionally weak. Where one strand of thought stressed the malleability and psychiatric vulnerability of the Jews, another emphasised their distinctive acumen and psychological constancy. Such qualities were then said to be an ancient racial endowment. The German economist Werner Sombart summed up such thinking shortly before the First World War, when he observed that the Jews had inherited special capacities of endurance, chameleon-like adaptability and powers of suggestion, because they had been forced, as a race, to think themselves into the place of the other, simply in order to survive.[47]

How much the author of Svengali happened to know about earlier Victorian instances linking Judaism with mesmerism (occasionally), and with neurasthenia and hysteria (quite frequently), we cannot be sure. Yet it was certainly the case that the psychiatric concern as well as the figurative bond between mesmerism and the Jews had become gradually more prominent during the age. It would be strange, for instance, if Du Maurier were ignorant of the story of Jenny Lind's aforementioned Jewish 'enchanters' – from the illustrious Meyerbeer and Mendelssohn to the less renowned Otto Goldschmidt. If he did know of the 'sorcery' charges lev-elled against Benjamin Disraeli, Du Maurier was no doubt ignorant of the fact that certain rabbis in faraway places took an interest in Mesmer's prac-tice.[48] He may or may not have read about that double mythology whereby ritual murder charges were in turn related to sinister trances induced by elders in the community. Anyway, attempts to settle the limits of 'what Du Maurier knew' should not be pursued too seriously in this context; after all, such a quiz is reminiscent of the very parlour games that hooked the public during the 'Trilby boom' of the mid 1890s. What is in question is not just direct influence, but the wider cultural and social determinants that produced this kind of imaginative linkage in the first place, and that could 'make sense' in the period.

Close to hand was a particular episode from the 1870s that involved (depending on whom you believed) either seduction or sedation. The case of the travelling Jewish dentist Paul Lévy and the poor gentile woman Berthe Braquehais remained somewhat obscure in the first instance, but the piquant details (initially heard behind closed doors) were to be recycled at scientific congresses and in books on hypnotism. The fact that the man was Jewish was usually mentioned merely *en passant*. Little was made of the racial provenance at the time, although the ambiguous sexual scenario – to say nothing of rumours of an ensuing pregnancy – did arouse curiosity amongst the specialists. Lévy was accused of raping the young woman in Rouen, at the Hotel d'Angleterre where he was lodging. Braquehais claimed that the dentist had put her into a special state of trance whilst she awaited the inspection of her teeth. Moreover, the 'lucid sleep' and ensuing sexual intercourse were said to have occurred despite the presence of her mother. One question was whether the liaison had occurred; another was whether she had really been stupefied. In the latter case, while drugs were considered a possibility, hypnosis was viewed as the most likely candidate. The suspect was said to have mastered her mind and then ingeniously taken advantage of her supine body (on several occasions) on his horizontally-folding dentist's chair. Meanwhile the unwitting maternal chaperone sat in the same room with her back turned! Lévy admitted intercourse had taken place but claimed it was consensual. His version was not believed and he received a ten-year sentence.[49]

Such legal cases focused attention on the possibility of Jewish hypnosis, but the link was also made more casually and rhetorically in the final decades of the century. Anti-Semitic writings of the 1880s and 1890s routinely explored the possibility of a specific racial ability to bamboozle others and occasionally related such ideas directly to the image of hypnotism. Thus, for instance, disgruntled Victorian commentators implied that financial schemes involved mesmeric manipulation. In Arnold White's scurrilous tract, *The Modern Jew*, published in London in 1899, it was stated that 'in the art of hypnotising large communities of shareholders into the belief that something is to be made out of nothing . . . there is no equal to the Jew'. Amidst the multiple dangers posed by the Jews, the art of paralysing the self-protective instincts of the gentile was the one that worried White most of all. The Jews knew what they were about. Where, say, the Irishman was characteristically bestialised in Victorian caricatures (not least, of course, in *Punch*), the Jew was cast as over-developed, sinisterly 'appraising' from without. In White's text, the Jew was also likened to a remote doctor figure, coolly judging the feverish and incapacitated patients. With his finger constantly on the pulse of public opinion, the Jew 'diagnoses the fever and the unrest afflicting the nation he honours with his presence with clinical success and also with the detachment of mind peculiar to the race'.[50]

It goes without saying that these were not the only variants of Victorian writing on the Jews. Indeed there was a powerful and famous tradition of Victorian philo-Semitism which for the most part did not cast the Jew in quite these terms, and certainly not with the same pejorative intent.[51] The point is that the connection was made and that it became a significant motif in late-nineteenth-century culture as well as in the formal writings of racial theorists. Obvious though that may seem, it has not been highlighted either by historians of mesmerism or of anti-Semitism. Whilst the racial and mesmeric concerns with psychological 'take-over' have been studied separately, their *relationship* with one another has not been drawn out in the existing historical literature. Nor did *fin-de-siècle* readers and critics of Du Maurier's novel make much of the conjoined magnetic and anti-Semitic elements of Svengali's portrait. On the contrary, Du Maurier's supporters tried to exculpate him from the charge of racial bigotry by claiming that Svengali had been demonised only by later imitators. The Jew's 'bad press', it was argued, was based more on sequels and subsequent embellishments than on Du Maurier's presentation of the original character.[52] More recently Du Maurier's biographer, Professor Leonée Ormond, has claimed that because the author had various Jewish friends and because Svengali is specifically an Oriental Jew, the depiction 'must not be seen as the expression of an unthinking and general prejudice'.[53]

Helpful though the biography is in other respects, this specific claim is unlikely to settle the matter. In the novel, as well as in the plays and poems which followed, Svengali is represented as dirty, ill-mannered and gross, as well as strangely desirable and impressive; moreover these attributes are linked to, and seen as representative of, his Jewishness. Filthy Svengali is contrasted with the clean Englishmen; indeed he roars with laughter at their having daily baths. Du Maurier's Jew is unquestionably sinister and sordid, greedy and predatory, albeit partly in the cause of fine music. While no defence can be offered of that odious representation, one can contend that the attribution of mesmeric power and thwarted artistic ambition made the character strikingly more complex than would appear at first glance.

Information available about Du Maurier's life confirms both his associations with and preoccupation about the Jews. Amongst his close personal acquaintances, for instance, was Emmanuel Oscar Mennhem Deutsch, a scholar and theologian who worked at the British Museum. Du Maurier saw the main target of his fictional and pictorial attacks on religion as directed not against the Jews, but rather against the sanctimonious and hypocritical representatives of the Church of England: there was nothing that got up his nose more than 'the average Parson'. Yet whatever his friendships with individual Jews, his drawings and writings participated sporadically and casually in the anti-Semitism of the day. Svengali was not a 'propaganda image' or part of some strategic, 'thought-out' rhetorical attack on Judaism; its sources and implications were both more serendipitous and more unconscious. The character was an inspired figure of fantasy and whimsy, whose aggressive implications Du Maurier might well have disclaimed; all this, however, must remain conjecture since the author's extant comments on his story are so few.

Du Maurier's work nicely exemplifies a tension apparent more broadly in Victorian languages of 'tolerance' and 'liberality'. Often the author sought to go against the base prejudices and stereotypical assumptions common in his era, as when he described Barty's Jewish schoolmates in *The Martian* (1896). Amidst the children of various aristocrats, sailors, rentiers, public officials and others, who people the educational institution in Paris that the intrepid young hero attends, were 'several very rich Jews, who were neither very clever nor very stupid, but as a rule, rather popular'.[54] Du Maurier evidently challenges any reader who would run ahead of his description and assume the Jews must always be vile. Indeed Barty marries a Jewess, against the grain of his very own prejudices. Du Maurier would no doubt have balked at the grosser hatred of many of his contemporaries, yet one also encounters him recoiling from 'the Jew'. Some Victorian critics drew attention to this kind of conflict within the same person, even identifying such a double perspective as a typical feature of English political psychology. In short, it was noted that racial distaste co-existed with the very liberal and enlightened points of view that, in theory, disavowed those same prejudices. The fact that anti-Semitism was not open and crude, it was argued, did not mean it was absent or without effect. Disraeli himself made the point in 1847, in a parliamentary debate on Jewish emancipation:

[Y]ou are influenced by the darkest superstitions of the darkest ages that ever existed in this country. It is this feeling that has been kept out of the debate; indeed that has been secret in yourselves – enlightened as you are – and that is unknowingly influencing you as it is influencing others abroad.[55]

Or as a reviewer (who initially signed himself merely 'A Jew') observed in 1877, while considering the public reception of George Eliot's *Daniel Deronda*, and in particular attitudes to her portrayal of the Jewish visionary Mordecai:

Let us not be misunderstood: the past generation of Englishmen has been so generous to Jews that we should be ungrateful if we accused cultured Englishmen of the present day of being *consciously* repelled by the idea of a poor Jew being worthy of admiration. But fifteen centuries of hatred are not to be wiped out by any legislative enactment . . . There yet remains a deep unconscious undercurrent of prejudice against the Jew which conscientious Englishmen have often to fight against as part of that lower nature, a survival of the less perfect development of our ancestors which impedes the Ascent of Man.[56]

Today one might be less inclined to see such emotional struggles as a biological function of ancestral influences. Nonetheless such a Victorian 'doctrine of survivals' is relevant enough to the case in hand. What was surely at the heart of this critique is the existence of unacknowledged, or even unconscious, hatred and contempt, that finds an object in 'the Jew'. This unwitting racial hatred can be glimpsed, it is suggested here, even in so mild, open-minded and bohemian an author as Du Maurier. Here was not some venomous and boorish version of racial invective, but the pernicious whimsy of a gentle man at odds with himself. The amusing creation of Svengali typified a strain of veiled hostility, far more difficult to get hold of and analyse than the frank rantings of Victorian bigots, at home or abroad.[57] The very qualities of hatred and resentment were then projected into the object – Svengali – who became the 'conductor' of precisely this kind of covert malice and violence. The Jew in turn was seen to project his supposed dumb helplessness and impotence into *his* victim; he was seemingly strengthened and enriched by virtue of controlling his object so completely.

Du Maurier appealed to the uncanny and the occult; his portrayals of people and their mental experience characteristically explored borderline conditions – phenomena lying at or just beyond the edge of sanity, or rational knowledge – not least through the processes of hypnosis, telepathy and dreams. His books were not written as psychological treatises, prosaic political diatribes or racial propaganda exercises, of which there were no small number in the late nineteenth century; instead, he offered rather dreamy, bitter-sweet evocations of the past, or rhapsodic accounts of undiscovered realms of human possibility, beyond the reach of humdrum scientific certainties or of any known rationalist methodology. Enchantment and strangeness – especially enchantment by strangers – became his very themes. 'The Chosen People' were cast as agents of miraculous transportations (through, for instance, the male Jew's hypnotic power or the Jewess's romantic allure) but also as the sources of the basest corruption. *The Martian* features the Sephardi Leah Gibson who is tall and dark with large captivating black eyes. She embodies 'a type that sometimes just now and again, can be so pathetically noble and beautiful in a woman, so suggestive of chastity and the most passionate love combined – love conjugal and filial and maternal – love that implies all the big practical obligations and responsibilities of human life, that the mere term "Jewess" (and especially its French equivalent) brings to my mind some vague, mysterious, exotically poetic image of all I love best in a woman'.[58] The anti-Semitic component, in other words, was complex and fragmentary; it was, moreover, distributed sporadically, 'casually', in the margins of the nostalgic fables spun by this immensely popular writer. In his various fictions, *Peter Ibbetson*, *Trilby* and *The Martian*, Du Maurier introduced his readers to all manner of extra-planetary and paranormal experiences not seen by the naked eye. Bodies and minds – earthly and extra-terrestrial – mixed together in weird combinations. He presents supernatural factors, occult practices, miraculous invasions and projections of thought through space and time. Racial and cosmic mysteries are frequently interspersed in these stories. A creature from space – Martia – who comes to earth and eventually inhabits Barty's head, in the novelist's posthumously published tale, is herself a victim of racial engineering on her home planet. Du Maurier (or at least his narrator) has some sympathy with such processes of 'selection'.

Like numerous other deficient denizens of Mars, Martia can inhabit the brains and bodies of a variety of creatures – a bird, beast, insect, even a fish – who remain 'unconscious of her presence'. For a while, she even lives inside a small Pomeranian dog belonging to a hard-up Jewish family in Cologne. She revels in the pervasive smells of fried fish in their house. Eventually, however, she gives up her domicile with the dog in favour of directly 'inhabiting' men, women and children. Hyperbole and bathos vie with each other, but Du Maurier consistently drives home the message that there are more wonders in heaven and earth than are dreamt of in nineteenth-century materialist philosophy and psychiatry. A conception of the unconscious is clear enough in his work, albeit without Freud's specific understanding of the idea. The term here, as in so much psychiatry and fiction of the period, characteristically refers to a pool of ancestral memories which, for reasons that altogether transcend the individual, are unavailable to the conscious mind.[59] Du Maurier cast thought-transference and inter-personal inspiration in various terms: a woman's dreams inserted into the head of a sleeping man, mesmeric rapport within a racially heterogeneous couple, even, as mentioned, a space traveller's strange residence within an artist's mind. Such fantastic answers to the enigma of how creative thinking occurs were beyond the limits of sober scientists, but the questions themselves were not.

Fragments from Du Maurier's diary hint that the very proximity to Jews could unsettle him, leaving him 'out of sorts'; as though such acquaintances were just not proper Englishmen. Du Maurier himself, as one chronicler observed, was, despite his Continental education, deeply English in his 'manners'.[60] He had some difficulty including the Jews within the terms of this 'Englishness', although this did not make him unsympathetic to 'their' culture. When he attended a Jewish wedding in London in April 1867, he recorded the event quite warmly in his diary: 'old Levy cried & so did old Phillips – kept our hats on, which felt very strange – music – all the unproper parts of the service in Hebrew'. But was it by chance that three days later, in his next entry, he seemed to have the following 'allergic' reaction: 'Muscular Christianity fit that always comes over me in spring – doing dumb-bells with bedroom chairs'?[61] In a book about his late father-in-law, C.C. Hoyer Millar reveals how varied and open was Du Maurier's social circle. The company he kept was literary, artistic, cosmopolitan. While certain Jews might be included, it is also made apparent that Jews evoked on occasion a certain distaste. Millar offers an intriguing example in reporting how he accompanied his wife (Du Maurier's daughter) to the

house of one Marc-André Raffalovich. Millar dubbed him 'a strange little
Russian Jew' in a reference which conveyed, of course, more than the man's
provenance or physical stature. Wilde also referred to him as 'little
André'.[62] Raffalovich had established a literary salon near the Royal Albert
Hall after his arrival in London in the 1880s. Whether directly relevant to
the composition of Svengali or not, Millar's account of the diminutive,
exotic and even charming host certainly provides a related instance of fascination and repulsion, as conceived in the world of the Du Mauriers. As
Millar put it:

> Late in the eighties, there arrived in London a strange little Russian Jew,
> André Raffalovich by name who brought with him many good intro-
> ductions. He took a large flat at the end of Albert Hall Mansions, next to
> the Albert Hall, and began entertaining on a considerable scale.[63]

Certainly Raffalovich had eclectic artistic, scientific and intellectual tastes,
including a particular concern with the occult (where his curiosity had been
stimulated by a cousin, George Raffalovich, who had written on the subject).[64] André took an interest in late-Victorian literature and the theme of
'decadence'; he wrote poetry, socialised with Wilde and his circle, but
remained something of an outsider – both a diagnostic observer of events
and a 'specimen' under scrutiny by his new London friends. Even by Wilde's
standards, Raffalovich had a reputation for excess, not least in his hospitality.
He was viewed as somewhat vulgar, too Svengalian, as it were, in his attempts
to captivate his guests. While his lavish food and drink were accepted by
artists and writers, he was spoken about with a certain condescension, some
of his guests evidently feeling that they patronised their host by accepting his
invitations. Kept waiting at the door with some companions for longer than
he liked, Wilde requested 'a table for six' when finally admitted to the sump-
tuous apartment. Although he had converted from Judaism to Catholicism
in 1896, Raffalovich was cast, in the conventional anti-Semitic terms of the
day, as too Jewish by half, striving too much for effect. His morals and sexual
tastes were also felt to be unclear. There were *sotto voce* jokes about his 'chaperone house-keeper who looked after the *ménage*'.[65] Wilde even declared
Raffalovich's poetry 'unhealthy', recoiling 'from the odour of the hot-house',
which he detected in his verse. Raffalovich was later to make his own critical
diagnoses of Wilde and referred to his detestable egotism.[66]

In the case of Raffalovich, as of Svengali (also accused of inhabiting an
unsavoury *ménage*), the disdain and disquiet of onlookers were inseparable

from wider racial and social assumptions about position and worth. In any event, the malicious intent of the Jewish fascinator is clear in Du Maurier's own text and the gallery of Svengali characters which followed. The squalid, invasive and mesmerising image of the Jew continued to feature in the plays and screen versions of *Trilby*. Indeed in the film adaptation from the stage hit,[67] dirty clothes and dark make-up mark the Jew. Furthermore, the very spacing of the figures on screen emphasised the threatening distance between mesmerist and mesmerised, Jew and gentile. In this film, Svengali (Sir Herbert Beerbohm Tree) is in a dominant and isolated position, reviled by the characters, yet for much of the time the object of the curious gaze of both the woman and men. Even before he has appeared, the three artists are seen scrutinising a picture of him. Once Svengali enters the frame, it is impossible to ignore him, however many other people there are in the scene. He has a heavy pointed beard, a worn coat and hat, dark wild hair, swarthy complexion, hooked nose and large, staring eyes. In one very early shot, these huge orbs themselves come to dominate the screen; we see nothing but two white discs. Hypnotically alluring, Svengali is nonetheless made up to be horrifying. He exemplified what Charles Dickens had earlier called 'the fascination of repulsion'.

In the film, Trilby hears music from the studio of the British artists as she comes down the stairs. She is enticed by the sound. As she enters, Svengali turns to her and then back to the piano. The camera carefully registers their eye contact. Svengali's ogling look captivates and disturbs Trilby. Meanwhile her pining admirer Billee watches helplessly from the side of the screen as the crafty mesmerist focuses his gaze and masters Trilby. All the other men are forced to gape impotently as he works his ocular and mesmeric magic. Soon Svengali, holding the woman's face in his hand, looks deep into her mouth, appreciating her vocal potential. He tests and explores, putting his head to her chest to hear the sound as she speaks. As Trilby swoons with one of her recurrent headaches, Billee reaches toward her, but she turns imploringly to Svengali. Her body goes limp. Svengali is again in motion at the front of the group, taking control. He asks her to look him in the eye as he makes movements with his hands, back and forth, his body swaying toward and away from her face. At one point he stares directly at the camera. He continues to move rhythmically and to touch her face. She remains still, looking up to him from her seated position. The others are bystanders. Gradually the group recognise that she has been hypnotised. Billee shouts at Svengali who in return grips him firmly and moves him away from Trilby. In retaliation, Taffy takes holds of

Scene from the 1914 film, *Trilby*, with Wilton Lackaye as Svengali.

Svengali. But it is the latter who has the power. Only he can release Trilby from her mental imprisonment, as he demonstrates, a few minutes later, liberating her from her trance by a few hand gestures. She is now free of her headache and kisses Svengali's hand in acknowledgement.

In a subsequent scene of the film, however, the sense of impotence suffered by the others in the face of Svengali is reversed. Now the Jew enters the room to find Trilby and Billee together. He is forced to witness their intimacy, looking on as the unnoticed and unwanted third person. We see him moving in the background, stealthily watching and eavesdropping, half-hidden behind a screen. It is not long before he has a chance to take his revenge, exploiting Billee's scruples about Trilby modelling naked. This time it is she who is half-hidden from our view. Svengali brings Billee into the room, forcing him to witness her undressed state, disabusing him of any illusion about her sexual modesty. The young man covers his eyes with horror, attacks Svengali, then flees the room. The painters look on, bemused. Tree emphasises the insinuating quality of the Jew, his lewdness as he confronts Billee with the girl's sexuality. The young lover rushes away from the artists' quarter, threatening (much to the joy of Svengali) to leave Paris altogether. He is persuaded by the matronly Mme Vinard to return, and there is a happy reunion between the lovers and the promise of marriage. The Jew is aghast. He sings, ominously, to them about the joys of love lasting only a moment. And so it goes on, through the various twists and turns of the melodrama.

There was debate about the special gifts and ethnic origins of Herbert Beerbohm Tree, the actor who first immortalised Svengali on stage and in film mirrored the discussion of the fictional character's own indeterminate 'racial genius'. Letting loose his own spirit, Tree was said to have haunted and bewitched his audiences.[68] He was famous for his performances in a number of Jewish parts, including Shylock, Fagin and Svengali, apparently finding in the last of these, 'a character after his own heart, eccentric, colourful, extravagant, melodramatic'.[69] Tree's repertoire fuelled the speculation about his own racial origins. Was the half-Lithuanian actor, who led a double life with two families, also Jewish?[70] Was the gentile acting a Jew, or *vice versa*? On occasion, such questions were considered in more abstract terms. Thus not whether such and such a Jew had such and such qualities, but rather whether some intrinsic relationship existed between the capacity for contrived and manipulative performance and this 'race'. There were even economists who argued that the Jews' long familiarity with trade had become an inherited skill at feigning.[71] Jews were said to be able to veil their feelings better during negotiations; again such qualities of concealment and performance were often considered to be 'in the blood'. The success of actresses such as Rachel Félix and Sarah Bernhardt prompted various ugly racial satires, as well as double-edged 'apologies' for the Jews. Commentators often made the rhetorical shift between particular cases and general maxims – individual Jews and Jewry at large. Thus in 1893 the French writer Anatole Leroy-Beaulieu declared that he saw beneath the frail exterior of the Jew an intense but morbid theatrical vitality: 'The Jew may be likened to those lean actresses, the *Rachels* and *Sarahs*, who spit blood, and seem to have but a spark of life left, and yet who, when they have stepped upon the stage, put forth indomitable strength and energy.'

Leroy-Beaulieu argued that modern leaders of the time such as the German socialist Ferdinand Lassalle, the French republican Léon Gambetta and, above all, the British conservative Benjamin Disraeli disclosed how very successfully Jews could perform on the political stage. They had become adept at a kind of contrived performance, their mesmerising effect achieved through seductive speech. Again the writer draws our attention to the disturbing magnetic attractiveness of Jews:

> These have shown us the Jew as master of the spoken word, swaying assemblies and fascinating the masses, as the prophet of these latter days, proclaiming to the people the gospel of democracy, an actor again, if you will, tragedian and comedian by turns, but with a swing and a fire, a force of animal vitality and a glow of inspiration such as was hardly to be looked for in the old blood of Israel.[72]

The association of hypnotism, Judaism and acting also attracted the passing attention of the philosopher Friedrich Nietzsche at around the same time. In *The Gay Science*, he offered a dizzying set of associations, bringing together the allure of acting, women, the working classes and Judaism. Racial, social and sexual tendencies to dissimulation were considered alongside one another in his aphorisms.[73] Nietzsche was interested in the inner nature of one who delights in artifice. Were there certain social types, he asked, who particularly manifested this craving to live inside a role and a mask? Such characteristics have easily and inevitably developed amongst the lower classes, 'who had to cut their coat according to the cloth, always adapting themselves to new circumstances' until they virtually became the coat they wore.[74] These propensities, he added, accumulated from generation to generation, producing a domineering, unreasonable and intractable character. Out of this type, it was possible to see the emergence of the actor or the 'artist' – the zany, the teller of lies, the buffoon. Such performers were highly adept at 'seeming'. Nietzsche then considered Jews in the same terms. They also possessed the art of adaptability to an exceptional degree. Indeed the philosopher went further in his sketch of the masterful actor:

This train of thought suggests immediately that one might see them virtually as a world-historical arrangement for the production of actors, a veritable breeding ground for actors. And it really is high time to ask: what good actor today is *not* – a Jew? The Jew as born 'man of letters', as the true master of the European press, also exercises his power by virtue of his histrionic gifts; for the man of letters is essentially an actor: He plays the 'expert', the 'specialist'.

Having touched on the lower classes and Jews (as well as diplomats), Nietzsche came to the question of women and this, in turn, brought him from acting to hypnosis.

Reflect on the whole history of women: do they not *have* to be first of all and above all else actresses? Listen to physicians who have hypnotised women; finally love them – let yourself be 'hypnotised by them'! What is always the end result? That they 'put on something' even when they take off everything. Woman is so artistic.[75]

One might refer here to the misogyny and contempt, already so widely remarked in Nietzsche's attitude, and leave it at that, but for my purpose it is important to notice specifically this 'playful' conjuncture of Jews, women and hypnotism which seemed to have such a grip on the thought and fiction of the time.

Others entered into this debate about the nature of emotional simulation, albeit in less cryptic terms than those of Nietzsche. There were specific explorations of the hypnotic propensities of the period's most illustrious players. Tree's abilities, for instance, divided the critics not only in terms of race but also in terms of entrancement. Was he hypnotic or just histrionic? Du Maurier's son-in-law later recalled Tree in the role of Svengali as 'fantastic, weird and comical in turns'. He felt the performance rose to 'great heights of tragic intensity'.[76] The aptly named Ernest Hart, a sober-minded medical commentator on hypnotism, argued that where Du Maurier had been scientifically precise in his presentation of Svengali's powers, Tree had gone wild, abandoning all accuracy or subtlety: 'It is the hypnotism of the platform and the stage play, and not that of Nature and pathology.' Yet Hart admired the intensity of Tree's acting, the vivid sensation of horror which he aroused in the viewer through his rendition of that spider, demon, modern Mephistopheles – Svengali:

As an impersonation it is one of the highest efforts of histrionic skill seen in modern times. Svengali has a 'force' which he passes into Trilby; he hypnotises her from behind unseen; he draws her to him from another room by 'force of will'; he is exhausted by the transference to her of 'his life'. All this is very effective from the stage point of view, but it clothes a vulgar error with the glamour of genius, and it possibly may renew for a time the vogue of the follies and frauds of the sham 'hypnotism, mesmerism and new magic', which I had hoped almost to have driven from the notice of reasonable men. Meantime all London will be drawn to see a most remarkable presentment of the platform 'mesmerist' outwardly at his best, or at his worst.[77]

The virtuosity was apparently informed by an ambiguous stage power. Not only was Tree's background racially shady but so, too, was the process by which he captured the hearts of his audiences. What kind of psychological state had he really entered in order to play a part so convincingly? His powers of persuasion on stage led some to ask whether effective actors and actresses really might be, or indeed had to be, 'out of their heads' in order to play others with conviction.[78] What kind of psychological condition ought the performers to induce in themselves, in order, *truly*, to act? How far could the impression of being 'transported' by one's part itself be dissimulated?

George Bernard Shaw took a jaundiced view of actors who entered into paroxysms of emotion, and thought ill of the exaggerated style Tree adopted in playing Svengali. He objected to the way the artist played up the 'Jewishness' and egotism of Du Maurier's original. Tree, he complained, overdid 'the stagey, the malignant, the diabolic, the wandering'.[79] Indeed Shaw's contempt for such theatrical excess was clear:

Imagine, above all, Svengali taken seriously at his own foolish valuation, blazed upon with limelights, spreading himself intolerably over the whole play with nothing fresh to add to the first five minutes of him – Svengali defying heaven, declaring that henceforth he is his own God, and then tumbling down in a paroxysm of heart disease (the blasphemer rebuked you see) and having to be revived by draughts of brandy.

The renowned critic and playwright considered this to be ludicrous, and a travesty of the original:

I derived much cynical amusement from this most absurd scene; but if I were Mr. du Maurier, I should ask whether the theatre is really in such an abject condition that all daintiness and seriousness of thought and feeling must be struck out of a book and replaced by vulgar nonsense.[80]

Shaw and others debated how far players legitimately (or illegitimately) distorted the audience's mental state, its potential suggestibility; and, conversely, to what extent audiences created an excitable or even deranged condition in the actor. Once again Shaw responded caustically, noting the way in which casts sometimes worked themselves up into an absurd emotional lather. In a hostile account of the procedure of another well-known actor, Sir Henry Irving (whom he felt had neither 'grip' nor brains), Shaw wrote: 'The condition in which he works is a somnambulistic one: he hypnotizes himself into a sort of dreamy energy, and is intoxicated by the humming of his words in his nose.'[81] Others, including the influential theatre critic William Archer, were more touched, lauding the actor for his extraordinary 'magnetic' presence. It was as though Irving's very body was possessed of an 'electro-magnet'. The audience were enthralled by his glistening eyes that transmuted so dramatically from a melancholic to a visionary, sinister or penetrating look.[82] Stanislavski was also impressed with the invisible currents Irving mobilised as he performed – 'something [that] streams out of you, some current from your eyes, from the ends of your fingers or out of your pores'.[83] Stanislavski argued that to achieve greatness, the actor had to draw upon emotional forces that stemmed from the dark areas of the mind. Indeed while training and discipline were crucial, the true artist had to be prepared, at a certain point, to allow the experience to tear away from his control, thereby tapping into what he called the 'superconscious'. As he wrote about one of his own triumphs on the stage: 'I understood that in a moment of strong upheaval which I mistook for inspiration, it was not I who controlled my body, but it was my body that controlled me.'[84] The performer had to channel and be channelled by these 'superconscious' currents. Only where inhibition was removed could a true characterisation emerge.

In a similar vein, Tree suggested that children were natural actors, only losing their capacity when burdened by the self-consciousness of gathering maturity. Tree himself was viewed by many of his admiring contemporaries as a natural who fully succeeded in freeing himself from inhibition. He was, as Max Beerbohm recalled, so effortlessly able to mesmerise the audience;

his presence was 'electrifying', his effect 'fascinating', 'haunting' and 'bewitching'.[85] For these reasons, and in contrast to the critical view of Bernard Shaw, another theatre reviewer, John Ranken Towse, particularly appreciated Tree's performance as the 'dirty spider', Svengali:

> The swift, noiseless, cat-like movements, watchful eyes and ghastly face, incessant restlessness, and the curiously skilful blend of fawning and arrogance, contributed to an abnormal, but not wholly incredible, individuality which will long live in the memory. The egotism, meanness, cynical selfishness, and innate ferocity of the creature were vividly exposed; but in all its viciousness and degradation – and herein lay the special excellence of the portrayal – there was the constant intimation of the artistic sense, the love of music for its own sake as well as its rewards, which was the villain's one redeeming grace.[86]

In so many images of the time, Jews are seen insidiously to penetrate the object. Through a mixture of fawning and arrogance, they play upon gentiles, asserting mastery; Jews, it was said, knew how to do it as well if not better than anyone else since they had always been obliged (according to Nietzsche and others) to 'play a part' in order to survive. Svengali provided the case *par excellence* of the 1890s. If the grotesque egoism of the display were clear enough, so was the demonic ability. Both aspects of the character were taken as exemplary, symbolising far more than an individual part. Svengali was viewed, then, as an illustration of a complex 'character type'. The Svengali of book, stage and screen possessed this abnormally pronounced individuality, but he also acted with the consummate 'know-how' and immobilising skill that typified his race.

* * *

That self-styled 'godless Jew' who invented psychoanalysis in the 1890s, Sigmund Freud, held a variety of views about the role of suggestion in his practice. On one occasion, long after he had given up the technique of hypnosis, he was reported to have confided to his aristocratic Russian patient, dubbed the 'Wolf Man', that psychoanalysis was in fact nothing but hypnosis; at other times he clearly reached a very different conclusion about the extraordinary technique he had pioneered. Nobody can know for sure what was actually said between Freud and that particular patient at the time, and whether, as has been reported, the latter really described the former as a 'Jewish swindler [who] wants to use me from behind and shit on my head'.[87] Whether such a 'report' was a case of memory or false memory, embellished recollection or retrospective fantasy we cannot be sure. Certainly, however, there was no shortage of people who openly viewed Freud thus, albeit such sentiments were usually expressed in less graphic terms.

In that interview, which took place late in his life, the Wolf Man drew attention to the dangers of hypnotism and Freud's apparent remark that psychoanalysis *is* hypnosis:

> When I do what transference shows me, it is really like being hypnotised by someone. That's the influence. I can remember Freud saying, 'Hypnosis, what do you mean, hypnosis, everything we do is hypnosis too.' Then why did he discontinue hypnosis? I cannot remember.[88]

Influential cultural critics of psychoanalysis today still draw on these long-standing uncertainties about the role of suggestion and hypnosis in the 'talking cure', although they generally avoid the anti-Semitic adjunct, 'Jewish swindler', so prevalent earlier in the century. Despite Freud's own highly idiosyncratic and complex relationship to Judaism, his early critics often thought that his work typified the 'Jewish system' or the quintessential 'Jewish approach', the product of trans-generational mental traits. Contemplating Freud's theory of the mind, the eminent English social psychologist William McDougall, for instance, mused in 1921: 'Maybe it is true of the Jewish race'.[89] Freud was certainly familiar with such insinuations or charges from rivals. He heard that the French psychologist Pierre Janet had linked psychoanalysis to a specific Viennese sexual *angst*, a speculation which Freud rejected as 'exceptionally senseless', but behind which, he suspected, lay anti-Semitism.[90] Freud's dismissal of Janet's reported charge is to be found in his history of the psychoanalytic movement, where he also speaks of the gulf that divided him from Carl Jung.

Freud acknowledged Jung's efforts to overcome his racial prejudice.[91] The fact of Jung's enduring anti-Semitism contains a certain irony given that he had been rapidly 'promoted' by Freud, in part to offset racialised dismissals of psychoanalysis. Freud once remarked to his close colleague Karl Abraham that the Swiss physician should be treated with special tolerance, since it was harder for him, as the son of a pastor, to accept psychoanalysis than it was for a Jew.[92] Yet Jung remained a symptom of the disease he had been introduced into psychoanalysis to cure. In his view, after the rupture, psychoanalysis *was* a disease, and one which related to Judaism. He wrote in a letter of the 'essentially corrosive nature' of the work of Freud

as well as his fellow Jew Alfred Adler.[93] In a notorious and still much discussed paper of 1934, entitled 'The State of Psychotherapy Today', Jung
sought to describe the peculiarity of Freud and Adler, more generally of the
Jews at large, through appeals to the differences of racial inheritance in the
unconscious.[94]

Jung's argument here reflected a commonly held view in the inter-war
period: namely that psychoanalysis had an especially pernicious effect on
gentile minds. It was apparently a system of thought stemming from
innately Jewish propensities and peculiarities, and could not be generalised,
or at least only through a kind of dogmatic imposition. Jung points out that
the way in which the patient resists and counters, his ability to see through
the doctor's artifices, his 'little game of prestige', should not be underesti-
mated.[95] The idea that it is possible to describe 'the Jewish mind' and to differentiate it from 'the gentile mind' is itself taken for granted. To discuss the
matter as though the mental apparatus of different races is the same strikes
Jung not only as absurd but also as dangerous.

It should be pointed out that an argument about racial-psychological
differences was also being explored (and even half entertained) by Freud,
too, at this time, albeit in terms which usually clouded the divide between
psychic fantasy, myth and history. Jung's speculations at least find an echo
in Freud's controversial study *Moses and Monotheism*, which appeared during the same decade, to the outrage of some Jewish groups and to the regret
of some of Freud's own followers. While not marked by the derogatory
tone towards Judaism – or the flirtation with myths of Aryanism – so
evident in the Jung paper (as elsewhere in his work and life), Freud suspected that Jews *were* constitutionally marked by a different ancestral psychology, indeed by an indestructible unconscious mental content. He
suggested, for instance, that the Jews had inherited *and repressed* the
acquired characteristic of guilt in relation to the fantasy of the primal murder of God (a crime repeated in the murder of Moses and symbolically
expiated by Christians in the sacrifice of Christ the son). Christianity
seemed to know of this guilt, in so far as the death of the son was a sacrifice
for that patricide. For what else, so the argument went, was Christ 'redeem-
ing' if not the murder of the father?[96]

Jung, however, proceeded differently. He combined a stark racial
hypothesis with his criticisms of psychoanalysis, a practice which he related
to Jewish psychological peculiarity. He viewed Freud and his followers as
imposing a 'morass' of ideas about infantile perverse sexual wishes on all
and sundry. In contrast to the neurotic barrenness of thought that these

Jews or even 'the Jewish race as a whole' suffer and seek to universalise, Jung posits an Aryan soul still in its rich infancy. This soul, full of potential, is also vulnerable to distortion and contamination. The Jews, who have a wider consciousness and are thus less vulnerable than the gentiles, are a real threat to this fledgling and vibrant collective mentality. It is surely not surprising that Jung's essay has been interpreted as the expression of a National Socialist 'fellow-traveller':

Freud and Adler have beheld very clearly the shadow that accompanies us all. The Jews have this peculiarity in common with women; being physically weaker, they have to aim at the chinks in the armour of their adversary, and thanks to the technique which has been forced on them through the centuries, the Jews themselves are best protected where others are vulnerable. Because, again, of their civilization, more than twice as ancient as ours, they are vastly more conscious than we of human weaknesses, of the shadow-side of things, and hence in this respect much less vulnerable than we are . . . As a member of a race with a three-thousand-year-old civilization, the Jew, like the cultured Chinese, has a wider area of psychological consciousness than we. Consequently it is *in general* less dangerous for the Jew to put a negative value on the unconscious. The 'Aryan' unconscious, on the other hand, contains explosive forces and seeds of a future yet to be born, and these may not be devalued as nursery romanticism without psychic danger. The still youthful Germanic peoples are fully capable of creating new cultural forms that still lie dormant in the darkness of the unconscious of every individual – seeds bursting with energy and capable of mighty expansion. The Jew, who is something of a nomad, has never yet created a cultural form of his own and as far as we can see never will, since all his instincts and talents require a more or less civilized nation to act as host for their development.

The Jewish race as a whole – at least this is my experience – possesses an unconscious which can be compared with the 'Aryan' only with reserve. Creative individuals apart, the average Jew is far too conscious and differentiated to go about pregnant with the tensions of unborn futures. The 'Aryan' unconscious has a higher potential than the Jewish; that is both the advantage and disadvantage of a youthfulness not yet fully weaned from barbarism. In my opinion it has been a grave error in medical psychology up till now to apply Jewish categories – which are not even binding on all Jews – indiscriminately to Germanic and Slavic Christendom. Because of this the most precious secret of the Germanic peoples – their creative and intuitive depth of soul – has been explained as a morass of banal infantilism, while my own warning voice has for decades been suspected of anti-Semitism. This suspicion emanated from Freud. He did not understand the Germanic psyche any more than did his Germanic followers. Has the formidable phenomenon of National Socialism, on which the whole world gazes with astonished eyes, taught them better?[97]

Despite Jung's caveat here, as elsewhere in his writings and letters, that such Jewish categories are not to be seen as binding on all Jews, the reader is left in no doubt of the basic psychological distinction between the races. There is little ambiguity about where the author lines up as he contrasts 'we' and 'them' in this portrayal of Jew and Aryan,[98] although his argument does become more blurred at points. Thus a link is made between Jews and women, as well as between the Jews and the 'shadow-side of things', even if it is also said that the Aryan unconscious is pregnant with the future and is yet to be fully known. The dominant diagnosis, however, is clear enough: the 'womanly' physical weakness of Jews necessitates their adoption of particular techniques of defence and attack. Also implied is the Jews' propensity to use their knowledge in order to get at those beyond the faith (aggressive actions as the best form of protection). There is an assumption of special racial sensitivities here and of invisible forms of shielding; a past which enables the Jew to confront the unconscious with less risk to himself. While the one group is described as very old indeed, the other is youthful – and in that fundamental inequality of ages, Jung detects serious dangers of psychic manipulation and disturbance.

While the Jews are described as the beneficiaries of a longer history, the passage contains breathless allusions to the dawning Aryan future. Jung refers to the Jews as nomadic, uncreative, feeding on the 'host' civilisation. They not only feed off the gentiles, but also impose something damaging upon them. At least on this score, Jung implicitly repudiated Freud's scepticism about the reality of the psychoanalyst's omnipotent force of suggestion.

With his patients reclining on a couch, and his own chair placed behind their heads, Freud deliberately eschewed the eye-to-eye contact that had been such a consistent feature of nineteenth-century hypnotic entertainment and medico-psychiatric treatment. One reason he gave for this particular innovation was that he could not bear to be looked at all day long by his patients, but perhaps more importantly it served to emancipate the

patient from the traditionally powerful gaze of the physician or the psychiatrist. On the other hand, recognition of the patient's enormous emotional
investment in the analyst, with all its displacements and condensations of
earlier relationships, was to become central to Freud's own theorisation of
the patient's 'transference' to the analyst, a clinical concept very significantly developed by his followers. In any event, his critics were not slow to
find continuities between the props of Freud's consulting room, to say
nothing of the persona of the analyst and the charismatic traditions of
mesmerism and hypnotism. Thus Jung insisted on the malign potential for
'suggestion' that remained implicit in the analytic operation. He offered the
haunting vision of psychoanalytical Jews, sadly lacking in the capacity for
'pregnant futures', imposing their negative categories on others.
Meanwhile, he chillingly anticipated that it was the '"Aryan" unconscious'
that 'contains seeds of a future yet to be born'.[99]

8
Evil Eye

Then Svengali, scowling, would play Chopin's funeral march more divinely than ever; and where the pretty soft part comes in, he would whisper to Trilby, 'That is Svengali coming to look at you in your little mahogany glass case!'

And here let me say that these vicious imaginations of Svengali's, which look so tame in English print, sounded much more ghastly in French, pronounced with a Hebrew-German accent, and uttered in his hoarse, rasping nasal throaty rook's caw, his big yellow teeth baring themselves in a mongrel canine snarl, his heavy upper eyelids drooping over his insolent black eyes.

Du Maurier, *Trilby*[1]

In a lyrical passage in *Trilby* on the transfer of the look of love between wife and husband, mother and child, Du Maurier intimated the profound significance of eye contact in the shaping and relating of selves:

That beautiful look of love surprised (which makes all women's eyes look the same) came into [Taffy's wife's] whenever she looked at Taffy, and filled his heart with tender compunction, and a queer sense of his own unworthiness.

Then a boy was born to them, and that look fell on the boy, and the good Taffy caught it as it passed him by, and he felt a helpless, absurd jealousy, that was none the less painful for being so ridiculous! and then that look fell on another boy, and yet another, so that it was through these boys that she looked at their father. Then *his* eyes caught the look, and kept it for their own use; and he grew never to look at his wife without it; and as no daughter came, she retained for life the monopoly of that most sweet and expressive regard.[2]

In the life and work of Du Maurier vision was attributed with the most precious and intense significance. To a quite exceptional degree, he was interested in the way exchanges of looks reflected and transformed human relationships, for good or evil. He focused upon the power of eyes, always concerned to get things sharp and clear, but at the same time charting the moment when an individual's sight becomes unreliable or fades away altogether, through blindness, madness, hypnosis or death. The artist's traumatic loss of vision in his left eye and his ensuing dread of total blindness, charged his whole awareness of sight with a terrifying sense of its vulnerability:

> To live day by day in dread of total blindness! Continually to face the possibility of utter uselessness, worthlessness, helplessness! To wake, and strive in vain to pierce the darkness of night! To lie and wonder if indeed it be the night! To watch and watch for the first streak of dawn, and at its coming to feel a cloud of agony and terror pass away! . . . Small wonder that Mr. Du Maurier murmurs: 'It has poisoned my existence.'[3]

In Henry James' mind, there was no doubt which of Du Maurier's senses was the most important and powerful. Indeed '[i]t seemed to me that he almost *saw* the voice, as he saw the features and limbs, and quite as if this had been but one of the subtler secrets of his impaired vision.' Even with only one functioning eye, his sight, 'was beyond any other I had known, and whatever it had lost, what it had kept was surprising. He had been turned out originally with a wondrous apparatus, an organ worthy of one of those heroes whom he delighted to endow with superfine senses.'[4]

At several points in his work, Freud described sight and blindness as symbols of potency and castration. Surely, however, the recurring ocular themes in Du Maurier's work cannot satisfactorily be explained that way. Freud's own critical remarks, elsewhere, about the value of symbolic generalisations should anyway make one cautious about such a claim, or about the idea that a concern with the eye and with sight simply condenses and displaces other anxieties. As many clinicians and theorists have shown, the preciousness of our visual apparatus, and the importance, in reality and phantasy, of being benevolently or malevolently *seen*, are of immense and complex psychological significance.[5] This is not the place to pursue such matters further, other than to note how Du Maurier returned again and again both to the problem of vision and to the variable psychic effect of external observation upon the subject. Du Maurier viewed his own melancholic side as inseparable from the trauma of near-blindness in his youth. The shocking impact of his early impairment is clear enough, but we can only speculate on what other factors, in his case, may have given such enduring meaning to that experience. He often drew attention later on to the medical healers who charged so heavily and delivered so little in his time of crisis abroad, as he traipsed from specialist to specialist in search of explanation and cure.[6] Du Maurier's novels sentimentally valorised 'good' eyes and drew attention to the penetrative effect of a hostile gaze. Indeed bad eyes often triumphed over good. In this respect, the depiction of Svengali's eyes – or, rather, of his malign powers of observation – also reflected the long-standing myth that Jews possessed envious eyes, which could actually damage or even destroy the object regarded. This concrete quality of the evil gaze was further elaborated in the stage version. In Paul Potter's 1895 dramatisation of the story, Trilby declares to the Jew: 'I shiver and sicken when your eyes meet mine. I would rather suffer torture than let you look at me.'[7]

The ocular theme in *Trilby* has been remarked upon by various critics, one recently going so far as to suggest that the novel concerns 'the most demonic male gaze in English literature'.[8] Svengali's companions must either avert their eyes or seek to face him down, challenging his dangerous appraisal. Svengali is thus temporarily cowed into submission by Taffy, or rather by the 'stern, choleric, invincible blue eye of the hated Northern gentile'[9] (the Jew's rancour unfortunately becomes all the greater thereafter). Du Maurier frequently takes the temperature of relationships via such benign and malign contacts, hypnotic or otherwise, describing heated looks of love, chilling visual domination or the freezing gaze of indifference. The hapless Billee's own increasingly frantic preoccupation with eye contact reaches a climax when Svengali and the hypnotised Trilby snub him:

> Little Billee's heart was in his mouth. He caught Svengali's eye, and saw him speak to her. She turned her head and looked at him standing there – they both did. Little Billee bowed. She stared at him with a cold stare of disdain, and cut him dead – so did Svengali.[10]

Concern about the invasive – and potentially evil – impact of the eye is central to the novel, and is also more widely evident in Victorian accounts of the hypnotic operation. Such representations were informed by much older speculations about the eye's capacity to shape and corrupt the object of vision, through its 'effluvia'. In these discussions it is not simply in some metaphorical sense that the viewer 'cuts dead' or 'stares through' the object viewed: in certain nineteenth-century reports about the state of fascination, the eyes are understood quite literally to have a physical effect upon the body that is looked at. Long-standing (and long-contested) theories that had persisted from the period of classical Greece to the Renaissance about the forces that were projected out by the looking eye had not completely vanished by the late nineteenth century, and were sometimes subsumed into new magnetic and electrical theories of 'fascination'. A pamphlet of 1890, *Soul-Subtlety: or, How to Fascinate*, saw the power of fascination as 'part of those wondrous, far reaching occult powers, electric or magnetic, which have some influence over every atom in existence, whether mineral, vegetable, or animal.'[11] The paralysing effect of certain kinds of eye were described in nineteenth-century fiction and some of the specialist literature on trances and hypnosis. Whilst the mesmerist's eyes were widely seen as consequential, it was recognised that there were also other ways than a commanding stare to make men and women fall into those special states of lucid slumber: there was nothing to prevent the blind being treated (or mis-treated) by the hypnotist as well.

A reversal of the theme of the male mesmerist's fascinating eye was offered in a tale briefly alluded to earlier that appeared at about the same time as *Trilby*. Conan Doyle's 'The Parasite' (1894) involves a sexually rapacious and hypnotically dangerous woman from the West Indies, Miss Penelossa. She succeeds in overpowering an eminent man, Professor Gilroy, through a captivatingly intense stare. As her victim declares:

> My eyes were fixed upon Miss Penelossa's face, but as I gazed the fea-tures seemed to blur and to fade away. I was conscious only of her own eyes looking down at me, grey, deep, inscrutable. Larger they grew and larger, until they changed suddenly into two mountain lakes towards which I seemed to be falling with horrible rapidity.[12]

He is hypnotically enslaved by this 'devil woman', this 'hellish parasite within me', and is liberated only through her death.[13] It was, however, Svengali and Trilby that brought the intertwined theme of the mesmeric

and evil eye to the greatest prominence for late nineteenth-century readers and audiences. Beerbohm Tree's original rendition (for stage and
screen) of Svengali's malignant and omnipotent stare was certainly
remarked at the time. A much later film version made in 1955, starring
Donald Wolfit as Svengali and Hildegarde Neff as Trilby (and with the
famous opera singer Elizabeth Schwarzkopf providing her voice) still
played powerfully upon the image of the mesmerist's deadly visual mastery, although the film also vaguely alluded to the notion of a hidden psychoanalyst. Here Trilby reclines (on the couch?), dreamily musing, whilst
Svengali looms over her, overwhelming. Gradually her capacity for free
thought is transformed into automaton-like subservience. Svengali
reaches the young woman with his 'long, dirty fingers', his stare, his insinuating voice. His will is macabre and irresistible. A silhouette image of this
wandering low-life musician early on in the film hints, but never spells
out, the racial attribution in the original tale. There was no explicit anti-
Semitism and, in that sense, the production was typical of a shift in the
terms of acceptable representation within mainstream culture after the
Second World War. Yet Wolfit still conveys something of the accou-
trements of the Victorian stage Jew: black beard, prominent nose, ragged
clothes, swarthy complexion. Even an echo of Dickens seems to come
through in the portrayal: just as in *Oliver Twist,* the Jewish Fagin is shown
to have a frightening and corrupting hold over the socially dispossessed, so
Svengali exerts his domination over a rootless waif. It is the woman's
orphan condition that makes her especially vulnerable to the psychological manipulation of this outsider. The film emphasises the death of
Trilby's father and its relationship to her suggestibility. His dying
prophecy had been that others would come to do her harm in the world
once he was no longer there to protect her. And so it comes to pass.

Trilby's friends warn her to look out. Yet she is curious, keen to meet
and confront Svengali, who has, as an onlooker explicitly puts it, 'the evil
eye'. The film script inserts this precise reference which is, in fact, not so
directly stated in the original story, although the notion of the Jew's possession of an envious gaze has a very long literary and mythological history
which is vaguely recalled in Du Maurier's novel, and in the subsequent play.
Matthew Lewis' widely read 'Gothic' tale *The Monk* (1796) had made passing reference to the fearsome appearance of the wandering Jew and indicated that his large, black and sparkling eyes were repositories of deep
mysteries: 'yet there was something in his look which the moment that I
saw him, inspired me with a secret awe, not to say horror.'[14] Closer to the

Poster for the 1955 film *Svengali*.

time of Du Maurier, the eponymous hero of *Daniel Deronda* was several times half-jokingly accused of possessing the evil eye.[15]

Wolfit highlights, but does not, of course, simply invent, the association between Svengali and the evil eye. In all versions, Svengali is perceived not only to be jealously wresting the prized possession – the woman – from other men, but also enviously attacking the desired object herself. Taking our lead from the film's explicit references, perhaps Svengali could be viewed as a modern conflation of older mythological features – the wandering Jew and the Jew with the evil eye. The possibility that the hypnotist's ocular domination might somehow relate to the old legend of the evil eye was itself considered in certain esoteric scientific debates of Svengali's own time; experts speculated about whether patients might themselves unwittingly be influenced by such myths, their suggestibility thus exacerbated by the erroneous belief that the eye could actually transform its object.[16] While it was argued that the evil eye was a primitive belief, *fin-de-siècle* writers recognised that this was not confined to dead or remote cultures. Neither was it a view that late-Victorian writers necessarily sought to dismiss *tout court.* It was, after all, a tendency of much intellectual work in this period to challenge the idea that natural science had, even potentially, the answers to all the world's unresolved mysteries.

The strong commitment to the powers of human reason that characterised so much Enlightenment thought was not infrequently challenged in the last decades of the nineteenth century; it even became fashionable for scientists to suspend their materialistic judgements and explore enigmas of the occult with open minds – the Italian criminal anthropologist Cesare Lombroso who, in his later years, participated remarkably uncritically in spiritualist seances, provides one of the most spectacular instances of this kind of *volte face. Borderland* was the characteristic title of a journal of the period, one of a number to pay renewed attention to the significance of folklore and the occult. Those hapless characters in the stories of Conan Doyle, Robert Louis Stevenson or Bram Stoker who haughtily dismissed traditional beliefs as mere redundant superstition were made to suffer heavily for their hubris. In such a context, the evil eye was a 'borderland' topic if ever there was one, worthy of renewed exploration.

The evil eye had long been associated with the Jews, even though this was by no means a necessary or exclusive ingredient in the myth. If Jews were often presented as carriers of the evil eye in the medieval and early modern periods, they had also been perceived as affording the gentile protection against the danger of hostile scrutiny.[17] Pre-modern visions of the Jews as highly equivocal figures, the bearers of poisons *and* remedies, the symbols both of doctoring and of disease, were resuscitated and re-explored here and there in Victorian discussions. Thus the central but contested roles of both Judaism and Islam in the long history of Western medicine and healing were studied and even occasionally catalogued afresh in the 1890s.[18] The distinguished German scientist Rudolph Virchow, speaking at a medical conference in Rome in 1894, remarked on the incalculable contribution made by both Jews and Arabs:

> In early medieval times it was the Jews and the Arabs who made a definite impression upon the progress of medical science. In our times Hebrew manuscripts have been brought to light which show with what zeal and learning Jewish physicians of early medieval times were active in the preservation and advancement of medicine. We may in truth say

that down to these times the hereditary talent of the Jews, which has contributed so much that is great to science can often be discerned.[19]

This kind of historical interest in Jewish medicine and primitive superstitions cropped up in a variety of places in those final Victorian years. An 1895 study by Frederick Thomas Elworthy, entitled *The Evil Eye*, paid some attention to the long tradition of Jewish protective amulets against the evil eye, products for which there had been substantial gentile demand.[20] The author drew together folklore, fascination and race, suggesting that mesmerism and hypnotism were but the latest examples of ancient superstitions and arts of entrancement.[21] Alongside accounts of the power of phylacteries, there were also contemporaneous explorations of how the Jews became the symbols and carriers of sickness. The recollection of such historical fantasies easily tipped over into their modern endorsement and elaboration. It was in such dialogue with the anti-Semitic past that a number of commentators came both to renew and substantially re-write medieval and early modern opinions where, as mentioned, Jews had often been seen as both the source of ills and of their cure.

In German, *Judenblick* (the Jew's look) signifies the evil eye, but an obvious caveat must be added: portrayal of the Jews' sullen, resentful or chilly eyes have by no means been restricted to German-speaking states.[22] While often feared and reviled in medieval and early modern societies, the Jews had also been ascribed singular powers, access to mysteries, and familiarity with potent but sinister recipes against the evil eye. At the same time tales and rumours of Jewish hatred, from the evil eye to ritual murder, circulated in many forms and places. 'Ritual murder' is a broad term for sacrificial killing, while the so-called 'blood libel' concerned more specific tales in which the blood of the murdered Christian (usually a small male child) was alleged to be used in Jewish feasts and celebrations.[23] Again, there were numerous variants of the narrative; material gathered from Russia and Poland, for example, shows how Jews were thought to use Christian blood to smear the eyes of their newborn babies since Jewish children 'are always born blind'. Theories about the constitutional blindness or myopia of the Jews found expression in diverse locations across the century, sometimes intermingled with references to ritual killing of gentiles.[24]

Many anti-Jewish writings in the eighteenth and nineteenth centuries bewilderingly mixed old and new elements, shaping as well as merely repeating 'traditional' views, incorporating personal commentaries and fantasies or juxtaposing scriptural quotations with specific political

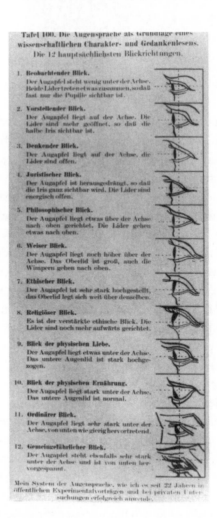

Tafel 100. Die Augensprache als Grundlage eines
wissenschaftlichen Charakter- und Gedankenlesens.
Die 12 hauptsächlichsten Blickrichtungen.

1. Beobachtender Blick.
Der Augapfel steht wenig unter der Achse.
Beide Lider treten etwas zusammen, so daß
fast nur die Pupille sichtbar ist.

2. Vorstellender Blick.
Der Augapfel liegt auf der Achse. Die
Lider sind mehr geöffnet, so daß die
halbe Iris sichtbar ist.

3. Denkender Blick.
Der Augapfel liegt auf der Achse, die
Lider sind offen.

4. Juristischer Blick.
Der Augapfel ist herausgedrängt, so daß
die Iris ganz sichtbar wird. Die Lider sind
energisch offen.

5. Philosophischer Blick.
Der Augapfel liegt etwas über der Achse
nach oben gerichtet. Die Lider gehen
etwas nach oben.

6. Weiser Blick.
Der Augapfel liegt noch höher über der
Achse. Das Oberlid ist groß, auch die
Wimpern gehen nach oben.

7. Ethischer Blick.
Der Augapfel ist sehr stark hochgestellt,
das Oberlid legt sich weit über denselben.

8. Religiöser Blick.
Es ist der verstärkte ethische Blick. Die
Lider sind noch mehr aufwärts gerichtet.

9. Blick der physischen Liebe.
Der Augapfel liegt etwas unter der Achse.
Das untere Augenlid ist stark hochge-
zogen.

10. Blick der physischen Ernährung.
Der Augapfel liegt stark unter der Achse.
Das untere Augenlid ist normal.

11. Ordinärer Blick.
Der Augapfel liegt sehr stark unter der
Achse, von unten wie gierig hervortretend.

12. Gemeingefährlicher Blick.
Der Augapfel steht ebenfalls sehr stark
unter der Achse und ist von unten her-
vorgespannt.

Mein System der Augensprache, wie ich es seit 22 Jahren in
öffentlichen Experimentalvorträgen und bei privaten Unter-
suchungen erfolgreich anwende.

The physiognomy of the gaze.

observations. Certainly references to Jewish ocular powers (or deficiencies)
often drew on older images and references, some taken from medieval
times, others from the Bible. Thus in an impassioned protest at the possibility of the naturalisation of the Jews, the Reverend William Romaine
(writing in England in the mid-eighteenth century) had referred to
Deuteronomy to argue that since God had indeed scourged the Jews by giving them a trembling heart, failing eyes and sorrow of mind, it would be
wrong for others to display too much tolerance. The Jews were rightly tormented by guilt. To seek to absolve them of their crimes and to naturalise
them would be to take on their blindness, to fall into an 'infatuation' that
could lead only to calamity: 'Blindness always precedes a judgement', he
warned.[25] Romaine offers a cautionary note, too, about mistaking Jews for
non-Jews and asks the following question: if Jews dress, behave and generally

'appear' like everyone else, how can they be seen for what they really are? In response, he reassures his reader that there is a way. Even emancipated Jews, however they get themselves up, can be distinguished through bodily signs, above all through their eyes:

> It is not his dirty skin, for there are other people as nasty; neither is it the Make of his Body, for the Dutch are every whit as odd, aukward (sic) figures as the *Jews*. But look at his eyes. Don't you see a malignant Blackness underneath them, which gives them such a Cast, as bespeaks Guilt and Murder? You can never mistake a *Jew* by this Mark, it throws such a dead livid Aspect over all his Features, that he carries Evidence enough in his Face to convict him of being a Crucifier.[26]

In Deuteronomy, Moses announces a long list of punishments for those who would not hearken diligently unto the voice of God. They include being smitten with madness, blindness and astonishment of heart: 'And thou shalt grope at noon-day, as the blind gropeth in darkness'. If sighted, the transgressor would be driven mad by what he saw. The evil eye would also befall such people. In place of a benign fraternal eye, a man would find that 'his eye shall be evil toward his brother, and toward the wife of his bosom, and toward the remnant of his children which he shall leave'. The woman's eye could also be malignly directed toward her husband, son and daughter.[27] Evidently such biblical references were not forgotten in some of these much later diatribes, but the evil was usually seen as directed not at other members of the Jewish family, but at gentiles.

Sheer deficiency and neediness, as well as intense envy of gentiles repeated over the centuries, were often assumed to be entirely natural motives for any present-day crimes alleged against the Jews. To the surprise of many European liberals, ritual-murder myths seemed to be flourishing anew in many areas during the late nineteenth century. A widely discussed episode had occurred in Hungary in the 1880s where Jews were suspected of the ritual murder of a young Christian girl; even those who did not directly endorse the notion of such instincts sometimes travelled a long way down the speculative path that regarded modern Jews as the special heirs of ancient atavistic urges. In response to the Hungarian case, the *Spectator* speculated on whether there might conceivably be a Jewish sect (somehow emanating from 'Hindooism') which had remained committed to human sacrifice.[28] The case turned on the testimony of the thirteen-year-old son of a synagogue official, who accused his own father of capturing the virgin, killing her and gathering up her blood in two dishes. Surveying these events in the East, the French doyen of the theory of suggestion, Dr Bernheim, concluded that deep emotional forces were at work in the son's reaction to the legal process: 'Under the power of this strong suggestive influence, the hypnotised brain meticulously constructs the scene evoked by the police officer. He has seen it all – the victim prostrate . . . the person performing the sacrifice plunging his knife in her throat, the blood pouring out . . . The retroactive hallucination has been created . . . and the memory of the imaginary vision is so vivid that he cannot forget it.'[29] Further cases were recorded in the years leading up to the First World War. Thus rumours of deadly Israelite crimes were whipped up in 1904 by a Catholic priest in Limerick (leading to attacks on the local Jewish population), while much further to the east the case of Mendel Beilis, a Jewish superintendent at a Kiev brickworks, brought to trial on the charge of ritual murder in 1913, led to an international outcry. It should not be overlooked that many prominent British writers, politicians and churchmen joined in the chorus of protests against the Russian charges.[30]

Various scholars have meticulously documented such ritual murder tales in European history, showing how Jews were accused of using blood for everything from the anointing of rabbis to circumcision rituals, from the prevention of fits to the eradication of bodily odours, from the manufacture of amulets against the evil eye to love potions, from the conception of secret medicines to the fabrication of paints to adorn the bodies of the dead.[31] By the eve of the Reformation, an elaborate Christian folklore on such sorcery had emerged, including reference to the Jewish symbols that could be used to guard against unforeseen dangers. It is not the original medieval and early modern histories of these practices and ideas that primarily concerns us here, however, but rather their exploration, appropriation and 'quotation' in the Victorian period.[32]

The historical literature shows how Jewish physicians were sometimes viewed by gentiles as having unique capabilities, which merited social concessions. The fact of such earlier historical 'toleration' was itself noted afresh by occasional late-Victorian inquirers.[33] Clearly there were often complex and ambivalent attitudes to Jewish healers at European courts. It had at times been possible for doctors to be exempted from the 'disabilities' suffered by the rest of the Jewish people. Thus Alphonse of Poitiers, the brother of Louis IX, 'the most rabidly anti-Jewish prince of the time', pleaded for treatment from a Jew who might restore him his sight. Pope Martin V in 1421 granted Spanish royalty the privilege of employing Jewish physicians. In 1652, the clergy of Frankfurt petitioned the City Council to complain about excessive tolerance in this regard: 'To employ Jewish doctors means nothing else than to cuddle serpents in our bosom.'[34] Any historical inventory of such rhetorical expressions and cultural fantasies would necessarily involve more sustained attention, but certain features do stand out in sharp relief; for instance, the repeated perception of the Jews as effective healers but also as potentially *lethal* magicians.[35]

These old and contradictory images of the Jew – healer and killer – provoked fresh speculation in the 1890s, notably so, for example, in relation to the notorious case of Roderigo Lopez, a Portuguese Jewish physician who had worked at St. Bartholomew's Hospital, treated Queen Elizabeth I, and was hanged at Tyburn in 1594, charged (by Essex) with seeking to poison the monarch in return for a large sum of money paid by the Spanish crown.[36] Accusations of ritual murder had reached their zenith in the fifteenth and sixteenth centuries and were regularly tied to complaints about Jews' seductive ability to worm their way inside. 'The worst of it is that they seduce a great many imprudent and weak persons with their satanic illusions, their fortune-telling, their charms and magic tricks and witcheries, and make them believe that the future can be foretold, that stolen goods and hidden treasures can be recovered, and much else can be revealed.' Thus did Pope Pius V justify his expulsion of the Jews from the Papal States in 1569.[37] The possibility of Jewish magic serving benign healing purposes was canvassed, but this tendency was dwarfed by the far more powerful currents of suspicion about Jewish knowledge and ability.[38]

It would be misleading, however, were the reader left with the impression that the blood and eye myths sketched here were in any way the exclusive preserve of either Jewish tradition or of anti-Semitic invective, whether in the Renaissance, Reformation or modern period. My purpose in briefly outlining these examples is two-fold: first, to trace the degree to which there had *on occasion* been a racial element to the history of perceptions of the evil eye; second, to show how the representations of visual contact which did feature so heavily in the accounts of mesmeric and hypnotic technique in the nineteenth century sometimes carried the trace, at least, of such older views and images. The evil eye is a highly variegated mythology. There is an extensive anthropological and historical literature on the subject, demonstrating common elements between cultures and across centuries, but also important differences in the perceived threat and in the nature of possible remedies. In some cases the gaze of a pictorial image could be viewed as physically dangerous to the beholder; Ernst Gombrich remarks that in the art of Byzantium as well as Ethiopia, evil figures such as Judas are never depicted staring out of pictures lest their evil eye damage the onlooker.[39]

In modern times, belief in the strikingly dangerous physical effects of the evil eye is still apparent in many communities in and beyond Europe. While it would be rare to find doctors declaring (as, for instance, the English physician Thomas Browne did in the seventeenth century) that the rays of the eyes actually carry forth a subtle poison that infects the brain of the object, the fear of such directly material consequences of looking have not necessarily disappeared from peasant communities.[40] The evil eye did not die out with the nineteenth century and injunctions to 'keep the evil eye away' are still common enough in many contexts today, although the belief system, in its blatant and extreme form, has increasingly become confined to remote rural areas or to particular groups especially enclosed by tradition. Before turning to the study of mesmerism, the Italian scholar Clara Gallini produced interesting research on evil-eye beliefs in several Sardinian villages and towns in the early 1970s. She has shown how directly and seriously some of her interviewees took their belief in the violence of the stare as well as in the malevolence of the tongue. In a series of discussions with local people, she recounts how the onlooker was felt to be capable of magically destroying the object. Gallini suggests that the meaning of the murderous gaze is not simply metaphorical but is intended quite literally. Many of her interviewees were convinced of the extraordinary aggression of the eye, its capacity to fire and wound. In this setting, the direction of the glance was perceived as extremely precise, while the range of its effects could be virtually limitless and related to almost any imaginable ill. Whether the evil eye was seen as the responsibility of the person through whom it operates was less clear but, whatever the intention behind it, the evil eye was understood to achieve an actual transformation in the nature of the thing malignly observed. The eye was likened to a cannibalistic force, consuming the target in a sadistic and all-consuming frenzy: 'The evil eye is a type of greed by which one "eats with one's eyes" the person or the thing.'[41]

Analogous assumptions are to be found in Lawrence Di Stasi's *Malocchio* (1981), which turns from the anthropological to the autobiographical, and includes a record of the place of the evil eye in the author's Italo-American childhood. This account describes the rituals of oil, water and prayers which followed when a two-year-old fell ill after becoming the object of the 'admiring' gaze of a visitor. Strangers' praise of children was often followed with a protective family appeal, 'God bless you', lest the guest's blessing was motivated by the evil eye. An appreciative regard was often believed to be the evil eye in disguise, since it was widely recognised that jealousy and envy were never far away when it came to the scrutiny of the neighbour's baby. On the other hand there was a further twist within the legend; the figure of the *jettatore* provided for the possibility of those who, through no apparent fault of their own, damaged the object upon which their gaze fell. Some people were said to be born with eyes that harmed whatever they happened to see, regardless of their intention.[42] The *jettatore* might be a person of special status – for instance, a nobleman or priest. In some more extreme accounts all clergymen were said to be afflicted. Pope Pius IX (1792–1878) was widely regarded as possessing this defect (despite his kindness). In one account, it was claimed that everything he blessed turned into a disaster:

> When he blessed our cause against Austria in 1848, we were winning battle after battle, doing famously. Suddenly everything goes to pieces. The other day he went to Santa Agnese to have a great festival, and down goes the floor in collapse, and the people are all smashed together. Then he visits the column to the Madonna in the Piazza di Spagna, and he blesses it and the workmen, and of course one of the workmen falls from the scaffolding the same day and kills himself. There is nothing so fatal as his blessing.[43]

In other words, the theory of the *jettatore* allowed for the possibility that someone might be the unwitting carrier of a damaging gaze – thus the eye itself, and not the person who possessed it, corrupted or destroyed the object. Conversely, it was often assumed that certain rancorous people sought out the evil eye. Those who were said to desire to possess it were often spinsters or childless wives. But whether the bearer was innocent or guilty of desiring the malevolence of their own look, the destructive effects were clear enough; the eye could provoke sufferings from head to toe, and could equally damage inanimate objects. Babies, pregnant or breast-feeding women and their children, cattle and crops were particularly vulnerable to attack.

It would be fanciful, of course, to argue that the sinister, hypnotising figures at issue in the present study are direct legacies of the evil-eye myth. Certainly I am not aware of material that would imply Du Maurier intended any such link, even though one can demonstrate the topic was, in some sense, 'in circulation' in the 1890s. The evil eye came up for varied discussion, for example, at an international congress on folklore held in London in 1891.[44] Between the world of 'evil eye' and the late-Victorian literature of the dangerous hypnotiser there are obvious differences, not only in the status and function of the representation but also in the very scenario described. Traditionally, the evil eye is most associated with the malign gaze of women occupying specific and often insecure places in their community; such old beliefs were frequently associated with envy of fertility or, even more directly, the fear of a third party's attack on the maternal function; none of which simply 'translates' into the mythology surrounding hypnosis.

Yet it is difficult to read anthropological accounts of the evil eye without some acknowledgement of its imaginative purchase on the literature of Victorian mesmerism and hypnotism. And it is also difficult to think about the dynamics of the evil eye without some reference to the account of prim- itive mental processes elaborated by Freud's follower, Melanie Klein. One of her most crucial concerns, after all, was to explore the nature and effects of envy in the psychic economy, as well as the enormous anxieties it stirs up.[45] Unavailable though such a vocabulary was at the time, of course, it is striking that scholars in the 1890s did relate folk belief in the evil eye and the *jettatore* to envy. Thus an 1890s study of the evil eye in rural Scotland illustrated how envy was perceived to be provoked in villages by a woman's fecundity. The reader is presented with a number of compelling illustrations relating the malign gaze to dairy farming: cows would become sick, butter would not churn and milk would go sour under the impact of the eye; young cattle were particularly at risk. The report's author, Dr Robert Maclagan, argued that the evil eye emerged from age-old features of the human per- sonality. Again, this study was one amongst several from the period, chart- ing the remarkable historical and geographical range of such views.

As these examples suggest, the late nineteenth century witnessed signif- icant European interest in the collation of ocular myths from around the globe – scholarly articles, reviews and specialist studies appeared. Maclagan argued that innate human propensities (for instance, to jealousy and envy), already expressed in ancient tradition and primitive mythology, had combined with Judeo-Christianity's 'Thou shalt not covet' to produce potent conflict and the stuff of legend.[46] According to his account, women, particularly those past child-bearing age, were more likely than men to be ascribed the evil eye. The suspect was generally disliked or under suspicion for some other reason. The possessor of the eye gained no material benefit from the damage done. In so far as it succeeded at all, the evil eye destroyed its object rather than appropriating it on behalf of the onlooker. Maclagan described the complex play of glances made and avoided in some Scottish communities where the belief prevailed. Women who were anxious to avoid a charge of bringing misfortune upon others would avert their eyes. After all, the unlucky recipient of the look might hold the gazer responsible for any subsequent ill-fortune:

> In one village, where twice a week a number of fishermen pass, the women and girls of the village try to keep out of sight of the men on their way to the fishing ground, lest, if by chance a fisher should see one of them and he was unlucky immediately thereafter, he would report to the rest his want of luck and whom he had met, and she would be marked as one of the unlucky.[47]

In many cultures, protective amulets are found against the evil eye. Again, Italy provides many of the best-known examples. The sign of the horn, *il corno*, is a good defence; those anxious that they may have received the look are advised to make the sign of the horn (*mano cornuta*). In one ancient Roman protective device Priapus, the phallic god also known as 'Fascinus', was used. In Latin the word *fascinum* may mean fascination of the evil eye as well as phallus.[48] Interestingly, the sign of the horn was the method of protection used by the great diva Adelina Patti (a singer to whom Du Maurier refers, along with Jenny Lind, in extolling Trilby's supreme virtuosity). Patti was a notorious believer in 'the eye'; on tour in the United States, her hostility to another singer in the touring company, the soprano Etelka Gerster, was intense. Who knows whether such upsets contributed in any way to Gerster's later treatment for hysteria by the illustrious Doctor Charcot. Patti, in any case, apparently held the unfortunate woman responsible for every misfortune, from false notes to Californian earthquakes; Gerster, she believed, had the evil eye. As an American impresario observed in a wry retrospective assessment of the singer:

> 'Gerster' was her first exclamation when she found the earth shaking beneath her at San Francisco . . . Whenever Gerster's name was mentioned . . . Mdme Patti made with her fingers the horn which is supposed to counteract or avert the effect of the evil eye; and once, when the two rivals were staying at the same hotel, Madame Patti, passing in the dark the room occupied by Mdme Gerster, extended her first and fourth fingers in the direction of the supposed sorceress, when she found herself nearly tapping the forehead of Mdme Gerster's husband, Dr Gardini, who, at that moment, was putting his boots out before going to bed . . .[49]

The material presented here clearly contradicts the claim that racial assumptions have necessarily dominated traditional views of the evil eye. It does, however, suggest that Du Maurier's depiction of the special qualities of the gaze reflected wider currents of thought and cultural fantasy in the period, and not merely the vicissitudes of the author's mental life and medical trauma. His contemporaries would not have been surprised by the representation of the Jew's glance as so piercing and intense that it could unsettle the gentile, with or without the latter's conscious knowledge.[50] In the same period, after all, the French anti-Semitic campaigner Edouard Drumont was discomforted by what he perceived to be the expressive, sad, gazelle-like eyes of the Jews; typically, he thought he saw concealed in them a terrible, interminable and fully controlled hatred.[51] In an influential study of the Jews and modern capitalism written in 1911, Werner Sombart, a professor of economics in Berlin, observed not only the 'Chosen People's' extraordinary knowledge of the gentile heart, but their remarkable intellectual penetration of the objects they scrutinised. 'They are able with their keen intellects to probe, as it were, into every pore, and to see the inside of a man as only Röntgen Rays would show him.'[52]

The conventional ascription of enigmatic depths, haunting beauty, even a certain hypnotic quality in the Jewess's eyes has been widely remarked. Nineteenth-century literary descriptions of such captivating eyes were often banal, or at least familiar enough, although more subtle writers tended to disturb rather than merely to reproduce them. The issue became more complex, for instance, when the 'fascination' was shown to emanate as much from the Jewess's self-perception as from the viewer's construction. Here is the American novelist Nathaniel Hawthorne in *The Marble Faun* (1860) describing the eyes of Miriam, who 'had what was usually thought to be a Jewish aspect'. (Miriam's racial origins and social circumstances are shrouded in uncertainty.) They were highly mysterious, 'dark eyes, into which you might look as deeply as your glance would go, and still be conscious of a depth that you had not sounded, though it lay open to the day'. Hawthorne leaves it unclear whether particular 'racial' qualities of appearance are self-evident properties or merely relational, drawing their Jewishness or 'Italianicity', for instance, from affiliation to some other quality. This easily leads to a permanent process of slippage, where each aspect is racialised merely by virtue of its discursive linkage with another 'feature', whose substantial reality is actually in doubt: 'if she were really of Jewish blood, then this was Jewish hair, and a dark glory such as crowns no Christian maiden's head'.[53] In Miriam's case, the mystery of origins

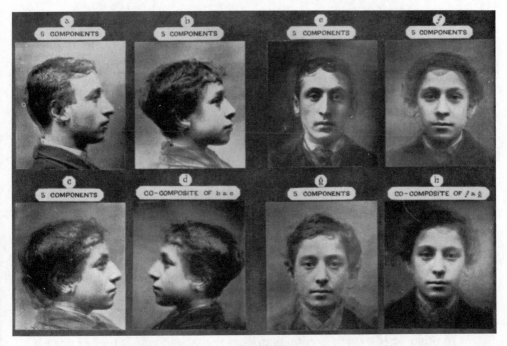

Composite photographs by Francis Galton, published in 1914.

makes all judgements, even as to her appearance, profoundly uncertain. In more commonplace tales and formulations, the notion of the Jews' peculiar eyes (as well as blood, hair, smell and so forth) was expressed more crudely. Yet even within the most crass discussions of the Jewish 'race' in the period, the reader may occasionally detect the writer's unease, or at least a recognition of the uncertain position of the gentile onlooker. Indeed this was often the very point: the Jew unsettled the non-Jewish interlocutor or viewer.

Victorian medicine, psychiatry, biology and anthropology were all strikingly brought to bear in pursuit of fixed racial features.[54] The alleged moral and innate physical differences between Jew and gentile drew attention from grand scientists as well as the most humdrum hacks. Even Darwin viewed the Jews as being of 'uniform appearance', regardless of their geographical location. His cousin, Francis Galton, the inspiration behind the eugenics movement, characteristically took things further. He photographed Jewish people and sought to collate the information in his 'composite photography machine'. He hoped to find the common denominator of appearance within particular social or racial groups. In pursuit of the 'typical

modern Jewish face', Galton remarked the icy gaze he observed in his photographic subjects. In what must rank as one of the most striking of all projections of the Victorian writer's attitude on to his object, he referred to
their 'cold, scanning gaze': 'I felt, rightly or wrongly, that every one of them
was coolly appraising me at market value, without the slightest interest of
any other kind.'[55]

The validity of such generalisations about the nature of Jewish character, bodies and faces was commonly confirmed, as was the thesis of unifor-
mity. According to the French racial theorist Joseph Gobineau, the 'French,
German and Polish Jews – they all look alike. I have had the opportunity
of examining closely one of the last kind. His features and profile clearly
betrayed his origin. His eyes especially were unforgettable.' Jews were 'seen'
to be different, to have, for instance, uniformly swollen, bulging or expres-
sionless eyes.[56] We may recall the late-nineteenth-century French writer on
political affairs Leroy-Beaulieu at this point in the discussion; he, too, was
convinced that the Jew's passion 'flares out only in the fire of his glance'.[57]
In other words, many commentators in the second half of the nineteenth
century argued that there was a distinguishable Jewish 'racial body' as well
as a specifically Jewish eye, revelatory of character and fashioned by a long
history of persecution and ethnic 'aloofness'.

That Jews possessed distinctive eyes, as well as the defining feature of the
'Jewish nose', was a recurrent observation within Victorian fiction. In one of
Thackeray's burlesques, London's Jews have eyes 'black as night'.[58] The motif
had featured with a different gloss in the novels of Benjamin Disraeli. He
dwelt on Sidonia's intelligent yet inscrutable look, and presented Eva with her
'proud eye', rescuing Tancred from captivity in the desert.[59] It was claimed
that careful examination of Jews' eyes revealed the history, tribulations and
deep values of the person. This is Tancred's view of Eva:

> But it was in the eye and its overspreading arch that all the Orient spake,
> and you read at once of the starry vaults of Araby and the splendour of
> Chaldean skies. Dark, brilliant, with pupil of great size and prominent
> from its socket, its expression and effect, notwithstanding the long eye-
> lid of the Desert, would have been those of a terrible fascination, had not
> the depth of the curve in which it reposed softened the spell and modi-
> fied irresistible power by ineffable tenderness.[60]

Both idealising and denigrating reflections on Jews' eyes in fact occur
with such careless frequency as to be part of the common currency of the

Victorian age. In the East End of London one might apparently detect a Jewess with ease, in the last years of the century, merely by staring at her as she met the gaze of the observer: her eyes 'shone with the Hebrew fire which has consumed its own smoke ever since the chosen people became vagabonds on the face of the earth, and her beaked nose was a facsimile of the Hebrew noses which ornament the stone monuments in the British Museum'.[61] In an intriguing novel, *When it was Dark*, published in 1903, the villainous lapsed Jew Schuabe has 'keen detective eyes':

> His features are Semitic, but without a trace of that fullness, and some-times coarseness, which often marks the Jew who has come to the mid-dle period of life. The eyes were large and black, but without animation, in ordinary use-and-wont. They did not light up as he spoke, but yet the expression was not veiled or obscured. They were coldly, terribly *aware*, with something of the sinister and untroubled regard one sees in a rep-tile's eyes.[62]

Schuabe plots to shake Christian confidence in the Resurrection, by plant-ing a false 'ancient' confession of a hoax involving the removal of Christ's body. When news of this is published, moral anarchy erupts around the world. In this fiction the rootless, destructive Jew, dislocated from his own community, finally goes mad, but not before bringing about something close to paranoid psychosis across the globe by successfully robbing Christians of their foundational belief. It so happened that Freud was rather taken by the tale, mentioning it appreciatively in his major study of group psychology after the First World War, although he did not take heed of the prominent anti-Semitic theme running like red thread through the novel, which depicts its villain as conspiratorial, rancorous and possessed of a deep and malign acumen.

It could be argued that the demonic Jew encountered in the illuminat-ing pages of *When it was Dark* and other such stories of the *fin de siècle* were simply heirs to centuries-old fears of Jewish omnipotence and omniscience, metonymically represented by the feature of the eye itself. Numerous twen-tieth-century descriptions, furthermore, remain equally committed to this imaginative terrain, and to the idea that the eye can 'stand in' for the qual-ity of the whole person. Would not the unnaturally compelling and power-ful gaze of the genius or of the madman form part of any modern 'dictionary of received ideas'? Today's charismatic political operators always seem to have – or, at least, are ascribed – captivating and even mesmerising eyes.[63] For many commentators the mystery would seem to reside in the physical body, rather than in psychological and cultural projections. Admittedly it would be glib to dismiss these ocular distinctions as merely cultural fantasies, social stereotypes in the mind of the 'onlooker'. Not all eyes are the same, not all 'looks' have the same quality, but how certain kinds of gaze acquire – or are attributed – hypnotic and special penetrative powers certainly merits critical and historical attention.

Many celebrated and notorious descriptions of the genius and the madman in modern culture and politics routinely draw attention to the eye; the dominating glare of various 'schemers' and 'fixers' is virtually taken for granted. Perhaps Rasputin provides the best-known early twentieth-century example; admirers as well as critics muttered that he could contract and enlarge his pupils at will, as though his orbs were vast lakes in which the onlooker might drown.[64] Charges that Rasputin made direct and malign use of his knowledge of hypnotic techniques were part of the general whispering campaign against him.[65] In modern culture, the charismatic artist is equally likely to be identified as extraordinary through his very eye – most famously perhaps in the case of Picasso and his hypnotising look.[66] Portraits of modern dictators – Hitler, Mussolini and Stalin – all document 'eye-witness' accounts of the tyrants' exceptionally disturbing and entrancing gaze.[67]

The dictatorial eye, special qualities of the voice and other physical or behavioural features that accentuate the hypnotic lure of certain fascist tyrants has often been described by both admirers and critics. Thomas Mann's *Mario and the Magician* (1929), discussed in chapter three, offers a depiction of a sinister hunchback mesmerist eventually murdered by his humiliated subject. Mann's mesmerist, like many of his predecessors, has 'piercing eyes', as well as a number of other flamboyant features. The alluring *and* repugnant stare remains a consistent feature of the portrait of the mesmerist, although *why* this should be the case has never been satisfactorily explained and has remained a source of continuing puzzlement. Freud himself addressed the question, hardly more conclusively, in *Group Psychology*:

> The hypnotist asserts that he is in possession of a mysterious power that robs the subject of his own will; or, which is the same thing, the subject believes it of him. This mysterious power (which is even now often described popularly as 'animal magnetism') must be the same power that is looked upon by primitive people as the source of taboo, the same

that emanates from kings and chieftains and makes it dangerous to approach them (*mana*). The hypnotist, then, is supposed to be in possession of this power; and how does he manifest it? By telling the subject to look him in the eyes; his most typical method of hypnotizing is by his look. But it is precisely the *sight* of the chieftain that is dangerous and unbearable for primitive peoples, just as later that of the Godhead is for mortals. Even Moses had to act as an intermediary between his people and Jehovah, since the people could not support the sight of God; and when he returned from the presence of God his face shone – some of the *mana* had been transferred on to him, just as happens with the intermediary among primitive people.[68]

A link has been suggested in this chapter between certain Victorian representations of hypnotism and the recollection of earlier tropes and myths. At the same time, it is important to keep in mind the novelty of so much of the modern discussion and experience of hypnosis and allied practices, as well as the discontinuities which mark the Victorian literature on anti-Semitism. Indeed, even much older visions of Jewish suffering and endurance acquired, during that era, quite new theoretical elaborations, imaginative twists and scientific rationalisations. These developments will be the subject of the next chapter.

9
The Training of Sorrow

She had elected to be suppressed, through some unfitness, physical or mental or moral, which rendered it inexpedient that she should become a mother of Martians, for they are very particular about that sort of thing in Mars: we shall have to be so here some day, or else we shall degenerate and become extinct; or even worse!

Du Maurier, *The Martian*[1]

'I am too horrified for words at this monstrous horrible sentence against the poor martyr Dreyfus. If only all Europe would express its horror and indignation. I trust there will be a severe retribution.'[2] Queen Victoria's passionate telegraph to her Prime Minister about the martyrdom of Alfred Dreyfus typified the views of significant sectors of the English establishment in the late 1890s. Her feelings were echoed by government ministers and amplified in *The Times*. Dreyfus had become a household name. Hostility to the treatment meted out to this soldier by the French army and state reflected not only a debate about anti-Semitism in Europe, but Victorian criticism of foreign foul play, corruption and breach of the law. In framing a Jew, French officers were perceived to have debased their own code of honour, disregarded proper impartiality and ridden roughshod over the Captain's rights – all of which were seen as symptomatic indications of Gallic arrogance.

No contrast with English institutions could have been clearer, at least in the view of the Queen. France was seen as fatally flawed by its history of absolutism, revolution, Catholicism and demagoguery. In an interesting recent study of the subject, the historian Robert Tombs argues that anti-Dreyfusard voices in Britain came very largely, if not exclusively, from the fringes, rather than from the establishment centre; thus, from disgruntled Catholic Irish commentators on the one hand and some socialists on the other.[3] In addition to distaste for the machinations of foreign governments, a number of commentators in the 1890s cast their critical eyes upon the history of racial intolerance on their own side of the Channel, rejoicing in the contrast between an intolerant past and a generous-hearted present. Critics were divided about the degree to which Shakespeare wronged the Jews through his portrayal of Shylock, but the subject was certainly of some significance at the time, part of a wider cultural interest in cataloguing and debating historical injuries 'against a race who possessed as many virtues and as few vices as the majority of Christians of the time', as an article in the *English Historical Review* tentatively put it in 1894.[4]

The Dreyfus Affair focused attention on the plight of an individual, but also upon other themes such as the nature of crowd psychology and the role of occult forces in public affairs. Mob violence occurred in towns across France, social behaviour which in turn became the focus of considerable intellectual scrutiny. In fact the major French advocate of the theory of suggestion, Hyppolite Bernheim, was himself Jewish and happened to come from Mulhouse, the same town as the family of Captain Dreyfus. Bernheim sought to use scientific and medical knowledge to understand the irrational forces of group behaviour in general, and anti-Semitic passions in particular. It was a period in which French intellectuals, and the very idea of intellectuals, were shaped by 'the Affair'; but it was also a time when individual writers were accused by crowd psychologists such as Gustave Le Bon of descending psychologically to the very same level as 'the mob' from whom they sought to differentiate themselves.

Le Bon was an anti-Dreyfusard, but his ideas were used by a miscellany of intellectuals with varied political sympathies. Participants in the controversy in France were often cast by their critics as mindless mob members. Images of debased Jews, mad beasts and weak-minded women were used (singly or in combination) to characterise the supporters of Dreyfus, while charges of exploiting black arts, low demagoguery, propaganda and even hypnotism proliferated on both sides.[5] In the later 1890s, the question of hypnotism entered still more directly into the Dreyfus Affair. A noted somnambulist, Léonie Leboulanger, made contact with the sister of the prisoner, proclaiming that she *knew* he was innocent; the officer's character and the true nature of events had apparently been revealed to her while she was in a trance. Her testimony was, of course, eminently contestable; Léonie herself was known as a multiple personality, supposedly inhabited by three different personae, each of which would emerge at particular points in the process of her entrancement, and all of whom displayed very different characters and views. She was hardly the most credible of witnesses. Nonetheless various newspapers, seriously or in jest, reported the incident of the '*somnambule fameuse dans le monde des occultistes*' who had so unexpectedly intervened in the crisis, and perhaps shed a new and disturbing light upon the matter.[6] Léonie had a long-standing working relationship with various doctors; she was the pet hypnotic subject of a well-respected physician in Normandy, Joseph Gibert, but was also investigated and studied by a number of others, including the pioneering doctor and psychologist Pierre Janet, the author of *L'Automatisme psychologique* which had appeared in 1889. Not surprisingly, opponents of Dreyfus used the story of this bizarre, multiple-voiced 'witness' with greater alacrity than his defenders. They countered Léonie's testimony, claiming that Jews and liberals were forced to rely on such mystification for lack of more rational grounds, the very argument about irrationalism that the Dreyfusards had made against their enemies.

Such obscure and occult aspects of the saga – as the incident involving Léonie – were, admittedly, sideshows comprising a footnote at most in the major discussions of Dreyfus in the 1890s, both in France and abroad. The alarming mass mobilisations in Paris and other cities, both for and against Dreyfus, were certainly closely watched, regarded by a variety of observers, from Victoria down, as signs of a foreign state in serious crisis. Clearly the social, cultural and intellectual contexts in which anti-Semitic ideas circulated in the two countries were in very many respects as distinct as were their consequences. The bitter divisions provoked by the Dreyfus controversy in France, to say nothing of the virulence of anti-Semitism in the Hapsburg Empire – let alone the social turmoil and hatred that underlay and followed the Russian Pogroms – were all of a different order to any racial debates or conflicts that occurred in Britain during those years. Yet this side of the Channel, there were certainly vociferous anti-Semitic diatribes at the time, as well as quieter, more restrained expressions of racial distaste in the years leading up to the long-drawn-out Dreyfus saga. It is only with regard to the ambivalence of the liberal English intelligentsia both towards the anti-Semitic passions of Continental thinkers *and* towards Jews in general – and East European immigrant Jews in particular – that one can begin to understand the cultural determinants of Du Maurier's portrait of Svengali.

While critical political, cultural and social differences must be acknowledged between England and France, much of the discussion that now follows concerns those more extreme and antagonistic late-Victorian voices that challenged racial tolerance and lamented Jewish assimilation.[7] Before coming to such English commentaries, however, more needs to be said about the clamour surrounding Dreyfus since it was by far the most dramatic, well publicised and politically divisive individual racial tragedy of the 1890s. Parisian commentators who were already writing on the difference between the 'real' French and the 'French' Jews, would not have been surprised by reports, late in 1894, that a Jewish officer (who had been promoted to the General Staff) had passed secrets to the Germans. Few political crimes could have been more heinous. It would be almost impossible, after all, to exaggerate the impact on French opinion of defeat in the Franco-Prussian War (1870), and the extent of anxious national self-examination in subsequent decades. There was an enduring 'German crisis of French thought' and this still gave special significance to the image of a Jew betraying France to that triumphant and increasingly powerful neighbour.[8]

Dreyfus was sent to Devil's Island, but doubts about the basis of his conviction remained. A movement for his release, led by his family and by various sympathisers including the future French leader, Georges Clemenceau, gathered pace. By 1896 discussion of Dreyfus' possible innocence was taking place even in the higher echelons of the French army itself, although it was only in the following year that the intensity of the protests peaked. Zola's famous, corruscatingly critical letter, 'J'accuse', was published in January 1898, the year in which another army officer (having confessed that the evidence used in the case was indeed forged) committed suicide. Dreyfus' sentence was subsequently annulled, but it was only in 1906 that he was formally pardoned.

The florid accounts of conspiracy and treachery that found their fullest expression in the Dreyfus Affair, were part and parcel of anti-Semitic political discussion in late nineteenth-century France. Even without assumptions of direct espionage, it was frequently argued that the Jews had a racially disintegrative effect on the society in which they lived. Disloyalty was to be expected. The case of the Jewish officer had caused a national and international scandal of major proportions, dramatically splitting French opinion. The stakes for the national destiny were viewed on both sides of the argument as immense. For the prominent author and passionate anti-Dreyfusard Maurice Barrès, the Affair was a tragic indication of a general state of collapse in French culture. In his view, France had ceased to be a

Captain Dreyfus being led away to prison, January 1895.

nation (in any organic sense) and had become, in the long wake of the Enlightenment and the French Revolution, merely an abstract and theoretical 'people'. The presence and even prominence of the Jews were symptoms of this sorry condition, the festering abscess on the decaying state.[9] In the shadow of the initial trial and the resulting furore, it was possible for anti-Dreyfusards to conclude that the individual's actual innocence or guilt was entirely secondary to the national predicament. As Tzvetan Todorov, a recent commentator on racial myths, describes the logic of such a position:

> If Dreyfus is proved guilty, the French army will be the stronger for it: that is good for France. If on the contrary Dreyfus is shown to be innocent, that discredits the army and harms the nation. Conclusion: whatever the 'absolute' truth of the matter, *French* justice requires that Dreyfus be condemned. Even if Dreyfus is innocent, the Dreyfusards are necessarily guilty.[10]

It was as though the very presence of such 'aliens' and their defenders ruined society; the Jews' successful entry into society presented the 'true Frenchman' with a maddeningly provocative predicament and a profound sense of impotence. Pro-Dreyfusard protests were themselves viewed as evidence of national disarray, even as an active destruction of French interests: 'Their plot divides and disarms France, and this delights them. Even if their client were innocent, they would remain criminals.' Such arguments presupposed that Dreyfus could not be judged according to 'French' standards, for he belonged to a different race.[11] Rather than a question of human rights, the issue was conceived in the terminology of ethnology, or even zoology. Dreyfus apparently illustrated the behaviour of a different human species, the Jewish species, which Frenchmen did not really have the right to judge: 'We would not pillory him on Devil's Island, but as a living witness, as an object lesson, we would set him up near a chair of comparative ethnology.'[12]

For writers such as Drumont and Barrès, Jews had no choice; they were simply and perpetually different:

> According to this viewpoint, the physical signs of Jewishness are clearly recognisable from a distance. The moral features of the Jews oppose those of the French. Jews are guilty of not blending into the nation, of remaining cosmopolites in every country; for a Jew, being a foreigner is not a transitory state but an essence. Not only are Jews not at home, like Italian or Polish émigrés, but they have no home; they are people without a fatherland – whereas human beings are only what the fatherland makes them; Jews are thus nothing at all.[13]

In some Victorian texts, one can identify similar assumptions to those above, and a similarly shrill tone; in short, expressions very much at odds with those used by the horrified but restrained monarch. Consider Arnold White's diatribes on the subject in the 1880s and 1890s. This polemical commentator on urban and racial affairs expressed in no uncertain terms his concern at the secret agenda of the alien, envious and resilient Jewish people who had been moving into London. He railed against lax immigration policies – his simple call for practical action at the ports emanated logically enough, after all, from the nightmare of race he presented in his writings. White pulled together a range of disturbing images. Britain, it seemed, was faced with an unmanageable human flood, deluged by equivocal outsiders who were conspiratorial, parasitic and degenerate in nature.

He feared the Jews would constitute a kind of tumour, a compact and deadly mass inside the body of the city. Where others dreaded the consequences of racial intermixing, White pointed to Jewish arrogance in refusing to intermarry with gentiles. Their undesirability lay in their very distinctness, their resistance to assimilation. Biological, religious and social perils merged together in his much-discussed but still shocking racial portrait of the age. The Jews had been steeled by a history of suffering, and had thus acquired an evolutionary advantage which could be used against their 'hosts'.[14]

Whereas in earlier times it was above all the Jew as enemy of Christendom, the Jew denying Christ, the son of God, who most powerfully shadowed gentile argument, by the later nineteenth century a quite different preoccupation had become dominant: conscious allegiance was now a far less salient issue than inherited blood, brains, eyes or bones. Such preoccupations with the physical aspects of racial identity were not entirely the invention of the Victorian period. Perhaps, indeed, the sharpness of the contrast between the modern and pre-modern vocabularies of anti-Semitism has sometimes been exaggerated in the process of refuting the argument for mere continuity. But it is surely true that the kind of authority on which such ideas were based did significantly shift away from religious terms of reference and the question of the individual's intent. Biology and materialist psychology increasingly held sway in such discussions.[15] The period witnessed the emergence of new scientific movements committed to racial engineering; the word 'eugenics' itself was coined in 1883 by Galton. While always contested, certainly vigorously so in Britain, and enjoying varying fortunes and histories in different countries, eugenics was taken by its advocates to be relevant to every facet of social policy, and to speak to the urgent crises of the great cities. Debates about the relative worth of the different sections of the resident population came together with anxious prognostications about the implications of 'adding in' so much 'poor' immigrant blood to Victorian or Edwardian society.

London, Paris and other great capitals, declared a growing number of doom-merchants and xenophobes both within and beyond the eugenics movement, could not continue to accept all and sundry from abroad; to do so was to turn the city into the world's sewer. It was not the case that all of those who supported eugenics supported this particular racial cause, neither did they all draw on the same florid vocabulary. Nonetheless, White was by no means alone in making recourse to the imagery of faeces, offal, vermin or rubbish, expressions that gave at least some shape to the profound and inchoate sense of disturbance and bewilderment provoked in him and others by this so-called 'alien invasion'.[16] The stridency of such racial excoriation and condescension betrayed not confident cultural mastery but the most profound underlying anxiety. In this writing, legitimate and widely circulating economic and social concerns about metropolitan poverty, employment and housing were suffused with the most paranoid fantasies and an imagery redolent of an acute state of psychic persecution.

English and French authors such as White or Drumont wrote as men who feared they were fighting a losing battle against such persecutions. Some of these preoccupations were aired by White and others in the evidence given to the Royal Commission on Alien Immigration in Britain, an inquiry which paved the way for the Aliens Act of 1905. Whilst many views inimical to White's were also expressed, the result of such judicious deliberations was a tightening up of the rules for entry into the country, via an attempt to exclude the loosely defined category of 'undesirable aliens'.[17] White had long insisted that the Jews were involved in a global network of conspiracy; they 'maintain a secret and indissoluble bond of common interest', presenting a single front to their enemy, corroding empires from within – especially the British Empire. Judaism itself was a secret worldwide organisation, committed to insidious forms of colonisation. A similar view was expressed by Georges Vacher de Lapouge, a professor from the University of Montpellier. The language of racial inferiority and necessary 'culling' predominated. For Vacher de Lapouge, disaster lay ahead in modern polyglot culture.[18] He denounced 'the Semites' as a serious demographic peril. If one was not careful, he warned in the 1890s, the Jews would do to half of Europe what the British had done to India. What he found so remarkable was that the current 'conquest' of France was being achieved without resistance, and without bloodshed. It was a silent take-over.[19]

Warnings about the risks of British 'toleration' of the Jews were diversely expressed. There were, as mentioned earlier, numerous public ruminations on the implications of the political career of Disraeli. Retrospective assessments, liberal or otherwise, continued to focus on his racial background and peculiarly intense allure. Disraeli was often thought to have played a devious 'Jewish' game, his populist encouragement of imperialism, for instance, reflecting his cynical nature grander conspiratorial ambitions.[20] What Arnold White sought to provide, however, was not only a commentary on foreign affairs but a critique of British 'generosity', for which, in his view, one could just as well substitute the word 'folly'.

Although he formally rejected the antics of late nineteenth-century French and Russian rabble-rousers, he counselled that pogroms and other persecutions might follow here were the present 'crisis' to continue. White diagnosed the Dreyfus Affair as a sign of fundamental racial incompatibility that was as true of Britain as it was of France. This was the important issue, he argued; the Dreyfus case went beyond the question of individual injustice, even though by the time White produced *The Modern Jew* in 1899 it was clear enough to those who really wished to know that the prisoner had been wrongfully charged and that the evidence against him had been forged. Other writers took an equally pessimistic view of the prospects of Jewish loyalty to the nation, although there was no set-piece anti-Semitic event in Britain on the scale of the Dreyfus Affair to crystallise the domestic debate. London society in the mid-1890s was more preoccupied with the *cause célèbre* of the trial of Oscar Wilde.

As anti-Semitic rhetoric and mob actions had gathered pace in European countries during the last quarter of the nineteenth century, some Victorian commentators (and not all of them on the social and political margins) directly applauded draconian government action against the Jews abroad and advocated its application at home. 'The Russians have punched some Hebrew heads irregularly,' Edward A. Freeman had remarked, appreciatively yet flippantly, in the 1880s, before taking up a prestigious chair of modern history at Oxford. Freeman was a major authority on the history of Europe with a particular *penchant* for racial theorising. He excoriated 'the sentimentalists' who denounced the Russian actions: it was all 'jew humbug' (sic). Every nation was entitled to 'wallop' its own unwelcome aliens without outside interference, although his personal preference was simply to 'kick them out'. Admittedly this commentator had similarly murderous inclinations towards other supposedly inferior peoples as well – 'This would be a grand land', he mused, on a lecture tour of the United States in 1881, 'if only every Irishman would kill a negro, and be hanged for it.' The Jews, however, constituted a more chronic preoccupation for Freeman, although he was not invariably to be found so crudely sticking the boot in when he discussed the issue. During his travels to America, he sometimes attempted a more magnanimous tone, even a studied detachment. Indeed, given his capacity for reflex racial invective, what is striking here is his relative restraint. Perhaps perplexed by this 'New World', Freeman refrained from pejorative comment in a letter home in which he noted the presence of synagogues. He expressed perhaps a little surprise but no immediate rancour when he mentioned having dined with a Jew whilst in transit; he appeared equally subdued when he added that he had 'seen another in a train'.[21] But he was not always so fastidiously poe-faced in his intellectual confrontations with that 'race'.

While White, Freeman and many others pontificated, in violent terms, about the world's bloody history and inevitable ruthless struggle, Du Maurier was exploring these stock questions – or rather these questions of 'stock' – in his gentler fictions, and was employing a range of evocative epithets as he pondered inter-racial sexual unions.[22] His less-than-flattering portrayal of a particular 'Negroid-Jew' reflected a common fascination with, and recoil from, such racial hybridity in European theory and fiction that was increasingly evident in numerous texts during the second half of the century.[23] In *Peter Ibbetson*, Jewish and black blood run together to produce the monstrous Colonel Ibbetson, Peter's uncle. The Colonel is clearly Jewish enough to be cast as 'a regular Shylock', one who had ruined Peter's father, but his class position is vague and his 'pedigree' complex. His father is an archdeacon, his mother the heiress of an immensely rich pawnbroker, Mendoza, 'a Portuguese Jew with a dash of coloured blood in his veins besides, it was said'. These inherited traces are manifest in the Colonel himself:

> indeed this remote African strain still showed itself in Uncle Ibbetson's thick lips, wide-open nostrils, and big black eyes with yellow whites – and especially in his long, splay, lark-heeled feet, which gave both himself and the best bootmaker in London a great deal of trouble.
>
> Otherwise, and in spite of his ugly face, he was not without a certain soldier-like air of distinction, being very tall and powerfully built. He wore stays, and an excellent wig, for he was prematurely bald; and he carried his hat on one side, which (in my untutored eyes) made him look very much like a '*swell*', but not quite like a *gentleman*.[24]

Such passing comments in Du Maurier's novels may be seen as very much the ideological products of the age. Increasingly since about 1850, nationhood was being cast in terms of immutable blood and race rather than being a question of moral choice, religious or social affiliation. In Britain's case, the consequences of inter-racial sexual liaisons, let alone marriage, in the Raj or in Africa, had aroused growing concern and hostility.[25] In the later years of the century, various thinkers lamented the 'class struggle' within the European nations on the grounds that such mistakenly warring groups shared a national identity; indeed, membership of the same 'imperial race'. One's nationality, apparently, was inborn rather than made – the idea that one could change one's nationality merely by taking up residence elsewhere was vigorously contested.[26] The 'Diaspora' of Jews thus presented itself as a particular anthropological problem, explored in a plethora of studies, such as *Jewish France, Israel among the Nations, The Modern Jew, England under the Jews* – all titles of significant English and French studies from the *fin-de-siècle* years. Although penned by different authors and with varying styles, they shared certain deep concerns about the corrosive role of the Jews inside the political state, or even the fatal encroachment and seduction of the gentile mind. All these works used the 'natural history' of the Jews – their long 'training of sorrow' – to explain the race's group psychology and destabilising effect. Such books aimed to get beyond the particular features of this or that individual or specific community, in order to speak of the 'Chosen People' at large and of their problematic impact on a wider society.

It is true that these works were not exactly 'original'; they disclosed little but stereotypes, recycled images from the wider racial evolutionary conversations of the period; but nonetheless they are worth highlighting since they exemplify significant currents of thought and provide us with a clue to the racial aspect and cultural purchase of the Svengali myth. While obviously one would turn to different sources for a convincing investigation of the actual social or political circumstances of the Jews a century ago, nonetheless these inquiries are important because of the cultural fantasies and preoccupations they disclose, not least the idea that it was possible to identify some general racial project on the part of the Jews. Moreover, the Jews are perceived to have shared ambitions and longings of a quite contradictory kind. On the one hand, the reader's attention is drawn to the Jews' closed cultural and historical identity, their social and sexual aloofness, their fears of 'blood pollution' *by* gentiles. On the other hand, the Semite's intrusive relationship *with* the gentile is repeatedly lamented in this literature: sexual or emotional invasion, psychological designs and economic interference are all anxiously discussed; racial parasitism and colonising intent are indicted. 'The Yiddishites', to use the term employed by that most incensed of writers, Joseph Banister, apparently took the gentiles by surprise, took them to pieces and laid claim to all that was of value in the victims. Banister's extreme, populist tract, *England Under the Jews* (1901) made the point as starkly as had Drumont, in his notorious late-nineteenth-century work *La France juive*. Drumont spoke of the 'Jewification' of the gentile, and of the racial corrosion of '*la Grande Nation*' itself.

Parasitism was of course a frequent racial charge. Even the vice-president of the Jewish Historical Society of England, Lucien Woolf, went along with some of these stereotypes. In an article on anti-Semitism for the eleventh edition of the *Encyclopaedia Britannica* (1910–11), he expressed the view that urban European Jews who had descended from pastoral Semites were especially prone to engage in 'parasitic activities'.[27] If some commentators held the Jews under suspicion for their sexual abstinence, others, such as Banister, noted that the 'trophy' of the gentile woman was always deeply prized, despite Jewish protestations to the contrary. In *England Under the Jews*, he declared:

It is, of course, denied but is nevertheless true, that no Jew is more of a hero among his fellow tribesmen than the one who can boast of having accomplished the ruin of some friendless unprotected Christian girl.[28]

Diagnoses of the Jews as a 'lecherous breed' (Banister) have a long history and have lived on into more recent culture – the Jews in the twentieth century have often enough been linked with a nightmarish world of sexual violence and moral desecration, cast either as the essential perpetrator *or* the age-old victim of florid sexual crimes. There is a link, I suggest, between the perception of an essential racial 'victimhood' and the attribution of a terrifying power of retribution. Similar arguments have been advanced before in analyses of anti-Semitism, for instance in Jean-Paul Sartre's celebrated book on the subject, *Portrait of the Anti-Semite*, published soon after the Second World War. Sartre remarked on the switch from images of passive endurance to the accusation that the Jews actively instigated their own and other people's suffering. He drew attention to the violent, eroticised perception of the 'beautiful Jewess', hinting at how the object of the fantasy was then understood to violate the mind of the anti-Semite. The very phrase 'beautiful Jewess', he implied, signals and represses certain historical images of violence and trauma. It was observed that Jewish women's rape by Cossacks and others was itself often eroticised in the process of being described.[29] The sexualised aggression and invasiveness in quasi-pornographic accounts is just as often projected on to the Jew, who becomes in turn a deeply threatening violator. Of this propensity, a reviewer of a recent study of T.S. Eliot's anti-Semitism has gone further, describing an 'unconscious – but still present – conception of the Jew in the English collective psyche, as a satyr-like figure of venality and sexual obsession'.[30] In such visions, the Jews seek not so much racial separation as a complete penetration and possession of others. The sexual, the political, the racial and the psychological dimensions of these fears had at times been articulated quite separately in the nineteenth century, but sometimes they also became entangled with one another. Moreover, many of the racial and mesmeric discussions explored above give expression both to a dread *and* to a longing for such 'alien' conquest. It seemed that the Jews could reverse their own pitiable state by transferring humiliation to gentiles. And depictions of the gentile's desire *for* abjection (for instance at the hands of an alien) were, on occasion, understood as a function of a special hereditary vulnerability to hypnotic manipulation.

The Victorian period was the era *par excellence* of racial and evolutionary speculation, so often involving the establishment of clear hierarchies of moral and physical value, and with black-and-white judgements about potential levels of attainment as well. Yet the Jews appeared to strain these theories to breaking point. They were understood to constitute a special case, especially taxing to anthropological theorists, the legion commentators in the human sciences who gloomily manned the look-out towers on behalf of the racial future, increasingly advocating state interference in the patterns of human reproduction, rather than a continuing biological free-for-all. The social meaning of Darwin's seminal work, *The Origin of Species* (1859), was tirelessly debated, while his specific vision of natural selection and fitness was loosely applied (including by the author himself) to individuals, groups and nations. In these terms, were not the Jews 'fit', manifesting in their very endurance as a group, their biological hardiness? And if that argument was accepted, what were the implications for Jewish-gentile relations? These questions were often posed at a physical, demographic *and* psychological level. Svengali's strength (it was explained in the 1890s by a Du Maurier follower) stemmed from his suffering.[31] The Jews apparently were empowered by their history; they had been hardened over centuries, formidably equipped for life's vicious theatre. Part of their armoury, it was claimed, lay in their special capacity to entice and scheme: they were both admired and denounced for their skill in working the system, labouring away, plotting, exploiting the rights they had been granted, entering inside their 'host's' space in more ways than one.

Reading the influential English and French anti-Semitic texts from around the turn of the century one cannot but be struck, amidst the profusion of charges, by this fear of the Jew's capacity to transform weakness into strength – the Jew cast as omniscient and even omnipotent, whether in the psychological, financial, cultural, demographic or political sphere.

Millennia of hardship, it was argued, had given the Jews a mental acuity which was then wielded like a weapon. A broad Lamarckianism was generally at stake in such thinking: it was assumed that environmentally and socially acquired characteristics were simply passed on, bodily and mentally, to the next generation; misery in earlier epochs had bred the very strength of future generations. As White warned in *The Modern Jew*: 'Intellectual superiority, Oriental subtlety, and the training of sorrow accredit the Jews with a complex and mysterious power denied to any other living race.'[32] Armed with these acquired strengths, White's persecuted Jew became a potentially formidable persecutor.[33]

To return to the origins of our story, it may be recalled that Svengali and Trilby had first been offered up by Du Maurier to Henry James, in rudimentary form, in the late 1880s.[34] After the plot was initially recounted to him, James had written a brief outline, describing how a servant girl was to be 'mesmerized and made to sing by a little foreign Jew who has mesmeric power [and] infinite feeling'.[35] The off-hand attribution 'little' sits oddly alongside the rather grandiose hypnotic abilities and psychologically penetrative capacities that the man in question is said to possess over the woman. The character is to have disturbing skills at his disposal and is to play his music into, and through, this intermediary. James' sketch of *Trilby* indicates that differences of rank, gender, racial identity and, presumably, age are all at stake. The prototype mesmerist of James' recollection is decidedly alien, a 'foreign Jew'. There were, as we have seen, those in the period in which James was writing who would have taken that adjective as self-evident since it was frequently argued that Jews were quintessentially foreign and could, indeed, be nothing but foreign. In any land into which they happened to wander, they would remain outsiders. However much 'toleration' or 'emancipation' a 'liberal nineteenth century' had allowed, Jews could not equal, let alone become, gentiles, because they were constituted differently, *as a race*. Similarly sceptical views can be found amongst the various sympathetic accounts of the Jews in this period. Aaron the Jew, the eponymous hero of a novel (from the same year as the book version of *Trilby*, 1894), by the prolific Jewish writer Benjamin Farjeon. He concludes: 'Once a Jew always a Jew, whether he follows the Mosaic laws or disregards them.'[36] (Farjeon was also to be the author of a novel and a play on the theme of mesmeric dangers.) Farjeon's novel both quoted and painfully confirmed the view that to convert to or from Judaism was not really possible.

Whether the Jews were cast as malign because of their propensity to infiltrate others, or because of their refusal to merge, gloomy racial forecasts multiplied. Each possibility had its proponents. Innumerable variations on the metaphors of unfitness, parasitism, vampirism, corrosion and so forth were available for commentators exercised by the danger of racial difference – or racial fusion – in the age of Svengali. Either way, it was said that political and social toleration, as well as the removal of career barriers, had made the task of differentiating the body and mind, in addition to the social practices, of Jews, all the more urgent and important.[37] The word 'Jew' had many connotations in Victorian Britain; sometimes it merged together with a more generalised imagery of a romantic Orient, whether personified as wise or sinisterly threatening.[38] Disraeli himself had played a part in developing certain mystical 'eastern' associations in his novels, notably via the omniscient figure of Sidonia. 'In spite of centuries, of tens of centuries, of degradation,' he declares, 'the Jewish mind exercises a vast influence on the affairs of Europe.'[39] In Victorian racial discussion, Jews and Muslims were sometimes grouped together to form a misty and inscrutable outsider, but at other points Jews were carefully isolated.[40] By the late nineteenth century, it was in any case less the romanticised or reviled vision of the Orient in general which occupied centre stage in political discussions of the Jew in Britain, but rather the implications of the exodus of poor and unassimilated newcomers from Russia. The new arrivals were met with a complex and ambivalent response by the already resident Jewish population, fearful, amongst other things, of an indiscriminate English backlash against all Jews, a major assault on the liberties and possibilities that had been achieved.

In summary, the Jews occupied a particularly complex position within these traditions of intellectual thought and the human sciences. The figure of the wandering Jew, for example, was coming to be understood in a new psychiatric terminology associated most notably with Charcot and his followers. The Jew also occupied a particularly problematic place in racial hierarchies of the period, viewed as literally and metaphorically stateless, neither unequivocally higher nor lower, black nor white, European nor extra-European, thereby complicating or even wrecking the anthropological schemes so fastidiously set out in the Victorian period. The very necessity of exodus for the Jews, as narrated in the Bible, was incorporated into theories of their peculiar biological and psychological constitutions. It was not only Dr Meige at the Salpêtrière Hospital who found the Jews to be classic hysterics, or worse, obsessed with the need to voyage, from country to country and from clinic to clinic.[41] The point was that the significant population movements of Jews in the later decades of the century, precipitated

WHAT'S IN A NAME?

" What a prethuth noothenth it ith! Jutht becauth ma Thirname
happenth to be Abramth, and ma Parenth chrithened me Motheth,
lotth o' People theem to thuthpect I mutht be o' Hebrew ecthtracthion!
Whereath a thwear a haven't got a thingle drop o' Hebrew blood in
all ma veinth, 'thelpme!'"

Cartoon by George
Du Maurier, 1883.

by poverty, pogroms and other persecutions, turned what might otherwise
have been an arcane intellectual debate into an urgent political question.[42]
The movement of Jews into Western European capitals generated intense
preoccupations not only about urban living conditions, housing and jobs
for the metropolitan working classes, but also about the biological future of
the indigenous population. It was a debate about entrapment and take-over
in both the most fantastical *and* the most material of senses. Whether racial
mixing (or 'miscegenation') led to healthy or degenerate stock was keenly
debated during the second half of the century, such discussions drawing on
or challenging the ideas of various significant racial theorists around the
middle of the century who insisted, rather tragically, that the passage of civilisation depended on the very inter-breeding which went on to destroy it.[43]

Perhaps the most dramatic illustration of the unease and malaise provoked by the very idea of the Jews' place in European culture is provided in
the middle of the nineteenth century by Richard Wagner (or 'Blagner' as

Du Maurier facetiously dubbed him later).[44] His vitriolic essay *Judaism in Music*, published without the author's name in 1850, was a kind of landmark, exemplifying particularly clearly how the location and meaning of the Jews in Europe was provoking fevered and desperate forms of theorising, so many rearguard efforts to re-establish the stable racial polarities that the 'advancing' Jews were perceived to have threatened. Wagner sought to analyse the Jews' seductive, enchanting but ultimately superficial relationship to the arts, attempting, as it were, a diagnosis of Svengali, *avant la lettre*. Wagner's account continued to inform debate in later decades. A supplement, added in 1869, revealed his identity and developed further complaints about the ways in which Jews continued to wound and persecute him as well as to embitter his public; there was no recognition of hatred on his side, only the ambition, apparently, of a deep and thorough investigation. It was the Jews who were deemed pitiless. He held them particularly responsible for cruelty to animals as well as to men, a vice stemming from their purely instrumental view of nature. By the 1870s, Wagner came to extend this claim, arguing that the Jews lusted after blood and corpses; he somehow connected such psychological pathologies with the mass extermination of animals in the Paris slaughterhouse as well as the terrible killing of the modern battlefield.[45]

Whilst Judaism continued to haunt Wagner in his later life, he had first written the essay in a vain attempt to identify the problem once and for all, to be done with the Jews; emotionally, racially, artistically, the composer sought to rid himself and modern culture of that impossible 'race'. This involved an attempt to 'understand' the 'involuntary repulsion' which Jews provoked in him. The notion that such 'natural antipathy' on the part of the gentile was merely 'bad manners' had led the 'Hebrews' into disastrous self-deception. Wagner's 'invariable dislike of the Jew' was rationalised via familiar stereotypes. He referred to the money-counter's 'busy fingers', to gold-gatherers and to a whole people marked out by an 'unpleasantly incongruous' appearance. Wagner was convinced that the Jew could not play the role of the gentile without there being a sense of 'the ludicrousness of such a proceeding'. Members of this race were unable to make true artistic pronouncements. Never on the inside of the community, the Jew 'converses in the tongue of the people amongst whom he dwells from age to age, but he does this invariably after the manner of a foreigner.' Such people speak babble, like 'stupid birds' in an 'apish tongue'. They are parrots, muttering in strange ways – hissing, buzzing, grunting, confusedly babbling. Wagner's prose has a torrential quality: venomous clauses tumble over one another, as though there is an insatiable desire to describe every facet of his own distaste. But in that overflow – or 'overkill' – of language he achieves a purpose, implies indeed a determination for accuracy. There is no stopping him till he finds the *mot juste* amidst the general cascade of pejorative terms. Wagner wants to get to the crux of the peculiarity of these people in each sphere of their lives. Jewish music is deemed discordant, 'strange, odd, indifferent, unnatural and distorted'. To listen to these sounds is always to hear the mangling of beauty and truth, like hearing a poem of Goethe recited 'in the Jewish gibberish'.[46]

In his essay, Wagner was countering a diametrically opposed view, on occasion advanced by Jews themselves, which held that they possessed a special or even unique musical genius. Disraeli has Sidonia boast that Jews are the most gifted people in the realm of sound:

> The ear, the voice, the fancy teeming with combinations, the imagination fervent with picture and emotion, that came from the Caucasus and which we have preserved unpolluted, have endowed us with almost the exclusive privilege of music; that science of harmonious sounds which the ancients recognised as most divine, and deified in the person of their most beautiful creation.

Sidonia goes on to speak of the choruses and orchestras of Europe staffed by Jews who have concealed their real names, in order to 'conciliate the dark aversion' of gentiles. It is as though Disraeli himself, rather than just his character, exults in the belief that modern musical performance is dominated by the 'sweet singers of Israel'; when admiring Rossini, Mendelssohn and Meyerbeer, or listening to the voice of a Pasta or a Grisi, the audience are said to be in the presence of the quintessential musical genius of the Jews. In Disraeli/Sidonia's words, 'Almost every great composer, skilled musician, almost every voice that ravishes you with its transporting strains, springs from our tribes.' The confident conclusion: 'musical Europe is ours'.[47] This was evidently quite at odds with the representation to be found in Wagner, or for that matter in Knox's contemporaneous book, *The Races of Men* (1850), where it was argued that the Jew has no ear for music, or any real love of science or literature.[48]

For Wagner, the Jews are parasites and are doomed to that existence in perpetuity; they can never play a part in that crucial 'joint emanation of an ancient community'.[49] The substitution of paper money for primitive gold was the Jews' way of corrupting the modern world.[50] They vitiate and bewitch, fawn and intrude – their degraded values normalised as the moral system of everyday life, just as mere paper money was a kind of legalised counterfeit passed off as the real thing and then adopted by everyone. Wagner noted the strange sleight of hand involved, as paper money became currency, the marker of value, for Jew and gentile alike. He considered the whole money system an elaborate hoax in which the Jews were profoundly implicated. There was no better instance here for Wagner of insidious cultural suggestibility.

Wagner's Jews were seen to corrupt gentiles but to remain, in themselves, stubbornly resistant to infiltration or dilution. Two thousand years of cohabitation within European societies 'have not sufficed to eradicate peculiarities of the Semitic mode of expression, which has defeated all culture through the strange obstinacy of the Jewish nature'. Only in the solemn musical service dedicated to Jehovah, and in the life of the synagogue, can a spiritual source be found. Yet whatever its original purity, Judaism itself has descended into the greatest corruption. It has no inner life. Thus the Jew should return to the fold even though it cannot offer any real sustenance. The Jews' best hope, he says, is to retreat inside their own racial community. In music, the Jews supposedly reveal all the deficiencies of their speech in general: they are cold, passionless, unsentimental, aroused only by selfish interests, namely material profit or personal vanity. Wagner declares that the Jews have been quite unable to grasp the nature of true beauty and thus to be creative in the plastic arts. How, then, did they rise to prominence in music? Answer: usury brought in a fortune which they could exploit in a society that increasingly exalted money. A debased education system was similarly open to abuse. The educated Jew took an 'infinity of trouble to eradicate the more salient signs by which his humble *confrère* is distinguished'. In fact such Jews merely cut themselves off from their race, isolating themselves from their old society without being capable of fully assimilating into a new community. They end 'without friends or sympathy'. The Jews can have a Christian baptism, but they cannot *become* true Christians.

In the chapter on Felix Mendelssohn the tone changes somewhat. Albeit grudgingly, Wagner cannot but feel respect; he finds himself compelled to recognise 'the ripest specific talent' in the man. Yet he detects something lacking, a factor which precludes the possibility of the admittedly remarkable composer joining the hallowed tradition of Bach-Mozart-Beethoven, that chain of 'genuine music heroes'. In Mendelssohn one may be excited by the power of imagination, but one also registers the crippling deficiency, the tragedy of a real talent trapped inside the body and mind of an ignoble race. The Jewish composer *per se* is a peculiarly modern symptom, a function of the 'worm-eaten corpse of the age': 'It is only when the inner death of a body becomes apparent that exterior elements have the power to seize upon it; though only to destroy it. Then it is, that, maybe, the flesh of this body is transformed into a mass of swarming worm-life; but, at sight of that, who would dare assert that the body still lives?'[51] A highly gifted poetical Jew such as Heinrich Heine only triumphs in an age of cynicism, such as the nineteenth century, when true poetising has become a lie.

Some commentators speculated that Wagner wanted to repudiate once and for all the Jewish blood he feared ran through his own body. Certainly this could be linked with the idea that the Germans needed to eliminate not only the Jew 'without' but also the Jewishness which, so it was intuited, had penetrated the German soul. Nietzsche for one suspected Wagner's racial identify was less than pure. It was mooted that Wagner's railings against the 'outsider race' were really a desperate attempt to reject the qualities he dreaded were his own.[52] In pamphlets such as *Was Richard Wagner a Jew?*, written by O.G. Sonneck and published in 1912, and indeed in the introduction to the English translation of Wagner's essay, Nietzsche's 'accusation' was debated. Was Wagner a gentile? Was he a true German? Had he really descended from a Jew named Geyer? If that was the truth, how were these antecedents disguised? Did he know it when he wrote his diatribe? And if so, as Sonneck asks, 'is it conceivable that Wagner in that case would have had the audacity to launch on the public over his own signature, an enlarged and in its additional matter equally anti-Semitic edition of "Das Judenthum in der Musik" in 1869?' The matter was then summarily dismissed as too ridiculous for words: 'However such speculations, too, would be sheer waste of time in view of the fact that Wagner is not known to have ever entertained the slightest doubt of his Christian, or rather, German origin.' We know the great composer was a gentile in so far as we can ever know anything genealogical for sure, concluded this obscure contributor to a Music Teacher's Association discussion of 1911. Yet we can never be quite certain, since gentile paternity, like all paternity, is shrouded in doubt. 'To conclude the analysis of this phase of the matter, it is of course possible that Wagner was not Friedrich Wagner's son, just as it is possible that none of us is the child of the man whose name we bear, but among decent-minded, level-headed, and unprejudiced folk such theoretical possibilities do not count for practical purposes. The probability that we are the sons of our legal fathers amounts for us to a certainty, unless absolute proof to the contrary be produced.'[53]

Wagner had taken some pains to show how the Jews had effectively intruded into the 'host culture'; they were seen to have succeeded in vitiating morality, art and spiritual values. 'An alien Jewishness has pushed itself . . . into the German literary world', as Wagner's friend, the playwright Heinrich Laube, put it.[54] This idea of triumphant Jewish 'entry' into the gentile's valued institutions was commonplace. Take another notorious vision of the image of the burrowing alien from a different political radical in this period:

> [The Jews have] one foot in the bank and the other in the Socialist movement, and with their posterior planted on the German daily press – they have got hold of all the newspapers – and you can imagine what a nauseating literature results from all this. Now the whole Jewish world – which constitutes one exploiting sect, one people of leeches, one single devouring parasite closely and intimately bound together not only across national boundaries, but also across all divergence of political opinion – this Jewish world today stands in large part at the disposal of Marx on the one hand, and of Rothschild on the other.[55]

Thus did the anarchist Bakunin denounce Marx's 'furious synagogue' as only one aspect of the problem of the Jewish conspiracy. Marx's rival Pierre Proudhon argued in similar terms, most unguardedly of all in his private notebooks. It was the natural state of the Jews, he claimed, to live dispersed amongst others, as bloodsuckers. The Jews were anti-social, obstinate and evil, but they dissimulated. Their fanaticism had fed through into the fanatical wings of Christianity. 'I hate that nation', Proudhon insisted. He wanted to abolish the synagogues, forbid the Jews employment, destroy their cult, expel them to Jerusalem (except for those married to true French folk) and even, in his most chilling formulation, exterminate this people who constituted an enemy to human kind.[56] Proudhon railed against Jewish secret spies disseminated in the host culture, against those evil, irascible, envious, bitter beings (from the Rothschilds to Marx) 'who hate us'. This is his conclusion: 'By fire or fusion or by expulsion the Jews must disappear . . . What the peoples of the middle ages hated by instinct I hate upon reflection and irrevocably.'[57]

Although nobody was able to halt his progress at the frontiers of France or England, Svengali himself was described as an intrusive wanderer and dangerous alien. He bore witness to the fear of an unwelcome foreign 'descent' and involuntary embrace. But this depiction of the invasive Jew gave expression not only to hostility, but also to a kind of fascination. In the localised case of Svengali, and in the phenomenon of mesmerism in general, one repeatedly encounters this ambiguous 'structure of feeling': commentators simultaneously frightened *and* excited their readers with reports about worlds of helpless desire, enchantment and horror in the hands of such lowly trance merchants. In *The Bells* (discussed in chapter seven), the Jew figured both as a victim and as a persecuting 'superego', or, at least, as a reproaching ghost. In a slightly different form, this was the view of Leroy-Beaulieu in his curiously double-edged attack on conventional anti-Semitism in the 1890s, *Israel among the Nations*. Here the Jews are seen to have become strong (and fearsome) through triumph over adversity. Long ages of suffering had made them ever sharper, more calculating and penetrating. 'Every race develops a code of morals that accords with the conditions of its existence.' The Israelite mind has become a precise and formidable instrument to wield against gentiles. Through the necessity of ancestral calculation, through the 'natural selection' of forbears who could cope with adversity (from sharp-eyed money-changers to wise rabbis), the modern Jew is judged to be the beneficiary of the very obstacles placed in front of earlier generations. Members of the race possess talents, a special shrewdness, imparted by their less fortunate ancestors. The Jew instinctively knows how to take the measure of the gentile, to assess accurately men of all ranks, in all states of emotion or fortune: 'for centuries he was able to gauge them at leisure: were they not all clients of Israel?'

Mocked and attacked, the 'little' Jew has to be permanently 'on guard', for 'the Jews bear not in their bodies only, but in their souls, traces of the cruelties to which they were subjected for fifteen centuries'. Despite or, indeed, because of the ruin of his body, the Jew's mind is exceptionally acute. His 'superiority' lies not in some Greek balance of body and soul, but precisely in mental triumph over an enfeebled frame: 'No other race has so often proved the fallacy of the *mens sana in corpore sano*.' The Jews are less carnal than gentiles, less gross in their appetites. Vigilance and suspicion have become second nature. The Jews can acclimatise easily in each and every environment, even though deep down their nature is unchanging. Leroy-Beaulieu again:

There is in every Jew a secret power of metamorphosis which has often amazed me. He is able to undergo any transformation while scarcely ever losing the impress of his race, just as he preserves on his body the mark of his religion. He has the remarkable faculty of new skin, without at bottom ceasing to be a Jew. He is thus the man who modifies himself most, and yet changes least. In this respect he is perhaps unique. There is something Protean in him. The ease with which he transforms himself borders on the miraculous.[58]

The historian who has written most prolifically about *fin-de-siècle* anti-Semitism in recent years, Sander Gilman, has drawn on such remarks as those of Leroy-Beaulieu to explore the exotic and idealising aspects of the racial repertoire as well as the denigration of the Jew's body and mind. Gilman is alert to the ways in which acclamation and damnation may converge in the end. In a recent study, *Smart Jews*, he concentrates not on sexual or bodily myths, but on intelligence. He is as suspicious of the intellectual 'praise' showered collectively on the Jews by gentiles (or by Jews themselves) as of the opposite. The notion of the superior intelligence of the 'chosen people' is a myth the origins of which can be located firmly in the age of biological racism that also generated so many accounts of racial deficiency and idiocy. Just as much as any overtly pejorative labelling, assumptions of unusual Semitic intelligence characteristically take for granted the very category of 'race' which many population geneticists as well as historians would now seek to question. Attempts to discriminate the vices and virtues of different 'types' of Jews are equally to be dismissed. Gilman claims that arguments for the intellectual superiority of Ashkenasi Jews over Sephardi Jews can be linked with antiquated claims that races improved the further north or east (within limits) the ethnographer happened to cast his eye.

Gilman's striking arguments and copious illustrative material have effectively alerted us to the *historical* construction of the 'Jew's body' or the 'Jew's mind', although there are some limitations to the binary model of 'otherness' which so often informs this kind of approach. Gilman characteristically argues, for instance, that the category of the Jew has been used in anti-Semitism to define what the Aryan was not. He draws attention to how a model of negation has operated in racial thought – variants of the category known as 'Jew' made to contain the projected anxieties of the 'non-Jew', while the latter is made safe and secure. The implication is often that such cultural tendencies to 'splitting' have successfully pulled the categories of Jew and gentile apart, effectively providing the desired defence. Having shown, for instance, how an idea of the Aryan has been constructed, and how the reviled Jewishness has been evacuated, Gilman writes that '[t]here was no need to "protect" aspects of this [Aryan] image because no necessary link remained between the Jew and the Aryan like the one between the male and the female'.[59] Certainly anti-Semitic writing often seeks to sort out that psychological and conceptual mess once and for all. Dreams of a regenerated and undivided psyche at home in a purified milieu link much of such literature. Yet so also does the lament that the 'Jewification' of the gentile is irreversible and therefore the hope of social separation is doomed to failure.

There has been considerable interest within recent literary criticism as well as social theory in further exploring and refining the historical depiction that Gilman and others have so usefully and tellingly established. In short, it is important to recognise that the Jew often represents not so much an absolute opposite as the breakdown of a logic of opposition and hierarchy. It is not the case that such an argument is entirely new in the historiography of anti-Semitism, but it has been put with a particular force in recent years. The sociologist Zygmunt Bauman, for example, has argued not only that the Jews have been constituted as foreign to the European 'host culture', but have also been viewed as undermining the clear definition of gentile culture and identity as such: '[The Jew] stands for the treacherousness of friends, for the cunning disguise of the enemies, for fallibility of order, vulnerability of the inside.'[60] Jews and gypsies, Bauman suggests, those quintessential non-national nations, provide a reminder of the relativity of *all* nationhood.[61] The Jew is 'strangerhood incarnated', as he puts it, and yet resides problematically *within* the host culture. A much older saying, perhaps first to be found in later Roman literature but more definitely in medieval commentary, put the point as follows: 'No enemy of the Christian faith is closer and more unavoidable to us than a Jew.'[62]

Other cultural commentators have advanced related arguments to Bauman's. Thus in some suggestive remarks on the logic of anti-Semitism within the thought world of the Nazis, the cultural theorist Slavoj Zizek explores the distinctiveness of the perception of the Jews. He also develops this argument, viewing the Jews as not just another stigmatised and reviled group, but as a racial entity that threatens the conceptual system itself:

In Nazi ideology, all human races form a hierarchical harmonious Whole (the 'destiny' of the Aryans at the top is to rule, while the Blacks, Chinese and others have to serve) – all races *except the Jews*: they have no proper place: their very 'identity' is a fake, it consists in trespassing frontiers, in introducing unrest, antagonism, in destabilising the social fabric. As such, Jews plot with other races and prevent them from putting up with their proper place — they function as a hidden Master aiming at a world domination: they are a counter-image of the Aryans themselves, a kind of negative, perverted double; this is why they must be exterminated, while other races have only to be forced to occupy their proper place.[63]

This is not the place to follow all the twists and turns of these discussions, or to multiply examples of this kind of theoretical approach to the question, by now very common in the secondary literature. But it is important to stress one or two features that are particularly salient in the present context. In the first instance, as Zizek remarks, we can see 'the Jew' as loaded with particularly paradoxical symbolic meanings. Complicated and perhaps irresolvable social, cultural and economic antagonisms came to be located in the compelling imagery of Jewish exploitation. A whole range of contrasting features converge in 'the Jews' : they are seen to be voluptuous *and* impotent, dirty *and* fastidious, rich and ever anxious about their poverty, all powerful and yet constantly in search of power, blind but sharp-eyed, and so on. Zizek then points out that this preliminary explanation fails to address the obsessional nature and the 'fascinating force' of the Jew within the history of racial constructions. (It is this 'fascinating force' that found perhaps its most scintillating Victorian embodiment in Svengali. Not just the Jew as symbol of obscure longings and desires, but as the figure who realises an omnipotent dream, moulding the object just as he wills).

In anti-Semitism, Jews become a receptacle for all those qualities it is comfortable to disown (avarice, lust, egotism, and so on). In turn the Jew is understood to interfere with the gentile, to strip the object of meaning, to fill her with his own fantasies and emotions. In such representation, Zizek implies, Jews serve as a kind of 'lightning conductor' for unwanted parts of the self and for uncontainable social forces. But they also present a category problem — not clearly pertaining to one race or place, neither black nor white, European nor non-European. And if they do not have a clear place, perhaps their homelessness is itself their defining feature. Jews become the emblem of the unrealisable nature of the idealised, unified human group, of the unachievable idyll of a fully harmonious social order. They even bear witness, in Zizek's provocative formulation, to 'the structural impossibility of "society"'.[64] They are made the depository of what would otherwise be recognised as disintegrative forces within 'the community'. The psychic projection of such disintegrative powers into the Jew enables various utopian political philosophies to take into account the inevitable failure of their own project since, it is argued, Jews can both be localised as a category, yet are also seen to have spread everywhere already and to be quite uncontainable. The internal negativity of society itself is channelled into the Jew. But this channelling can never fully succeed; indeed the Jew looms larger and larger, in anti-Semitic thought, like some mirror-image of the megalomania apparent in its own discourse.

10
Night at
the Opera

" ' ET MAINTENANT DORS, MA MIGNONNE ! ' "

Some one came into the empty box, and stood for a moment in front, gazing at the house. A tall man, deathly pale, with long black hair and a beard.

It was Svengali.

He caught sight of Taffy and met his eyes, and Taffy said: 'Good God! Look! look!'

Then Little Billee and the Laird got up and looked.

And Svengali for a moment glared at them. And the expression of his face was so terrible with wonder, rage, and fear that they were quite appalled – and then he sat down, still glaring at Taffy, the whites of his eyes showing at the top and his teeth bared in a spasmodic grin of hate.

Du Maurier, *Trilby*[1]

Svengali and Trilby were knockabout characters of melodrama, who encapsulated in an accessible form some of the expectations and preoccupations aroused by scientific theories and cultural ideas that were 'in the air' in Europe through the 1880s and 1890s. Du Maurier pondered unexplained mysteries of the material and immaterial world; yet he assumed no specialised technical knowledge on the part of his readers. Where Freud was caught up in an elaborate and erudite dialogue with medico-psychiatry, the human sciences and the classics of world literature, Du Maurier was steeped in Victorian sentimental yarns and filled his stories with references to the period's best known showmen, musicians and celebrities. In focusing on hypnosis, Du Maurier both reflected and helped to shape public anxieties; he highlighted a theme that was absolutely central to medical, psychiatric and criminological debates, and to emerging critiques of mass culture in the 1890s.[2]

Trepidation about the power and abuse of hypnosis may be understandable and even sometimes justifiable, then as now; but when the underlying apprehensions become petrified into 'Svengalian' form something more interesting and ominous is at stake. A central purpose of the preceding chapters has been to identify and explain Svengali's mesmerism in historical terms, tracing the tangled lines of racial and psychological thought that lay behind his representation. Admittedly, this book has also devoted space to literary gossip, ephemeral quarrels and the delightful absurdities of a craze that could result in so many 'spin-off' products, marketed above all across the Atlantic: from Trilby hams to hats. But to explore the 'smoke and mirrors' involved in the saga and its cultural reception at the *fin de siècle* is not merely to indulge in some antiquarian tour. The particular kind of English cultural whimsicality at stake here is worth taking more seriously in its own right, precisely because its more paranoid motifs are so much less noted or discussed than the gross hatreds that marked the outright racial invective of the day. While the most shrill political anti-Semitism may have been more prevalent in St. Petersburg, Vienna or Paris than London, some of the same underlying passions were assimilated and reflected in this more 'innocuous' popular form. The insistent frivolity of this bohemian story of the parasitic mesmerist should not conceal the importance of the underlying representation.

Even without the nasty racial edge that the caricature once had, contemporary use of the Svengali image may be as much a way of evading as providing explanation of unconscious processes. Myths can serve both to familiarise and explain away what is puzzling. The myth of Svengali encodes a specific *kind* of malign alliance and establishes a clear division of roles between the participants: active/passive, corrupter/corrupted, hypnotiser/hypnotised. 'Svengali' implies a destabilising and obscure psychological intervention whilst paradoxically confirming a fixed, highly stylised scenario of 'alien' conquest.

If Du Maurier's Svengali was an unmistakable product of the late-Victorian years, he cannot fully be explained within that time frame, remaining, over a century later, the name *par excellence* for the entrancing and maverick manipulator. Whilst focusing on the nineteenth century, I have tried also to evoke something of Svengali's afterlife. Perhaps there is no definitive composite portrait that can be drawn from the hundreds of Svengali figures who have been depicted in modern journalism, pictures, doggerel verse, stories and films. Nonetheless, even if there are numerous variations on the theme, certain features are generally assumed, if rarely quite spelled out when the term is casually used. Motivated by malice, ambition or lust, possessed of a sinister knowledge, Svengalis are often shown directing the hapless main actor on the public stage. Since the Svengali cannot be the king or queen, he will do the next best thing and mastermind the actions of the token political leader or soloist, and even seek to orchestrate the ensuing popular applause. Svengali still slips easily into the conversation of political pundits for whom spin, hype and gullibility are the terms of reference for understanding the real machinations of power. It is tempting to see something essentially *fin de siècle* about the assumptions of moral and psychological enfeeblement that often accompany these accounts at the millennium. Yet the contexts are surely fundamentally different and historians rightly warn against facile equations of one turn of the century with another. A recent compendium on 'how centuries end' showed how little rather than how much really united the cultural preoccupations of 'the nineties' in the last seven centuries.[3]

A century ago, critics frequently insisted that moral depravity and suggestibility reflected biological degeneracy and argued that this condition was widespread amongst modern artists and philosophers. An elaborate 'scientific' ensemble of ideas on race and heredity was deemed relevant, indeed indispensable, to the discussion. Creative writers constantly engaged with the terms of these prevalent medico-psychiatric pronouncements on degeneration (althoug more cautious practitioners might wince at the generalities being banded about by such popularisers of science as Max Nordau). The stories of Du Maurier, to say nothing of Maupassant, Huysmans, Zola or Conrad, the paintings of Ensor, the dramas of Ibsen, the philosophy of William James and Nietzsche, are frequently unintelligible without some awareness of these powerful and intensely contested concerns.

Mainstream newspaper pundits today may well still lament the debasement of traditional social values, the undermining of solid relationships, the corrosion of authentic beliefs (often seen as the precious patrimony of the Victorian period), yet the specific racial and medico-psychiatric language of the 1890s has largely withered away. Certainly, 'automatism' is still a frequent talking point, and the politicians, with their false grins, shameless lies and synthetic catchphrases, are viewed as symptomatic of a much more extensive malaise. Some of our contemporary social anxieties about psychological influence and mass 'automatism' contain, no doubt, a kernel of imagery and theory from that past. While the 1890s knew nothing of

'spin doctors', there was no shortage of hand-wringing about the prominent hypnotists and backstage fixers who really shaped decisions while fostering the democratic illusions of the public. The fear of 'demos' is, of
course, much older still, but the 1890s was the decade in which crowd science and elite theory came of age, and such questions were posed with
unmistakable urgency.

Hypnosis itself is still fashionable today both as public spectacle and as
a form of therapy. Celebrated hypnotists appear on TV, the trance-inducer
once again in the starring role, not entirely unlike the dubious stars whose
names were cited in amazement or alarm in newspapers of the late nineteenth century. Meanwhile punters 'under the influence' are encouraged to
turn themselves into clowns for the cameras. Such triumphs of bedazzle-
ment are questioned as well as publicised now and then in front-page
reports relating to various ugly court cases – members of the public out
for damages, claiming to have suffered irrecoverably from the hypnotist's
disgusting 'entertainment' – again echoing certain notorious forensic
debates and legal polemics of the last century. Lawyers are in evidence as
well, even claiming that unfortunate participants have been driven to madness by the charismatic mind magicians on stage.[4]

But it is perhaps in the sphere of psychotherapy rather than hypnosis
that current anxieties about suggestibility are now played out. A febrile air
of crisis now surrounds the entire subject. Brash headlines and florid articles in recent years have insisted that pliant patients have invented memories – or retracted them – for no other reason than to please their
healers. It is the latter, apparently, who are the real 'movers and shakers' of
such concocted sexual tales; the armchair confessor is no longer the listener
or interpreter but the veiled author of the entire affair. If not reducible to
simple manipulator and stooge, the therapeutic duo are represented in a
kind of enchanted dance, or a *crime à deux*, spinning fantasies into histories, stories into events.

Pundits often place psychoanalysis in the dock, lumping it together
indiscriminately with other twentieth-century 'cults' and 'fads'; it is castigated for having set such therapeutic excesses going in the first place
(influencing to ill effect even those practitioners who have nothing to do
with its specific 'talking cure'). Psychoanalysis is painted by its critics as a
historical monolith, entirely unreconstructed since its inception, as though
Freud *was* Svengali and the entire movement his helpless Trilby. Freud
himself is said never really to have abandoned hypnosis, despite his own
best (or worst) endeavours. And if he wasn't actually setting modern

Svengalidom in train, maybe Freud was just another old mountebank, dressed up in bourgeois Viennese clothing. If psychoanalysis was formally an invention of the 1890s, it is also sometimes viewed as but an elaborate footnote to the 'animal magnetism' that Mesmer had brought to public attention in Vienna a century before Freud.

The predicament, real or imagined, of the gullible client influenced by the devious 'Svengalian' therapist persists as a stock talking point in much current media conversation of the 'healing arts'. Of course, manipulation, suggestion and interference may well operate in fact, rather than just in paranoid cultural fantasies. It is right to challenge misguided zeal (and worse) within the therapeutic professions. The damage that can be caused by such interactions, where the practitioner becomes the collusive 'part-ner', inattentive to the transference and counter-transference forces oper-ating in the room with the patient, demand severe scrutiny and challenge. The cajoling and insinuations of therapists *parti pris* on the matter, say, of sexual abuse have been compellingly chronicled in a number of recent books, such as Mark Prendergast's controversial exposé, *Victims of Memory* (1996), although the accusation of indoctrination (while no doubt some-times merited) can too easily be used to deny the desires, fantasies and active role of patients; it is what patients do with the set experience and with the figure of their analyst that is necessarily a central object of exploration, and which forms the most direct and therapeutically mutative evidence in psychoanalysis. But many polemical studies often imply, simply, the impo-sition of a singular and malign Freudian intent, a dangerous assault rou-tinely carried out upon a supine object.

It remains extremely difficult to sort out how far direct experience, his-torical stereotype and cultural hype inform the cases of abusive 'ventrilo-quism' – false memories or forgettings – regularly reported. A recent influential critique of such wrongs is symptomatically entitled *Making Monsters*, while a heading in Prendergast's account warns of 'FREUD'S MENTAL EXTRACTIONS'.[5] Freud is accused of 'grandiose conceit', in either planting the seeds for the 'current epidemic of incest accusations', or denying altogether the truth of sexual abuse, with putatively devastating effects on his patients and the culture at large.[6] Until recently, it is claimed, everyone fell for such 'Freudian stories' hook, line and sinker: 'Freud's pro-nouncements have been treated almost as holy psychological writ.'[7] The whole painful subject of sexual abuse, memory and false memory raises a host of complex ethical, technical, theoretical and legal issues, but it may be noted here that cultural fantasies of a 'Svengali-like' figure play at least some part in mystifying conceptions of the patient-doctor interplay, and particularly in images of psychoanalysis, to this day. Serious cases of manipulation and bad faith there undoubtedly are, but we are surely also in the presence of an unhelpful stereotype as well – a formula that is used to make the complex simple, and the plural singular. In place of the emblematic 1890s Svengali who sought to make the subject forget herself and become his mouthpiece, one encounters a kind of template in which the malign latter-day Svengali makes the patient 'remember' a story that never occurred. War often breaks out between commentators predisposed to view such stories as generally true and those who are deeply suspicious of the motives of therapists or analysts *per se*, and of the very fact that they 'dredge up the past'. Yet while sometimes the actual outlines of terrible events in a childhood can be reconstructed (in a manner that would satisfy, say, the requirements of the courts), analysts and patients may very often have to face the fact that the external record of 'what precisely happened' can never be known for sure. The extent to which psychoanalysis should set out to reconstruct, in forensic manner, the definitive truth of the past has anyway been the subject of much debate and change within the field; yet generalised and reductive denunciations of the old analytical 'fixations' with abuse, or its blanket denial, remain the order of the day.

Turning to a newspaper, on the day I write this, I find the columnist Julie Burchill denouncing the 'criminally irresponsible psychotherapy racket' and laying the blame for 'the culture of complaint' and 'the repulsive habit of self-analysis' at Freud's door; a somewhat orthodox view, perhaps, for so sparkling an iconoclast.[8] As the psychotherapist Susie Orbach complained in the same paper, in a series entitled 'shrink wrap', ill-informed and hostile descriptions routinely 'depict silver-tongued Svengalis enticing the vulnerable, acting as advisers, using them as mouthpieces for their own ideas'.[9] She points to the way in which a scenario involving demonic practitioners has as its corollary the image of helpless, beguiled patients. Such a representation, she argues, has been given free rein in our culture, while there is usually a dearth of proper information and balanced judgement in the media about the actual services available, and the complex ideas, controversies and models out of which they have developed. 'Svengali' persists in such public discourse as a usefully misleading expression for what are actually diverse practices and traditions, beautifully telescoping complex and often contradictory group psychological processes into the clear-cut lines of an old melodrama.

The Svengali of everyday conversation is a forceful puppet master, cast in numerous contemporary accounts of political machinations, as the 'subject supposed to know'.[10] His uncanny powers were, of course, evoked by Du Maurier himself in the original story. And yet, as the final instalments of *Trilby* appeared in 1894, it was clear that the mesmerist was not going to get the last laugh. The moral of the story was much discussed at the time. For some Victorian sentimentalists, it was simply a charming 'fairy tale', in which 'a beautiful loveable nature [is] brought finally to an end which forces tears to the eyes of conscience'.[11] It has been argued here, however, that the tale's meanings and morals were rather more diverse and culturally significant than that. The specific hypnotic encounter of Svengali and Trilby was the dazzling culmination of older mesmeric excitements and dreads, as well as of racial fear and fascination. He exemplified that 'Jewish' confusion of categories, his bizarre magnetism causing his object to be attracted and repelled all at once, even attracted *by* repulsion. Through hypnosis, Svengali was shown to make the subject feel his own state of helplessness; he forces his target to incorporate his helpless ego within herself. The woman became a mouthpiece, the vehicle of his 'Jewish' desperation and his dreams of unhampered liberty and greatness. In some versions of the tale in the 1890s, Svengali's powers were seen as illusory (a feature of his ludicrous vanity), in others as effective, producing an observable change in the nature of the object.

Quite how Du Maurier arrived at his astonishingly successful hypnotic formula – or even the name Svengali – remains unclear. It is always to some extent, of course, a mystery how subjects settle upon their authors, or for that matter how historical topics crystallise for their researchers. Storytellers and readers have found many ways to render the blind spots of personal curiosity, the enigmas of composition or the puzzle of how one 'happens' upon a plot. In Du Maurier's own case, there were some heated discussions about the creative origins of his protagonists during his lifetime; even angry debates about what he had borrowed or plagiarised from earlier writers. The tale directly alluded to the work of others and made reference to previous work. Not the least important was the fact that the name (if not the character) of Trilby existed in a much earlier poem by the Frenchman Nodier and that the phrase 'Little Billee' had been coined by Thackeray.[12] Such precedents were used by at least one fly-by-night theatre company in America to deny that the story belonged to Du Maurier at all, and therefore that *Harper's New Monthly Magazine* had any legal right to demand payments. The author was awkwardly positioned: sometimes in the role of the plaintiff, at other points, the accused – although he and his work were never actually put in the dock, despite Whistler's embarrassing threat to bring an action. Du Maurier left it to his publishers to defuse that particular crisis, as well as to protect his legal rights against the burgeoning crowd of imitators and unlicensed entrepreneurs.

Such matters went beyond laws of copyright (important though that issue was at the time),[13] entering into the extensive public commentary surrounding the story – so many questions about the imponderable 'borrowings' of art. If Du Maurier's 'inspiration' evidently had its deeply personal sources, it was also an amalgam of wider cultural fantasies and existing narratives. Beyond the explicit literary allusions and the openly discussed 'poisoning' personal experiences about which we know from the author and his friends (for instance, the threat of losing his sight, or the disturbing mesmeric experiments he conducted with the man he dubbed 'Mephistopheles') lay a less penetrable web of memories, readings, associations and ideas that evidently informed Du Maurier's invention. In interviews and writings, the author offered only the most oblique pointers to how his life-long interest in the occult related to what he termed the 'realistic dreaming' of his childhood.[14] We cannot second guess the promptings of his unrecorded dreams, still less pursue further a 'wild analysis' of his unconscious motives; rather the aim has been to set out the available intellectual, cultural and political ingredients from which he concocted so idiosyncratic and influential a recipe. Above all, this book has endeavoured to reconstruct a particular association of ideas involving mesmerism and the Jews that recurred in the culture, in various guises, and for reasons that went beyond the invention, monomania or malice of any single author or group.

Whilst the Jew occupied a crucial role as repository of Victorian ambivalence about capitalism (for instance, in the stock figure of the rapacious but irresistible financial 'bloodsucker'), the alien hypnotist also became a kind of conduit for a much wider contemporary unease concerning the nature of irrational social influences and psychological transmissions. The image of the bewitching and inveigling Jew brought together a range of fears: not only of exploitation and parasitism, but the prospect of a kind of enchantment, in which an abject and dirty alien figure successfully entered into and distorted the victim's mind and body. The Svengalian narrative brought together two widely rehearsed historical concerns: the hypnotic man's wrongful possession of the woman *and* the Jew's capacity to invade the gentile. The Jew at issue here was a fantasised object into which a variety of psychologically unwanted features was projected. But via the image of hypnosis, the reviled and envious figure was then, as it were, imaginatively re-internalised, perceived as a terrifying psychic 'insider', the resurgent master in the house of the unsuspecting gentile's ego.

Svengali is portrayed as a massive egotist, but his position is always seen from outside. The reader never sees eye to eye with this villain, never shares *his* perspective on the story in which he is implicated and which in the end destroys him. Svengali is allowed little by way of personal confession or explanation; he can be compared in that respect with several other classic *fin de siècle* personae who are forbidden a full subjective presence or even a chance to speak convincingly of themselves, anywhere in the text. The insistent point about Dracula, Mr Hyde, or Svengali is their impact on others, and the reader is not invited to enter very far into their 'monstrous' states of mind. The excitement hinges on their destructive effect on surrounding characters, achieved by physical or psychic means; they embody a kind of danger which ultimately colonises their prey from *within*. Despite this propensity to deny subjectivity to their villains, it was precisely the genius of such stories to cast into question the dichotomous terms and assumptions offered in their own narratives, to show the degree to which the monsters' very presence was desired and conjured by the supposedly hapless victim. Stoker, Stevenson, even Du Maurier, muddied the waters, clouding the moral and psychological oppositions on which their stories simultaneously depended: conscious/unconscious, man/woman, inside/outside, west/east, ape/human, subject/object, virtue/vice, Jew/gentile, the self-possessed/the hypnotised, and so on.

In so far as Du Maurier's Svengali existed in the first person singular, this only served to indicate his impossible egotism, bringing home the fact that he was a dangerously (or ridiculously) grandiose Jew, seeking to conquer the world. The problem of freeing the character from such hostile 'objectification', even when he spoke as 'I', can equally well be seen in the 'defence' that was attempted in at least one of the spin-off products of the 1890s, *Extracts from the Diary of Moritz Svengali*, penned by an obscure writer Alfred Welch whose work was published in America. The aim was to offer Svengali's perspective, through his 'personal notes', but this text merely confirmed the fact that Svengali could not be written from within, or salvaged from the racial presuppositions of the age. Welch jokily complained that Du Maurier was unable to get inside the character, because of the governing assumptions of his Anglo-French identity and his affection for the musician's rival: 'It will be readily understood that neither Mr du Maurier's national preferences nor his friendship for Mr Bagot would be likely to lead him to regard Svengali favourably.'

Welch points out that *Trilby* has some more benign passages; his 'new' account of Svengali sought to build on those positive elements, describing a man capable of kindness who is splendid in appearance, a true artist and inspiration, a genuine admirer of talent. But the terms of the characterisation remain no less questionable than those of the original novel or the play. What we are offered is less the Jew's viewpoint than a plea for mitigating factors to be taken into account when sentencing the villain. It could almost have been written by the political scientist Leroy-Beaulieu, whose lukewarm praise and Lamarckian explanation of the Jews' psyche figured in the previous chapter. Welch invites his reader to remember the history of suffering, the training of sorrow, endured by Svengali. His sinister mesmeric desires are now partly explained away in terms of his difficult early life; his darker motivation is linked to the barrenness of his youth, his flight from poverty, the trauma of persecution. After all, Welch implies, here is a man who has grown up amidst the snarling faces and scornful attitudes of the Poles.

The account begins in the 1850s, in the 'shadow of the Ghetto'. Svengali records his fervent desire to get away from the 'contemptuous petty officials' who insult the Jews. The reader is told of the dirt and squalor, the repulsive and degrading life he is forced to lead in eastern Europe. He rails against poverty, but also against the abjection of the Jewish community, even perhaps repudiating the condition of Jewishness itself.[15] As he travels away from the ghetto toward Paris, Svengali finds both the atmosphere and the sky changing. Emerging from servitude, he struggles to adjust his eyes to the brighter western light. He describes breathing a new air of freedom and meeting up with a group of courteous artists from Britain. Svengali is shown partially to rise above his original milieu, preserving and exploiting a musical talent and hypnotic gifts, despite that background so full of sufferings. He has 'big black eyes' and a stern air of command, key ingredients of the hypnotist, but even in his precious experience of liberty, he is all too well aware of the humiliating nature of his own position as an immigrant in Paris, 'like a dog from the mud of the Ghettos'. From his place as lonely and permanent outsider, Svengali describes how he comes to dominate Trilby, yet is always frustrated by his inability to evoke her love. He can only truly have control of her when she is mesmerically 'possessed', and he can never be sure even then that he has fully obliterated her memory of other affective ties.[16]

While Welch's account insists that some allowance be made for Svengali, this should not lead one to ignore the fact of his personal repulsiveness. 'Dirtiness' is a Svengalian feature in *The Diary* as in the other turn of the century representations of the mesmeric Jew. Moreover the racial hatred and obsession is projected on to Svengali, coming back from him with great force: here it is exclusively the Jew who is busy evaluating the others in reductive eugenic terms. Thus when Trilby appears, he swiftly moves to measure her physical qualities, musing on the advantages of racial hybridity, as Du Maurier himself had done in insisting on the benefits of some 'minim' of Jewish blood: 'It seems that the English are a good stock on which to graft some other variety. A little Scotch or Irish or almost any other strain wonderfully improves the individual.' As Svengali records his fantasies about sexual union with Trilby, he is also calculating the financial and biological gain.

Despite the generosity he experiences in Paris, Svengali remains embittered, envious, rancorous. When he temporarily loses Trilby, he is thrown back into the pitiable condition of a lonely wandering Jew. Welch shows that, faced by misfortune, it is in Svengali's character to make the worst of things, weakening and destroying his objects. All such tales of Svengali sooner or later make the point that none of us really get over our wounds, least of all the Jews. And those who have the most wounds are the most to be feared, for their hatred and desire for revenge will be the most terrible. There are echoes of Fagin in all of this. Like Dickens' villain, Svengali is here conceived as a kind of reptile of the streets, slinking along by gloomy walls. In the twilight, Svengali watches, 'with envious eyes', men returning home to their wives. He does possess music, however, a field in which his companions are utterly ignorant, and he uses that capacity to take charge of the woman. As he ruminates: 'They do not understand music either, and she spends her time with them while I could play with her voice like on a flute, and she will not attend to me when the little artist is near to look upon.' Trilby is the prize of this feud over artistic and ethnic possession. She is the coveted object who is always to be 'unconscious of her triumph'.

Welch describes how Svengali meets Trilby on the stairs, quickly capturing her attention with his hypnotic passes. He revels in his possession: 'she is mine – all mine; and all the little Englishmen and the big Englishmen cannot take her from me.' Through subliminal management of her mind and voice, he shapes her career. Before long, her hypnotic 'education' is complete, and her musical ascent begins. Welch displays Svengali and Trilby triumphant, the couple showered with vast riches, while the

audiences are transfixed and paralysed by the experience of their own adoration: 'The enthusiasm was almost terrifying – it was like madness'.
What they are in fact hearing, Svengali knows, is 'her voice guided by my
heart and brain'. Yet they remain oblivious of the truth. The admiring
crowd is wholly taken over by a strange ardour, in fact driven 'frantic with
enthusiasm'.

Hypnosis is shown to produce strange allegiances, to undo social bonds,
consciousness itself, yet *The Diary* also insists on the indelible underlying
patterns of race and national affiliation. Svengali's immutable constitution
is emphasised in contrast to British or English (the two are run together
here) 'character'. According to Svengali himself, the English all share a
national insularity and parochialism which run much deeper than any class
divide:

> I saw the three artists again to-day in the Place de la Concorde. With our
> English friends the appetite for the air of Bohemia does not last very
> long. It is not a congenial climate. They go back to their beer and skit-
> tles or port and fox-hunting – it is all the same – after a very short
> excursion in to foreign realms. An Englishman is an Englishman before
> he is a citizen of any broader country. I wonder whether it is because
> they find their own ways so infinitely better than others, or because the
> routine of established customs is a safe shield behind which to hide.[17]

Even in this avowedly sympathetic account, it seems eventually that both
Englishmen and Jews have to agree more on the differences than the simi-
larities between them. Racial foundations ground social and psychological
experiences, even though both Du Maurier and Welch reveal that they are
aware such categories are anything but pure.

All of Du Maurier's novels, to say nothing of the spoofs and speculations
which followed, epitomised a maudlin and melodramatic style of the day
that many grander critics and philosophers despised. Yet in the figure of the
exploitative, beguiling conductor and his touching victim, Du Maurier had
hit on a curiously resonant symbol. Letters from friends and enemies surely
alerted him that something strangely irrational was happening, not only
within the tale but also in public responses to his plot, even as the novel was
first being serialised. It is hard to tell now how far the 'overwrought' reaction of the readership was being knowingly parodied rather than simply
'lived', at least by some of Du Maurier's own artistic circle, but of the wider
passion and clamour, the author could not remain in any doubt. A typical

example of the histrionic posturing and hyped-up mood was provided by the painter Edward Burne-Jones, who wrote to Du Maurier begging that his fictional night at the opera should end well for the heroine. Trilby's life, he insisted, *must* be spared:

> Meantime a far more important matter is this – are you going to kill Trilby – or be kind to her? I cannot have her killed. You may polish off as many men as you like in the process of her career – & they must endure their fate with courage, proud to be crushed by such feet – but no harm beyond a heartache or so to Trilby – as you love me.

Du Maurier replied that whilst she would have to die, he would do the deed as gently as he could, admitting that she was precious to him as well:

> I am delighted (& immensely flattered) that you should like my dear Trilby well enough to intercede for her – she is to me almost as a child of my body! Alas – she is committed to depart this life next August – but in such a pleasant and comfortable manner that you will be pleased – a true euthanasia.[18]

In fact it is Svengali who is the first of the trio of lovers to go, indirectly precipitating the deaths of Trilby and then Little Billee, by virtue of his own collapse at a final fateful concert. La Svengali's London debut had been expected to offer a crowning triumph. The glassy-eyed diva is to sing before a great and expectant crowd, that includes her much bewildered friends, Taffy, the Laird and Little Billee. Having finally caught up with her again, after all the vices and vicissitudes of their separation, they have come to hear the transformed Queen of Song, the soprano of sopranos, at the peak of her powers. In fact to sing like a nightingale, as we know, she depends completely on the physical presence and eye contact of the mesmerist. Nobody in the audience knows the precise extent of the influence of the *maestro*, nor are they party to the secret that he is on his last legs. It is not the physical assaults of Taffy and Gecko, mortifying though they are, which finally finish off Svengali, as he takes up, once again, that lonely vigil in his private box. Rather, it is his own long disregarded infirmity of constitution. Disastrously for Trilby, he suffers a heart attack just ahead of her crucial London performance. With Svengali slumped and out of view, the spell is broken, the singer disorientated and her voice restored to its old tuneless rasp. Pandemonium ensues at the theatre. In due course, she recovers con-

"'SVENGALI! . . . SVENGALI! . . . SVENGALI! . . .'"

Illustration for *Trilby* by George Du Maurier, 1896.

sciousness and is reunited with her friends, but fails to regain health and vitality. Trilby's own decline is made lingering and poignant, evidently inspired by Dumas' *La Dame aux camélias*. Her friends are shocked to find that she retains a certain regard for Svengali, even an affection, his name on her lips to the end. Beyond the singer's physical deterioration and death, Little Billee, also broken, finally passes away and it is left to Taffy and his wife, Little Billee's sister, to close the novel, picking up the pieces of the story in a final nostalgic tourist trip back to Paris, where (via a chance encounter with the contrite Gecko) they learn the truth about Svengali's plot to mesmerise and transform Trilby.

Despite all the build-up, and in contrast with the heroine's subsequent demise, Du Maurier's notification of Svengali's death at the opera had been brief enough: 'Monsieur Svengali had suddenly died in that box – of apoplexy or heart disease.'[19] It was as if this terse message captured the suddenly shrunken status of the dead villain. But first Paul Potter and then Beerbohm Tree worked over the climactic scene, making sure that its dramatic import was fully realised at the theatre. Du Maurier referred to the transformation of his own 'rambling scenes' into the unforgettable drama of hypnotic influence as Potter's 'happiest of happy thoughts'.[20] Svengali's rise and fall was to be brought home unmistakably to the public. Critics winced at the grotesque exaggerated style – the sheer vulgarity – that was involved in such a production. Kate Terry Gielgud recorded caustically in her notebook:

> It was surely quite bad enough to have Svengali in the flesh haunting every moment of the play, eavesdropping, soliloquising, piano-playing, praying, cursing and mesmerising; but that after he is dead – at any rate after his really magnificent death scene – with a back fall across a table so that his head hung upside down to the audience with open eyes and protruded tongue – a ghastly spectacle – after this he must needs put in an appearance as a portrait in a frame (delugeɑ with limelight, of course), at sight of which Trilby shrieks and presumably expires, so that Little Billee's blue blood may not be sullied by an alliance with one who sat 'for the altogether'.[21]

A critic in the *Cambridge Review* was equally cutting about the props and general contrivance involved in the final scenes: 'If the resources of the spirit world cannot produce a better portrait than that which causes Trilby's death in the last scene would it not be better for Svengali to appear in person?'[22] Others were more powerfully affected by the ending and by the celebrated actor's startling performance in the lead role. Tree conveyed with every ounce of his body the mesmeric force and haunting eye, the intense rage and defiance of the Jew. His Svengali gloated about his victory over the surrounding men and women, declared his immortality as well as his contempt for their religion. He even claimed to be divine:

> You talk to me of right, or religion of your God (*Finger to teeth*). That for your religion – I laugh at it – I laugh at everything – everybody – I am afraid of nothing – I am myself, Svengali – I am my own god.

But even as he uttered the words, he staggered and gasped, feeling the weak beat of his heart. And so the illusion of power was steadily dissolved, revealed scene by scene as self-deception, nothing but an empty performance. The once exultant Jew was forced to abandon the pretension that he was a law unto himself. No sooner had he boasted of his strength, than he was to be seen begging in vain for a reprieve from death:

> God – do not let me die! (*Gasps*) Let me live another year – another month – another hour! I will repent – Oh, God of Israel! Shema Yisroel Adonai Eloheno Adonai Echod! (*Continues gibbering*).[23]

Tree was an old hand at such theatre; he knew how to milk his audience, playing up Svengali's fall and comeuppance for all they were worth. Night after night, the old megalomaniac could be seen on the stage, boxed ever further into his lonely corner, shrinking inexorably into nothingness.

Notes

1 Svengali

1. Max Beerbohm, quoting a London critic, and recalling his half-brother, Sir Herbert Beerbohm Tree's stage triumph as Svengali in 1895. Beerbohm 1920, p. 100.
2. Du Maurier 1994, pp. 9–10.
3. See the second edition of the *Oxford English Dictionary* which defines 'Svengali' as one who exercises a controlling mesmeric influence on another, frequently for a sinister purpose. The first reference curiously is given as 1914, an entry from Kipling's *Divers Creatures*: 'I'm glad Zvengali's back where he belongs'. This refers to a dog with a mesmeric stare. Examples drawn from the 1930s, 1960s and 1970s are also provided. As the present study shows, however, earlier examples of Svengali's entry into the language, from the '*Trilby* boom' years of the 1890s, could also surely have been added.
4. Anon.1896b.
5. Du Maurier certainly has some eminent detractors. The highly distinguished literary critic, Professor Frank Kermode, for example, finds precious little to admire in Du Maurier's writing; indeed he regards *Trilby* as amongst the worst novels he can recall ever having read (personal communication).
6. Hitler 1992, p. 282.
7. Consider the metaphors employed in this account of Jewish power in a turn of the century publication, *Labour Leader*, on the left of British politics: 'The Rothschild leeches have for years hung on with distended suckers to the body politic of Europe. This family of infamous usurers, the foundation of whose fortunes was laid deep in the mire of cheating and scoundrels, has spread itself out over Europe like a network. It is a gigantic conspiracy, manifold and comprehensive. There is a Rothschild – a devoted member of the family – in every capital of Europe. Vienna, St Petersburg, Paris, London, Berlin, are each and all garrisoned and held for family purposes by members of this gang. This blood-sucking crew has been the cause of untold mischief and misery in Europe during the present century, and has piled up its prodigious wealth chiefly through fomenting wars between States which ought never to have quarrelled. Wherever there is trouble in Europe, wherever rumours of war circulate and men's minds are distraught with fear of change and calamity, you may be sure that a hook-nosed Rothschild is at his games somewhere near the region of disturbance.' Quoted in Holmes 1979, pp. 83–84. Compare this remark by the German journalist and political radical, Wilhelm Marr, in *The Victory of Judaism over Germanism* (1879): 'The very struggle for existence is no longer

possible without Jewry taking its commission.' Quoted in Gay 1992, p. 215.

8. Millar 1937, p. 145.

9. In 1922, for instance, when D.H. Lawrence's *Aaron's Rod* appeared, with its own musical and mesmeric themes, it was assumed that the reader was familiar with Du Maurier. Lawrence has the Marchesa declare: 'So I will be like Trilby, and sing a little French song. Though not Malbrouk, and without a Svengali to keep me in tune'; Lawrence 1980, p. 298.

10. *Guardian*, review section, 19 July 1996, p. 2.

11. *Sunday Times*, 'world news' section, 29 September 1996, p. 22.

12. *Observer*, review section, 18 January 1998, p. 2.

13. For an exception, see the piece in the *New Statesman* entitled, 'A victim of anti-Semitism?' (Glanville 1998).

14. *Guardian*, 26 February 1996, p. 1. Mandelson himself responded in a subsequent article to the charge, pleading not guilty and expressing perplexity at how he came to acquire the shady appellation: 'If the whole thing is that innocent, where does the talk of me as a Svengali come from? I like to think of my own case as something of an accident of history.' *Guardian*, 'the week' section, 28 September 1996, p. 2. The piece appeared under the heading: 'Out of the darkness. Machiavelli, evil genius, king of spin doctors?' A typical Steve Bell cartoon (reproduced on p. 8, above) of the influential Mandelson has him hanging from the ceiling at the Liberal Democratic Party conference in the form of an enormous spider; *Guardian* (24 September 1997, p. 18). Indeed this has become his regular cartoon embodiment. The name 'Rasputin' has also been attached to Mandelson; see, for instance, *Guardian*, 14 January 1999, p. 10. An advertising and public relations man, Tim Bell, was referred to in the same newspaper as Mrs Thatcher's Svengali of the 1980s (16 July 1997, p. 1) while still more recently, Matthew Freud (Sigmund's great grandson) has been dubbed the new Svengali to politicians and pop stars alike (19 November 1999, p. 24).

15. Figes 1996, p. 31.

16. Christiansen 1984, p. 98.

17. Eliot 1979, pp. 532–33.

18. Hawkins 1990, p. 97.

19. Rogan 1988, p. 275.

20. For these references to the so-called 'Svengali Spice', see *Mail on Sunday*, 9 November 1997, pp. 1, 3, and the review section, pp. 10–14.

21. Harbinson 1975, pp 101–103.

22. Guralnick 1994, p. 240.

23. Spitz 1989, pp. 179, 176.

24. Rogan concluded his history of 'starmakers' and 'Svengalis' with some reflections on the male, Jewish and homosexual domination of British musical management in the 1950s and 1960s. The ubiquity of the 'Jewish Svengali', he suggests, was quite simply an occupational fact about the business. There is a certain myopia in this discussion; for whatever the ethnic background or sexual orientation of musical managers, Rogan's account takes for granted the very image of Svengali which the present inquiry is seeking to historicise. Hence for Rogan it is, as it were, a statistical question as to how many Jewish, gay, black or women Svengalis there are at any one time, not a historical and psychological question about the desires and fears projected into such a figure in the first place.

25. W. Archer, *Theatrical World* (1896), quoted in Taylor 1996, p. xxiii.

26. Hart [1896] 1982, p. 207.

27. Du Maurier 1994, p. 11.

28. Wilson 1957, p. 79.

29. Kelly 1996, p. 2.

30. Kiessling 1977.

31. 'The Hypnotism of "Trilby"', *British Medical Journal* (20 November 1895), reprinted in Hart 1982, p. 207.

32. Bowen 1939, p. 40.

33. Levi 1989, p. 144.

34. 'They hatch cockatrice's eggs, and weave the spider's web: he that eateth of their eggs dieth, and that which is crushed breaketh out into a viper. Their webs shall not become garments, neither shall they cover themselves with their works: their works *are* works of iniquity, and the act of violence *is* in their hands.' Isaiah 59: 5–6.

35. Drawing on patients' dreams, Abraham (1927) located the creature as a figure representing the mother or the mother's genitals. A patient brought him a picture of a spider as recollected from a dream and was astonished to find himself recognising, in his own drawing, the female sexual organs. Moreover, in the middle of his own illustration, surrounded by hair, the body of the spider suggested something unquestionably like a penis. Abraham suggested that the creature represents the penis embedded in the female genitals: 'The "Wicked" mother who, according to Freud's view, is represented by the spider, is clearly a mother formed in the shape of a man, of whose male organ and masculine pleasure in attack the boy is afraid – just as young girls are timid in regard to men. The patient's feeling towards spiders can be best described by the word "uncanny".' He relates the fact that the spider kills its victim by sucking its blood to its imaginative appropriation as symbol of castration. In Freud's own rendition, 'a spider in dreams is a symbol of the mother, but of the *phallic* mother, of whom we are afraid; so that the fear of spiders expressed dread of mother-incest and horror of the female genitals'; Freud 1932, p. 24.

36. See chapter nine, above.

37. The term 'psychotherapy' was in circulation from the 1880s; Gauld 1992, p. 298.

2   The Violence of Publicity

1. James 1897, p. 607.

2. Bright 1895, p. 422.

3. That fact raises in different form questions about the merchandising of a personality and a product which many of the following pages will address. The Du Maurier cigarette was first manufactured in 1929 by Peter Jackson (Tobacco) Ltd, a subsidiary of Imperial Tobacco. A further tipped version of the cigarette was launched in 1936. Money went to Gerald and, after his death, to his family. My thanks to the archivist of the Hampstead Museum, Burgh House, London, for this information; Harding 1989, p. 168.

4. Daphne Du Maurier 1963.

5. Berry 1970.

6. George's father had dispatched him to study at the Birkbeck Chemical Laboratory at University College London. He did briefly go on to set up practice as an analytic chemist, but spent more and more time singing and sketching. His former professor at UCL remarked presciently that Du Maurier would make 'a shocking bad chemist'; quoted in anon. 1896b.

7. For further details, see Leonée Ormond's life of Du Maurier (1969).

8. Anon. 1896b.

9. Even before Du Maurier embarked on his novels, Henry James noted this chauvinist aspect of his illustrations: 'Du Maurier has done the "low" foreigner of London (or of his native) streets – the foreigner whose unspeakable baseness prompts the Anglo-Saxon observer to breathe the Pharisee's vow of thanks that he is not as these people are; but as we have seen he has done the low Englishman quite as well'; James 1888, p. 363.

10. Du Maurier 1994, p. 166.

11. See for instance, *Journal of the Society for Psychical Research*, 1 (1884). In 1884, an American psychical society was also established to pursue such issues. The *Oxford English Dictionary* indicates that the word 'automatism' in the specific new sense of a psychic

phenomenon that appears sponta- neously in consciousness, or any action performed subconsciously, uncon- sciously, undirected by the mind or will of the normal personality, can first be found in a discussion by Myers in the 1884 proceedings of the Society for Psychical Research. Other usages of the word are recorded as early as the sev- enteenth century. In the sense of 'auto- matic' or acting mechanically, it can be detected in the first half of the nine- teenth century.

12. These remarks occur in the context of Freud's discussion of dreams and occultism, in the *New Introductory Lectures* (Freud 1932, p. 55).
13. James 1897, p. 607.
14. Du Maurier 1994, p. 272
15. *Annual Register* 1896, p. 126
16. Anon. 1895 ('Three English novels'), p. 269.
17. The idea that Dracula's features, as presented in Stoker's novel, were to be read as markers of Jewishness has pro- voked speculation; see, for instance, Halberstam 1993.
18. Du Maurier 1994, p. 6. The argument that a modest 'homeopathic' dose of the Jews would be good for the English stock was also specifically made in racial writings of the turn of the cen- tury; see Zatlin 1981, p. 128.
19. See chapter ten.
20. Daphne Du Maurier 1951, p. 76.
21. Daphne Du Maurier 1951, pp. 115, 150.
22. Gilder and Gilder 1895, p. 23.
23. Gilder and Gilder 1895, p. 23.
24. James 1888, p. 347.
25. See, for instance, Foldy 1997.
26. Grossman 1996, p. 526. I draw heavily on Grossman's thoughtful article in this passage on Wilde and Du Maurier. Wilde was often criticised for his lack of moral fibre, his paradoxical wit, his impenetrable masks, his sheer and unabashed delight in unnaturalness. And to a considerable degree, Du Maurier (far earlier than the Marquis of Queensbury) had immortalised the

view of Wilde as the quintessential poser in his *Punch* cartoons. This is not to claim that Du Maurier's Svengali was an 'imitation' of Wilde: the differ- ences are too many and too obvious to recite. But for readers familiar with the image of Oscar as the overweening, conceited, sexually flamboyant and pernicious Irishman (and what readers in the 1890s would not have been?) Du Maurier's egotistical, mocking and mesmerising conductor who destroys an Irishwoman, would have had a spe- cial resonance.

27. Thus in Du Maurier's story, while Little Billee's painting is classical and restrained, his British friends' creative work sentimental and *ersatz*, Svengali's genius could be viewed as stereotypically Wildean – protean, brilliant, showy, opportunistic and false. Svengali suc- ceeds in all but the highest and best music, we are told, and yet in most of the lesser registers of art he makes a mesmerising impression; see Grossman 1996.
28. Quoted in Grossman 1996, p. 539n.
29. Lord Henry makes the point that *all* influence is bad influence, but such a homily was to no avail in the case of Dorian or ultimately of Wilde:

   Because to influence a person is to give him one's own soul. He does not think his natural thoughts, or burn with his natural passions. His virtues are not real to him. His sins, if there are such things as sins, are borrowed. He becomes an echo of someone else's music, an actor of a part that has not been written for him. (Wilde [1890] 1976, p. 16)

30. Grossman (1996) is the most recent commentator to advance this view.
31. *Pall Mall Gazette*, 19 May 1894, p. 2.
32. Du Maurier 1947, p. 650.
33. In an unforgettable letter to the Home Secretary on 2 July 1896, Wilde sought remittance of the sentence for his crimes on the grounds of diminished responsibility and by arguing that 'the

fearful system of solitary cellular confinement' and the general degradation of prison life could only drive him ever further into insanity and despair. He referred to his own 'sexual madness' and his 'horrible form of erotomania'. These conditions, he conceded, had been recognised by modern pathological science as a function of degeneracy. In support of this view of himself, he cited the work of two eminent specialists, Cesare Lombroso and Max Nordau. Wilde 1962, pp. 401–406.

34. Ionides 1996, p. 63.

35. In a previous celebrated case in 1877, the litigious Whistler had won the spectacular sum of one farthing damages after the art critic John Ruskin had derided him for 'flinging a pot of paint into the public's face'.

36. For further details, see the appendix to Du Maurier 1994. Note that it was not the first time Du Maurier had caricatured Whistler. In 1862, he had produced a facetious sketch of the painter alongside Felix Moscheles, in a private letter to Mrs Roche; see 'unpublished items' in the bibliography.

37. Various substitute sketches were considered, including the depiction of a figure called Kretsch, a Jew from an eminent soap boiling company of Bermondsey. In the end, Du Maurier came up with the name of 'Anthony', and based his characterisation partly on a Swiss painter with whom he had once shared a studio in Germany. Thus when the novel appeared in book form, the character was no longer a Whistler look-alike, but a substitute figure, the outlandish, if morally more anodyne, 'yellow-haired Anthony, a Swiss who became a household name in two hemispheres'. See the appendix to Du Maurier 1994.

38. *Pall Mall Gazette*, 15 May 1894, p. 2.

39. Quoted in Weintraub, 1974, pp. 387–88.

40. Quoted in Weintraub, 1974, p. 387.

41. Anon. 1894, p. 2.

42. Gilder and Gilder, 1895, p. 17; see also Weintraub 1974, ch. 32, 'L'Affaire Trilby'.

43. Jackson 1913.

44. Anon. 1895 ('Three English novels'), p. 270.

45. *British Medical Journal*, 16 November 1895, reprinted in Hart 1982, pp. 209-10.

46. Gilder and Gilder 1895; see also the material on George Du Maurier, including the 'Du Maurier scrapbook', in the files of the Hampstead Museum, Burgh House, London (see 'unpublished items' in the bibliography for further details).

47. Purcell 1977, p. 71; Whiteley 1948, p. 32; in his introduction to *Svengali* (Du Maurier 1973), Peter Alexander adds (in a remark which captures the vastness of the operation, even if it is wide of the mark in terms of Du Maurier's own fortunes): 'There is nothing that has been achieved in any merchandising operation that has bettered that of "Trilby" – the only difference being with the lax state of copyright existing in the 1890's, poor George Du Maurier made nothing from all this exploitation of his work!' (p. 18). The royalty statements, contracts and some other correspondence relating to Du Maurier's *Trilby* and associated products (calendars, dolls, musical versions etc.) can be consulted in the archives of the publisher, Harper and Bros, at the Butler Library, Columbia University, or in the microfilm reproduction of these papers produced by the publisher, Chadwyck-Healey. Details concerning the contractual arrangements for stage rights (for instance with Beerbohm Tree) are included in this collection as well as an affidavit signed by Du Maurier (8 May 1895), declaring that his *Trilby* was not derived from Nodier, whose work he said that he could not recall ever having read; see reel 50 of the microfilm series; for full details see the unpublished items section of the bibliography. On *Harper's* decision to give Du Maurier a royalty on sales of *Trilby*, despite the fact that Du Maurier origi-

nally signed a contract settling for a lump sum, see Bright 1895, p. 419.

48. Thus, for instance, one Isaac Hull Platt gave a paper in the United States before the Fellowship of Ethical Research in which he defended the honour of the novel. He argued that Du Maurier's critics were religious pedants and dogmatists who confused the letter for the spirit of religion. Platt insisted on the humanity of the story, whatever the marital and sexual status of the heroine; he suggested that if the novel transgressed conventional mores, it was because the latter needed amending, not because the former needed censuring. A wider distinction could be made between real religious truth and mere ceremonial form: 'It may come to be regarded as not altogether immoral to hold that that which is impure is not made pure by a sacerdotal function, and that true sexual kinship is not determined by a particular form of ecclesiastical or civil marriage, but by spiritual affinities inherent in the soul.' Platt advocated a more fundamental revision of values; for where acquiescence in the institution of marriage is motivated by lucre or title, it is no better than any other sexual relationship. He urged the audience to abandon the idea of 'a vengeful implacable deity', extolling the benefits of an ethics based on the potential of the human being and which would assert the 'infinite capacity of development in the human soul'. Sex can be holy and spiritual or gross and material; there is nothing in the act as such which is shameful; it is all a question of the moral attitude (or lack of it). Platt then proceeded to explore different motivations for sexual activity: 'The impelling motive to the sex relation in mankind may be roughly enumerated, proceeding from lowest to highest, as follows' (in ascending order): pursuit of gain; gross animal desire; friendship; romantic love; true spiritual sentiment. Platt 1895, pp. 9–11.

49. Gilder and Gilder 1895, p. 22.

50. Quoted in Gilder and Gilder 1895, p. 22. A later serendipitous find of 400 old *Trilbys* at the St. Louis Public Library also revealed the extent of the clamour (Winterich 1929, p. 105).

51. Returning from a weekend with Du Maurier in Folkestone, James wrote of his friend's depression, 'in spite of the chink – what say I the "chink" – the deafening roar – of sordid gold flowing in to him.' James himself 'came back feeling an even worse failure than usual'; letter to Gosse, quoted in Edel 1969, p. 134.

52. James 1897, p. 607.

53. C.C. Hoyer Millar, disputed this version of events, claiming that it was he who accompanied Du Maurier, his father-in-law, on the fateful walk, which, according to his recollection, took place between Hampstead and Highgate villages; Millar 1937.

54. James 1947, p. 97; see also Edel 1969, p. 163.

55. Moscheles 1896.

56. Du Maurier's friend Luke Ionides claimed Svengali was based on a Greek student they had known in Paris, an able musician who claimed mesmeric powers and erroneously believed that ladies fell in love with him at a glance; see Ionides 1996, p. 63. For some speculations about an earlier version of Svengali in a lost magazine article by Du Maurier, see Harding 1989, p. 24.

57. Moscheles 1896, p. 59.

58. Beerbohm 1920, pp. 97, 201.

59. Gielgud 1980, p. 35. She took a critical view of the standard of acting and found the entire production unpardonably crude. Cf. Trewin 1996, pp. 36–37.

60. Anon. (*The Sketch*) 1895.

61. Purcell 1977, pp. 69, 71.

62. Winterich 1929, p. 105.

63. The early short was sometimes known as 'The Poster Girls and the Hypnotist', at others as 'Svengali and the Posters'. Under the title 'Svengali' there was a

1931 Warner Bros production, directed by Archie L. Mayo, starring John Barrymore and Marian Marsh. In 1946, in a different vein, one could see a short Technicolor production of Mighty Mouse and Svengali's Cat, from Twentieth Century Fox. This combined features of the Pied Piper with the Svengalian saga, in a drama of mesmerised mice. In 1955, there was the British production, directed by Noel Langley and starring Donald Wolfit as Svengali with Hildegarde Neff as Trilby. Neither was this the last. In 1983 came a film by Anthony Harvey starring Peter O'Toole and Jodie Foster. Under the title of 'Trilby', the list was still longer, starting from 'Trilby and Little Billee' in 1896, a brief film featuring the studio scene from the novel. There were various adaptations before the First World War, 'Trilby and Svengali' from Kinematograph Company and 'Trilby' from Standard Feature Films, as well as a version directed by Harold Shaw, from the London Film Company. A subsequent interpretation was directed by Maurice Torneur under the auspices of the Equitable Motion Pictures Corporation, starring Clara Kimball Young as Trilby and Wilton Lackaye as Svengali. A production in the early 1920s was directed by James Young. Over half a century later in 1976, the BBC presented *Trilby* as a 'Play of the Month', scripted by Hugh Whitemore and directed by Piers Haggard.

64. James 1897, p. 607.
65. Gilder and Gilder 1895, p. 8.
66. Gilder and Gilder 1895, p. 20.
67. Muskerry 1896, p. 1. The play was first performed at the Theatre Royal, Richmond on 11 May 1896.
68. In Du Maurier's story, Svengali 'spoke fluent French with a German accent, and humorous German twists and idioms, and his voice was very thin and mean and harsh, and often broke into a disagreeable falsetto'; Du Maurier 1893–94, p. 172.

69. There are various other allusions to the eye. Taff, for instance, refers light-heartedly to his 'callous optics'. Compare Svengali's address to the sceptical Thrillby: 'I am not only a musician, but also a mesmerist. I have music at my finger's ends and fascination in my eyes. (Squinting) See, I fascinate you – so! THRIL. Not a bit! You're squinting' (Muskerry 1896, p. 7).
70. Muskerry 1896, p. 7.
71. Quoted in Edel, 1969, p. 165.

3 Mesmerism

1. Potter [1895] 1996, p. 219.
2. Zweig 1933, p. 59.
3. Tatar 1978; Fara 1995; Moll 1906.
4. Pattie 1994, p. 55.
5. Mesmer 1785, p. 49.
6. On the connection between mesmerism and eighteenth-century electrical theories, see Darnton 1968 and Tatar 1978, ch. 2.
7. In the subsequent history, mesmerism was to be explained in quite different ways: it was pulled back towards prevailing theories of hidden spiritual powers as well as towards emerging materialist explanations. The spirit-orientated interpretation, developed, for instance, by one of Mesmer's followers, Bergasse, placed mesmerism back in contact with a set of esoteric 'illuminist' ideas which had re-emerged in the work of Swedenborg and others during the eighteenth century. Illuminism was said to derive from ancient Egyptian knowledge, preserved by the Jews, the Alexandrians and Essenians and to have seeped, via the Crusades and many subsequent detours, into the margins of the Enlightenment. Illuminism also flourished in various circles of Freemasonry; see Stedman Jones's introduction to Fourier 1996.
8. Her visual problems were said to have begun between her third and fourth

years; Pattie 1994, p. 57.

9. Pattie 1994, pp. 57–64.

10. Zweig 1933. See also Crabtree 1993, pp. 10–11.

11. This account draws on *The Gentleman's Magazine* (Anon. 1785, p. 175). See also Mesmer 1781a, p. 40; Gauld 1992, p. 3. Fraulein Paradis' youthfulness was exaggerated by some adversaries; thus *The Gentleman's Magazine* claimed she was thirteen, whilst Mesmer himself stated more accurately that she was eighteen (Mesmer 1781a).

12. Contrast the critical view in *The Gentleman's Magazine* with the very different and strikingly insouciant account of the doctor himself (Mesmer 1781a, p. 42). Mesmer argued that it was the enforced separation between himself and Fraulein Paradis which brought on her convulsions.

13. Moll made much the same point, when he rejected 'the contemptible group of Mesmer's professional slanderers' (Moll 1906, p. 8).

14. Harte 1902, vol. 1, p. 52.

15. It was Baron Anton Stoërck who acted as go-between on behalf of the displeased Empress. Stoërck was a powerful scientific figure; he was a well-known pharmacologist and toxicologist, President of the Faculty of Medicine in Vienna and one of the Emperor's doctors. Mesmer complained bitterly that Stoërck and others (including Herr Barth, a Professor of Anatomy and specialist in eye diseases) had witnessed the girl's improvement themselves, but had then expediently (and in his view enviously) chosen to deny it. They remained unmoved by all his subsequent protestations.

16. He cannot have been universally held to be in disgrace, however, since he departed with a letter of recommendation from a government minister addressed to the Austrian ambassador in Paris (Pattie 1994, p. 66). A report (which was apparently apocryphal) had it that Mesmer attended one of Paradis' concerts in Paris in 1784, leading to further gossip about his dubious liaison with her seven years earlier (Pattie 1979).

17. Fara 1995, p. 169, n. 131.

18. De Puységur, for instance, considered the eye more susceptible than any other organ. He declared: 'it is by a light rubbing of the eye that I charge my subjects, and bring on somnambulism; and it is also by a very light friction on the eye that I operate a sudden discharge, from which results awakening into their natural state' (quoted in Harte 1902, vol. 1, p. 100).

19. These and surrounding remarks draw heavily on Gauld's history of hypnotism (1992) as well as the cogent account of the British tradition in Winter 1998.

20. The first 'Lodge of Harmony' was set up at the Hôtel Coigny in Paris in 1784. In addition to administering animal magnetism to the poor, the Lodge (soon expanded into the 'Society') provided lectures, including some given by Mesmer himself. Suitable participants were awarded a diploma permitting them to set up treatment facilities in a particular named town; Gauld 1992, p. 10

21. Within royal circles, he had managed to interest Charles d'Eslon, physician-in-ordinary to the king's brother (whose support for Mesmer resulted in his dismissal from the roll of *docteurs régents*). Other followers included an Alsatian banker, Guillaume Kornmann, whose son had been cured of various eye ailments by magnetic means.

22. It was only in the later 1830s, however, with Charles Poyen and his 'trance-maidens', that the technique really caught on in America. As a medical student, Poyen had spent time in Paris where he learned the magnetic craft. His followers included the former watchmaker and mesmeric performer, Phineas Parkhurst Quimby (Tatar 1978).

23. Mann 1975, pp. 126–27.

24. 'It seems safe, therefore, to draw one conclusion from the pulp literature of the 1780's: the reading public of that era was intoxicated with the power of science, and it was bewildered by the real and imaginary forces with which scientists peopled the universe. Because the public could not distinguish the real from the imaginary, it seized on any invisible fluid, any scientific-sounding hypothesis that promised to explain the wonders of nature' (Darnton 1968, p. 23). Fred Kaplan (1974) has extended this argument to the early nineteenth century, claiming that early Victorian confusions between metaphysics and science explain the popular success of mesmerism.

25. Darnton writes so compellingly of the eighteenth century's weird and abundant cosmologies that it is easy to pass over the assumption that nineteenth-century people were less 'intoxicated'. He suggests that in failing to be able to differentiate 'science' from 'pseudo-science', Mesmer's contemporaries were more prone to a kind of naïve enthusiasm; they saw less sceptically, making out the phenomena of their world as best they could with the collection of animalistic, vitalistic, and mechanistic theories that they had inherited from their predecessors; Darnton 1968, pp. 13–14.

26. Harrington 1988. According to the *Oxford English Dictionary*, 'mesmerism' was first used in English, in 1802; 'hypnotism' can be dated to 1843.

27. Darnton 1968.

28. Harte 1902, vol. 1, p. 64.

29. Thuillier 1988, pp. 11–12. For some contemporary views about the social heterogeneity of Mesmer's patients, see Tatar 1978, p. 20.

30. Charles Fourier was perhaps the most puzzling and also amongst the most significant heirs to this set of ideas. On Fourier's relationship to mesmerism and the esoteric currents of eighteenth-

century illuminism, see Stedman Jones in Fourier 1996.

31. Harte 1902, vol. 1, p. 13n.

32. Mesmer 1781a.

33. Other participants in these official inquiries included the astronomer Jean Bailly and the botanist Bernard Jussieu. The commissioners were sceptical about explanations involving magnetic fluids. It was significant, however, that Jussieu dissented from the main thrust of the report and came up with a personal theory that mesmerism derived not from magnetism but from animal heat. He published his own (less antagonistic) paper on the subject; see Chertok 1989. Soon after these inquiries, Mesmer left France, but a range of followers remained to do battle on his behalf.

34. This report was initially deemed too favourable to mesmerism and was not published. A new commission was ordered, which produced a more hostile commentary, denying the existence of the magnetic phenomenon; Chertok 1989. This in turn generated protests by supporters of mesmerism; see, for example, Berna 1838.

35. Chertok 1989.

36. Darnton 1968, p. 58.

37. For the wider shift into psychological explanations of mesmerism, see Chertok 1989.

38. Cavailhon 1882, p. 3.

39. Parssinen 1977, p. 103. For *Punch*, see anon. 1851a.

40. Parssinen 1977.

41. Fara 1995, p. 154.

42. Anon. 1860, p. 52.

43. *The Magnetic Review*, vol. 1, no. 1 (new series), (June 1878), pp. ii–xv.

44. Winter has shown the degree to which clerics participated in the debate. Thus Thomas Arnold, Henry Wilberforce and Richard Whateley sought to use Mesmer's science to discredit 'papist' infatuation with miracles. Others deployed it to bolster

Roman Catholicism, declaring the procedure an example of the divine presence. There were less spiritual claims as well, such as that mesmerism could be used for personal enrichment, or for purposes of law enforcement: mesmeric futurologists predicted that the science would lead to the location of stolen property and even to the successful identification of thieves; Winter 1992, pp. 46–49.

45. *The Zoist*, 23 (October 1848), pp. 213–37; ibid., 25 (April 1849), pp. 196–200. Elliotson sought to legitimate mesmerism in medical circles by insisting on his own scientific, rather than commercial, motivation.

46. Kaplan 1975.

47. Braid (1795–1860) coined the term 'hypnosis' to describe a combined state of slumber and uncanny concentration. Whilst some doctors urged the acceptance of mesmerism into the therapeutic repertoire, this remained a minority view. The implication of quackery, the growing association of mesmerism with phrenology, the vitriolic disputes around Elliotson at University College London, all added weight to the case of those who opposed both mesmerism in particular and psychological approaches to mental disorders in general. Thomas Wakley declared in the *Lancet* that 'mesmerism is too gross a humbug to admit of any further serious notice.' Braid suffered from some vilification *both* by orthodox doctors and by orthodox mesmerists (Clark 1981, pp. 278–80).

48. Braid 1852, pp. 10, 53, 56.

49. Bramwell 1903, p. 41.

50. Bramwell 1903, p. 41. It should also be recorded here that while the original theory of mesmerism concerned magnetic fluids, there was also a broader contemporary recognition of the complex powers of eye contact itself. As Fara has shown (1995), the early history of mesmerism coincided with a powerful Romantic view in which eyes were understood to shape, quasi-magnetically, the experience of the suffering lover.

51. Bramwell 1903, p. 41.

52. Braid 1852, p. 66.

53. Tatar 1978, pp. 152, 156.

54. See chapter six, above.

55. Letter to John Welsh, 13 December 1844; (Carlyle 1883, vol. 2, pp. 22–24). The expressiveness of the eyes is crucial to the account of how rapport is achieved in many of these anecdotes. Several studies of mesmerism in literary representation are available. 'Dickens and Mesmerism', for instance, has been the object of a full-length study in its own right (Kaplan 1975); other such inquiries have followed.

56. Anon. 1844.

57. Forel 1906.

58. Harris 1989.

59. Chertok 1989.

60. Bernheim 1891a.

61. Bernheim's forensic, psychological and therapeutic ideas aroused very considerable interest in France and abroad. A recent novel, *Freud à Nancy*, has sought imaginatively to reconstruct these richly suggestive personal encounters in the 1880s; Picard 1997.

62. The 'classical theory' of punishment, as derived in particular from the work of Beccaria and Bentham, had made the rationally calculating individual its mainstay. It was very difficult to reconcile such conceptions of the criminal with the visions of automatism, blind passion and hypnotic possession flourishing in the later period. In 1866, Ambroise Auguste Liébeault had strongly warned that the *somnambule* could be induced to commit crimes.

63. Cavailhon 1882, p. 17.

64. Micale 1990 and 1991.

65. Blavatsky 1972, p. 28.

66. On Charcot's influence in Britain, see Ellenberger 1970, p. 94.

67. Lerner 1998.

68. Freud 1893, pp. 16, 17, 9, 10.

4   Hearts and Minds

1. Du Maurier 1994, p. 199.
2. This anecdote, relating to a performance in Moscow in 1881, was reported by Russian psychiatrist. The theory of 'nervous mimicry' or 'neuromimesis' that was canvassed at the time had already been explored by doctors much earlier in the nineteenth century; Vrettos 1995, p. 81.
3. Geyl 1986, p. 146.
4. In *Electricité animal* (1805), Dr Jacques Henri Désiré Petetin, a physician from Lyon, argued that electrical fluids within the nervous system were responsible for powerful emotional effects. He sought to apply 'artificial electricity' to remove imbalances in the electrical fluids of the body; Crabtree 1993, p. 10.
5. Crabtree 1993, p. 10.
6. Quoted in Brod 1956, p. 39. Heine was referring to the impact that the politically energetic writer and journalist Börne had on him when they had met in 1815. Heine was German *and* Jewish by birth; as such, Svengali proudly claimed racial allegiance with him: 'We have got a poet too . . . His name is Heinrich Heine' (Du Maurier 1994, p. 81). The composer Richard Wagner also made a song and dance about the poet, but of a very different kind, insisting that as a Jew Heine could not be a true German; his conversion counted for nothing (Wagner 1910).
7. Harrison 1886, p. 431.
8. It was in an operatic burlesque of *Trilby* by Joseph W. Herbert and Charles Puerner that the villain was renamed 'Spaghetti'.
9. *"Thrillby," A Shocker in one Scene and Several Spasm (sic)* (Muskerry 1896, p. 7).
10. Moscheles 1899, pp. 249–50; emphasis added.
11. Mack Smith 1994.
12. Butler n.d., p. 50; see also Hibbert 1987 and Beales 1991 for numerous other examples.
13. The ways in which such racial constructions related to shifting domestic political circumstances and perceptions has been explored in detail in a major study of the subject, *Englishmen and Jews* (Feldman 1994); for the specific demonisation of Disraeli, see Wohl 1995; Ragussis 1995.
14. See chapter seven.
15. It was the contention of Charcot's adversary, Dr Bernheim, that the whole hypnotic process could be understood in terms of suggestion. On the other hand, he argued that this was induced at the level of the nervous system; in short, that suggestion has a *physical* cause or effect.
16. *Lancet*, 25 March 1843, p. 937. The article explored insanity and somnambulism, and their relationship to the notion of the individual's responsibility for his actions under the law. See also Hacking 1995, pp. 221–22; and for a broader discussion of Wakley's role in the career of the mesmerist John Elliotson, see Winter 1998.
17. Winter 1998.
18. Amongst those to take a special interest in such terms in the 1890s was the philosopher William James. Morton Prince, the American pioneer of theories of multiple personality disorder who came to lead the Boston school of psychology, also used the word 'dissociation' in print in 1890, after his visit to France. Janet by contrast dropped it after the appearance of his philosophy thesis, *Psychological Automatism* (1889), and became increasingly sceptical. These remarks are drawn from Hacking's survey (1995).
19. Quoted in Harrington 1988, p. 228; this article also has a good account of the emergence of 'transfer'; see also Carroy 1991. In an 1845 discussion of magnetism Aubin Gauthier had already noted how morbidity crossed from the magnetiser to the magnetised (hence the importance of the mesmerist's healthy bodily and mental state); Gauthier 1845; cf. *Premier Congrès*

international de l'hypnotisme 1889, p. 159, for a statement on the significance of the hypnotist's health to the treatment of the patient.

20. Richer and de la Tourette 1889, p. 111.
21. The translations are from Hacking 1995, pp. 206–207. See also Ribot 1912, pp. 38–39, 107.
22. Hacking 1995, p. 64.
23. Ellenberger 1970. In his study of the subject, Hacking argues that in fact multiple personality does not teach anything much about what it is to be a person, to have a self and a mind; or at least, its implications remain very unclear. Nonetheless he shows how, historically, it has been taken to have enormous significance (Hacking 1995, p. 222).
24. Quoted in Ginneken 1992, p. 25.
25. 'Reading as a means of culture', *Sharpe's London Magazine* (1867), quoted in Mays 1995, p. 171. For some periodical discussions, *circa* 1900, about the implications of new fads, mass amusement, popular leisure and boredom, see Rosenberg and White 1957, p. 391.
26. Tarde 1890, p. 84.
27. For the history of crowd psychology, see Nye 1975; Barrows 1981, Ginneken 1992.
28. See Hughes 1958. 'Charisma' was a concept centrally at issue in the work of Max Weber. He differentiated institutional forms (whereby, for instance, certain robes, or the throne itself, acquired sacred meanings), from the overwhelming allure of such historical figures as Christ or Napoleon. Either way, Weber considered the modern world of action and instrumental rationality at odds with such factors. Charisma primarily belonged to an earlier set of social forces. The shaman, the witch-doctor or the prophet were not truly contemporary any more than such visceral forms of activity as ritual intoxication or self-mortification were congruent with the nature of the modern age. Weber assumed that moder-

nity signified, in principle, the decline of such forces, although he seemed equally impressed by their recalcitrant survival. Eisenstadt 1968; Lindholm 1990.

29. Such ideas were greatly elaborated and developed by Freud, who contended, by the time of *The Ego and the Id* (1923) that even a portion of the ego was unconscious. Certainly the crucial distinction between the conscious and unconscious remained, but the terms for understanding their relations were shifting. In a paper written during the First World War, entitled 'The Unconscious', Freud had already pointed out that in analytic encounters, neither participants could be sure of where their knowledge was coming from, since one unconscious spoke to another – in other words, without passing through the consciousness of either person.
30. Ginneken 1992. The second half of the nineteenth century has been described as the 'golden age of hypnotism' (Chertok 1989). Significantly, writers such as Tarde published what was in effect research on social psychology in specialist journals on hypnotism; thus, for instance, a piece on 'social somnambulism' appeared in the *Revue de l'hypnotisme*; see 'Les lois de l'imitation: le somnambulisme social'; *Revue*, 5 (1891), pp. 1–7.
31. Tarde 1890, p. 85.
32. Tarde 1890, ch. 7.
33. Tarde 1890, p. 97.
34. Chanon 1980.
35. Quoted in Brantlinger 1990, p. 103.
36. On the increasingly febrile hyping of 'goods' by a burgeoning advertising industry in the fifty years after the Great Exhibition of 1851, see Richards 1990.
37. Barthes 1957.
38. For a recent discussion of these issues, see Winter 1998.
39. Williams 1982; Weart 1988.
40. Quoted in Williams 1982, pp. 87–88.

41. Harrison 1886, p. 18.
42. In fact many of the new popular periodicals, circulating and railway libraries, which had mushroomed in the 1840s and 1850s, did seek to educate and inspire, as well as to amuse; Fraser 1981, pp. 74–75, 225. The remarkable sales of *Uncle Tom's Cabin*, which reached the British market in 1852, was the case *par excellence* of a maudlin style used to edify and activate.
43. Moscheles, who was a pupil of Beethoven, recounted how he had been instructed by a footman to ring the servants' bell when he appeared at a nobleman's house to give piano lessons to his daughter; Bowen 1939, p. 42. Lablache's gesture is described in ibid., p. 40.
44. Gay 1996, p. 35; see also p. 12 ff.
45. Baldick 1983.
46. The writer went on to track the process of religious suggestion, renewal and disillusionment across three novels in the 1890s, zigzagging from Catholic *Paris* to the Papal labyrinth itself. Zola's novel *Lourdes* also soon became a Catholic hate object in its own right, finding its way onto the Vatican index of forbidden books, which further fuelled the fire of the writer's complex anti-clerical passion. Amidst these tribulations he produced a fantastically tortuous saga of moral corruption, bureaucratic impenetrability, religious illusion and political frustration: *Rome* was a remarkably Kafkaesque novel, *avant la lettre*.
47. Harris 1999, p. 11.
48. Ellenberger 1970, pp. 164–65; Blackbourn 1995. In his history of hypnosis, Moll specifically referred to Lourdes as an example of modern suggestibility. Or again: 'An idea implanted in hypnosis takes root like a belief in Lourdes in a faithful Catholic.' (Moll 1906, p. 316). The first international congress of hypnotism also used Lourdes as a kind of template for suggestibility at large (*Premier Congrès international de l'hypnotisme* 1889, p. 94);

similarly, Bernheim discusses Lourdes as a classic example of modern suggestibility (see Bernheim 1891b).
49. Blackbourn 1995, p. 189.
50. Blackbourn 1995, p. 407.
51. Fraser 1981, p. 225.
52. Ackroyd 1990, p. 943.
53. Harrison 1886, p. 26.
54. An abbreviation of 'fanatic', the *Oxford English Dictionary* records its first use, in the United States in 1889, to mean a keen spectator of sport, although in the form 'fann' it had already been used in 1862. On the other hand 'craze', in the sense of 'insane or irrational fancy', occurs earlier (1813). But the *OED* records a new connotation of 'craze', a 'capricious and usually temporary enthusiasm' which emerged in the late nineteenth century. Thus a piece in the *Fortnightly Review* in 1887 referred, in this distinctive sense, to 'a quiet craze touching everything that pertains to Napoleon the Great and the Napoleonic legend'. Du Maurier himself had been one of the foremost English satirists of upper and middle class fashion and fashion victims, as his obituarist in *The Times* particularly stressed (anon. 1896b).
55. Other American fads of the 1890s included pigs-in-clover puzzles, a game that involved batting a balloon around ('Pillow-Dex') and a form of checkers called Halma; Skolnik 1978, p. 23; cf. Vermorel and Vermorel 1989.
56. Fishwick and Browne 1970, pp. 21, 23.
57. Quoted in Foldy 1997, p. 50.
58. Briggs 1988, p. 326.
59. Brantlinger 1990, p. 101.
60. James 1962b, vol. 9, pp. 185–230.

5   The Sexual Charge

1. Du Maurier 1994, p. 199.
2. 'The advantages of animal magnetism'; anon. 1841.
3. Visiting mesmerists such as 'Baron' Dupotet, Alexis and Adolphe Didier, J.B.

Marcillet, Adolphe Kiste and Charles Lafontaine were much discussed in Britain at the time.

4. Harte 1902, vol. 2, p. 61.

5. Winter 1992, p. 16, n. 7. In the 1790s, English mesmerists were already insistently differentiating their technique and ethics from those of 'their foreign brethren' (Kaplan 1974).

6. Winter 1992 and 1998.

7. Cavailhon 1882, pp. 36, 37. Professional hypnotisers such as Hansen and Donato are described, *inter alia*, in Ellenberger 1970, p. 85; Gauld 1992. For closely related debates on medical and popular hypnotic practices in wartime and Weimar Germany, see Lerner 1998. The emphasis on mastery of the visual field has long remained a central feature of hypnotic technique. In an inter-war popular manual in Italy, for instance, it was claimed that personal magnetism often depends on nothing more than charismatic eye contact (Paladino 1933). The manual advises the would-be hypnotist to practise in front of a mirror and to cultivate an unblinking commanding gaze.

8. Cavailhon 1882, p. 2. Donato did not like the term 'hypnotism', with its implication that the subject was asleep. For an influential contemporary discussion of Donato's hypnotic powers, see Morselli 1886.

9. Cavailhon 1882, p. xlvi.

10. Gallini 1983. On legal sanctions against mesmerism in Donato's country, Belgium, during the 1890s, see Lobet 1891.

11. By 1890 a law which prohibited unlicensed public performances had been enacted in France. Similar legislation was passed in Austria, Italy and the German state of Baden; Gallini 1983; Harris 1989; Lerner 1998.

12. Burrows 1912.

13. See Jordan 1895, verses 11, 20, 21, 68, 115.

14. Harris 1985 and 1989.

15. By the 1880s, Bernheim, Liégeois and others concertedly argued that case; Harris 1989; Gauld 1992, p. 497.

16. *Premier Congrès internationale de l'hypnotisme* 1889; Duyckaerts 1992. Prominent participants at the Congress included Charcot, Bernheim, Richet, Mesnet and Lombroso. Delegates came from many countries and from as far afield as Mexico, Haiti and Venezuela. Dr Myers (doyen of 'psychical research') was there, as was the philosopher William James.

17. Some of the 'serious-minded' neurologists of the age in fact become interested in hypnotism after seeing popular performances in the 1870s and 1880s by Hansen, in Germany, or Donato in Belgium, France and Italy; Ellenberger 1970, p. 85.

18. On the persistence of mesmerism, and claims for its material basis, see Harrington 1988. Harrington shows that, despite the rise of neurological explanations of hypnotism in the late nineteenth century, particularly associated with the work and reputation of Charcot, 'animal magnetism' never quite disappeared. Indeed it made a 'come-back', via the work of Victor Jean-Marie Burq (1822–84) who had long been experimenting with the application of metallic plates to afflicted parts of his clients' bodies. At the request of Claude Bernard, to whom Burq had appealed for support, the magnetist's claims were seriously investigated by Charcot and his pupils. What Harrington calls 'neo-mesmerism' remained part of the repertoire of explanations for the enigmatic and still much debated phenomenon of induced trance states in the late nineteenth century. In short, a materialist account of how magnetism or some hitherto unknown metallic property affected the body, perhaps the nervous system, continued to be advanced long after Braid had coined the term 'hypnotism' in the 1840s.

19. Lyster was chorus master and assistant

conductor to Boscha. He described the Master's power to provoke fascination and repulsion, with his guttural voice, dark features and flamboyant clothes. He was entrancing and somewhat fearsome. Under his influence, Anna thrilled her audiences. Lyster claimed her music lessons had been carried out under hypnosis; Alexander's introduction to Du Maurier 1973.

20. Northcott 1920, pp. 85–99.

21. Thus in 1889 Albert de Rochas, an energetic investigator of the occult, had taken a model named Lina and put her in deep trance. Under his sway, she was able to sing with aplomb and dance with great agility. Soon after 1900, Professor Leon Silvani announced in San Francisco that he had turned a tone-deaf girl called Viola West into a 'singing nightingale' through hypnotism. Between 1903 and 1906, a Swiss hypnotist, Emile Magnin, created an act around a woman who would dance and sing at the man's bidding. These examples are drawn from Alexander's introduction to Du Maurier 1973.

22. Moscheles 1896, pp. 45, 47, 52, 56, 59.

23. Winter 1998.

24. The former tale features a sinister Italian monk from Palermo who, through drugs and other nefarious methods, takes over the body and mind of the narrator's wife, Louisa. The latter story concerns a woman's ambiguous suicide – or murder – raising the question of whether a somnambulist might be induced to take poison; anon. 1861 and 1862.

25. Anon. 1891; cf. Harte 1902, vol. 2, pp. 88–114.

26. Mesnet 1894, p. xiv.

27. Mesnet 1894, pp. xix, xiv, xvii.

28. For further instances of such sexual and criminological apprehensions, see Gallini 1983; Harris 1989; Gauld 1992.

29. Ellenberger 1970, pp. 161–65; cf. Tatar 1978.

30. Schaffer 1996, p. 56. My sketch of the trade in automata merely summarises

material provided in Schaffer's valuable article.

31. Ellenberger 1970, p. 60.

32. Schaffer 1996, p. 68.

33. This was not the Turk's first visit; he had initially been presented in London in 1783.

34. Willis' study, entitled *Attempt to Analyse the Automaton Chess Player*, revealed the illusion in 1820. The notorious hoax led to Maelzel's departure. He eventually died on board ship near Cuba in 1838, whilst the Turk was destroyed in a fire in Philadelphia in the early 1850s; Schaffer 1996.

35. Already in the official inquiry into Mesmer's work in the 1780s, one important participant (Bailly) had noted that animal magnetism was perilous to the decorous relations of the sexes. In the course of the nineteenth century, unease with the sexual and moral implications of the practice intensified.

36. Oldrà 1922, p. 35.

37. One of Mesmer's early followers, Deleuze, made the case for the utility of this amorous dimension, although others dissented from his view.

38. Harris 1985.

39. James [1874] 1962a, references to pp. 56, 261–62, 286, 295.

40. On several occasions in 1838, Dickens attended the doctor's mesmeric sessions and went on to refer to Elliotson as 'one of my most intimate and valued friends'. He was notably supportive of this increasingly beleaguered practitioner after his hospital had turned against him. Elliotson became family doctor to the Dickens family. Ackroyd reports that Dickens in turn tried to help him when in later life he became despondent and even suicidal. 'I am a believer,' Dickens later declared: 'I became so against all my preconceived opinions and impressions' (Ackroyd 1990, pp. 473–74).

41. Rosa's ill-fated proposed marriage to Edwin Drood had been decreed by a

parent, now dead: 'a husband has been chosen for her by will and bequest'; Dickens, 1895b, p. 17.

42. Jasper was one amongst several of Dickens' late villains whose faces concealed rather than revealed their nature. Unlike, say, Fagin or Sikes, these characters are socially respectable but secretly perverse. They cannot be *seen* in their lowliness or wickedness. Similarly, in another of Dickens' late novels, *Our Mutual Friend* (1865), the figure of Bradley Headstone is the epitome of decency on the surface, but deep down he has bestial impulses and deranged thoughts: 'he broke loose at night like a wild ill-tamed animal'. Headstone fostered the imp of his own perversity, nursing 'a kind of perverse pleasure akin to that which a sick man sometimes has in irritating a wound upon his body'. Dickens, 1895, p. 453.

43. Dickens, 1895b, pp. 109, 120, 51, 163.

6 Queen of Song

1. Dickens [1870] 1895b, p. 51.
2. Du Maurier 1994, p. 272.
3. Conan Doyle 1985, p. 37.
4. The contributor in question was Dr Tuckey. He presented a number of cases involving abrupt nervous collapse, situations in which the subject mysteriously lost her voice or manual dexterity. For his clinical account, as presented, to the Société d'Hypnologie et de Psychologie in 1893, see Tuckey 1894.
5. Carse 1948, p. 349.
6. Said 1991, p. 4; see also Peter Gay 1996.
7. Carse 1951, p. 126.
8. Carse 1948 and 1951, p. 97.
9. Carse 1951, p. 122.
10. Quoted in Carse 1951, p. 126.
11. Quoted in Bowen 1939, p. 308.
12. Quoted in Bowen 1939, p. 280.
13. Bowen 1939, p. 332.
14. Canetti 1984, p. 460.
15. Lebrecht 1991, p. 31.

16. Du Maurier 1994, p. 191.
17. A new group of performers, led by Lind, 'amid temptations difficult to be withstood, may be deemed worthy models of conduct in domestic life'; Foster 1850, p. 4.
18. Lind 1966, p. 111.
19. Anon. (*Lindiana*) 1847a, p. 36.
20. Rosenberg 1850, p. 37; see also Bulman 1956, p. 164.
21. Christiansen 1984, p. 94.
22. Even a legal dispute with a disappointed impresario was published by the plaintiff, and became a commercial success; on 'The Case of Bunn versus Jenny Lind', see Bulman 1956, p. 190.
23. Anon. (*Lindiana*) 1847b, p. 8.
24. Bulman 1956, p. 107.
25. Bulman 1956, p. 107.
26. Meyerbeer, Mendelssohn and Lind are all directly mentioned in *Trilby*.
27. Mendelssohn's adroit musical gestures, status and wealth were sometimes seen to raise him above his racial background altogether. As a commentator put it in 1939, '[h]ow clever of Mr Mendelssohn to have written a *Scottish Symphony!*' (Bowen 1939, p. 41).
28. Thackeray's specific target here is Disraeli's *Coningsby*; Thackeray 1879, pp. 28–29.
29. Christiansen 1995, p. 95.
30. Bulman 1956, pp. 278–79.
31. Foster 1850, p. 34. See also Bulman 1956, pp. 22, 57.
32. Foster 1850, p. 4. Note the poem published in 1847 entitled 'The Jenny Lind Mania'.
33. On Barnum's career as impresario and circus organiser, see Rosenberg and White 1957, p. 61. Barnum pioneered new forms of circus spectacular from the 1850s. He introduced American audiences not only to General Tom Thumb and Jenny Lind but also to the world's largest elephant, Jumbo. His purchase of the animal from the Royal Zoological Gardens in London in 1882 led to some protests.
34. Bulman 1956, pp. 250, 256.

35. Anon. 1847c, pp. 456, 457. For the doctor's own account, see Braid 1852, p. 34.
36. *British Medical Journal,* 16 November 1895, reprinted in Hart 1982, p. 209.

7   Racial Hypnosis

1. Du Maurier 1994, pp. 66–67.
2. The phrase is borrowed from George Eliot's *Daniel Deronda.*
3. Anon. (*Punch*) 1895c, p. 232.
4. Quotations from *Trilby* in Du Maurier 1994, respectively pp. 58, 6, 7, 48.
5. See particularly the discussion of Wagner's *Judaism in Music,* in chapter nine, above; Wagner 1910.
6. Eliot 1995, p. 626.
7. Luska [1885], 1984. There is no reason to think Du Maurier knew of this obscure tale, published in New York.
8. Boyle 1878, p. 11.
9. *Spectator* (2 November 1878), quoted in Wohl 1995, p. 404. Wohl gives various other contemporary instances in which Disraeli was ascribed supernatural powers.
10. Wohl 1995, p. 405
11. 'Comus' 1876, pp. 4–5. Such epithets were not unknown in the Gladstone household and more widely in non-conformist political discussion. Gladstone's niece, Lady Lucy Cavendish, fantasised: 'I shot Dizzy in a brougham, looking more horribly like a fiend than ever, green, with a glare in his eye'. Battiscombe 1956, p. 174.
12. By the last decades of the century, the Jews 'are now depicted as dangerously organised and scheming anti-Christians' (Wohl 1995, p. 380).
13. See Rather 1987; Wohl 1995.
14. Quoted in Wohl 1995, p. 404.
15. Anon. 1877, p. 14.
16. *Public Opinion,* (September 6, 1876), quoted in Wohl, 1995, p. 405.
17. J.W. Gould, 'The grand old Pilot', *Liberal World, A Monthly Journal and Review for Young Men* (1880), quoted in Wohl 1995, p. 405.
18. Kaplan 1975, p. 11; Winter 1992, p. 79.
19. Physicians considered themselves to be faced by a 'veritable army of nefarious magnetizers' intent on raping women and generally corrupting society; the ranks of these dangerous manipulators, 'typically included Jews, working-class men, criminals, magnetizing performers, amateur healers and household servants'; Harris 1989, p. 159.
20. Moll 1906, p. 5.
21. Moll 1906, p. 381.
22. It was adapted by Leopold Lewis from *Le Juif polonais,* by Émile Erckmann and Alexandre Chatrian. The original had first been performed in Paris in 1869. For another British adaptation of the text, see Ware 1872.
23. Mayer 1980.
24. Stanislavski 1924, p. 243.
25. Lewis n.d. [1871], pp. 29, 10, 14.
26. Kaplan 1975.
27. Dickens [1838] 1895a, pp. 115, 52, 91, 276, 317.
28. Dickens [1838] 1895a, pp. 249, 250, 327.
29. Ackroyd 1990, p. 1089; cf. Kaplan 1975, p. 239.
30. The death precipitates madness in Nancy's friend Bet.
31. Ackroyd 1990, pp. 546, 1090, 1098.
32. The reference persists in more recent cultural production; one of the key icons of anti-Semitism in Hollywood cinema, as we are told in a recent study, is 'the squinting, marginal, and disruptively askance look' of the Jew (Nochlin and Garb 1995, p. 240).
33. Esdaile [1850] 1957, p. 135; see also Winter 1998, ch. 8.
34. Although establishing any intentional link between India and Du Maurier's villain may be stretching things too far, one might note in passing the reference in the novel to 'fading Bengal fires' as Trilby finishes a song; Du Maurier 1994, p. 199.
35. See for instance, amongst numerous articles, 'The advantages of animal magnetism', anon. 1841; 'The oracle of som-

nambulism', anon. 1851a; 'Mesmeric bliss', anon. 1872. See also anon. 1853 and anon. 1860.

36. 'Mesmerism: its dangers and curiosities'; anon. 1844 , p. 100.

37. 'Among his pet hates we must not forget the gorgeous flunky and the guzzling alderman, the leering old fop, the rascally book-maker, the sweating Jew tradesman and the poor little snob (the 'Arry of his day)'; Du Maurier 1898, p. 41.

38. 'Hebrew of the Hebrews'; anon. 1874, p. 254.

39. See chapter nine.

40. Mosso 1896, p. 94.

41. Anon. 1894b, p. 149.

42. On the history of the legend, see Anderson 1965.

43. Drumont 1889, pp. xvii–xviii.

44. Meige 1893, pp. 7–8, 27, 54–55; Goldstein 1985; Hacking 1998.

45. In a recent book, *Mad Travellers*, Ian Hacking points out how Meige's inquiry into the 'wandering Jews' occurred in the context of the psychiatric theory of fugue, first elaborated in the work of a French doctor, Tissié, in the 1880s; see Hacking 1998, pp. 113–124; cf. Borch-Jacobsen 1999.

46. 'The Mission of the Jews' (anon. 1893–94b); 'The Russian and his Jew' (Bigelow 1893–94); 'Where is the wandering Jew now?' (anon. 1893–94a).

47. Sombart 1913, p. 278.

48. For some remarks, however, on the interest of one or two nineteenth-century rabbis in the powers of mesmerism, see Zimmels 1952, pp. 82, 134.

49. Brouardel 1879, pp 39–59. See also the compelling evocation of this and other such medico-legal trials in Harris 1989, pp. 187–8, and passim.

50. White 1899, pp. 158, 159.

51. On philo-Semitism in this period, see Manuel 1992, p. 40.

52. See the discussion in Gilder and Gilder 1895.

53. Ormond 1969, p. 454. Another biographer mentions (without adding any further comment) the 'Semitic fea-

tures' of Moscheles, the man who introduced Du Maurier to mesmerism; Kelly 1996, p. 5.

54. Du Maurier 1947, p. 469.

55. *Hansard* [1847], quoted in Ragussis 1997, p. 295.

56. 'A Jew' is in fact the prolific writer and folklorist Joseph Jacobs; see Jacobs 1877, p. 107; cf. Ragussis 1997, p. 296. Jacobs goes on to refer to 'unconscious Judaeophobia'.

57. Ragussis 1997.

58. Du Maurier 1947, p. 541.

59. Note how Freud himself differentiates Gustave Le Bon's undynamic late-nineteenth-century conception of the racial 'unconscious' from psychoanalytic understanding of the concept; Freud 1921, p. 75n.

60. Lucas 1934, p. 385.

61. Lucas 1934, p. 396.

62. Wilde made the reference in a letter written in 1886; Wilde 1962, p. 193.

63. Millar 1937, p. 76.

64. Marc-André Raffalovich (1864–1934), known as André, was the younger son of parents who had migrated from Odessa to Paris in 1863. His father became a prosperous banker who moved in elevated artistic and scientific circles. He and his wife claimed friendship with Claude Bernard, Ernest Renan and other well-known members of Parisian intellectual society; the Raffalovich's daughter, Sophie, also a writer, married the Irish Nationalist William O'Brien in 1890. André came to London in 1884. His intention of going from there to study at Oxford was abandoned due to health problems. He eventually moved to Edinburgh, with his lover, John Gray (also a prominent convert to Catholicism).

65. On André Raffalovich's relationship with his 'chaperone', Miss Florence Truscott Gribbel, see Sewell 1968, pp. 24–25.

66. Raffalovich would later make rather derogatory remarks about Wilde's

downfall, publishing a small book on the subject, *L'Affaire Oscar Wilde,* in Paris in 1895, which was to be incorporated into a larger work, *Uranisme et unisexualité,* which appeared in the Bibliothèque de Criminologie, edited by Dr Lacassagne. Henry Havelock Ellis quoted Raffalovich's commentary on Wilde in his sexological studies. Raffalovich claimed that Wilde had given the word 'artistic' a new sexual innuendo. He also noted that 'musical' was acquiring covert erotic implications in the period; Raffalovich 1896, pp. 188–89; cf. Smith 1970, p. 53.

67. National Film Archive Collection Print of Harold Shaw's version of 'Trilby' (1914). This was a version of Sir Herbert Tree and His Majesty's Theatre Company Production of 'Trilby', made by the London Film Co. Ltd.

68. Taylor 1996, p. xxiv.

69. Towse 1916, p. 446.

70. Taylor 1992, pp. 104–105; cf. Beerbohm 1920, p. ix.

71. Sombart 1913.

72. Leroy-Beaulieu, 1895, pp. 150, 244.

73. 'On the Problem of the actor', *The Gay Science* (1882), in Nietzsche 1974.

74. Compare Alexandre Dumas fils, who insisted that on stage the Jew must always be a buffoon; to which Leroy-Beaulieu adds, the Jew becomes a 'fantastic automaton', always confined to the same role (Leroy-Beaulieu 1895, p. 286).

75. Nietzsche 1974, pp. 316–17, section 361. The translator of this text by Nietzsche points out that the very word chosen in German here, 'Frauenzimmer', has derogatory implications.

76. Millar 1937, p. 154.

77. Hart [1896] 1982, p. 207.

78. In a major study, Albert Moll noted the link between actors and hypnotic subjects; Moll 1906, p. 153.

79. Shaw 1928, p. 232. In a recent article, George Taylor has shown that Tree's additions to his prompt copy of the play confirms this particular melodramatic emphasis on the character's egotism. Tree restored Svengali's gruesome 'Paris Morgue' reverie over Trilby's imagined dead body and also played up his blasphemy. The ensuing heart-attack is thus more directly presented as a punishment for the Jew's hubris; Taylor 1992, p. 109.

80. Shaw 1928, vol. 1, p. 231.

81. St John 1949, p. 208. Shaw rejected this kind of acting based on what he called 'the somnambulistic method and the artificial voice' (p. 208). See also Taylor 1992, p. 105.

82. Archer 1883, pp. 31, 47, 50.

83. Quoted in Taylor 1992, p. 105. Tree also lectured in the 1890s on the relationship between acting, imagination and unconscious behaviour; ibid.

84. Stanislavski 1924, pp. 169–70.

85. Beerbohm 1920, p. 185.

86. Towse 1916, pp. 446–47; Taylor 1992, p. 108. This theatre critic celebrated the wonderful performance with its perfect illusion of dirtiness and 'spidery' character, although he felt that Tree did not have the true greatness which was a prerequisite for playing tragic heroes.

87. When an interviewer relayed this supposedly verbatim remark back to him many years later, the old ex-analysand expressed incredulity at the idea he could have said such a thing. For the complex implications and political (mis)uses of these 'recollections' in current debates, see Forrester 1997, ch. 6.

88. Obholzer 1982, p. 38; see also Borch-Jacobsen 1996, p. 30. Bernheim, whose new studies on hypnosis Freud had translated in 1892, had also made the point that 'suggestive psychotherapy' might work just as effectively, if not more effectively, without hypnosis in the formal sense (Bernheim 1891a and b).

89. Quoted in Gay 1978, p. 117. McDougall nonetheless insisted on the friendliness of his challenge to Freud, and also went on to repudiate frank versions of anti-Semitism in the 1920s.

90. Freud 1914, pp. 39-40. See also Freud's Italian critic Morselli's discussion of how psychoanalysis conflates specifically Jewish neuroses about circumcision with the notion (fallacious in Morselli's view) of a universal castration complex; Morselli 1923, vol. 1, p. 178.
91. Freud 1914, p. 43.
92. Gay 1978, p. 121. Gay refers to Freud's position as that of a 'Godless Jew'. Whilst Freud may have called himself an 'old Semite', he repudiated the idea of a specifically Jewish science. In another sense, however, Freud viewed his outsider position as Jew as crucially enabling. It allowed him, he remarked (in a reference to Ibsen's play), to tolerate being 'an enemy of the people'; ibid., p. 137. Another scholar, Gilman (1993b), criticises Gay's account, emphasising racial rather than religious aspects of the perception of Jewishness in Freud and more widely in the period.
93. Quoted in Gilman 1993b, p. 31.
94. This was by no means the first time he had ventured into this territory; see Gilman 1993b, p. 31.
95. Jung 1970 [1934], p. 159.
96. The complex odyssey of Freud's thought on the matter, particularly from *Totem and Taboo* to *Moses and Monotheism* is discussed in Yerushalmi's elegant book, *Freud's Moses* (1991).
97. Jung 1970 [1934], pp. 165-66. See also Yerushalmi 1991, pp. 48–49.
98. It is not certain why the word 'Aryan' but not 'Jew' is placed in inverted commas in Jung's remarks. To argue that it was because the Jew is viewed as a more straightforward entity, not needing the qualification implied by such punctuation, does not seem entirely convincing, given the highly problematic nature of the whole Jewish issue in his thought. For a debate about the necessity or otherwise of such cautionary quotation marks around the word 'Jew' in contemporary critical discussions, see the introduction to Cheyette

and Marcus 1998.
99. For a series of discussions of Jung's 1934 paper and more generally of his relationship to Freud and to anti-Semitism, see Maidenbaum and Martin 1991.

8 Evil Eye

1. Du Maurier 1994, p. 82.
2. Du Maurier 1994, p. 265.
3. Bright 1895, pp 415–16.
4. James 1897, pp. 599, 601.
5. The psychological factors that may enable the patient to observe and to tolerate being observed have been the subject of much exploration, as has the nature of the symbolic investment in the eye as well as psychosomatic disorders of vision. These were explored in early psychoanalytic papers, *inter alia* by George Groddeck (1977) and William Inman (see 'Unpublished Sources' in the bibliography); for an important contemporary psychoanalytic discussion of the underlying processes, see Britton 1998, especially ch. 4.
6. For biographical details, see Ormond 1969.
7. Potter [1895] 1996, p. 236.
8. Kern 1996, p. 95.
9. This refers to Taffy's mastery of Svengali; Du Maurier 1994, p. 223.
10. Du Maurier 1994, p 213.
11. S—— 1890, p. 2. It was also explained that in order to fascinate, there must be an eye that can command steadfastness of vision as well as a resolute and concentrated will; ibid., p. 11. Cf. Connor 1998, p. 11. I draw more generally on Connor's essay in my account here.
12. Conan Doyle 1894, pp. 39–40.
13. The names of Richet, Charcot and Bernheim all feature in the story
14. Quoted in Valman 1996, p. 84.
15. Eliot 1995 [1876], pp. 329, 330, 409, 332.
16. See for instance the piece, 'Fascinateurs

et jettatores' in the *Revue de l'hypnotisme* (anon. 1888); see also Moll 1906, p. 78. Amongst the great believers in the evil eye, Moll particularly draws attention to southern Europeans and the Jews of North Africa, as well as Christians and Moslems throughout the Middle East.

17. On Jewish amulets that offered protection against the evil eye, see Trachtenberg 1939, pp. 54–56; Zimmels 1952, pp. 135–39 and 'The Evil Eye', *Jewish Encyclopaedia*, vol. 5, pp. 280–81; Hsia 1988. On the medieval assumption that sorcerers and their victims could be discerned by the fixed stare of their eyes, see Trachtenberg 1939, p. 13. Pre-medieval examples of the Jewish evil eye legend have also been noted. One fourth century edict, cited by Trachtenberg, forbade the Jews from blessing crops while standing in a field.

18. Friedenwald 1897.

19. Quoted in Friedenwald, 1977, vol. 1, p. 5.

20. Elworthy 1895. The extent to which the evil eye was connected to the Jews in and beyond the Middle Ages has been debated by historians; see Trachtenberg 1943, p. 70.

21. Elworthy 1895, p. 36.

22. See especially Gilman 1993a, pp. 42-63; Siebers 1983, p. 50 and, more generally, ch. 2, 'Anthropology and the Evil Eye'.

23. Dundes 1991.

24. Trachtenberg 1943, pp. 28, 152; Dubnov 1916–20, vol. 2, p. 77.

25. Romaine 1753, p. 1.

26. Romaine 1753, pp. 8-9; cf. Endelman 1979, p. 125.

27. Deuteronomy, ch. 28 in *The Holy Bible*.

28. Dundes 1991, p. 104.

29. Bernheim 1891b, p. 247.

30. It had taken two years for the case to come to court and for the defendant to be found not guilty. For the published protest involving many prominent public figures, including Rider Haggard, George Bernard Shaw, H.G. Wells, Arthur Conan Doyle, Thomas Hardy,

Frederick Harrison, Karl Pearson and Edwin Ray Lankester, see Hertz 1913.

31. Dubnov 1916–20, vol. 2, p. 77; Hsia 1988, p. 2. For late-nineteenth-century examples of these fears, see Leroy-Beaulieu 1895.

32. How the social realities of Jewish occupations in those pre-modern societies interlocked with such hostile, or at the very least, prescriptive, assumptions about Jewish nature is a complex question which has generated considerable research by historians. In a study of the myth of ritual murder in the early modern period, Po-Chia Hsia points out that some Jews took possession, as it were, of the distinct character they had been ascribed, thus becoming fortune tellers, healers or magicians. To explore this further would entail closer scrutiny of the way in which the very idea of a person was tied to the fulfilment – the 'enactment' – of a particular social role in those periods. Historians of the Jews and of anti-Semitism have documented how gentile myths were amalgamated with the rich magical stories to be found within the tradition of the *Kabbalah*. Gentile ideas about the Jews' special powers shaped the way people lived their lives, just as experiences of persecution and hardship impinged upon Jewish culture: 'Demons of all sorts populated the religious folklore of medieval Jewry; theirs was a world haunted by diseases and disasters, often induced by evil spirits. Magical formulas, gems, amulets, talismans, medical cures, omens, dreams, and divination, filled this imaginative universe founded on a real life of perpetual insecurity and frequent brutality' (Hsia 1988, p. 7).

33. See the discussion and references below.

34. Quoted in Trachtenberg 1943, p. 94.

35. Hsia 1988, p. 5.

36. The likelihood that the accusations were trumped up, or even that Lopez was framed, amidst the various court

intrigues of the time, have been much studied, including by historians working in the late nineteenth century. The literature shows that Lopez's Jewish background was at least a factor in accusations against him; he was, according to the Solicitor-General, 'that vile Jew', 'wily and covetous' (quoted in Hyamson 1908, p. 139). Another report described him as a 'Jewish doctor, worse than Judas himself', but it is difficult to assess the role of such rhetoric. For regardless of his Jewishness, he was vulnerable as a royal physician and foreigner in a period when suspicion of plots (particularly orchestrated from Spain) were so intense; Marcham 1927. Whilst *fin de siècle* commentators published scholarly articles on the Lopez affair and its significance as a source for Shakespeare's Shylock, *The Merchant of Venice* itself was frequently on tour: Irving was particularly admired in the title role; see Dimock 1894; Hale 1894. The Lopez case was also discussed at some length in a major study (under the auspices of the Jewish Historical Society of England) of the history of the Jews in England that was published during the Edwardian period; see Hyamson 1908.

37. Quoted in Trachtenberg 1943, p. 76. The expulsion was from Papal territory bar Rome and Ancona.

38. On the opportunities available to Jewish doctors in the Middle Ages, but also on the powerful apprehensions they aroused, see Shatzmiller 1994.

39. Gombrich 1960, p. 96.

40. Gifford 1958, p. 8 and *passim*.

41. Gallini 1973, pp. 102–103.

42. See De Martino 1963 on the evil eye's propensity to spy, grudge, harm, control and fascinate; the figure of the *jettatore* is explored in detail by De Martino in ch. 4.

43. Quoted in Di Stasi 1981, pp. 33–34.

44. At the Second International Folk-Lore Congress, the anthropologist E.B. Tylor presented material on charms and amulets that warded off the evil eye; Jacobs and Nutt 1891, pp. 387–93. For further studies of the evil eye from around this period, see Elworthy 1895; cf. Seligmann 1910 and 1922.

45. The psychoanalytic and, more specifically, Kleinian literature on envy, and the primitive infantile anxieties about the consequences of envy for both the subject and object, disabuses us of any notion that the underlying psychic beliefs at stake in the 'evil eye' are ever fully superseded or surpassed, whatever the personal, social and historical determinants. The classic discussion is to be found in Klein 1957. For a novel and thoughtful attempt to use Kleinian ideas about envy, infancy and the maternal function in the consideration of early modern witchcraft, see Roper 1994.

46. Maclagan 1902, pp. 3–4.

47. Maclagan 1902, pp. 28–29.

48. Di Stasi 1981, pp. 41–43.

49. The impresario J.H. Mapleson, quoted in Christiansen 1984, p. 102.

50. Leroy-Beaulieu 1895, p. 173.

51. Drumont 1889, p. xv.

52. Sombart 1913, p. 263.

53. Hawthorne 1937 [1860], p. 617.

54. The examples sketched in this passage are drawn from Sander Gilman's various essays on the subject (for instance, 1991 and 1993a).

55. Gilman 1991, p. 64; Gilman 1993a, p. 43 For a later and more illustrious literary example of this trope, consider the way D.H. Lawrence presents the Jewess Yvette, with her 'resentful brown eyes' in *The Virgin and the Gypsy* (1930). One detects the persistence of that enduring discourse of the 'Jew's body' (to say nothing of the gypsy's) of which the eye was itself one particularly prominent feature. The gypsy has 'black eyes, which seemed to shoot her [Yvette] in some vital, undiscovered place, unerring'. Yvette's eye contact with the gypsy also brings us back obliquely to the theme of som-

nambulism: 'The childlike, sleep-walking eyes of her moment of perfect virginity looked into his, unseeing. She was only aware of the dark strange effluence of him bathing her limbs, washing her at last purely will-less. She was aware of *him*, as a dark, complete power' (Lawrence 1970, pp. 55, 48).

56. Even the Jewish specialist on folk tales, Joseph Jacobs, concurred in Victorian findings as to the 'typicality' of the Jewish face in general and the eyes in particular. Admittedly he differed from Galton and company in the gloss he then put on this: he found social rather than natural explanations for the common elements of the observed physiognomy. In his commentary on photographic composites of Jewish schoolboys, it is clear how much ground Jacobs shared with Galton (see Jacobs 1891). His essay on 'Anthropological Types' in *The Jewish Encyclopaedia* noted that these 'eyes themselves are generally brilliant, both eyelids are heavy and bulging, and it seems to be the main characteristic of the Jewish eye that the upper lid covers a larger proportion of the pupil than among other persons. This may serve to give a sort of nervous furtive look to the eyes, which, when the pupils are small and set close together with semistabismus, gives keenness to some Jewish eyes.' Quoted in Gilman 1991, pp. 44; see also pp. 45, 49.

57. Leroy-Beaulieu 1895, p. 215.

58. Thackeray 1879, p. 18.

59. 'The deep and disciplined intelligence of Tancred, trained in all the philosophy and cultured with all the knowledge of the West, acted with magnetic power upon a consciousness, the bright vivacity of which was only equalled by its virgin ignorance of all that books can teach, and of those great convulsions which the studious hour can alone elaborate' (Disraeli 1847, vol. 3, pp. 64–65).

60. Disraeli 1847, vol. 2, p. 42.

61. Law 1891, p. 203.

62. Thorne 1903, pp. 71, 25.

63. On the central role attributed to eye contact in hypnosis, see, for example, Moll 1906, pp. 115–16.

64. Figes 1996, p. 31.

65. On Rasputin's powers of hypnosis, and more generally on his mesmerising eyes, see De Jonge 1982, pp. 75–78, 154 and *passim*. De Jonge's book also describes the various other alluring healers who captivated the Tsar and Tsarina before Rasputin's time; see also Katlov 1967, p. 425; Fuhrmann 1990, pp. 27–29

66. Here is Fernande Olivier, describing how she first met Picasso in 1904: his eyes were 'dark, profound, piercing, strange, almost staring'. Picasso's eyes, wrote Gertrude Stein, with regard to the same period, 'were more wonderful than even I remembered, so full and so brown, and his hands so dark and delicate and alert'. In 1920, when Maurice Raynal was disappointed with Picasso's latest exhibition, he wrote: 'Some of the stars in his eyes have gone out.' As John Berger concludes: 'The eyes in the head become a symbol for the whole man. In the films about Picasso you can see his eyes for yourself. They reveal – or so it seems to me – the inordinate intensity of the man's inner life and at the same time the solitariness of that life.

'Little by little we are being forced to consider the general nature, the trend of Picasso's subjective experience. How to define the spirit which he himself values more than his work, which charges his presence, and which burns in his eyes?' (Berger, 1965, pp. 14–15).

67. In the case of Hitler: 'The swiftness of the transition from one mood to another was startling: one moment his eyes would be filled with tears and pleading, the next blazing with fury, or glazed with the faraway look of the visionary.' (Bullock 1962, p. 377). Bullock notes how Hitler retained 'an

uncanny gift of personal magnetism which defies analysis'. 'This was connected with the curious power of his eyes, which are persistently said to have had some sort of hypnotic quality' (ibid.). In conversation with some followers, Hitler is said to have discussed in clinical fashion the process of influencing and dominating the masses; 'Le secret de la domination des masses', Rauschning 1939, 237–42; cf. Borch-Jacobsen, Michaud and Nancy 1984, p. 111. On the political legacies of Gustave Le Bon, see Nye 1975. Another pertinent example which could be included in this inventory of the 'hypnotising look' is provided by Mussolini; various contemporaries remarked on Mussolini's fascinating eyes, face and body; Passerini 1991, pp. 71–72.

68. Freud 1921, p. 125.

9   The Training of Sorrow

1. Du Maurier 1947, p. 674.
2. Queen Victoria to Lord Salisbury (9 September 1899); quoted in Tombs 1998, p. 495.
3. Tombs 1998. I rely more generally on Tombs' account in this passage.
4. Dimock 1894, p. 472. In response, a defence of Shakespeare's racial attitudes appeared in the *English Historical Review* a few months later; see Hale 1894.
5. As Carroy and Plas write, the adversaries of the Dreyfusards were able to reverse the more familiar argument about anti-Semitic obscurantism, claiming that the supposed 'friends of truth' were in fact magicians and somnambulists (1995, p. 51). Anti-Dreyfusards were also accused on occasion of being malign hypnotists; Forth 1998, pp. 74–75.
6. Carroy and Plas 1995, p. 47. This article also tells the story of Dreyfus and the 'somnambule' in more detail.
7. The focus in the present study is largely on British and French sources. While some German material has been pre-

sented in these chapters, for instance, Wagner's *Judaism in Music*, no attempt has been made here to explore the national context of such views, or the secondary literature that relates anti-Semitism to national history and, in particular, to 'the German question'. Suffice it to say that the imagery and theories highlighted here by and large in the English and French examples upon which I have drawn can certainly also be found in the German primary literature. How far there were specific German 'inflections' to such widespread metaphors of the Jew at issue in the current discussion has been debated by many scholars. Examples of the early modern sources that lay behind the nineteenth-century perception amongst German writers and artists of the Jews as burrowing, beguiling and formidably astute 'aliens' can be found in the specialist literature. For wide-ranging surveys of German material, see, for instance, Mosse 1970, Low 1979; Rose 1990. The case for the particularly powerful and influential consequences of the concept of 'Jew-ification' in Germany is made in Rose 1990, see especially p. 44. Gay (1978) notably challenges earlier scholars who have presented a monolithic image of the Jews in late nineteenth-century Germany. He stresses the variety of motives for, and forms of, anti-Semitism. For some, he argues, it was a form of social snobbery, for others the basis for a murderous eugenic programme; for some a function of family tradition, for others a scientific mission. Gay discusses the contradictory views of a number of major intellectuals at the time as well as numerous minor writers. On attitudes to East European Jews in particular, see Wertheimer 1987. For the emergence of the term 'anti-Semitic' in the late 1870s in Germany, see Gay 1992, p. 217. Milfull 1993 contains a recent set of discussions of German anti-

Semitism at large. There are suggestive remarks on the differences between French and German anti-Semitism, in relation to psychiatric ideas of 'travelling insanity' and the 'wandering Jew', in Hacking 1998, p. 121.

8. Digeon 1959.

9. Barrès 1899, p. 5.

10. Quoted in Todorov 1993, p. 58.

11. Quoted in Todorov 1993, p. 58.

12. Quoted in Todorov 1993, p. 58.

13. Todorov 1993, p. 247; see also the development of this theme in Bauman 1991 and Zizek 1989.

14. White 1899, p. xvi.

15. For a discussion of these changing concerns, see Manuel 1992, p. 293.

16. See for instance White 1899 and Banister 1901.

17. Feldman 1994.

18. Compare Hitler's later view in *Mein Kampf,* where the Jew epitomises all that is wrong with cosmopolitan and polyglot culture. Despite the confusing effects of multilingualism, the racial character of Jews remains forever intact. The Jew can speak a thousand languages, but he is still and always the same Jew (Hitler 1992, p. 283). The Jew always seeks, moreover, to keep the male line pure. The Jewish man rarely marries a Christian and when a Christian marries a Jewess the offspring take after the Jewish side (ibid., p. 286). 'With satanic joy in his face, the black-haired Jewish youth lurks in wait for the unsuspecting girl whom he defiles with his blood, thus stealing her from her people' (ibid., p. 295).

19. Vacher de Lapouge 1899, p. 467.

20. Rather 1987.

21. Gay 1993, p. 81; Freeman 1895, vol. 2, pp. 242, 245, 428.

22. There were some connections between anti-Jewish and anti-African stereotypes, evident, for example, in the common notion that they shared in a basic physical ugliness. In late-nineteenth and early-twentieth-century Germany, the racial linkage of Jews and blacks was

extensively developed. In Britain, it had already been considered by Knox in *The Races of Men* (1850); see Efron 1994, pp. 51–52.

23. See Nochlin and Garb 1995, pp. 38, 176.

24. Du Maurier 1891, pp. 131, 44.

25. Hyam 1990.

26. Hobsbawm 1990.

27. Woolf 1910–11, p. 134.

28. Banister 1901, p. 39.

29. Sartre 1948.

30. *Observer* (Review), 26 May 1996, p. 14 (Self 1996).

31. Welch 1897.

32. White 1899, p. xvi.

33. A similar argument had been advanced, in less shrill language, a few years earlier in the *English Historical Review;* see Hale 1894.

34. See p. 38, above.

35. James 1947, p. 97; see also Edel 1969, p. 163.

36. 'So powerful is the force of Judaism that it can never be entirely destroyed in the heart of one born in the ancient faith' (Farjeon 1894, vol. 2, p. 94). Or as Aaron knows directly in his own family: 'Ruth's instincts were in her blood; transmitted by parents whom she had never known . . . Heredity lay at the root of this domestic misery.' (vol. 3, p. 15).

37. In 1830, all public offices in England remained closed to Jews. Careers were blocked in Parliament as well as in the professions. Schoolteaching was also largely out of bounds and Jews were ineligible to take degrees at Oxford, to attend the medical schools or to pursue a career in the law. Between 1830 and 1871 all of these formal obstacles were removed (Feldman 1994). For reflections on wider European anxieties at the turn of the century about the loss of Jewish identity in the face of emancipation, see Le Rider 1993.

38. Banister, for instance, in arguing that Jews such as Felix Moscheles schemed to stir up pro-Boer opinion against the British during the Boer War, put it

down to their eastern origins. The Jews, he declared are basically an 'Asiatic tribe' of invaders; Banister 1901.

39. Disraeli 1844, vol. 2, pp. 200–201.

40. As Feldman (1994) has shown, hostile commentators often meant very different things by 'the Jew' or even the 'Eastern Jew'. Thus, for instance, the meanings of 'Jew' in the context of Eastern European immigration in the late nineteenth century need to be distinguished from those pertaining earlier to 'the Orient'. In the latter case there were sometimes romantic or exotic resonances, as well as a sinister sense that Jews and Muslims were but one meta-force: a synthesised 'East' at odds with Christendom. One biographer, Lord Cromer, identified the array of Oriental and Jewish features in Disraeli as follows: tawdry finery, mystification, love of intrigue, tenacity, luxuriance of imaginative faculties, addiction to plausible generalities, florid language, passionate outbursts of grief in words which made an Anglo-Saxon doubt their sincerity, spasmodic eruption of real kindness of heart despite the underlying cynicism of character, excesses of flattery (for personal gain) contrasted with extreme vituperation (for purposes of advertisement), the total absence of any moral principles as a guide to life. Jews were also perceived to be driven by an Old Testament lust for revenge. Referring to the period from early summer 1876 when Turkey's intransigent attitude to the Bulgarian uprising provoked one of the greatest furores in nineteenth-century British foreign policy, and in which the anti-Semitic aspect to anti-Disraeli feeling was given a new sharp edge, Wohl remarks: 'Repeatedly during the Eastern Crisis, Christian charity was contrasted to the alleged Oriental Jewish lust for eye-for-an-eye, tooth-for-a-tooth justice.' The Victorian vogue for staging *The*

Merchant of Venice is also to be noted (Wohl 1999, p. 390).

41. Meige 1893. On claims that the Jews were peculiarly prone to psychosis, see Pilcz 1902.

42. It has been estimated that the British Jewish population of 60,000 in 1880 had reached 300,000 by 1914 (Feldman 1994).

43. Such was the view, for instance, of the increasingly influential French racial commentator, Gobineau.

44. Du Maurier 1994, p. 200. One might speculate perhaps on the relationship between Wagner's account and Du Maurier's depiction of Svengali, although I am not aware of any direct evidence for the link. Du Maurier's appreciation of Wagner's music was perhaps intended to be marked posthumously by the choice of the Vorspiel to 'Parsifal' (along with music by Chopin, Schubert and Schumann) at his funeral; anon. 1896c.

45. Rose 1992, pp. 94, 145.

46. Quotations are from Wagner 1910, respectively pp. 4, 8, 10, 11, 23, 13, 29. Du Maurier refers flippantly to 'Blagner' with his contempt for morbid Gallic sentimentalism and Italian tune-tinklers. The acrobatics and virtuosity of 'Svengalismus' are not to his taste at all (Du Maurier 1994, p. 200).

47. Disraeli 1844, vol. 2, p. 207; cf. Efron 1994, p. 49. There were some more facetious Victorian accounts of the pretensions of the 'musical Chosen People', some penned by Jews. Thus, one might juxtapose the grand musical claims of Sidonia, or Svengali for that matter, with the ridiculous musical ambitions of the Jewish pawn-broker Mr Moss in Farjeon's *Aaron the Jew* (1894). Mr Moss is vain, self-interested and complacent, albeit redeemed by a certain benevolence of heart. He loves music and attempts to go in for opera. He studies Italian for the purpose of pursuing a singing career, longing to make his fortune as a tenor. He imag-

ines himself on theatre notices as 'Signor Mossini'. Unfortunately, he has no talent (Farjeon 1894).

48. Efron 1994, pp. 50–51.

49. Wagner 1910, p. 11.

50. Rose 1992, p. 70.

51. Wagner 1910, respectively, pp. 13, 19, 33, 45–46.

52. In Nietzsche's ironic assessment, the very anti-Semitism which Wagner espoused marked him out as a probable Jew. In Nietzsche's discourse this needs to be understood as part of a complex, multi-layered relationship to the question of Judaism and anti-Semitism, about which much has been written both in criticism and in defence. Nietzsche lauded Heine and, in contrast to the pseudo-brilliance of Wagner, who had become all too 'German', he presented the musical genius of the Jewish Offenbach as well as Mendelssohn. Nietzsche also drew attention to that German zeal to be 'true Germans' which in its very excess was self-defeating and pathetic. Rather than demonstrating some inalienable difference between Jews and gentiles, the Germans who proclaimed their racial purity so loud in fact disclosed their fear of being confounded with the Jews. In *The Gay Science* (1974), he also sometimes reflected back attributions of filthiness at the self-professedly 'pure' anti-Jewish commentator. At the same time *The Gay Science* sometimes reiterates the grotesque racial assumptions the philosopher elsewhere repudiates. But for a defence, see Kofman 1994, pp. 21, 24. In a different way, Sartre made the same argument, declaring that it is not the Jew who creates anti-Semitism, but anti-Semitism which creates the Jew. If Jews did not exist, anti-Semitism would have invented them. Sartre even compares the anti-Semite to a hysteric in whom revulsion passes from mind to body. Moreover behind the revulsion lies a secret desire: 'Thus, one of the ele-

ments which make up his hatred is a profound sexual attraction towards the Jews. This arises, in the first place, from a fascinated curiosity about Evil. But above all, I believe, it arises from sadism.' (Sartre 1948, pp. 8, 10, 38, 120). A critique of the anti-Semitic assumptions informing Sartre's own attack on anti-Semitism, can be found in Nochlin and Garb (eds) 1995.

53. Sonneck 1912, pp. 20, 19. Numerous caricaturists from the 1870s had depicted Wagner with a Jewish face; Newman 1976, vol. 2, pp. 610–13.

54. Quoted in Rose 1992, p. 41.

55. Bakunin, 'Rapports personnels avec Marx', quoted in Silberner 1952, p. 101. The Jews, Bakunin, argues, adored a murderous God, and this was the source of their devouring propensities in the world.

56. Proudhon 1961, p. 337.

57. Quoted in Rose 1992, p. 64.

58. Leroy-Beaulieu 1895, pp. 208, 180, 148, 177, 178. Similar arguments are developed in Sombart 1913. Here the Jews are credited with mental precision, phenomenal egotism, sharp but narrow vision, energy and mobility. Collectively, they have 'calculating, dissecting and combining minds' (p. 261).

59. Gilman 1993b, p. 9.

60. Bauman 1991, p. 61 and Bauman 1998.

61. In a critique of Bauman's argument, Gillian Rose pointed out that there is a danger of sliding from a description of how the Jews have been seen as 'other' towards an endorsement of the view that the Jews actually *are* 'the other'. She was sceptical of the quasi-Lamarckianism which so often runs through these arguments, thus, for instance, challenging Bauman's view that somehow via their historical experience of deracination the Jews actually are naturally better equipped to deal with, and be creative within, a rootless modernity (Rose 1993).

62. Quoted in Manuel 1992, p. 1.

63. Zizek 1989, pp. 128-9. He also offers a more surprising argument, claiming that the Jew is the object of racism *par excellence*, across history, because of the fearsome inaccessibility of the Jewish God. This God becomes, in Zizek's Lacanian psychoanalytic reading, 'the very embodiment of the desire of the Other in its terrifying abyss'.

64. Zizek 1989, p. 126.

10 Night at the Opera

1. Du Maurier 1994, p. 226.

2. On the emergence of new forms of mass culture and the development of new forms of diagnosis about its putatively debilitating effects in the 1890s, see, for instance, Rosenberg and White 1957. Democratisation, capitalism and Americanisation were all variously held responsible for the apparent decline in values and tastes.

3. Briggs and Snowman (eds) 1996.

4. A particularly prominent legal case involving the well-known hypnotist Paul McKenna and a participant member of his audience became a major newspaper talking point in Britain throughout the early summer of 1998.

5. The section heading is from Prendergast 1996, p. 459. See also Ofshe and Watters 1994 and Crews 1995, pp, 60, 72. A further sharp attack on Freud (as well as on some of his earlier critics) in relation to the seduction theory and false memory has recently been offered by Webster (1996). A study by Mollon (1998) explores the contemporary complexities of the abuse debate and its implications for psychotherapists in a less heated manner. The possibility that psychoanalysts might inculcate false memory was sceptically discussed by Freud himself, although perhaps in light of subsequent polemics, he would have done well to devote more space and thought to the matter at an earlier stage. He tended to disparage the view

that the analyst had power simply to transfer his or her own views wholesale to the patient. In a discussion at the end of his 'Wolf Man' case, Freud ruefully contemplated the idea that the patient might be but the passive recipient of the analyst's whims:

> The old-fashioned psychotherapist, it might be maintained, used to suggest to his patient that he was cured, that he had overcome his inhibitions, and so on; whilst the psychoanalyst, on this view, suggests to him that when he was a child he had some experience or other, which he must now recollect in order to be cured . . . What was argued first was that they were not realities but phantasies. But what is argued now is evidently that they are phantasies not of the patient but of the analyst himself, who forces them upon the person under analysis on account of some complexes of his own. (Freud 1918, p. 52)

6. The phrases are drawn from Ofshe and Watters 1994, pp. 296, 298, and Prendergast 1996, p. 471. The public discussion on both sides of the Atlantic turns not just on whether, say, memory of seduction may be but fantasy (the complex and easily misrepresented ground across which Freud himself travelled in the 1890s), but also on whose 'constructions' are actually at issue in the process of 'retrieval'. The best-known of these current 'counterblasts' ascribes Freud with an enormous historical responsibility for manipulating, distorting and assaulting the truth. He is said to be the true historical sponsor of 'false memory syndrome' and today's 'incest Pied Pipers'; Crews 1995, p. 72.

7. Prendergast 1996, p. 459.

8. 'Sad Sacks', *Guardian*, weekend section, 15 May 1999, p. 5.

9. *Guardian*, weekend supplement, 10 February 1996 (Orbach 1996).

10. The phrase belongs to the French psychoanalyst Jacques Lacan whose own extraordinary powers of intellectual and emotional domination might perhaps have merited further scrutiny here. A book on the subject by the philosopher Mikkel Borch-Jacobsen, renowned for his earlier studies of 'emotional ties', is entitled *Lacan, the Absolute Master* (1991).

11. Anon. 1895d ('Three English novels'), p. 270.

12. In addition, Du Maurier acknowledges the influence of a poem featuring Trilby by Alfred de Musset; Bright 1895, p. 419.

13. See Purcell 1977.

14. Quoted in Bright 1895, p. 419.

15. This can be linked to other examples; on the participation of Jews in anti-Semitism, see Gilman 1991.

16. The pathos of Svengali's exclusion is also emphasised in some of the films, particularly in the 1955 version.

17. Welch 1897, pp. 74, 16, iv, 23, 40, 16, 54, 19, 77, 68, 55, 64.

18. Burne-Jones' letter was in response to a note from Du Maurier, congratulating him on his baronetcy; (Burne-Jones Papers XIX, 4 [February, 1894]; see 'unpublished items', in the bibliography).

19. Du Maurier 1994, p. 228.

20. Bright 1895, p. 421.

21. Gielgud 1980, pp. 35–36.

22. Anon. 1896a, p. 138.

23. Potter 1996, p. 244. The words, which start the Jewish morning and evening prayer, translate as: 'Hear, O Israel, the lord our God, the lord is one'.

Bibliography

Unpublished Sources

Du Maurier, George, 'Scrapbook' and miscellaneous archives, Hampstead Museum, Burgh House, London.

Du Maurier, George, letter to Mrs E. Roche (1862). British Library Manuscripts Collection, ref. 46345 f 124.

Du Maurier George, Correspondence with Edward Burne-Jones, February 1894; Burne-Jones Papers, XIX, 4, Fitzwilliam Museum, Cambridge.

Harper and Bros, Publisher's Archives, The Butler Library, Columbia University, reproduced on microfilm by Chadwyck-Healey, Cambridge and Tenneck, 1982.

Inman Papers, [miscellaneous published and unpublished writings by William Inman] Archives of the Library of the Institute of Psychoanalysis, London.

Whistler, James McNeill, letter to Du Maurier [1894], Glasgow University Library (MS Whistler D 177).

Published Sources

(Place of publication is London unless otherwise stated.)

Abraham, Karl (1927). 'The Spider as a Dream Symbol' [1922], *Selected Papers on Psycho-Analysis*, ch. 19.

Ackroyd, Peter (1990). *Dickens.*

Ainger, Canon (1897). 'George du Maurier in Hampstead', *The Hampstead Annual*, 12–19.

Anderson, George K (1965). *The Legend of the Wandering Jew*, Providence.

Annual Register (1896). *A Review of Public Events at Home and Abroad for the Year 1895*, n.s.

Anon. (1785). 'An account of Mademoiselle Theresa Paradis of Vienna, the celebrated blind performer on the piano forte', *The Gentleman's Magazine* 55: 175–76.

Anon. (1841). 'The advantages of animal magnetism', *Punch*, 1: 10.

Anon. (1844a). 'Mesmerism; its dangers and curiosities', *Punch* 6: 100.

Anon. (1847a). *Lindiana: An Interesting Narrative of the Life of Jenny Lind*.

Anon. (1847b). *Memoir of Jenny Lind*.

Anon. (1847c). 'Jenny Lind and hypnotism', *Phrenological Journal and Magazine of Moral Science*, 20: 456–58.

Anon. (1851a). 'The oracle of somnambulism', *Punch*, 20: 104.

Anon. (1851b). 'Prudence and mesmerism at Hungerford Hall', *Punch*, 20: 184–85.

Anon. (1853). 'Mesmerism', *Punch*, 24: 147.

Anon. (1860). 'Restorative in slumber', *Punch* 38: 52.

Anon. (1861). 'The poisoned mind', *Once a Week*, 5: 715–24.

Anon. (1862-3). 'The Notting Hill mystery', *Once a Week*, 7: 617–22 and 8: 1-6, 29-35, 57–64, 85–91.

Anon. (1872). 'Mesmeric bliss', *Punch*, 62: 261.

Anon. (1874). 'Hebrew of the Hebrews', *Punch*, 64: 254.

Anon. (1877). *Britain at the Bar: A Scene from the Judgement of Nations: A Dramatic Poem*.

Anon. (1888). 'Fascinateurs et jettatores', *Revue de l'hypnotisme*, 2: 284–86.

Anon. (1891). *The Power of Mesmerism: a Highly Erotic Narrative of Voluptuous Facts and Fancies*, printed for the Nihilists, Moscow.

Anon. (1893–94a). 'Where is the wandering Jew now?', *Harper's New Monthly Magazine*, 27: 313–14

Anon. (1893–94b). 'The mission of the Jews', *Harper's New Monthly Magazine*, 27: 259–66.

Anon. (1894a). '"Trilby": an open letter', *Lika Joko*, (20 October), 1–2.

Anon. (1894b). 'Le Juif errant à la Salpêtrière', *Revue de l'hypnotisme*, 8: 146–50.

Anon. (1895a). 'Dresses at the theatre', *The Sketch*, (30 October).

Anon. (1895b). [Discussion of *Trilby*], *Illustrated London News*, (9 November), 573.

Anon. (1895c). 'The marvellous feat of Tree-ilby Svengalivanised!', *Punch*, (21 December 1895) 232.

Anon. (1895d). 'Three English novels', *Atlantic Monthly*, 75: 266–70.

Anon. (1896a). 'The new theatre', *Cambridge Review*, 18: 138.

Anon. (1896b). 'Death of Mr. Du Maurier', *The Times*, (9 October), p. 6.

Anon. (1896c). 'Funeral of Mr Du Maurier', *The Times* (14 October), p. 4.

Appignanesi, Lisa and Forrester, John (1991). *Freud's Women*.

Archer, William (1883). *Henry Irving: Actor and Manager. A Critical Study*.

Baldick, Chris (1983). *The Social Mission of English Criticism, 1848-1932*, Oxford.

Banister, Joseph (1901). *England under the Jews*.

Barrès, Maurice (1899). *La Terre et les morts (sur quelles realités fonder la conscience française)*, Paris.

Barrows, Susanna (1981). *Distorting Mirrors: Visions of the Crowd in Late-Nineteenth-Century France*, New Haven.

Barthes, Roland (1957). *Mythologies*, Paris.

Battiscombe, Georgina (1956). *Mrs Gladstone. The Portrait of a Marriage*.

Bauman, Zygmunt (1991). *Modernity and Ambivalence*, Oxford.

—— (1998). 'Allosemitism: premodern, modern, postmodern' in *Modernity, Culture and 'the Jew'*, ed. Bryan Cheyette and Laura Marcus, Oxford, ch. 8.

Beales, Derek (1991). 'Garibaldi in England: the politics of Italian enthusiasm', *Society and Politics in the Age of the Risorgimento: Essays in Honour of Denis Mack Smith*, Cambridge, ch. 8.

Beerbohm, Max (1920). *Herbert Beerbohm Tree: Some Memories of Him and his Art.*

Berger, John (1965). *Success and Failure of Picasso*, Harmondsworth.

Berna, Didier Jules. (1838). *Magnétisme animal. Examen et réfutation du rapport fait par M.E-F Dubois (D'Amiens) à L'Academie Royale de Médecine*, Paris.

Bernheim, Hippolyte (1891a). *Hypnotisme, suggestion, psychothérapie*, Paris.

—— (1891b). *De la Suggestion et de ses applications à la thérapeutique*, 3rd edn, Paris.

Berry, Paul (1970). *By Royal Appointment: A Biography of Mary Anne Clarke, Mistress of the Duke of York.*

Bigelow, Poultney (1893–94). 'The Russian and his Jew', *Harper's New Monthly Magazine*, 27: 603–08.

Blackbourn, David (1995). *The Marpingen Visions: Rationalism, Religion and the Rise of Modern Germany.*

Blavatsky, Helena Patrova (1972). *Dynamics of the Psychic World: Comments by H.P. Blavatsky on Magic, Mediumship, Psychism and the Powers of the Spirit*, comp. Lina Psaltis, Wheaton, Illinois.

Borch-Jacobsen, Mikkel (1996). 'Neurotica: Freud and the seduction theory', *October*, 76: 30–39.

—— (1999). 'What made Albert run?', [review of Ian Hacking's *Mad Travellers*], *London Review of Books* (27 May), 21: 9–10.

Borch-Jacobsen, Mikkel, Michaud, Eric, Nancy, Jean-Luc (1984). *Hypnoses*, Paris.

Bowen, Catherine Drinker (1939). *'Free Artist': The Story of Anton and Nicholas Rubinstein*, New York.

Boyle, A. (1878). *The Sympathy and Action of England in the Late Eastern Crisis and What Came of Them.*

Braid, James (1852). *Magic, Witchcraft, Animal Magnetism, Hypnotism and Electro-Biology*, 3rd edn.

Bramwell, J. Milne (1903). *Hypnotism: Its History, Practice and Theory.*

Brantlinger, Patrick (1990). 'Mass Media and Culture in Fin-de-Siècle Europe', in *Fin-de-Siècle and its Legacy*, ed. Porter and M. Teich, Cambridge, ch. 6.

Bratley, George H. (1904). *The Art of Fascination: A Popular Exposition of the Sun's Etheric Force, Which, When Transmitted, is Personal Magnetism*, Harrogate.

Briggs, Asa (1988). *Victorian Things.*

Briggs, Asa and Snowman, Daniel (eds) (1996). *Fins de Siècle: How Centuries End*, New Haven.

Bright, Addison (1895). 'Mr Du Maurier at home', *The Idler*, 8: 415–22.

Britton, Ronald (1998). *Belief and Imagination: Explorations in Psychoanalysis.*

Brod, Max (1956). *Heinrich Heine: The Artist in Revolt.*

Brouardel, Paul (1879). 'Accusation de viol accompli pendant le sommeil hypnotique: relation médico-légale de l'affaire Lévy, dentiste à Rouen', *Annales d'hygiène publique et de médicine légale*, 3rd ser. 1: 39–59.

Bullock, Alan (1962). *Hitler*, rev. edn.

Bulman, Joan (1956). *Jenny Lind: A Biography*.

Buranelli, Vincent (1975). *The Wizard from Vienna*.

Burrows, J.F. ('Karlyn') (1912). *Secrets of Stage Hypnotism, Stage Electricity and Bloodless Surgery*.

Butler, Josephine (1901?). *In Memoriam, Harriet Meuricoffre, By Her Sister*.

Canetti, Elias (1984). *Crowds and Power*, Harmondsworth.

Carlyle, Jane Welsh (1883). *Letters and Memorials*, ed. James Anthony Froude, 3 vols.

Carroy, Jacqueline (1991). *Hypnose, suggestion et psychologie*, Paris.

Carroy, Jacqueline and Plas, Régine (1995). 'Dreyfus et la somnambule', *Critique*, 572: 36–59.

Carse, Adam (1948). *The Orchestra from Beethoven to Berlioz: A History of the Orchestra in the First Half of the Nineteenth Century, and of the Development of Orchestral Baton-Conducting*, Cambridge.

—— (1951). *The Life of Jullien: Adventurer, Showman-Conductor and Establisher of the Promenade Concerts in England, together with a History of those Concerts*, Cambridge.

Cavailhon, Édouard (1882). *La Fascination magnétique precédée d'une preface par Donato*, Paris.

Chanon, Michael (1980). *The Dream that Kicks: The Prehistory and Early Years of Cinema in Britain*.

Charcot, Jean-Martin (1991). *Clinical Lectures on Diseases of the Nervous System*, reprint of the 1899 translation, ed. and introduced by Ruth Harris, Tavistock Classics in the History of Psychiatry.

Chertok, Léon (1989). *Hypnose et suggestion*, Paris.

Cheyette, Bryan (1995). 'Neither Black nor White: The Figure of "the Jew" in Imperial British Literature', in *The Jew in the Text: Modernity and the Construction of Identity*, edited by Linda Nochlin, and Tamar Garb, ch. 1.

Cheyette, Bryan and Marcus, Laura (eds) (1998). *Modernity, Culture and 'the Jew'*, Oxford.

Christiansen, Rupert (1995). *Prima Donna: A History*.

Clark, Michael (1981). 'The rejection of psychological approaches to mental disorder in late nineteenth-century British psychiatry' in *Madhouses, Mad-doctors and Madmen: The Social History of Psychiatry in the Victorian Era*, ed. Andrew Scull, pp. 271–312.

'Comus' (1876). *The Devil's Visit to Bulgaria and Other Lands*, Brighton.

Connor, Steve (1998). 'Fascination, skin and the screen', *Critical Quarterly*, 40: 10–23.

Crabtree, Adam (1993). *From Mesmer to Freud: Magnetic Sleep and the Roots of Psychological Healing*, New Haven.

Crews, Frederick (ed.) (1995). *The Memory Wars: Freud's Legacy in Dispute*, New York.

Darnton, Robert (1968). *Mesmerism and the End of the Enlightenment in France*, Cambridge.

De Jonge Alex (1982). *The Life and Times of Grigorii Rasputin.*

De Martino, Ernesto (1963). *Italie du sud et magie,* Paris.

Dickens, Charles (1895a). *The Adventures of Oliver Twist* [1838]. (Chapman Hall ed.)

—— (1895b). *Our Mutual Friend* [1865]. (Chapman Hall ed.)

—— (1895c). *The Mystery of Edwin Drood* [1870]. (Chapman Hall ed.)

Digeon, Claude (1959). *La Crise allemande de la pensée française (1870–1914),* Paris.

Dimock, Arthur (1894). 'The conspiracy of Dr Lopez', *English Historical Review* 9: 440–72.

Disraeli, Benjamin (1844). *Coningsby: or the New Generation.*

—— (1847). *Tancred; or the New Crusade,* 3 vols.

Di Stasi, Lawrence (1981). *Mal Occhio: The Underside of Vision,* San Francisco.

Doyle, Arthur Conan (1894). *The Parasite.*

—— (1985). *The Penguin Complete Sherlock Holmes,* Harmondsworth.

Drumont, Edouard (1889). *La Fin d'un monde,* Paris.

Dubnov, Semen Markovich (1916–20). *History of the Jews in Russia and Poland from the Earliest Times until the Present Day,* tr. from the Russian, 3 vols, Philadelphia.

Dumont, Theron Q. (1914). *The Advanced Course in Personal Magnetism,* Chicago.

Du Maurier, Daphne (ed.) (1951). *The Young George Du Maurier. A Selection of his Letters 1860–67,* with a biographical appendix by Derek Pepys Whiteley.

—— (1963). *The Glass Blowers.*

Du Maurier, George (1891). *Society Pictures.*

—— (1893–94). 'Trilby', *Harper's New Monthly Magazine,* vol. 27, pp. 168–89, 329–50, 567–87, 721–41, 825–47 and vol. 28, pp. 67–87, 260–84, 351–74.

—— *Trilby* (1894). (Osgood McIlvaine and Company edn).

—— (1898). *Social Pictorial Satire: Reminiscences and Appreciations of English Illustrators of the Past Generation.*

—— (1947). *The Novels of George Du Maurier,* with introductions by John Masefield and Daphne Du Maurier.

—— (1973). *Svengali,* ed. and introduced by Peter Alexander.

—— (1994). *Trilby,* ed. and introduced by Daniel Pick, Harmondsworth.

Dundes, Alan (ed.) (1991). *The Blood Libel Legend,* Madison, Wisconsin.

Duyckaerts, François (1992). *Joseph Delboeuf: philosophe et hypnotiseur,* Paris.

Eckardt, Wolf von, Gilman, Sander L. and Chamberlain, J. Edward (1988). *Oscar Wilde's London.*

Edel, Leon (1969). *Henry James: The Treacherous Years 1895–1901.*

Efron, John M. (1994). *Defenders of the Race: Jewish Doctors and Race Science in Fin-de-Siècle Europe,* New Haven.

Eisenstadt, Shmuel Noah (ed.) (1968). *Max Weber on Charisma and Institution Building,* Chicago.

Ellenberger, Henri (1970). *The Discovery of the Unconscious: The History and Evolution of Dynamic Psychiatry,* New York.

Eliot, George (1979). *The Mill on the Floss* [1860], Harmondsworth.

—— (1995). *Daniel Deronda* [1876], Harmondsworth.

Elworthy, Frederick Thomas (1895). *The Evil Eye.*

Endelman, Todd M. (1979). *The Jews of Georgian England 1714–1830: Tradition and Change in a Liberal Society,* Philadelphia.

Erckmann, Émile and Chatrian, Alexandre (1869). *Le Juif polonais,* Paris.

Esdaile, James (1957). *Hypnosis, Medicine and Surgery,* originally titled *Mesmerism in India,* [1850], New York.

Fara, Patricia (1995). 'An attractive therapy: animal magnetism in eighteenth-century England', *History of Science,* 33: 127–77.

Farjeon, Benjamin Leopold (1894). *Aaron the Jew: a Novel,* 3 vols.

Feldman, David (1994). *Englishmen and Jews: Social Relations and Political Culture 1840–1914,* New Haven.

Figes, Orlando (1996). *A People's Tragedy: The Russian Revolution, 1891–1924.*

Fishwick, Marshal and Browne, Ray B. (1970). *Icons of Popular Culture,* Bowling Green, Ohio.

Flaubert, Gustave (1976). *Bouvard and Pécuchet,* trans. A.J. Krailsheimer, Harmondsworth.

Foldy, Michael (1997). *The Trials of Oscar Wilde: Deviance, Morality, and Late-Victorian Society,* New Haven.

Forel, August (1906). *Hypnotism or Suggestion and Psychotherapy.*

Forrester, John (1990). *The Seductions of Psychoanalysis,* Cambridge.

—— (1997). *Dispatches from the Freud Wars,* Cambridge, Mass.

Forth, Christopher (1998). 'Intellectuals, crowds and body politics of the Dreyfus Affair', *Historical Reflections/Réflexions historiques,* 24: 63–91.

Foster, George G. (1850). *Memoir of Jenny Lind,* New York.

Fourier, Charles (1996). *The Theory of the Four Movements* [1808], edited by Gareth Stedman Jones, Cambridge.

Foveau de Courmelles, François Victor (1891). *Hypnotism.*

Fraser, Wittamish (1981). *The Coming of the Mass Market, 1850–1914.*

Freeman, Edward A. (1895). *Life and Letters,* ed. William Richard Wood Stephens, 2 vols.

Freud, Sigmund, (1888). 'Hysteria', *Standard Edition of the Complete Psychological Works,* vol. I: 39–59.

—— (1891). 'Hypnosis', *Standard Edition of the Complete Psychological Works,* Vol. 1: 103–114.

—— (1893). 'Charcot', *Standard Edition of the Complete Psychological Works,* Vol. 3: 9–23.

—— (1914). 'History of the Psychoanalytic Movement', *Standard Edition of the Complete Psychological Works,* Vol. 14: 1–66.

—— (1918). 'From the History of an Infantile Neurosis', *Standard Edition of the Complete Psychological Works,* Vol. 17: 1–122.

—— (1921). 'Group Psychology and the Analysis of the Ego', *Standard Edition of the Complete Psychological Works,* Vol. 18: 65–144.

—— (1932). *New Introductory Lectures, Standard Edition of the Complete Psychological Works,* Vol. 22: 3–182.

Friedenwald, Aaron (1897). *Jewish Physicians and the Contributions of the Jews to the Science of Medicine,* Philadelphia.

Friedenwald, Harry (1977). *The Jews and Medicine: Essays*, 3 vols [1944], Baltimore.

Fuhrmann, Joseph T. (1990). *Rasputin: A Life*, New York.

Gainer, Brian (1972). *The Alien Invasion: The Origins of the Aliens Act of 1905*.

Gallini, Clara (1973). *Dono e malocchio*, Palermo.

—— (1983). *La sonnambula meravigliosa. Magnetismo e ipnotismo nell'ottocento italiano*, Milan.

Galton, Francis (1865). 'Hereditary talent and character', *Macmillan's Magazine*, 12: 157–66.

Gauld, Alan (1992). *A History of Hypnotism*, Cambridge.

Gauthier, Aubin (1845). *Traité pratique du magnétisme et du somnambulisme*, Paris.

Gay, Peter (1978). *Freud, Jews and Other Germans: Masters and Victims in Modern Culture*, Oxford.

—— (1993). *The Cultivation of Hatred, The Bourgeois Experience: Victoria to Freud*, vol. 3.

—— (1996). *The Naked Heart, The Bourgeois Experience: Victoria to Freud*, vol. 4.

Gay, Ruth (1992). *The Jews of Germany: A Historical Portrait*, New Haven.

Geyl, Peter (1986). *Napoleon: For and Against* [1949], Harmondsworth.

Gielgud, Kate Terry (1980). *A Victorian Playgoer*.

Gifford, Edward, S. (1958). *The Evil Eye: Studies in the Folklore of Vision*, New York.

Gilder, Joseph B. and Jeannette L. (1895). *Trilbyana: The Rise and Progress of a Popular Novel*, New York.

Gilman, Sander (1991). *The Jew's Body*.

—— (1993a). *The Case of Sigmund Freud: Medicine and Identity at the Fin de Siècle*, Baltimore.

—— (1993b) *Freud, Race and Gender*, Princeton.

—— (1995). 'Salomé, Syphilis, Sarah Bernhardt', in *The Jew in the Text: Modernity and the Construction of Identity*, ed. by Linda Nochlin and Tamar Garb, ch. 5.

—— (1996). *Smart Jews: The Construction of the Image of Jewish Superior Intelligence*, Lincoln, Nebraska.

Ginneken, Jaap Van (1992). *Crowds, Psychology and Politics, 1871–99*, Cambridge.

Glanville, Jo (1998). 'A victim of anti-Semitism?', *New Statesman*, (17 July), 10.

Goldstein, Jan (1985). 'The wandering Jew and the problem of psychiatric anti-Semitism in *fin-de-siècle* France', *Journal of Contemporary History* 20: 521–52.

Gombrich, Ernst (1960). *Art and Illusion*.

Groddeck, George (1977). *The Meaning of Illness*.

Grossman, Jonathan H. (1996). 'The mythic Svengali: anti-aestheticism in *Trilby*', *Studies in the Novel* 28:525–42.

Guralnick, Peter (1994). *Last Train to Memphis: The Rise of Elvis Presley*, Boston.

Hacking, Ian (1995). *Rewriting the Soul: Multiple Personality and the Sciences of Memory*, Princeton.

—— (1998). *Mad Travellers: Reflections on the Reality of Transient Mental Illness*, Charlottesville.

Halberstam, Judith (1993). 'Technologies of monstrosity: Bram Stoker's *Dracula*', *Victorian Studies*, 36, 333–52.

Hale, John W (1894). 'Shakespeare and the Jews', *English Historical Review,* 9: 652–61.

Harbinson, W.A. (1975). *Elvis Presley: An Illustrated Biography.*

Harding, James (1989). *Gerald Du Maurier: A Biography.*

Harrington, Anne (1988). 'Hysteria, hypnosis, and the lure of the invisible: the rise of neo-mesmerism in *fin-de-siècle* French psychiatry', *The Anatomy of Madness,* ed. by W.F. Bynum, Roy Porter and Michael Shepherd, vol. 3, ch. 8.

Harris, Ruth (1985). 'Murder under hypnosis in the case of Gabrielle Bompard: Psychiatry in the courtroom in Belle Époque Paris', *The Anatomy of Madness,* ed. W.F. Bynum, Roy Porter and Michael Shepherd, vol. 2, ch. 10.

—— (1989). *Murders and Madness. Medicine, Law, and Society in the Fin de Siècle,* Oxford.

—— (1999). *Lourdes: Body and Spirit in the Secular Age.*

Harrison, Frederick (1886). *The Choice of Books and Other Literary Pieces.*

Hart, Ernest (1982). *Hypnotism, Mesmerism and the New Witchcraft* [1896], including an appendix, 'The Hypnotism of "Trilby"', from the *British Medical Journal,* 20 November 1895, New York.

Harte, Richard (1902). *Hypnotism and the Doctors,* 2 vols.

Hartmann, Carl Robert Eduard von (1884). *Philosophy of the Unconscious,* 3 vols

Hawkins, Harriet (1990). *Classics and Trash: Tradition and Taboos in High Literature and Popular Modern Genres,* Brighton.

Hawthorne, Nathaniel (1937). *The Marble Faun, or The Romance of Monte Beni* [1860], in *The Complete Novels and Selected Tales of Nathaniel Hawthorne,* New York.

Hertz, J.H. (1913). *The Kieff Ritual Murder Accusation: Protests from Leading Christians in Europe.*

Hibbert, Christopher (1987). *Garibaldi and his Enemies* [1965], Harmondsworth.

Hitler, Adolf (1992). *Mein Kampf,* with an introduction by D. Cameron Watt.

Hobsbawm, Eric (1990). *Nations and Nationalism since 1780: Programme, Myth, Reality,* Cambridge.

Hoffman, E.T.A. (1992). 'The Sandman' [1816], in *The Golden Pot and other Tales,* Harmondsworth.

The Holy Bible containing the Old and New Testaments (1887). Oxford.

Holmes, Colin (ed.) (1978). *Immigrants and Minorities in British Society.*

—— (1979). *Anti-Semitism in British Society 1876–1939.*

Hsia, R. Po-Chia (1988). *The Myth of Ritual Murder: Jews and Magic in Reformation Germany,* New Haven.

Hughes, H. Stuart (1958). *Consciousness and Society: The Reorientation of European Social Thought, 1890–1930.*

Hyam, Ronald (1990). *Empire and Sexuality, The British Experience,* Manchester.

Hyamson, Albert M. (1908). *A History of the Jews in England.*

Hyman, Louis (1972). *The Jews of Ireland: from Earliest Times to the Year 1910,* Shannon.

Ionides, Luke (1996). *Memories* [1925], Ludlow.

Jackson, Holbrook (1913). *The Eighteen Nineties: A Review of Art and Ideas at the Close of the Nineteenth Century.*

Jacobs, Joseph, ['A Jew'] (1877). 'Mordechai: a protest against the critics', *Macmillan's Magazine*, 36: 101–11.

—— (1891). *Jewish Statistics, Social, Vital and Anthropometric*.

Jacobs, Joseph and Nutt, Alfred (eds) (1891). *The Second International Folk-Lore Congress: Papers and Transactions*.

James, Henry (1888). 'George Du Maurier', *Partial Portraits*, chapter 10.

—— (1897). 'George Du Maurier', *Harper's New Monthly Magazine*, 34: 594–609.

—— (1947). *The Notebook of Henry James*, ed. F.O. Matthiessen and Kenneth B. Murdock, New York.

—— (1962a). 'Professor Fargo' [1874], in *The Complete Tales of Henry James*, ed. and introduced by Leon Edel, 1962, vol. 3 (1873–75).

—— (1962b) 'The Next Time' [1895], in *The Complete Tales*, vol. 9 (1892–98).

Jay, Martin (1993). *Downcast Eyes: The Denigration of Vision in Twentieth-Century French Thought*, Los Angeles.

Jewish Encyclopaedia, The (1903). 'The Evil Eye', vol. 5, pp. 280–81.

Jordan, Leopold (1895). *Drilby Re-Versed*, illustrated by Philip and Earle Ackerman, New York.

Journal of the Society for Psychical Research, 1 (1884).

Jung, Carl Gustav (1970). 'The State of Psychotherapy Today' ('Zur gegenwärtigen Lage der Psychotherapie') [1934] in *Civilization in Transition, Collected Works*, vol. 10, 2nd edn, Princeton.

Kaplan, Fred (1974). '"The mesmeric mania": the early Victorians and animal magnetism', *Journal of the History of Ideas*, 35: 691–702.

—— (1975). *Dickens and Mesmerism: The Hidden Springs of Fiction*, Princeton.

Katlov, George (1967). *Russia 1917: The February Revolution*.

Kautsky, Karl (1926). *Are the Jews a Race?*

Kelly, Richard (1983). *George Du Maurier*, Boston.

—— (1996). *The Art of George Du Maurier*, Aldershot.

Kern, Stephen (1996). *The Eyes of Love: The Gaze in English and French Paintings and Novels 1840–1900*.

Kiessling, Nicholas (1977). *The Incubus in English Literature: Provenance and Progeny*, Pullman.

Klein, Melanie (1957). 'Envy and Gratitude', *The Writings of Melanie Klein*, ed. R. Money-Kyrle, B. Joseph, E. O'Shaughnessy and H. Segal, vol. 3 [1975].

Kofman, Sarah (1994). *Le Mépris des Juifs: Nietzsche, les Juifs, l'anti-sémitisme*, Paris.

Kohn, Marek (1995). *The Race Gallery: The Return of Racial Science*.

Kristeva, Julia (1982). *Powers of Horror: An Essay on Abjection*, New York.

Lamont, L.M. (1912). *Thomas Armstrong, A Memoir, With Reminiscences of George Du Maurier and of James Whistler*.

Lanoire, M. (1940). 'Un Anglo-Francais, George Du Maurier', *Revue de Paris*, 47: 263–81.

Lapouge, Georges Vacher de (1899). *L'Aryen: son role social: cours libre de science politique professé à l'Université de Montpellier (1889–1890)*, Paris.

Law, John [pseudonym of Margaret Harkness] (1891). *In Darkest London*.

Lawrence, D.H. [1922] (1980). *Aaron's Rod*, Harmondsworth.

—— [1930] (1970). *the Virgin and the Gypsy*, Harmondsworth.

Lebrecht, Norman (1991). *The Maestro Myth: Great Conductors in Pursuit of Power*.

Le Rider, Jacques (1993). *Modernity and Crises of Identity: Culture and Society in Fin-de-Siècle Vienna*, Cambridge.

Lerner, Paul (1998). 'Hysterical cures: hypnosis, gender and performance in World War I and Weimar Germany', *History Workshop Journal*, 45: 79–101.

Leroy-Beaulieu, Anatole (1895). *Israel among the Nations: A Study of the Jews and anti-Semitism*.

Levi, Primo (1989). 'The Fear of Spiders', in *Other People's Trades*, pp. 141–45.

Lewis, Leopold (n.d.) [1871]. *The Bells*, A Drama in 3 Acts.

Lind, Jenny (1966). *The Lost Letters of Jenny Lind*.

Lindholm, Charles (1990). *Charisma*, Oxford.

Lobet, Léon (1891). *L'Hypnotisme en Belgique et le projet de loi*, Verviers.

Low, Alfred D. (1979). *Jews in the Eyes of Germans: From the Enlightenment to Imperial Germany*, Philadelphia.

Lucas, E.V. (1934). 'George du Maurier at Thirty Three', *Cornhill Magazine* 150: 385–410.

Luska, Sidney [Henry Harland] (1984). *As it was Written: A Jewish Musician's Story* [1885], New York.

McCail, R.C. (1977). The genesis of Du Maurier's *Trilby*, *Forum for Modern Language Studies*, 13: 12–15.

Mack Smith, Denis (1994). *Mazzini*, New Haven.

Mackay, Charles (1932). *Extraordinary Popular Delusions and the Madness of Crowds* [1841; 2nd edn 1851], New York.

Maclagan, Robert Craig (1902). *Evil Eye in the Western Highlands*.

The Magnetic Review: A Record of Curative Electric Science and Journal of Health.

Maidenbaum, Aryeh and Martin, Stephen A. (eds) (1991). *Lingering Shadows: Jungians, Freudians and Anti-Semitism*.

Mann, Thomas (1975). *Mario and the Magician and Other Stories*, Harmondsworth.

Mannoni, Octave (1971). *Freud: The Theory of the Unconscious*.

—— (1980). *Une Commencement qui n'en finit pas. Transfert, interpretation, théorie*, Paris.

Manuel, Frank (1992). *The Broken Staff: Judaism through Christian Eyes*, Cambridge, Mass.

Marcham, Frank (ed.) (1927). *The Prototype of Shylock. Lopez the Jew, Executed 1594: An Opinion by Gabriel Harvey*.

Mason, A.A. (1994). 'A psychoanalyst looks at a hypnotist: a study of *folie à deux*', *Psychoanalytic Quarterly*, 63: 641–79.

Mayer, David (ed.) (1980). *Henry Irving and The Bells*, Manchester.

Mays, Kelly J. (1995). 'Reading and Victorian periodicals', in *Literature in the Marketplace: Nineteenth-Century British Publishing and Reading Practices*, ed. John O. Jordan and Robert L. Patten, Cambridge.

Meige, Henri (1893). *Le Juif errant à la Salpetrière*, Paris.

Mesmer, Franz Anton (1781a). *Mémoire sur la découverte du magnétisme animal*, Paris.

—— (1781b). *Précis historique des faits relatifs au magnétisme-animal*, Paris.

—— (1785). *Aphorismes de M. Mesmer*, ed. M. Caullet de Veaumorel, third edn, Paris.

Mesnet, Ernest (1894). *Outrages à la pudeur: violences sur les organes sexuels de la femme dans le somnambulisme provoqué et la fascination. Étude médico-légale*, Paris.

Micale, Mark (1990). 'Charcot and the idea of hysteria in the male: gender, mental science, and medical diagnosis in late-nineteenth-century France', *Medical History*, 34: 363–411.

—— (1991). 'Hysteria Male/Hysteria Female: Reflections on Comparative Gender Construction in Nineteenth-Century France and Britain', in *Science and Sensibility: Gender and Scientific Enquiry, 1780–1945*, ed. Marina Benjamin, Oxford, ch. 7.

Micklethwait, D.J. (1971). [discussion of *Trilby*, copyright law, franchising etc.], *Law Quarterly Review*, 87: 19–20.

Milfull, John (ed.) (1993). *Why Germany? National Socialist Anti-Semitism and the European Context*, Oxford.

Millar, C.C. Hoyer (1937). *George du Maurier and Others*.

Moll, Albert (1906). *Hypnotism*, 6th edn, revised and enlarged.

Mollon, Phil (1998). *Remembering Trauma: A Psychotherapist's Guide to Memory and Illusion*, Chichester.

Morselli, Enrico (1886). *Il magnetismo animale: la fascinazione e gli stati ipnotici*, Turin.

—— (1923). *La psichanalisi*, Turin.

Moscheles, Felix (1896). *In Bohemia with Du Maurier. The First of a Series of Reminiscences with 63 Original Drawings by George D Maurier Illustrating the Artist's Life in the Fifties*.

—— (1899). *Fragments of an Autobiography*.

Mosse, George L. (1970). *Germans and Jews: The Right, the Left and the Search for a 'Third Force' in Pre-Nazi Germany*, New York.

Mosso, Angelo (1896). 'Mesmer e il magnetismo', *La vita italiana: conferenze tenute a Firenze nel 1896*, Milan.

Muskerry, William (1896). *"Thrillby," A Shocker in one Scene and Several Spasm (sic)*, with special songs composed by F. Osmond Carr.

Newman, Ernest (1976). *The Life of Richard Wagner* [1933], 4 vols, Cambridge.

Nietzsche, Friedrich (1974). *The Gay Science with a Prelude in Rhymes and an Appendix of Songs* [1882], translated from the second edn of 1887, New York.

Nochlin, Linda and Garb, Tamar (eds) (1995). *The Jew in the Text: Modernity and the Construction of Identity*.

Nodier, Charles (1887). *Trilby ou le Lutin d'Argail*, Lyon.

Nordau, Max (1895). *Degeneration*, translated from the second German edn, New York.

Northcott, Richard (1920). *The Life of Sir Henry R. Bishop*.

Nye, Robert (1975). *The Origins of Crowd Psychology: Gustave Le Bon and the Crisis of Mass Democracy in the Third Republic*.

Obholzer, Karin (1982). *The Wolf Man Sixty Years Later: Conversations with Freud's Controversial Patient*.

Ofshe, Richard and Watters, Ethan (1994). *Making Monsters: False Memories, Psychotherapy and Sexual Hysteria*, New York.

Oldrà, Antonio (1922). *Gli spiriti: breve studio sull'ipnotismo e sullo spiritismo*, Florence.

Orbach, Susie (1996). 'Shrink Rap . . .', *Guardian* (weekend section), 10 February 1996.

Ormond, Leonée (1969). *George Du Maurier*.

'A Painter' (1898). *Turner's Complete Guide to Theatrical Make-up*.

Paladino, G. (1933). *Metodo scientifico per sottomettere, da vicino e da lontano, gli altri alla propria volontà*, Lucca.

Parssinen, Terry M. (1977). 'Mesmeric performers', *Victorian Studies*, 21: 87–104.

Passerini, Luisa (1991). *Mussolini imaginario*, Bari.

Pattie, Frank A. (1979). 'A Mesmer-Paradis myth dispelled', *American Journal of Clinical Hypnosis*, 22: 29–31.

—— (1994). *Mesmer and Animal Magnetism: A Chapter in the History of Medicine*, Hamilton, New York.

Picard, Michel (1997). *Freud à Nancy*, Paris.

Pick, Daniel (1995). 'Freud's *Group Psychology* and the history of the crowd', *History Workshop Journal*, 40: 39–61.

Pilcz, Dr [no first name given] (1902). 'Sur les psychoses chez les Juifs', *Annales médico-psychologiques*, 15: 5–20.

Piquet, Martine (1996). 'Dans les griffes de Svengali: Caricature antisémite littéraire et graphique dans *Trilby* de George Du Maurier', *Cahiers victoriens et édouardiens*, 43: 73–88.

Platt, Isaac Hull (1895). *The Ethics of Trilby: with a Supplemental Note on Spiritual Affinity*, Philadelphia.

Poe, Edgar Allan (1967). 'The Facts in the Case of M. Valdemar' [1845], *Selected Writings*, Harmondsworth.

Poliakov, Léon (1974). *The Aryan Myth: A History of Racist and Nationalist Ideas in Europe*.

Porter, Roy (1985). 'Under the Influence: Mesmerism in England', *History Today* (September 1985), 23–29.

—— (1987). 'The Language of Quackery in England, 1660-1800', *The Social History of Language*, ed. Roy Porter and Peter Burke, ch. 4.

Potter, Paul (1996). Stage Adaptation of *Trilby* [1895], in *Trilby and other Plays*, ed. and introduced by George Taylor, Oxford.

Prendergast, Mark (1996). *Victims of Memory: Incest Accusations and Shattered Lives*.

Proudhon, P.-J. (1961). *Carnets*, vol. 2 [1847–8], ed. Pierre Haubtmann, Paris.

Purcell, Edward L. (1977). 'Trilby and Trilby Mania', *Journal of Popular Culture*, 11: 62–77.

Raffalovich, André (1896) *Uranisme et unisexualité: Etude sur différentes manifestations de l'instinct sexuel*, Paris.

Ragussis, Michael (1995). *Figures of Conversion: 'The Jewish Question' and English National Identity*.

—— (1997). 'The "secret" of English anti-Semitism: Anglo-Jewish studies and

Victorian studies', *Victorian Studies* 40: 295–307.

Rather, L.J. (1987). 'Disraeli, Freud and Jewish conspiracy theories', *Journal of the History of Ideas*, 47: 111–31.

Rauschning, Hermann Adolf Reinhold (1939). *Hitler Speaks: A Series of Political Conversations with Adolf Hitler on His Real Aims.*

Ribot, Théodule (1912). *Diseases of Memory: An Essay in the Positive Psychology.*

Richards, Thomas (1990). *The Commodity Culture of Victorian England. Advertising and Spectacle, 1851–1914*, Stanford.

Richer, Paul, and de la Tourette, Gilles (1889). *'Hypnotisme'*, Dictionnaire encyclopédique des sciences médicales, Paris, vol, 15, pp. 67–132.

Rogan, Johnny (1988). *Starmakers and Svengalis: The History of British Pop Management.*

Romaine, William (1753). *A Modest Apology for the Citizens and Merchants of London who Petitioned the House against Naturalizing the Jews*, third edn.

Roper, Lyndal (1994). *Oedipus and the Devil: Witchcraft, Sexuality and Religion in Early Modern Europe.*

Rose, Gillian (1993). *Judaism and Modernity: Philosophical Essays*, Oxford.

Rose, Paul Lawrence (1990). *Revolutionary Anti-Semitism in Germany from Kant to Wagner*, Princeton.

—— (1992). *Wagner: Race and Revolution.*

Rosenberg, Bernard and White, David Manning (eds) (1957). *Mass Culture: The Popular Arts in America*, Glencoe.

Rosenberg, Edgar (1960), *From Shylock to Svengali: Jewish Stereotypes in English Fiction*, Stanford.

Rosenberg, Charles G. (1850). *The Life of Jenny Lind*, New York.

Rouget, Gilbert (1980). *La Musique et la transe: Esquisse d'une théorie générale des relations de la musique et de la possession*, Paris.

S——, Miss Mary (1890). *Soul Subtlety; or How to Fascinate: A Great Secret Explained*, Birmingham.

Said, Edward (1991). *Musical Elaborations.*

St John, Christopher (1949). *Ellen Terry and George Bernard Shaw: A Correspondence.*

Sartre, Jean-Paul (1948). *Portrait of the Anti-Semite.*

Schaffer, Simon (1996). 'Babbage's Dancer and the Impressarios of Mechanism', in *Cultural Babbage*, ed. Francis Spufford and Jenny Uglow, pp. 53–80.

Self, Will (1996). 'The hollow man' [review of Anthony Julius, *T.S. Eliot, Anti-Semitism and Literary Form*], *Observer* (Review), 26 May 1996, p. 14.

Seligmann, Siegfried. (1910). *Der böse Blick und Verwandtes: Ein Beitrag zur Geschichte des Aberglaubens aller Zeiten und Völker*, 2 vols, Berlin.

—— (1922). *Die Zauberkraft des Auges und das Berufen: Ein Kapitel aus der Geschichte des Aberglaubens*, Hamburg.

Sewell, Brocard (1968). *Footnote to the Nineties: A Memoir of John Gray and André Raffalovich.*

Shatzmiller, Joseph (1994). *Jews, Medicine and Medieval Society*, Los Angeles.

Shaw, George Bernard (1928). *'Trilby* and "L'Ami des Femmes"', *Dramatic Opinions and Essays*, 2 vols, New York, vol. 1, ch. 30.

Showalter, Elaine (1991). *Sexual Anarchy: Gender and Culture at the Fin-de-Siècle.*

Siebers, Tobin (1983). *The Mirror of Medusa,* Los Angeles.

Silberner, Edmund (1952). 'Two studies on modern anti-Semitism, 1: The Jew hatred of Mikhail Bakunin', *Historia Judaica,* 14: 93–106.

Skolnik, Peter L. (1978). *Fads: America's Crazes, Fevers and Fancies,* New York.

Smith, Timothy D'Arch (1970). *Love in Earnest: Some Notes on the Lives and Writings of English 'Uranian' Poets from 1889 to 1930.*

Sombart, Werner (1913). *The Jews and Modern Capitalism* [1911], translated from the German.

Sonneck, O.G. (1912). *Was Richard Wagner a Jew?,* reprinted from the proceedings of the Music Teacher's Association for 1911.

Spitz, Bob (1989). *Dylan: A Biography,* New York.

Stanislavski, Constantin (1924). *My Life in Art,* Boston.

Stephan, Nancy Leys, and Gilman, Sander L. (1991). 'Appropriating the Idioms of Science', *The Bounds of Race: Perspectives on Hegemony and Resistance,* ed. Dominick La Capra, Ithaca, ch. 3.

Steyn, Juliet (1995). 'Charles Dickens' *Oliver Twist*: Fagin as Sign', in *The Jew in the Text: Modernity and the Construction of Identity,* ed. Linda Nochlin, and Tamar Garb, ch. 2.

Tarde, Gabriel (1890). *Les Lois de l'imitation: étude sociologique,* Paris.

Tatar, Maria M. (1978). *Spellbound: Studies on Mesmerism and Literature,* Princeton.

Taylor, George (1992). 'Svengali: Mesmerist and Aesthete', *British Theatre in the 1890s,* ed. Richard Foulkes, Cambridge, ch. 6.

—— (1996). Introduction to *Trilby and Other Plays,* Oxford.

Thackeray, William Makepeace (1879). 'Burlesques', in *The Works of Thackeray,* vol. 15.

Thorne, Guy [C. Ranger Gull] (1903). *When it was Dark.*

Thuillier, Jean (1988). *Franz Anton Mesmer ou l'ecstase magnétique,* Paris.

Todorov, Tzvetan (1993). *On Human Diversity: Nationalism, Racism, and Exoticism,* Cambridge Mass.

Tombs, Robert (1998). '"Lesser breeds without the law": The British establishment and the Dreyfus Affair, 1894–1899', *Historical Journal,* 41: 495–510.

Towse, John Ranken (1916). *Sixty Years of the Theatre: An Old Critic's Memories,* New York.

Trachtenberg, Joshua (1939). *Jewish Magic and Superstition: A Study in Folk Religion,* New York.

—— (1943). *The Devil and the Jews: The Medieval Conception of the Jew and its Relation to Modern Anti-Semitism,* New Haven.

Trewin, Wendy (1996). 'Punch and Trilby', *The Lady,* (9 December 1996), 36–37.

Tricht, Victor van (1892). *L'Hypnotisme,* Namur.

Tuckey, Charles Lloyd (1894). 'Quelques exemples de troubles nerveux observés chez des musiciens', *Revue de l'hypnotisme,* 8: 85–88.

Valman, Nadia (1996). 'Muscular Jews: Young England, gender and Jewishness in Disraeli's "political trilogy"', *Jewish History,* 10: 57–88.

Veith, Ilza (1965). *Hysteria: The History of a Disease,* Chicago.

Vermorel, Judy, and Vermorel Fred (1989). *Pandemonium! The Book of Fan Cults and Dance Crazes.*

Vrettos, Athena (1995). *Somatic Fictions: Imagining Illness in Victorian Culture*, Stanford.

Wagner, Richard (1910). *Judaism in Music (Das Judenthum in der Musik).* Being the Original Essay together with the Later Supplement [1850, 1869].

Wakley, Thomas (1843). Editorial comment, *Lancet* (25 March 1843), 937.

Ware, J. R. (1872). *The Polish Jew*, repr. in *The British Drama Illustrated*, vol. 12.

Weart, Spencer R. (1988). *Nuclear Fear: A History of Images*, Cambridge, Mass.

Webster, Richard (1996). *Freud's False Memories: Psychoanalysis and the Recovered Memory Movement*, pamphlet [also appended to paperback edition of *Why Freud was Wrong*], Southwold.

Weininger, Otto (1906). *Sex and Character* [1903], translated from the sixth German edn.

Weintraub, Stanley (1974). *Whistler. A Biography.*

Welch, Alfred (1897). *Extracts from the Diary of Moritz Svengali*, New York.

Wells, H.G. (1946). *Tono-Bungay* [1909], Harmondsworth.

Wertheimer, Jack (1987). *Unwelcome Strangers: East European Jews in Imperial Germany*, New York.

White, Arnold (1899). *The Modern Jew.*

Whiteley, Derek Pepys (1948). *George Du Maurier. His Life and Work*, 1948.

Williams, Rosalind (1982). *Dream Worlds: Mass Consumption in Late Nineteenth-Century France*, Los Angeles.

Wilde, Oscar (1962). *The Letters of Oscar Wilde*, ed. Rupert Hart-Davis.

—— (1976). *The Picture of Dorian Gray* [1890].

Wilson, Edmund (1957). *A Piece of My Mind: Reflections at Sixty.*

Winter, Alison (1992). '"The Island of Mesmeria": The Politics of Mesmerism in Early Victorian Britain', Ph.D., Cambridge.

—— (1998). *Mesmerised: Powers of Mind in Victorian Britain*, Chicago.

Winterich, John T. (1929). 'George du Maurier and *Trilby*', *Books and the Man*, New York, ch. 6.

Wohl, Anthony S. (1995). '"Dizzi-Ben-Dizzi": Disraeli as alien', *Journal of British Studies*, 34: 375–411.

Wood, T. Martin (1913). *George du Maurier. The Satirist of the Victorians. A Review of his Art and Personality.*

Woolf, Lucien (1910–11). 'Anti-Semitism', *Encyclopaedia Britannica*, eleventh edn, vol. 2, pp. 134–46.

Yerushalmi, Yosef Hayim (1991). *Freud's Moses: Judaism Terminable and Interminable*, New Haven.

Zatlin, Linda Gertner (1981). *The Nineteenth-Century Anglo-Jewish Novel*, Boston.

Zimmels, Hirsch Jacob (1952). *Magicians, Theologians and Doctors : Studies in Folk-Medicine as Reflected in the Rabbinical Responsa (12th–19th Centuries).*

Zizek, Slavoj (1989). *The Sublime Object of Ideology.*

Zweig, Stefan (1933). *Mental Healers: Franz Anton Mesmer, Mary Baker Eddy, Sigmund Freud.*

Index